LEAVING
Shadows

LITERATURE IN ENGLISH
BY CANADA'S UKRAINIANS

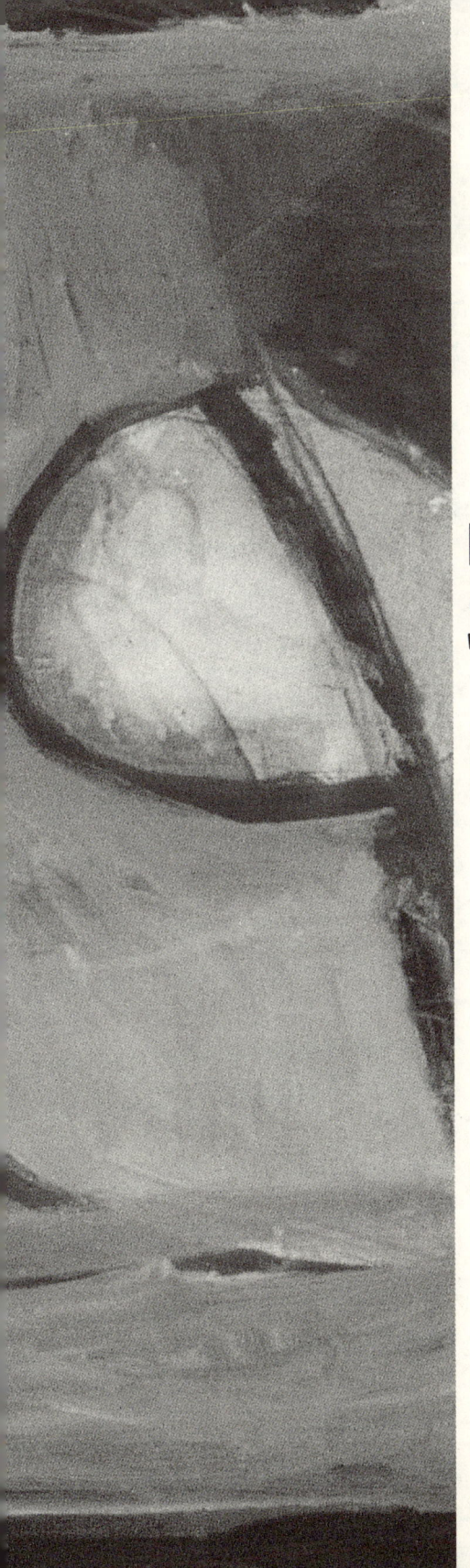

Lisa
GREKUL

LEAVING
Shadows

**LITERATURE IN ENGLISH
BY CANADA'S UKRAINIANS**

THE UNIVERSITY OF ALBERTA PRESS

Published by

The University of Alberta Press
Ring House 2
Edmonton, Alberta, Canada T6G 2E1

Lisa Grekul copyright © 2005
ISBN 0-88864-452-3

Library and Archives Canada Cataloguing in Publication

Grekul, Lisa, 1972-
  Leaving shadows : literature in English by Canada's Ukrainians / Lisa Grekul.

Includes bibliographical references and index.
ISBN 0-88864-452-3

  1. Canadian literature (English)–Ukrainian-Canadian authors–History and criticism. I. Title.
  PS8089.5.U5G74 2005
  C810.9'891791   C2005-905393-3

All rights reserved.
First edition, first printing, 2005.
Printed and bound in Canada by Houghton Boston Printers, Saskatoon.
Copyediting by Alethea Adair.
Index by Judy Dunlop.

No part of this publication may be produced, stored in a retrieval system, or transmitted in any forms or by any means, electronic, mechanical, photocopying, recording, or otherwise, without the prior written consent of the copyright owner or a licence from The Canadian Copyright Licensing Agency (Access Copyright). For an Access Copyright license, visit www.accesscopyright.ca or call toll free: 1-800-893-5777.

The University of Alberta Press is committed to protecting our natural environment. As part of our efforts, this book is printed on New Leaf Paper: it contains 100% post-consumer recycled fibres and is acid- and chlorine-free.

The University of Alberta Press gratefully acknowledges the support received for its publishing program from The Canada Council for the Arts. The University of Alberta Press also gratefully acknowledges the financial support of the Government of Canada through the Book Publishing Industry Development Program (BPIDP) and from the Alberta Foundation for the Arts for its publishing activities.

Cover and Titlepage: Tom Yurko, *Incubation*, 1992. Acrylic, coloured pencil on vinyl, 85.1 x 114.2 cm. Collection of the Alberta Foundation for the Arts. Used by permission of the artist.

Pages 1, 3, 11, 33: Walter Drohan, *Landscape*, 1958–1960. Oil on panel, 59.6 x 74.9 cm. Collection of the Alberta Foundation for the Arts. Used by permission of the artist.

Pages 47, 49, 63, 77, 89: Fran Slubik, *Spring in the Air*, 1989. Watercolour on paper, 50.2 x 65.7 cm. Collection of the Alberta Foundation for the Arts. Used by permission of the artist.

Pages 109, 111, 129, 153: Tadeusz Warszynski, *With Three Pebbles*, 1997. Etching, chine colle on paper, 25.1 x 33 cm. Collection of the Alberta Foundation for the Arts. Used by permission of the artist.

A volume in (cuRRents), a Canadian literature series.

Canada Council for the Arts   Conseil des Arts du Canada

Contents

vii   *Acknowledgements*
ix   *Introduction*
           Listening to *All of Baba's Children*

PART ONE
Re-reading the Past
Literary Representations of Ukrainian Canadians
1900 to 1970

3   ONE   Ukrainian Canadians: A Study in Assimilation

11   TWO   "Digesting" the "Foreign Mass": Ukrainian Canadians in Three Anglo-Canadian Novels

33   THREE   Re-reading the Female Ethnic Subject: Vera Lysenko's *Yellow Boots*

PART TWO
Re-claiming Identity
Ukrainian Canadian Writers and Multiculturalism
1971 to 1984

49   FOUR   Ethnic Revival versus Historical Revision: Ukrainian Canadians and Multiculturalism

63	FIVE	"We aren't buying black oxfords": The Ambivalent Politics of Hybridity in Maara Haas's *The Street Where I Live*
77	SIX	"We laugh, but we are sad": Oral History in George Ryga's *A Letter to My Son*
89	SEVEN	"easter bread and clouds": The Poetry of Andrew Suknaski

PART THREE
Re-imagined Communities
Transcultural Ukrainian Canadian Literature
1985 to 2005

111	EIGHT	From Multiculturalism to Transculturalism: Shifting Paradigms in the Search for Identity
129	NINE	From Canada to Ukraine—and Back: Janice Kulyk Keefer's *The Green Library* and *Honey and Ashes*
153	TEN	Between Borders, Beyond Bloodlines: Myrna Kostash's Creative Non-fiction
193		*Post-script* Monumental Culture and the Future of Ukrainian Canadian Literature
205		*Notes*
231		*Works Cited*
243		*Index*

Acknowledgements

I WISH TO THANK my former professors Glenn Deer, Laurie Ricou, and Bill New for the guidance they gave me as I was writing the first drafts of this book. Thanks also to Stephen Slemon, Susanna Egan, Carl Leggo, and Eva-Marie Kröller for their help at various stages of the project.

I am grateful to Linda Cameron, Director of the University of Alberta Press; and to Judy Dunlop, who produced a first-rate index. Many thanks to Denise Ahlefeldt for the creative energy she put into designing the book, and special thanks to Gail Lindt at the Provincial Archives of Alberta for helping Denise select the images that she used.

I am indebted to Alethea Adair, my editor, for her sharp eye and enormous generosity of spirit; working with her has been a wonderfully rewarding experience, one that I will never forget.

For their support and encouragement, I wish to thank my friends Laurie McNeill, Vicki Gray, and Rachel Poliquin. Though they may not have realized it, my students—Sasha Wiley, Belinda O'Loan, Wes Doyle, Margo Foster, and Sang Wu, especially—were sources of motivation and inspiration. Conversations with Kirk Bewer—about, among other things, German-ness and Ukrainian-ness—kept my belief in this project alive. Heartfelt thanks to Kirk, and to Gloria, Marshall, Jana, and Chad Grekul, and Jacqueline Pollard, for their boundless love.

Leaving Shadows, finally, is dedicated to Patrick O'Neill, who knows more than anyone what was sacrificed for it.

Introduction

Listening to *All of Baba's Children*

IN 1977, when Myrna Kostash published her first book, everyone in my family bought a copy. I was too young at the time to share my parents', aunts', and uncles' excitement about *All of Baba's Children*, but I grew up listening to stories about how Kostash conducted her research; how she spent several months in Two Hills getting to know the residents and learning about their history; how she went on to write about the community and its people. A small, predominantly Ukrainian Canadian town in northeastern Alberta, Two Hills is the community around which my maternal and paternal great-grandparents settled after immigrating to Canada from Ukraine at the turn of the twentieth century. My family members, especially those who still live in the Two Hills area, were thrilled when *All of Baba's Children* came out because the book put their community on the map. They were proud. No one had ever published a book about Two Hills before. But *All of Baba's Children* was more than a book about Two Hills: it was a book about Ukrainians written by a fellow Ukrainian, one of their own. They all bought copies and put them on display in prominent places—on coffee tables and fireplace mantles. My parents placed their copy in our living room bookshelf beside other important books—our set of encyclopedias, my dad's *Complete Works of Shakespeare*, the Bible.

That I grew up knowing few specific details about Kostash's book isn't altogether surprising—no one in my family had actually read *All of Baba's Children*, so no one talked about the actual content of the book. I knew that it was a novel and that one of my uncles, apparently, made an appearance in it as a minor character. Although I recall hearing that Kostash caused some controversy by making communists, or communism, part of her plot, I don't remember anyone in my family being particularly bothered by this. She might not have gotten all of her facts quite right, but my relatives were willing to forgive her for it. What mattered was that she had written a story about us, about Ukrainians. For members of my family, *All of Baba's Children* became a cultural artifact, on a par in many ways with Ukrainian Easter eggs and embroidered tablecloths—something to be displayed as a symbol of our culture.

For years, I didn't read *All of Baba's Children* either. I didn't take it down from my parents' bookshelf until 1997, when I was finishing my undergraduate degree in the Department of English at the University of Alberta and contemplating graduate studies in Canadian literature. I read it because I had noticed that we spent a good deal of time in my Canadian literature classes talking about the voices of minority writers—First Nations, Japanese, Chinese, Indo-, and African Canadians—whose experiences have been traditionally pushed to the margins of the Canadian literary institution. Listening to these voices seemed, and still seems, absolutely fundamental to the study of our national literature. Canadian literature and Canadian literary studies should reflect the experiences of all Canadians. But where were "my" people? Where were "our" voices? Why hadn't my classmates and I studied any Ukrainian Canadian writers in our Canadian literature courses?

So I began reading the only Ukrainian Canadian book that I thought existed, *All of Baba's Children*, which I discovered, much to my astonishment, wasn't a novel at all but rather a non-fictional, journalistic account of Two Hills history. More surprises were to come. The book didn't celebrate Ukrainian culture as I assumed that it would—Kostash wrote frankly about political and religious tensions within the Ukrainian Canadian community. She wrote about sexism, anti-Semitism, the inevitability of assimilation and cultural loss. Ironically, the book that my family members had held up as a testament to the vitality and resilience of Ukrainian culture in Canada told a different story.

I was outraged and I trace the starting point of this book back to that outrage, which has changed shape and focus several times over the last seven years as I've tried to understand why books like *All of Baba's Children*—why literary works by Ukrainian Canadians—have fallen through the cracks of Canadian literary studies. My deeply personal investment in the subject matter of this book means that, from beginning to end, it has been an emotionally-charged enterprise. I was angry with Kostash, initially, for what she wrote about Two Hills. If this was our only book, shouldn't it promote a more positive image of our ethnic group? I found her prose dense and difficult. Why couldn't she have written a novel, a story, something more accessible and entertaining? At the same time, I was embarrassed that my family members hadn't read what she had written. By putting Kostash's book on display without knowing what it was about, they seemed to be playing out, however unwittingly, the painful stereotype of the "dumb Ukrainian."

Once I started poking around the library, though, and discovered that *All of Baba's Children* was by no means the only Ukrainian Canadian book in print, I became embarrassed. I found Vera Lysenko, George Ryga, Andrew Suknaski, Janice Kulyk Keefer, Helen Potrebenko, Yuri Kupchenko, Gloria Kupchenko Frolick, Ludmilla Bereshko, Larry Warwaruk, Ted Galay, and Marusya Bociurkiw. I found novels, books of poetry, short stories, works of creative non-fiction, and drama, not to mention two anthologies, *Yarmarok: Ukrainian Writing in Canada Since the Second World War* (1987) and *Two Lands, New Visions: Stories from Canada and Ukraine* (1998). How could I not have known about this enormous body of writing? Now I felt like the "dumb Ukrainian."

In previous drafts of this book, reflecting on why Ukrainian Canadian literature has been ignored within the Canadian literary institution, I blamed the Ukrainian Canadian community, generally, and Ukrainian Canadian scholars, more specifically, for not supporting our writers. I outlined the extensive network of Ukrainian Canadian institutes, centers, and programs of study in this country[1] and then I laid out the impressive body of scholarship that has been done on Ukrainian and Ukrainian Canadian history, politics, culture, religious institutions, language, and folklore. What troubled me at the time—and what troubles me still, to some extent—is that, while some work has been done on Ukrainian Canadian literature, most of this scholarship is focused on authors from Ukraine (such as Taras Shevchenko and Ivan Franko); considerably less is focused on Ukrainian-language authors in Canada; and still less on English-language writers. The first book-length study of Ukrainian Canadian literature, M.I. Mandryka's *History of Ukrainian Literature in Canada* (1968), pays little attention to English-language writers. Frances Swyripa's *Ukrainian Canadians: A Survey of Their Portrayal in English-Language Works* (1978) concentrates on the representation of Ukrainian Canadians in government reports, church documents, newspapers, and some scholarly monographs—material written, for the most part, by non-Ukrainian Canadians. Aside from Sonia Mycak's *Canuke Literature: Critical Essays on Canadian Ukrainian Writing* (2001), the body of scholarship on English-language Ukrainian Canadian literature comprises a smattering of essays written by Carolyn Redl, Beverly Rasporich, Tamara Palmer Seiler, Alexandra Kruchka Glynn, and Sonia Mycak amoung others, published primarily in ethnic journals, such as the *Journal of Ukrainian Studies* and *Canadian Ethnic Studies*, and not in more mainstream literary periodicals, such as *Canadian Literature* or *Essays on Canadian Writing*. These studies largely fail to contextualize or historicize the development of the Ukrainian Canadian literary tradition, and focus on prose fiction and drama to the exclusion of poetry and creative non-fiction.

The conclusion that I drew, then, in the early stages, was that Ukrainian Canadian scholars—those in the unique position to publicize the existence and promote the value of Ukrainian Canadian literature to Ukrainian and non-Ukrainian Canadian readers alike—had in effect turned their backs on English-language Ukrainian Canadian writers. Why had they done so? I considered the possibility that the writers were seen as "not Ukrainian enough" because they chose to write in English. I thought about writers who have been critical of the Ukrainian Canadian community—Myrna Kostash and Helen Potrebenko, for instance, are outspoken in their leftism and feminism; Janice Kulyk Keefer confronts anti-Semitism among Ukrainians in Canada and Ukraine; Maara Haas and George Ryga have distanced themselves from the label of "Ukrainian Canadian" writer, preferring instead to be seen as "Canadian" writers, or simply as "writers."[2] And I wondered if scholars had dismissed these authors for fouling their own nest, so to speak.[3] I was especially angered by those scholars who had worked on Ukrainian Canadian literature but who hadn't taken their work beyond the confines of Ukrainian Canadian studies. Was their scholarship not strong enough? Were they taking the safe and easy road by publishing within the Ukrainian Canadian studies network, among like-blooded and like-minded scholars, guaranteed to share the same thinking?

Retrospectively, these questions and the emotion behind them seem at best naïve. In the process of working on this book, my attitudes toward Ukrainian Canadians—and Ukrainian Canadian scholars, in particular—have changed dramatically. When I started this study in earnest, as a Ph.D. student at the University of British Columbia, I was unprepared for how isolating the experience would be; how often I would be called on in casual conversation to defend the subject matter of my dissertation; and how difficult it would be for me to fight the pervasive assumption that my research was more personal hobby-horse than legitimate scholarly enterprise. Again and again I encountered professors and peers who questioned the existence of Ukrainian Canadian literature ("do you have enough material for a whole thesis?"); who questioned the literariness, or the aesthetic quality, of this literature ("but is it any *good*?"); who let me know in no uncertain terms that only a Ukrainian Canadian scholar would be interested in studying Ukrainian Canadian texts ("so then you must be Ukrainian yourself"); and who had no compunction about declaring that the project was irrelevant to ongoing debates in Canadian literary studies ("you're going to have a hard time publishing anything"). That these questions were asked—and asked with alarming frequency—speaks volumes about the current state of the Canadian literary institution vis-à-vis minority writing, not least of all because similar questions are not, and would not be, asked of a student working on First Nations, East Asian, South Asian, or African Canadian literatures. Why the different attitudes toward ethnic and "racialized" minority literatures?[4]

Prior to the 1980s, when multiculturalism began to dominate public discourse on Canadian identity, such questions *would* have been asked of any scholar working on any minority literature. To be sure, no one—then or now—would disagree that, despite its British and French colonial legacies, Canadian culture is marked by its diversity. "To read Canadian literature attentively is to realize how diverse Canadian culture is," says W.H. New in *A History of Canadian Literature* (2003). "It is the cultural plurality inside the country that most fundamentally shapes the way

Canadians define their political character, draw the dimensions of their literature, and voice their commitment to causes, institutions and individuality" (3-4). And yet the argument put forth by such critics as Linda Hutcheon and Marion Richmond—that the Canadian literary canon has always been, by definition, multicultural, and that Canadian literary studies have always incorporated minority writing—is shaky, at best (*Other Solitudes* 13). A few of the earliest Canadian writers to achieve canonical recognition, Laura Salverson, Frederick Philip Grove, A.M. Klein, did come from minority backgrounds (Padolsky, "Canadian Ethnic Minority" 373; Kamboureli, *Making a Difference* 1)—and certainly Watson Kirkconnell's substantial work on Canadian literature in languages other than English and French (including his annual review, from 1937 to 1965, in the *University of Toronto Quarterly*) suggests that minority writing was not entirely ignored. But as Winfried Siemerling's Introduction to *Writing Ethnicity: Cross-cultural Consciousness in Canadian and Québécois Literature* (1996) points out, "demographics, settlement patterns, political representation, and official policies of multiculturalism do not find their direct equivalences in either literature or literary studies" (4).

The desire on the part of many writers and literary scholars to cultivate more direct equivalences, bolstered by the emergence of multiculturalism as an ideology as well as a practice, was the driving force behind the explosion of minority literary production in the 1980s. In "Canadian Ethnic Minority Literature in English" (1994), Enoch Padolsky, surveying a broad range of literature by minority writers from, for example, Czech, Hungarian, Dutch, Arab, West Indian, East Asian and Ukrainian backgrounds, suggests that "in the post-Second World War period, and especially from the late 1970s onwards, the number of Canadian minority writers increased dramatically, along with the range of groups represented" (364). In *Scandalous Bodies: Diasporic Literature in English Canada* (2000), Smaro Kamboureli offers a list of anthologies that collectively support Padolsky's claim to illustrate the "concentrated unfolding" of both ethnic and "racialized" minority writing that occurred at the 1980s (131).[5] But whereas the body of "racialized" minority literature, and scholarship related to it, continued (and continues) to grow, the intense period of ethnic minority literary production was short-lived and made comparatively little impact on mainstream literary studies. Thus, Ukrainian Canadian literature becomes a highly illustrative case study of what has happened to other ethnic minority literatures over the past decade or so. Most of the Ukrainian Canadian texts I stumbled on, after reading *All of Baba's Children*, were published in the 1970s and 1980s. Relatively few have been published since.

I am not sure if anybody knows definitively why the "boom and bust" of ethnic minority writing happened. Padolsky suggests that, even as ethnic minority writers came to voice, their texts were too often published by small, minority-oriented presses, too rarely reviewed, and studied primarily by minority critics (375). Another explanation, and a broader one, is that multiculturalism, as empowering as it may have seemed initially, offered ethnic minority writers too little encouragement too late. When Janice Kulyk Keefer sardonically identifies the "heyday of multiculturalism in the 1970s" as a time when it was "suddenly 'fun to be ethnic'" ("Coming Across Bones" 89), she gestures toward the fundamental shortcomings of multiculturalism—namely that it masked the profound cultural and linguistic loss that had already occurred among second- and third-generation Canadians by promoting trite, "song and dance" expressions of ethnicity. It was not, in fact, "suddenly 'fun to be ethnic'"—it could not be. Kulyk Keefer says of this time period that she chose not to write about her ethnicity because she could not forget the "pain and shame" she "associated with being Ukrainian"; she could not forget that she had been "marked...by an ethnicity whose visible signs were the butt of ethnic jokes about hunkięs in sheepskin coats eating perogies" (89). The common thread that runs through virtually all Ukrainian Canadian texts published during—and after—the "heyday of multiculturalism" is a deep-seated dissatisfaction with discourses of multiculturalism, and an intense desire to dismantle the assumption that celebratory "song and dance" models of ethnicity adequately reflect the actual, lived experiences of Ukrainians in Canada—what Kulyk Keefer refers to as her "painfully split subjectivity" (87).

Painful though it may have been for some writers to engage in dialogue about the tensions between their ethnic and national identity, doing so was also—in Myrna Kostash's words—"very exciting" ("The Shock of White Cognition" 4). Reflecting on her emergence in the 1970s and 1980s, post-*All of Baba's Children*, as a "kind of spokesperson in western Canada for the idea of ethnicity," she says that she felt at the "leading edge" of cultural debates about "challenging the globalization of culture," and she began to envision "broader and broader Common Fronts of cultural subversives—feminists, immigrants, eco-guerillas, Metis, artists, gays and lesbians" (4). The excitement and the vision, however, didn't last long. If it was, in the 1970s, "suddenly 'fun to be ethnic,'" by 1990, the situation had changed: "suddenly," says Kostash, "I had nothing to say," no commentary to make on otherness, marginality, or cultures of resistance (4). With the "articulation of a whole new point of view in the discourse around culture and identity"—the "articulation of race and colour"—she was forced to acknowledge that, "in the new terms of the discourse, [she] was white. [She] was a member of a privileged *majority*. [She] was part of the problem, not the solution" (4). Although Kostash goes on to argue that "whiteness is provisional"—Canadians of "east European, including Jewish, origin have only recently become white"—and that "any of us who still carry the texts of bigotry imprinted in our memory have a duty to speak to that instability of racial meaning," she nonetheless recognizes the "shock of white cognition" as a silencing moment.

That silencing, I think, is what stunted the production and study of ethnic minority literature. In the race debates that raged in the 1990s,[6] as racialized minority writers and scholars—Himani Bannerji, Dionne Brand, Marlene Nourbese Philip, Lee Maracle, Lenore Keeshig-Tobias, Roy Miki, and others—urgently and emphatically voiced their criticisms of the ways in which multiculturalism overlooks racially-inflected structures of inclusion and exclusion, evoking difference in order to neutralize it (Bannerji 109), ethnic minority writers' complaints about multiculturalism began to look, if not immaterial, certainly feeble. As Kulyk Keefer puts it, the bottom line is that "given the overwhelming need to acknowledge and combat racism in this country," whatever she has to say about her experiences as a member of an ethnic minority group is "of marginal importance" (99). Though she may see her ethnicity as a "scar rather than as a scarf to be tied on or discarded at will, the colour of [her] skin is not going to adversely affect people treat [her] on the subway or in a store, whereas for persons of colour, it is often only the fact of their race that is seen at all, and acknowledged in the most insulting and aggressive ways" (99).

But it is precisely the privilege of being able to discard the scarf—the ability to pass—that has rendered ethnic minority writers speechless vis-à-vis their enduring feelings of otherness. Ironically, it is racialized minority writers' inability to change their marginalized status in the economy of race that has brought them to voice, and brought serious, focused attention to what they have to say. Indeed, talking about race debates in the past tense—as discussions marked by discrete beginnings and endings—is not accurate: the emergence and increasing popularity of writers from First Nations, East and South Asian, and African Canadian backgrounds attests to the fact that race issues continue to influence the shape and direction of the Canadian literary institution. Nor is it accurate to suggest that Canadian literature is the only context in which issues of race have come to the fore in recent years. Globally, and across disciplines, race has emerged as a dominant, perhaps the dominant, locus of critical dialogue on the phenomena related to diaspora (including transnationalism, transculturalism, hybridity, metissage, migration), which form, collectively, the latest "leading edge" in cultural studies. Though scholars have appropriated and redefined diaspora in myriad ways,[7] most—Paul Gilroy, Stuart Hall, Rey Chow, Ien Ang, Fred Wah, Roy Miki, Rajagopalan Radhakrishnan, Vijay Mishra—implicitly collapse racialized and diasporic identity. Insofar as ethnicity gave way to race in conversations about multiculturalism, it has never occupied a prominent position in dialogue about diaspora.

What happened to ethnicity in the 1990s was, without a doubt, necessary and, moreover, inevitable. As Kostash says, "just as feminism's ideal of gender solidarity…had had to yield to the analysis of historical, cultural and class cleavages among women…so too did multiculturalism's ideal of unity among minorities have to yield to specifics of race and colour" (4). Nor is there any doubt whatsoever that debates about race (racism, race relations, race and nation, race and diaspora) must continue. But the general tendency on the part of scholars to emphasize visible difference, to the exclusion of other forms or experiences of difference, homogenizes the category of "white" and replicates the kind of thinking that, within colonial discourse, reduced racialized subjects to other. Though the experience of otherness may be less pronounced and less problematic for ethnic minorities than it is for racialized minorities, in the realm of identity politics, whiteness becomes a liability when it is (mis)read as a sign of privilege, *tout court*. Kulyk Keefer gestures toward this liability when she says that "our joint task to work against racism of any kind is one I can only meaningfully undertake not as some designated bearer of white privilege but as my particularized, differentiated, historically situated self" (99). And when she adds that her "self" is "not turned nostalgically back to some pure golden past, or engaged simply with the traumas of the past" but "situated in the present, pulled between...a rapidly changing Canada, and a chaotically 'developing' Ukraine" (99), she announces the relevance of her experiences, as an ethnic minority, to debates about diaspora and diasporic identities. The same can be said of many of us. There are "points of connection" between visible and invisible minorities—in the context of debates about diaspora and nation—that have yet to be identified and explored (99).

Looking back now on my professors' and peers' skepticism about this project, I have a clearer understanding and a new appreciation for why Ukrainian Canadian scholars would gravitate toward other like-blooded and like-minded scholars. I understand how difficult it is for scholars empowered with "white privilege" to intervene in debates about race. We run the risk of making academic arguments that sound too close to "those immigrants are taking our jobs." But I don't think that space within academic discourse is a limited commodity. There is ample room for voices from across the spectrum of minority experience. And those voices should be able speak to each other about the ways in which their experiences diverge and connect.

• • •

This book follows a rough chronology of Ukrainian Canadian literary production in English during the twentieth century. I focus exclusively on literary works written in English, not only because my Ukrainian language skills are rudimentary, but because the rich tradition of Ukrainian-language literature produced in this country—much of it published prior to the 1950s in such newspapers as *Kanadiiskyi Farmer/Canadian Farmer*, *Robochyi Narod/Working People*, *Ranok/Dawn*, *Ukrainskyi Holos/Ukrainian Voice*, and *Kanadiiskyi Rusyn/Canadian Ruthenian*; some collected in *Yarmarok*—raises a unique series of concerns that differ from those raised by English-language texts. My specific interest lies in examining how writers who have lost (or in some cases never had) the facility to speak Ukrainian negotiate their ethnic identity in the dominant language and culture of English Canada—though even then the corpus is unwieldy. To be sure, this book functions in part as a literary history that traces the unfolding of the English-language tradition and that contextualizes it within the shifting cultural and political discourses of Canadian nationhood. But in order to avoid providing superficial commentary on a great many writers and texts, I have chosen to concentrate on select authors whose texts are representative of how they and other writers responded to significant historical, cultural, and political moments.

I have divided the study, then, into three parts, based on time periods—1900 to 1970, 1971 to 1984, and 1985 to 2005—in order to foreground three dominant models of nationhood—Canada as a former British colony, marked by ideologies and practices of assimilation; Canada as a multicultural state, open to cultural diversity, in policy if not in practice; Canada as a post-national community increasingly defined by the diasporic consciousness of many members. The point is to understand how Ukrainian Canadian authors have seen themselves vis-à-vis shifting notions of the "ideal" Canadian; how dominant definitions of Canadian-ness have affected them; how they have either unwittingly perpetuated or intentionally challenged these definitions in their writing: how, in short, they have experienced and expressed their identity as members of, and simultaneously outsiders within, Canadian society; how they have kept the idea of ethnicity "alive." Context is absolutely key to how the book is put together. Because writers both shape, and are shaped by, the world around them, I introduce each part with an overview of how Ukrainians were viewed, as well as how they viewed themselves, during the given historical moment.

While the project as a whole obviously centres on writing by Ukrainian Canadians, I devote a portion of Part One to situating this writing in the more specific context of Canadian literature by looking at three canonical Anglo-Canadian writers—Ralph Connor, Sinclair Ross, Margaret Laurence—whose portrayals of Ukrainian Canadian characters shed important light on the deeply-entrenched negative attitudes toward Ukrainian Canadians that Ukrainian Canadian writers have had to face. My decision to begin with close readings of Connor's *The Foreigner: A Tale of Saskatchewan* (1909), Ross's *As For Me and My House* (1941) a nd Laurence's *A Jest of God* (1966) is an important one because the

Ukrainian Canadian writers I go on to examine are—consciously or unconsciously, and with varying degrees of success—writing back to the (mis)representations of Ukrainian Canadians in Anglo-Canadian literary works. Hence, in Part One, 1900 to 1970, after examining the assimilationist rhetoric that characterizes Anglo-Canadian writers' depictions of Ukrainian Canadians, I turn my attention to Vera Lysenko's *Yellow Boots* (1954), the first English-language novel by a Ukrainian Canadian, and a text that, I argue, reinforces discourses of assimilation even as it appears to anticipate—and indeed embrace—multicultural models of nationhood and nationality.

In Part Two, 1970 to 1984, I look at Maara Haas's novel *The Street Where I Live* (1976), George Ryga's play *A Letter to My Son* (1981), and Andrew Suknaski's poetry (published in *Wood Mountain Poems*, 1976; *the ghosts call you poor*, 1978; and *In the Name of Narid*, 1981), texts that offer more critical commentary on the policies and practices of official multiculturalism. The writers in this portion of the book reject "song and dance" models of ethnicity, choosing instead to explore the complex, often fraught, histories of their families and communities.

Part Three, 1985 to 2005, identifies many Ukrainian Canadians' sense of themselves as diasporic subjects, with intense emotional attachments to the country from which their ancestors emigrated, through readings of texts by Janice Kulyk Keefer (*The Green Library*, 1996; *Honey and Ashes: A Story of Family*, 1998) and Myrna Kostash (*Bloodlines: A Journey Into Eastern Europe*, 1993; *The Doomed Bridegroom: A Memoir*, 1998). In this final portion of the book, I explore and evaluate Kulyk Keefer's and Kostash's attempts to (re)define their ethnic and national identity by "returning" to Ukraine. How does going "back"— and, importantly, writing about the experience—change the way they see themselves, as Ukrainians and as Canadians? How do their texts alter the way scholars have approached the concept of diaspora?

In short, the chapters that follow offer answers—at times implicit, at times explicit—to the questions I've been asked about Ukrainian Canadian literature over the past few years: is it any good? Do you have to be Ukrainian to read and appreciate it? How exactly is it relevant to ongoing debates in Canadian literary studies? Aesthetic and formal concerns (what writers achieve with language, structure, style, and genre; how they organize their texts; the subtle nuances of voice that shape their stories) are not absent from this book. As difficult as it is to define and rationalize, taste is an inherent part of the reading process for each of us. But as a literary scholar, I am interested less in articulating why the texts that I focus on are "good" than in determining how "good" Ukrainian Canadian writers are at using the tools of their craft for the specific purpose of articulating their ethnic identity. My objective is to understand why Ukrainian Canadian authors make the thematic and formal choices that they do in their writing; what changes to public discourse on ethnic and national identity they would like their writing to make; how the idea of ethnicity constantly changes shape, taking on new forms and expressions, in their texts.

Leaving Shadows is not exhaustive in terms of what can and needs to be said about the English-language Ukrainian Canadian literary tradition. A single-volume study simply cannot accommodate the body of Ukrainian Canadian literature in its entirety, nor is there space enough in this book for connections to be made between Ukrainian Canadian and other ethnic minority works. I hope, however, that readers will view this text as initial groundwork for further debates and discussions—as a first step toward developing an extensive archive of scholarship on Ukrainian Canadian writing. Such an archive, I expect, would include comparative work on Ukrainian-language texts, published in Canada as well as in Ukraine, and English-language texts; cross-cultural work on Ukrainian Canadian, Jewish, and Mennonite writing (the latter two groups are seen as distinct from Ukrainian Canadian communities, though many Jewish and Mennonite Canadian writers trace their roots back to Ukraine); and writing by queer Ukrainian Canadians, such as Marusya Bociurkiw, vis-à-vis other queer texts. A study of the large number of texts published in and after the 1990s by Canadians of Central and Eastern European descent who have travelled "back" to their ethnic homelands—Lisa Appignanesi, Irena Karafilly, Anna Porter, Modris Eksteins, Michael Ignatieff, and Tony Fabijancic, in addition to Janice Kulyk Keefer and Myrna Kostash—is waiting to be done. And Ukrainian Canadians' reactions to recent developments in Ukraine, the "Orange Revolution," should breathe new life into theoretical debates about the nature of diasporic ethnic communities. Collectively, the multiple directions in which the study of Ukrainian Canadian literature can be taken suggest the relevance of it to an audience of readers who are not exclusively Ukrainian Canadian.

In the end, though, I can't deny that my Ukrainian roots and a wish to reach out to others who share these roots have played no small part in spurring me on to write this book. And it was the experience of writing and publishing another book that helped me embrace (rather than apologize for) my desire to speak to other Ukrainian Canadians. The other book I'm referring to is *Kalyna's Song*, my first novel (published by Coteau in 2003), the semi-autobiographical coming-of-age story of a fourth-generation Ukrainian Canadian woman who grows up in northeastern Alberta and southern Africa. As I worked on both the novel and my Ph.D. thesis, my overarching goal was to share the Ukrainian Canadian experience with non-Ukrainian Canadian readers. But *Kalyna's Song*, like *All of Baba's Children*, reminded me that members of a minority group respond powerfully to stories by and about one of them. History repeated itself in my family as aunts, uncles, and cousins across the country bought copies of my book, as they had bought copies of Kostash's almost thirty years before, and *Kalyna's Song* elicited reactions from my relatives, as well as from friends and from people I'd never met before, that have become, for me, the most compelling commentary on how important the production and study of Ukrainian Canadian literature is to Ukrainian Canadians themselves. Several friends of mine who had never mentioned their Ukrainian heritage to me before came out of the ethnic closet, so to speak, after they read *Kalyna's Song*: the book, they said, made them understand their grandparents' and their parents'—and their own—ambivalent feelings about being Ukrainian; it gave them insight into their history; and it sparked a sense of pride in their ethnic heritage. They had never read the names of their communities in a book (Szypenitz, Vegreville, St. Paul), or their own names (Natalka, Marika, Orysia), or the words for Ukrainian foods (*holuptsi*, *perohy*, *nachinka*).

Reflecting on these responses to my novel, I've discovered that what I have referred to as rage might always have been something closer to grief, a deep sense of sadness for those Ukrainian Canadian readers who had forgotten, or simply had not thought about, their Ukrainian-ness until they had read the book. And it has become clear to me that both *Kalyna's Song* and *Leaving Shadows* are about much more than Ukrainian Canadians: these books are about all third-, fourth-, and fifth-generation ethnic Canadians who have been given the simultaneous gift and curse of passing; and they are about the precarious future of ethnicity itself.

What does ethnicity mean to us, the children of multiculturalism and the grandchildren of assimilation, who are many decades removed from our ancestral roots? We pass. We are not called upon to explain where we come from, as racialized minorities often are: it is assumed that we come from here. We are not "read" as different, anything other than "Canadian," because we wear no outward signs of difference: most of us don't speak our ethnic languages, we don't speak accented English, we don't practice customs and traditions that make our ethnic identity visible. But many of us nonetheless *feel* different, and that feeling is legitimate. The question is: what do we do with it? How do we keep it from passing away?

We can begin, I believe, by paying attention to the voices of ethnic writers, the voices of "all of Baba's children." They remind us that ethnicity hasn't disappeared or passed away, but that it could. They show us that we need to work at drawing ourselves out of the shadows of assimilation and "song and dance" multiculturalism if we want ethnicity to remain a part of Canadian culture. What I hope readers will take away from my discussions of Ukrainian Canadian writing is the realization that keeping ethnic identity alive requires acts of will, courage, and, above all, imagination. The writers whose work I focus on in this book understand the crucial role that literature plays in nurturing—imagining and re-imagining—ethnic identity.

Seeing your ethnic group's story in print (or some version of your family's story, or something very much like your own story) is a powerfully validating experience: it legitimizes where you come from and who you are. *Leaving Shadows*, like *Kalyna's Song*, announces that Ukrainians are part of the historical, political, cultural, and literary landscapes of Canada—that our stories are woven into the fabric of this country. This book sends a message to the fourth-, fifth-, and sixth-generation Ukrainian Canadians who are sitting these days in Canadian literature classrooms.

Write your stories down; make your voices heard.

PART ONE

RE-READING THE PAST

Literary Representations
of Ukrainian Canadians

1900 to 1970

ONE

Ukrainian Canadians
A Study in Assimilation

UKRAINIANS HAVE BEEN A PRESENCE IN CANADA since the late nineteenth century, and their history in this country, like that of many ethnic minority groups, is marked by a troubling paradox. Though the vast majority of Ukrainian immigrants were actively recruited by the Canadian government to settle the west—to perform, that is, the backbreaking work of farming, logging, and mining in the service of the nation—these same immigrants were simultaneously seen as "other" to the Anglo-Canadian "self": not only culturally different, but culturally undesirable; inferior, backward, and even threatening to Anglo-Canadian society. In the postcolonial and pre-multicultural period of Canadian history, assimilation was the word of the day. Immigrants from non-Anglo-Celtic backgrounds were expected to shed their ethnic languages and cultures in order to fit into Canadian society. During the first decades of the twentieth century, Ukrainian Canadians experienced especially intense discrimination and enormous pressure to become "Canadianized," and this comes through—either directly or indirectly—in literary representations of Ukrainian Canadians produced at the time.

One of the largest ethnic minorities in Canada, Ukrainians immigrated to Canada in three distinct waves: from the 1890s until 1914, approximately 170,000 Ukrainians settled in Canada; from 1919 to 1939, another 68,000 Ukrainians immigrated; and, between 1947 and 1952, a further 32,000 arrived.[1] The first wave of immigration (1890s to 1914) comprised largely uneducated, impoverished peasant farmers from the (then Austro-Hungarian) western provinces of Galicia, Bukovyna, and Transcarpathia. They were members of a "subjugated" (Swyripa, "From Sheepskin Coat" 12) nation who sought a fresh start overseas.[2] According to Jars Balan:

> [s]tatistics paint a grim picture of what life was like for peasants in the Austro-Hungarian empire in the latter half of the nineteenth century. And they show that while suffering was widespread throughout the lower classes, the most victimized group of all were the Ukrainians. They had not only the lowest standard of living (the per-capita income in Galicia was one-tenth that in the rest of Austria), but the highest mortality rate in the empire (hovering between forty and forty-eight deaths per thousand in the Ukrainian part of Galicia, compared to twenty-eight per thousand in the Polish part). In addition, Ukrainians had smaller landholdings and larger debts; were more afflicted with disease; and had less access to medical care than their peasant counterparts in other provinces. (*Salt and Braided Bread* 4)

Having heard stories about cheap, abundant land in Canada—"a quarter section of 160 acres for a $10.00 fee" (Gerus and Rea 7)—many Ukrainians were enticed to immigrate[3] and most formed rural bloc settlements in Manitoba, Saskatchewan, and Alberta.[4] During the early years of settlement, it was not uncommon for immigrant women to clear and cultivate land while immigrant men left their homesteads to obtain ready cash through mining, lumber, or railway work (Marunchak 88–89). In historical scholarship, much is made of the early Ukrainian pioneers' love of the land and their unshakeable faith in the new life that it promised them. Accounts of early homesteading experiences are rife with descriptions of the immigrants' physical and spiritual endurance in the face of hardship. Ukrainian settlers rapidly adjusted to their new surroundings—they not only built homes but also schools, churches, and reading societies (*chytalny*).[5] A number of Ukrainian-language newspapers were soon established in Canada (all in Winnipeg) by the relatively small number of educated individuals who immigrated in the first wave.[6]

Unlike immigrants of the first wave, immigrants of the second wave (1919 to 1939) comprised two "categories" of people: "war-impoverished peasants" and members of the "persecuted nationalistic intelligentsia" (Gerus and Rea 12). Most came from eastern Galicia, which had fallen under Polish rule following the first World War, and were fleeing the economically and politically oppressive Polish state.[7] Historians suggest that immigrants of the second wave were, on the whole, more educated and nationally conscious than those of the first wave, and, while the majority settled in the prairie provinces, a significant number of "interwar" immigrants remained in southern Ontario (Gerus and Rea 13). These new immigrants threw their support behind existing, usually pro-nationalist, Ukrainian political organizations, such as the Ukrainian Self Reliance League (founded in 1918), and they also established Canadian branches of associations founded in Ukraine, such as the "rather curious conservative-monarchist" United Hetman Organization, also established in 1918 (Gerus and Rea 14). Partly in response to the pro-communist Ukrainian Labour-Farmer Temple Association (1918), the Ukrainian National Federation was formed (1932)—strongly supported by militant nationalist immigrants of the second wave (Gerus and Rea 15). At the same time, a number of new church-related organizations were formed (most notably the Ukrainian Catholic Brotherhood [1932]), adding to the long list of existing organizations supported by the Ukrainian-Catholic and Ukrainian-Orthodox Churches.[8] In 1940, the Ukrainian Canadian Committee was formed, a "national committee, which spoke for all but the Communists who rejected it and were rejected by it," and which has since played "an indispensable role in the encouragement and preservation of Ukrainian cultural life" (Gerus and Rea 15). During and after the Second World War, Ukrainians continued to publish numerous newspapers and became increasingly involved in Canadian politics as, for example, elected representatives in provincial and federal governments.[9]

Immigrants of the third and final wave[10] (1947 to 1952) were primarily political dissidents and intellectuals, refugees from all parts of Ukraine seeking asylum from Stalin's oppressive communist regime; "forcibly removed to western Europe as Nazi slave labor, they refused repatriation to the Soviet Union...at the war's end" (Swyripa, "From Sheepskin Coat" 17). Many of these highly educated, politically active immigrants—referred to in derogatory terms as "DPs" or "Displaced Persons"—settled in large southern Ontario and Québec urban centres; most of them came from urban backgrounds in Ukraine and were therefore drawn to the "booming factories and business opportunities in the major cities of central Canada" (Balan, *Salt and Braided Bread* 12). Marunchak describes third-wave immigrants as "teachers, doctors, economists, engineers, lawyers, university lecturers…poets, writers, painters and journalists" (571). Although several Ukrainian organizations in Canada, including the Ukrainian Canadian Committee, provided assistance to the new immigrants, "acute tensions" quickly developed between the émigré community and the "established and overwhelmingly Canadian-born Ukrainian community" (Gerus and Rea 18). According to O.W. Gerus and J.E. Rea, the "reluctance and often outright refusal of the newcomers to join existing organizations, their nationalistic arrogance and elitism and their determination to convert the established organized life to their own political purpose—the liberation of Ukraine—was one source of difficulty" (18). Canadian-born Ukrainians, on the other hand, "considered themselves responsible for the good fortune of the newcomers" and "resented the seeming lack of gratitude on the part of the former DPs for the work of the pioneers in facilitating the resettlement of the refugees and for winning acceptance of the Ukrainian fact in Canada in the first place" (Gerus and Rea 18). Conflicts between new Ukrainian immigrants and Ukrainian Canadians are frequently—but briefly—touched upon by historians. More often than not, in their discussions of Ukrainians in post-Second World War Canada, scholars choose to focus on the cohesive nature of the Ukrainian Canadian community, emphasizing the collective achievements of Ukrainian Canadians in professional and cultural spheres.[11]

But while some Ukrainian Canadian scholars have emphasized the unity and cohesion of Ukrainians in Canada,[12] from the outset of immigration the homogeneity of the Ukrainian community in Canada has been less real than imagined. Ukrainian Canadians have long been divided along religious and political lines, not only between but also within immigrant waves. Immigrants carried with them existing "Old Country" tensions between members of the Ukrainian Greek-Catholic Church and the Ukrainian Greek-Orthodox Church, and between adherents of pro-Soviet and pro-nationalist ideologies. Mennonite and Jewish Ukrainians, though rarely mentioned in accounts of Ukrainian Canadian history, also immigrated to Canada. Descendants of Ukrainian immigrants differ, moreover, in terms of their ethnic and national allegiances; though some maintain strong ties with their Ukrainian heritage—in some cases constructed ties through the practice of culture, in other cases actual social, political, and economic ties with Ukraine—others identify themselves only nominally as "Ukrainian Canadian," and still others see themselves as simply "Canadian."

In the decades following Canada's independence in 1867 until at least the First World War, as W.H. New points out in *A History of Canadian Literature* (2003), nationalistic sentiment was "anglocentric" and "male-dominated." During this "age of expansion" and "definition," the "prevalent idea of nationalism declared a fundamental belief in cultural uniformity" (79). Frances Swyripa, in *Ukrainian Canadians: A Survey of Their Portrayal in English-language Works* (1978), concurs, drawing attention to documents published between 1896 and 1918 that foreground Anglo-Canadians' "concern for the British character of Canada and her national prosperity" (1). Government officials, educationalists, and missionaries who had travelled through Ukrainian bloc settlements on the prairies, observing the Ukrainian immigrants' "clothing, church and cottage architecture, food, living conditions, customs, and religious observations" (5), complained that "a lack of hygiene, general untidiness and overcrowding, a plain and unappetizing diet, and the presence of animals close to or in the house" were typical among Ukrainians (2). The immigrants' churches were seen as "authoritarian" and "ritualistic," and Ukrainians themselves superstitious, avaricious, and dishonest (3). Referring to Ukrainians as "Foreigners," "Galicians," "Sifton's Sheepskins," and "bohunks," some Anglo-Canadian observers went so far as to suggest that Ukrainians were racially inclined toward drunkenness, crime, and mental illness (8–9; 18). During the first two decades of the twentieth century, in fact, many Anglo-Canadians believed that Ukrainian immigrants, if left unassimilated, would corrupt Canadian society. The fate of respectable Anglo-Canada required the intervention of the state—the mobilization of "the church, the school, political clubs and organizations, the labour union, and both the English and native-language press" (19)—in acquainting Ukrainians with the "superiority of British-Canadian ideals, institutions, and way of life" (3). Departments of Education in Manitoba, Saskatchewan, and Alberta introduced the "teaching of the English language, British ideals, and Canadian ways" to Ukrainian students in public schools; Methodist and Presbyterian evangelists established missions among Ukrainian communities; and government officials from the Department of the Interior frequently visited Ukrainian communities, monitoring their progress along the path of "Canadianization."

But dominant ideas about what the "model" Canadian is, and dominant ideas, more generally, about what Canada means, are never fixed or stable. Gradually, as both New and Swyripa point out, in the decades following the First World War, the policies and practices of assimilation gave way to more inclusive attitudes toward ethnic immigrants and their descendants. According to New, between the First World War and 1959, social contexts in Canada became "less British" and "more American"; as Canada "proclaimed its 'maturity,'" Canadians "began to think of their cultural identity in political terms, replacing the racial and religious definition of culture that had so governed the latter years of the nineteenth century" (131). From 1960 until 1985—decades in which Native and Québécois peoples began to assert their own claims to "nationhood," and in which discourses of multiculturalism and feminism emerged—national definitions of Canadian culture changed again, this time acknowledging the ethnic, regional, and gendered diversity of its citizens (204). And, from 1986 to the turn of the twenty-first century, Canadians continued to reconsider and reconstruct their ideas of the nation, focusing more sharply on "race," ethnicity, sexuality, and diasporic consciousness (283–358). Swyripa similarly notes that, from the "original emphasis on Anglo-conformity" from 1896 to 1918, through the "the germination of a mosaic concept" from 1919 to 1945, to the "recent acceptance of a multicultural expression of Canadian identity" consolidated between 1946 and 1970, Canadian history is marked by "progress towards eventual acceptance of the concept of diversity" (ix–xi).

Without a doubt, scholars such as New and Swyripa are correct about the instability of public discourse on Canadian nationhood and nationality; we are a nation whose sense of itself is constantly under revision. Reading the ongoing process of revision, however, as a narrative of progress is problematic because past definitions of the nation never pass away completely; on the contrary, they leave indelible traces on the social, political, and cultural landscape of the country. Many Ukrainian Canadians who experienced assimilationist pressures—people of my grandparents' and parents' generation—passed on to their grandchildren and children the attitudes they internalized: shame about their ethnic culture; the desire to "pass," which found its expression in the Anglicization of Ukrainian first and last names—Mihkaylo to Mitchell or Harasym to Harrison, for example; and the use of English in the home instead of Ukrainian. As we will see in subsequent chapters of this book, virtually all second- and third-generation Ukrainian Canadians writing during the 1980s and 1990s—long after discourses of assimilation had given way to multiculturalism—are forced to contend with the fact that, by the time inclusiveness had become the norm, they had lost ties with their ethnic culture and language, either partially or completely. Recuperation of these ties becomes the primary motivation for their writing as they seek to reconnect with their Ukrainian roots.

Assimilationist discourse has also, unsurprisingly, left its mark on Anglo-Canadian literature—on texts about Ukrainian Canadians by writers from Anglo-Celtic backgrounds. Ralph Connor's *The Foreigner: A Tale of Saskatchewan* (1909), Sinclair Ross's *As For Me and My House* (1941), and Margaret Laurence's *A Jest of God* (1966), the novels I discuss at length in the following chapter, collectively illustrate the pervasiveness of negative attitudes toward Ukrainian Canadians in Canadian literature during roughly the first half of the twentieth century. Connor's novel more bluntly articulates its author's assimilationist rhetoric than either Ross's or Laurence's, but the "othering" of Ukrainian Canadian characters takes place to some extent in each text. And while *The Foreigner* is read and studied less often than *As For Me and My House* and *A Jest of God*, two arguably more canonical works of Canadian literature, all three novels need to be examined for the ways in which they set the literary stage for Ukrainian Canadian texts that followed. Overcoming firmly entrenched misrepresentations of Ukrainian Canadians became a prime motivation, and a simultaneously daunting task, for Ukrainian Canadian writers seeking to make their voices heard in English-language Canadian literature. Beginning with

Vera Lysenko, whose novel *Yellow Boots* (1954) marks the starting point of the English-language Ukrainian Canadian literary tradition, virtually all Ukrainian Canadian writers have grappled with the enduring aftermath of assimilation—how to "write back" to stereotypes of Ukrainian Canadians; how to recapture the distinct culture that was in many ways erased as Anglo-Canadians attempted to "digest" the Ukrainian Canadian "foreign mass."

TWO

"Digesting" the "Foreign Mass"
Ukrainian Canadians in Three Anglo-Canadian Novels

Ralph Connor's *The Foreigner: A Tale of Saskatchewan*

RALPH CONNOR'S *The Foreigner: A Tale of Saskatchewan* (1909), a frontier romance with unmistakably nationalistic and proselytizing undertones, is the first novelistic portrayal of Ukrainian immigrants in Canada. Connor—the pen name of Presbyterian clergyman Charles W. Gordon[1]—brings together characters of Slavic (Galician, Bukovynian, Russian) and Anglo-Celtic (English, Scottish, Irish) origins to depict Canada at the close of the nineteenth century and to dramatize Slavic immigrants' potentially harmful impact on the nascent nation. At the start of the novel, Connor paints a decidedly grim picture of Slavic groups in Canada—so grim, in fact, that the very fate of the nation hinges on the success or failure of Anglo-Canadians in assimilating Slavic foreigners to Anglo-Canadian society. Throughout the novel, as Connor narrates the transition of Canada from colony to nation, he carefully outlines the methodologies as well as the benefits of assimilation.

Oddly enough, given the book's title, the major portion of *The Foreigner* takes place in Winnipeg. In the opening paragraphs of the novel, Connor describes Winnipeg as the "cosmopolitan capital of the last of the Anglo-Saxon Empires" (11), a city "[n]ot far from the centre of the American continent, midway between the oceans east and west, midway between the Gulf and the Arctic Sea, on the rim of a plain, snow swept in winter, flower decked in summer, but, whether in winter or in summer, beautiful in its sunlit glory" (11).² This idyllic conception of the "City of the Plain," however, is almost immediately disrupted by Connor's introduction of the "more unfashionable northern section of the little city," the immigrant quarter peopled with newcomers "strange in costume and speech" (13). "With a sprinkling of Germans, Italian and Swiss," he writes, "it was almost solidly Slav."

> Slavs of all varieties from all provinces and speaking all dialects were there to be found: Slavs from Little Russia and from Great Russia, the alert Polak, the heavy Croatian, the haughty Magyar, and occasionally the stalwart Dalmatian from the Adriatic, in speech mostly Ruthenian, in religion orthodox Greek Catholic or Uniat and Roman Catholic. By their non-discriminating Anglo-Saxon fellow-citizens, they are called Galicians. (14)

Connor goes on to describe the Galicians' overcrowded living conditions (a result of their "traditional social instincts"), their unusual foods ("with the inevitable seasoning of garlic"), and their general uncleanliness (they are a people "devoid of hygienic scruples and disdainful of city sanitary laws") (15). In the introduction to the novel, then—before announcing either character or plot—Connor establishes the binary oppositions upon which his narrative is constructed: the "sunlit glory" of "Anglo-Saxon" Winnipeg versus the "huddling cluster of little black shacks" of the city's immigrant underbelly; the civilized, progressive Anglo-Saxons versus the primitive, backward Slavic hordes. Even as Connor romanticizes the way in which Canada draws together "peoples of all tribes and tongues" (12)—he foretells that the "blood strains of great races will mingle in the blood of a race greater than the greatest of them all" (n.p.)—he nonetheless conceives the relation between these races in Canada as strictly hierarchical, privileging Anglo-Celtic settlers over those who come from places other than the British Isles.

The Foreigner is rife with the stuff of romance—noble heroes questing for the side of good; shifty villains plotting murder and mayhem; and even the occasional damsel-in-distress—but the binary opposition of good-versus-evil that shapes the romance structure of the novel is crucial to Connor's understanding of the newly-formed nation. As Frances Swyripa argues, in the "confrontation between the manly, virtuous,

Christian Anglo-Saxon and the ignorant, emotional, and frequently immoral Galician" (*Ukrainian Canadians: A Survey* 12), Anglo-Saxons become the naturally superior agents of British colonialism, and Slavs become utterly foreign, innately inferior objects of colonization. Not surprisingly, *The Foreigner* reads today like a sort of postcolonial morality tale in which good (Anglo-Canada) ultimately triumphs over evil (Slavic immigrants).

Indeed, *The Foreigner* is a story of "the East meets the West" (24)—aptly set in a city situated geographically between the "oceans east and west"—in which ethnically-inflected notions of good and evil are absolute. Paulina Koval, second wife to Michael Kalmar and caretaker of his two children, Irma and Kalman, is a "slow-witted" (15), "undoubtedly slovenly" (23) and morally reprehensible Galician woman; Kalmar is a crafty and cunning Russian nihilist, capable of assuming many disguises, an "object of terror and of horror to many" (105); and Rosenblatt, Kalmar's archenemy, is an "unscrupulous" (61) Bukovynian opportunist, a wealthy entrepreneur who exploits his countrymen in the New World. Juxtaposed against these Galician, Russian, and Bukovynian characters—each manifesting different characteristics of the Slavic "other"—are the Anglo-Celtic characters of the story, superior by virtue of their British culture and values. Margaret French is a selfless Methodist missionary who works tirelessly among the Galicians, acknowledging that, though they are "poor ignorant creatures," they "really have kind hearts" (195–98). Her brother-in-law, Jack French, is one of the "hardy souls" in the "daring vanguard of an advancing civilization" (189), a tough but sensitive Saskatchewan rancher of "good old English stock" (190). And Jack's friend, Dr. Brown, is a Presbyterian reverend who bravely forsakes the conveniences of civilization to establish a mission among the Galicians. He will "teach them English," "doctor them," and "teach them some of the elements of domestic science"—"in short, do anything to make them good Christians and good Canadians, which is the same thing" (253).[3]

In keeping with the nationalist sentiment of his time—which was, according to W. H. New, "anglocentric, male-dominated, and justified by appeals to God and National Law" (*A History of Canadian Literature* 79)—Connor constructs a plot as convoluted as it is romantic. As with many of his novels, published at a time when sentimental novels, historical tales, and nature stories were popular, the storyline of *The Foreigner* "celebrate[s] the virility of religious belief, requiring the strength of civilization to be tested against hard pioneering circumstances" (109–10). The main concern of the novel—Kalman's coming-of-age under the guidance of Jack French and Dr. Brown—foregrounds the "muscular Christianity" of Connor's enterprise (New, *A History of Canadian Literature* 109). The central question is whether or not Kalman can be fully assimilated into Anglo-Canadian society. Near the beginning of the novel—before he is introduced to either French or Brown, the forces of Anglo-Canadian good—Kalman visits his father, who is in prison for attempting to murder Rosenblatt (and for accidentally killing another man in the process). Listening to Kalmar swear his oath of revenge, Kalman's passions are aroused: he vows that, should his father fail, he will kill Rosenblatt himself. But will Kalman fulfil his father's wishes? Will he be ruled by the "hereditary instincts" of his "Slavic blood" that "[cry] out for vengeance" (343)? Or is it possible that, through "those greatest of all Canadianising influences, the school and the mission" (158), he will shed his semi-barbaric bloodlust and embrace the civilized, Christian virtue of forgiveness?

Sent by Margaret French to live in Saskatchewan with Jack French, Kalman is tutored by both French and Brown in the English language and the Presbyterian religion; he is taught, moreover, to dress, eat, and work like a morally upstanding Anglo-Canadian. In the latter half of the novel, as Connor carefully outlines Kalman's transformation from a wild and ignorant little Slavic boy to a civilized and educated young Canadian man, he also articulates—through conversations between French and Brown—the ideological foundations of assimilation.[4] French, who believes that the Slavs are a "hopeless business," is skeptical of Brown's missionary activities. He says to Brown,

> [d]on't be an ass and throw yourself away. I know these people well. In a generation or two something may be done with them. You can't make a silk purse out of a sow's ear. Give it up. Take up a ranch and go cattle raising. That is my advice. I know them. You can't undo in your lifetime the results of three centuries. (253–54)

Brown, who is determined to establish a school, a Presbyterian church, and a hospital in the nearby Galician colony, counters French's laissez-faire attitude with a pragmatic and patriotic analysis of the nation's fate. "These people here," he explains to French, "exist as an undigested foreign mass. They must be digested and absorbed into the body politic. They must be taught our ways of thinking and living, or it will be a mighty bad thing for us in Western Canada" (255). Given French's own moral flaws, his low opinion of the Galicians is somewhat ironic. Though a man of rugged strength and forceful courage—in temper and spirit a true gentleman—French periodically drinks himself into oblivion, fights, swears, and neglects both his farm and his young charge. But through the character of French, Connor illustrates that, in teaching the foreigner the language, religion and customs that characterize Anglo-Canadian culture, the Anglo-Canadian is himself reminded of his role as society's cultural and moral paragon. Just as Brown ministers to Kalman, so too does he minister to French, advising him that he has "that boy's life"—and, simultaneously, the fate of the nation—"in [his] hands" (281). That French takes seriously his role in shaping the future of the boy—and the country—is evidenced not only by Kalman's successful assimilation but also by the "new order" of French's ranch at the close of the narrative. After five years of "steady application to duty," moreover, French achieves success "not in wealth alone, but in character and in influence" (373). In the process of postcolonial nation-building, Anglo-Canadian moral and cultural ideals are at once imparted to immigrants and strengthened in established citizens.

But it is the final scene of the novel that finally confirms—as it boldly dramatizes—the success of Kalman's assimilation. At the coal mine that Kalman has discovered—and that, of course, the villainous Rosenblatt seeks to claim for his own—all of the central characters meet in a violently grandiose finale. Kalmar kills Rosenblatt, Rosenblatt kills Kalmar, and Paulina dies defending Kalman from Rosenblatt. Importantly, though Kalmar fatally wounds Rosenblatt, he does so without the aid of his son. Kalman, in fact, struggles to *stop* his father from committing the murder: "[m]y father!" he begs, while physically restraining Kalmar. "Don't commit this crime! For my sake, for Christ's dear sake!" (365). So, while the narrative ends in a veritable bloodbath, the tragic nature of its conclusion is mitigated by Kalman's decision not to perpetuate in Canada his people's violent Old Country feuds. Whereas the novel's morally reprehensible Slavic characters all conveniently meet their end, Kalman—the newly-assimilated Canadian—sees the error of their ways and survives.[5]

What Connor seems to suggest is that the unassimilated foreigner has no future in Canada. Throughout *The Foreigner*, Connor makes explicit the fact that, though Slavic immigrants pose a threat to Anglo-Canadian society—"they'll run your country," warns Jack French in conversation with Brown—they *can* be taught, through the institutions of school and church, Anglo-Canadian customs, values and morals—"they'll run your country anyhow you put it," replies Brown, "therefore, you had better fit them for the job. You have got to make them Canadian" (256). In the novel's epilogue, Kalman goes on to attend Business College, run the Night Hawk Mining Company, and marry Marjorie Menzies, illustrating that the assimilated Slavic immigrant's future is a happy one.

Yet if Kalman becomes a symbolic figure of the future nation[6]—the Slavic foreigner-cum-model citizen who unites with the Anglo-Celtic lass to produce "a race greater than the greatest of them all" (n.p.)—it is less his generally Slavic than his specifically *Russian* inheritance that makes him particularly well-suited for the role; and it is, more specifically, his embrace of *Presbyterian* religion and his union with a Scottish woman that make him the ideal Canadian. Crucially, his gender, too, marks him as an ideal participant in future nation-building. With the exception of Margaret French, who plays a minor role in the novel by sending Kalman away, Kalman's mentors are all male. And Irma, Kalmar's daughter, is hardly mentioned in the novel. So Connor's notion of the ideal Canadian privileges Scottish ethnicity and the Presbyterian religion as well as maleness. Certainly, as I have already argued, many of the Slavic characters in *The Foreigner* are depicted in derogatory terms. But whereas the Galician and Bukovynian characters in the novel represent absolute poverty, ignorance, and barbarity, Kalmar's—and, by extension, Kalman's—status in the narrative is more ambiguous. While violent and vengeful, Kalmar is also vaguely aristocratic in bearing, an educated gentleman whose political machinations are noble insofar as they embrace the "cause of freedom" against a tyrannical government (150).[7] Not unlike his father, Kalman is at his most heroic when taking up the fight for freedom:

> [t]he song [he sang] was in the Ruthenian tongue, but was the heart cry of a Russian exile, a cry for freedom for his native land, for death to the tyrant, for vengeance on the traitor. Nowhere in all the Czar's dominions dared any man sing that song. As the boy's strong, clear voice rang out in the last cry for vengeance, there thrilled in his tones an intensity of passion that gripped hard the hearts of those who had known all their lives long the bitterness of tyranny unspeakable. (181)

When Kalman finally unites with Marjorie, she calls him "[t]he son of a hero, who paid out his life for a great cause" (382). Though he fears that she "could never love a foreigner," Marjorie cries, "Oh, Kalman, I have been there. I have seen the people, your father's people.... Were I Russian, I should be like your father!" (382–83). Kalman, then, becomes the perfect hero for Connor's novel because, on the one hand, as a successfully "Canadianized" Slavic foreigner, he fulfills the assimilationist theme of the narrative; on the other hand, as the son of an exiled Russian revolutionary, he embodies the narrative's romance. Bereft of a similarly glorified political cause, the Galician and Bukovynian characters, in contrast to the Russians, play minor roles within the text.[8]

Interestingly, while Connor devotes the first half of his novel to derogatory portrayals of the Galician immigrants in Winnipeg, their assimilation to Anglo-Canadian society is mentioned only briefly in the conclusion. In a single—albeit lengthy—paragraph describing Brown's work in the Galician colony, Connor notes that

> [t]he changes apparent in the colony, largely as a result of Dr. Brown's labours, were truly remarkable. The creating of a market for their produce by the advent of the railway, and for their labour by the development of the mine, brought the Galician people wealth, but the influence of Dr. Brown himself, and of his Home, and of his Hospital, was apparent in the life and character of the people, and especially of the younger generation. The old mud-plastered cabins were giving place to neat frame houses, each surrounded by its garden of vegetables and flowers. In dress, the sheep skin and the shawl were being exchanged for the ready-made suit and the hat of latest style.

The Hospital, with its staff of trained nurses under the direction of the young matron, the charming Miss Irma, by its ministrations to the sick, and more by the spirit that breathed through its whole service, wrought in the Galician a new temper and a new ideal. In the Training Home fifty Galician girls were being indoctrinated into that most noble of all science, the science of home-making, and were gaining practical experience in all the cognate sciences and arts. (372)

Connor's emphasis here on Dr. Brown—"*Dr. Brown's* labours," "*his* Home," "*his* Hospital" (emphasis added)—as well as his use of the passive voice—"[t]he old mud-plastered cabins *were giving* place," "the sheep skin and the shawl *were being exchanged*," "fifty Galician girls *were being indoctrinated*" (emphasis added)—reveal the extent to which Galicians are passive objects of Brown's Canadianizing acts. In other words, Galicians function in *The Foreigner* less as an illustration of the ways in which assimilation unites "peoples of all tribes and tongues" (12) than as an affirmation of Anglo-Canadians' social, political, and cultural dominance. Through Kalman's coming-of-age narrative, *The Foreigner* may well dramatize the success of assimilationist ideology in marrying East and West, "self" and "other"; Kalman, by choosing to embrace Canadian culture, illustrates that processes of assimilation can create the ideal Canadian. But by relegating Galicians to the margins of the story—the very place where they began—Connor reveals that this is, first and foremost, an Anglo-Canadian story.

Sinclair Ross's *As For Me and My House*

Following the publication of *The Foreigner*, Slavic characters appeared in a number of Canadian novels. In Martha Ostenso's novel *Wild Geese* (1925), for example, a Hungarian character, Anton Klovacz, appears; the narrator in Frederick Philip Grove's *A Search for America* (1927) meets briefly with a Russian man, Ivan; and the heroine of Morley Callaghan's *They Shall Inherit the Earth* (1935), Anna Prychoda, is Ukrainian (293). But Slavic characters play very minor roles in Ostenso's and Grove's texts, and in *They Shall Inherit the Earth* the main character's ethnicity is incidental. In Sinclair Ross's *As For Me and My House* (1941), by contrast, Steve Kulanich's role in the narrative is more significant, and his Slavic ethnicity is a crucial aspect of his characterization. In fact, Ross's novel, though written three decades after *The Foreigner*, invites comparison with Connor's novel: not unlike Kalman, who is taken into the Anglo-Canadian "family" of French and Ross, Steve is brought into the home of Mr. and Mrs. Philip Bentley, the main characters in *As For Me and My House*. These two texts, through the figure of the Slavic boy, reflect Anglo-Canadian attitudes toward Slavic minorities at two different, though connected, historical moments. In fact, the portrayal of Steve Kulanich in *As For Me and My House* illustrates the extent to which Anglo-Canadian definitions of national culture, established during the late nineteenth and early twentieth centuries, continued to pervade Canadian society well after the First World War. In the literary arena, realism replaced romance as a dominant generic strain, but, as New suggests, the "francophone and anglophone versions of Canada barely took each other into account, let alone additional cultures and languages" (*A History of Canadian Literature* 149). Despite Watson Kirkconnell's work on languages other than English, and the emergence of such minority writers as Ostenso and A.M. Klein, Canadian literature, outside of Québec, was still committed to upholding Anglo-Canadian norms.

In many ways, *As For Me and My House* requires less introduction than *The Foreigner*. Over the years since its publication, numerous Canadian literary critics have analyzed Ross's novel's narrative structure, its realist genre, gender and sexual politics, and, more generally, its contribution to the prairie literary tradition.[9] Set during the depression and narrated by the wife of Protestant minister Philip Bentley, *As For Me and My House* takes the form of Mrs. Bentley's diary entries written during the couple's brief stay in the small town of Horizon, Saskatchewan. After twelve years of marriage, the Bentleys' relationship is, in modern terms, dysfunctional: miserable about the direction their lives have taken but unable to discuss, much less change, their situation, they are imprisoned by both the social expectations of the "false-fronted" little town in which they live and the marital obligations of their "false-fronted" relationship. For Mrs. Bentley, their small and dark home becomes a metaphor not only for the claustrophobic, provincial atmosphere of Horizon (and, in fact, of all the small towns in which the Bentleys have lived) but also for the suffocating nature of the patriarchal marriage institution. That Philip always uses the same text for his first Sunday sermon in a new town—"As For Me and My House We Will Serve the Lord" (Joshua 24:15)—underscores the symbolic function of the house in the narrative and the irony of the Bentleys' unhappiness, for neither the minister nor his wife is even remotely content in "serving the Lord."

One of the central concerns in the novel is the couple's childlessness. Mrs. Bentley brings a twelve-year-old foster boy, Steve Kulanich, into their home in an attempt to fulfill Philip's parental longings. Steve, however, is taken away from the Bentleys and it is Philip's affair with Judith West that ultimately produces a son for the couple.[10] After Judith's death, the Bentleys adopt the baby, and it is in baby Philip's (not Steve's) eyes that Mrs. Bentley sees "a freshness," a "vacancy of beginning" (216), hope for the future.

Unlike Kalman Kalmar in *The Foreigner*, who is of Russian origin, Steve Kulanich's ancestry is more ambiguous. In Mrs. Bentley's first description of the boy, she writes, "Steve was the first name, Rumanian or Hungarian" (48). "At first glance," she says of his eyes, "you would take them for Oriental" (54). He speaks "good English" but the "force and inflection" in his voice "in contrast to [native English speakers'] monotones sounds a little impetuous" (55). Later, she reiterates that he is "Hungarian, or Rumanian, or Russian—we don't even know that" (66-67). What Mrs. Bentley assumes is that, as a Slav, Steve has "[b]lood behind him that's different" from hers and Philip's (66). Steve's mother is dead, and his father is a railway labourer who lives in a little shack by the station with some woman ("the only case of open immorality in the town" [48]).

Steve, like his father, is an outsider in the town. He is "sensitive," "high-strung," "hot-blooded," and "quick-fisted" (48)—a devout Roman Catholic, moreover, whose most precious belongings are a crucifix and a Sacred Heart picture of the Virgin. Mary Kirtz, in "'I am become a name': The Representation of Ukrainians in Ross, Laurence, Ryga and Atwood" (1992), makes the claim that, although Steve is "not named as a Ukrainian, those who know the history of Ukrainian Canadians during this period would likely identify him as such" (37). She goes on, then, to suggest that, in Mrs. Bentley's descriptions of Steve, he becomes "the Ukrainian as inscrutable oriental"; "the Ukrainian as spontaneous, loud-mouthed peasant"; "the Ukrainian as gypsy rover"; and "the Ukrainian as blasphemous idolater" (37). Yet, in the absence of any descriptions that specifically link him to Ukrainian ethnicity, this argument seems to me difficult to make—and somewhat beside the point. Ross may well have imagined Steve as Ukrainian, but insofar as the novel constructs Protestant Anglo-Canadians as "self," and non-Anglo-Canadians as "other," Steve's characterization requires only the vaguest of Slavic qualities to fulfill the function of "other" in the narrative. That he has Oriental features, speaks with an accent, and espouses the Roman Catholic faith is enough to mark him as different from—and threatening to—the community.[11]

Whereas, in *The Foreigner*, prominent Anglo-Canadian citizens such as Margaret French and Dr. Brown know the importance of, and actively engage in, assimilating Slavic immigrants to Anglo-Canadian society, the prominent citizens of Horizon reject the notion that the Slavic "other" can or even should be included in their society. The Twills, the Pratts, the Finleys, and the Wenderbys are outspoken in their belief that Steve cannot be changed, and they are equally outspoken in their disapproval of the Bentleys' decision to try. When Mrs. Bentley announces to a group of ladies that she has taken Steve into her home, she is met with a barrage of criticism: "[y]ou mean, of course," says one lady, "just till other arrangements can be made. Naturally you wouldn't think of keeping him." Another says, "[t]he Roman Catholics have so many places of their own that he could go to. If you really want a boy to adopt there are surely enough good Protestants." And a third warns of the dangers involved: "[y]ou've heard, I suppose, what the blood behind him is?" (73). At a church board meeting, too, a month later, the Bentleys are chastised for their imprudent decision to care for Steve. As Mrs. Bentley recalls,

[s]omeone said we would remember our position in the community, the example we are setting. Someone else, more kindly, said we might be given time to train the boy...still someone else reminded us that bad blood was bad blood and always would be. As Steve Kulanich he had been recognized for what he was and treated accordingly. As the minister's son there was the danger of his vicious habits being over looked and tolerated. It was to be hoped we realized our responsibilities, and were prepared to measure up to them. Someone else had caught a glimpse of the crucifix above his bed, and thumped on a pew, "No popery." (95)

The Bentleys may appear to have good Christian intentions in taking Steve under their wing, but their parishioners are openly hostile toward him: they see Steve—and any benevolence toward him—as a threat to their community. Though never explicitly articulated as such, Steve's potential for assimilation to Anglo-Canadian society is at the crux of the debate about him that takes place during the church board meeting. While the Bentleys are ostensibly willing to give Steve a chance to prove himself, the townspeople are unwilling to so much as entertain the possibility.

On the surface, at least, the Bentleys do try to help Steve fit into Horizon. They take him to the barber, buy him new clothes, give him a horse, and take him on family outings. They are liberal-minded enough to allow Steve his crucifix and Virgin Mary lithograph and even to speak on his behalf before school and church officials after he has bloodied another child's nose. Mrs. Bentley brings Steve into their home, however, not out of concern for his welfare but in the hope that he can fill the couple's childless void and, hence, help solve their marital problems. She is drawn to Steve because, like the Bentleys, he is an outsider in the community and because she believes that, in siding with him against the less tolerant citizens of Horizon, she and Philip might regain the closeness that they have lost over the years—they might at last come together against the small towns that have driven them apart. Not surprisingly, then, when Mrs. Bentley discovers that Steve's presence in the family effectively widens the distance between husband and wife—Philip enjoys spending time alone with the boy, lavishing him with the sort of love and affection that he has never shown her—her interest in the child wanes, and she finds herself caught in several contradictory roles vis-à-vis Steve. At times a nurturing mother to him—"getting out a clean shirt for Steve, brushing his hair at the kitchen sink and putting on soap to make it stay in place" (85)—at times a fellow outcast in the community—in playing one of his Slavic folk songs on the piano, she stumbles upon a common interest with the boy, and their secretly shared passion for this music becomes a kind of symbolic "conspiracy" (95)—she is nonetheless unable to shake her feeling of rivalry.[12] "I like Steve, and at the same time I resent him" she states, "I grudge every minute he and Philip are alone together" (69). So, when Steve is taken away to an orphanage by two Catholic priests, Mrs. Bentley is nothing short of relieved—it was "good," she writes, "to have [Philip] to [herself] again" (155). (The good citizens of Horizon are pleased with his departure. In their first show of warmth toward the boy, a small crowd gathers at the train station to say their farewells.) Mrs. Bentley can—and does—write Steve out of her diary in a single entry because her marriage has always taken precedence over his well-being.[13]

In the end, given her experience with Steve, Mrs. Bentley's ultimate embrace of Judith West's (and Philip's) baby seems all the more ironic: if Steve exacerbated tensions between husband and wife, how will the baby—a baby conceived, no less, through an adulterous relationship between Philip and another woman—affect the couple's relationship? Whether the baby functions as a genuine symbol of hope for the Bentleys' marriage or as an ironic symbol of hope, the fact remains that Steve is written out of the narrative whereas the baby remains central to the Bentleys' story. Steve is, in Kirtz's words, "expendable" and a "throwaway" because "[a]pparently even a bastard is better than the son of unknown parents if the former has the appropriate patriarchal lineage" ("'I am become a name'" 38). Steve cannot be accepted as a permanent member of either the Bentley family or the town of Horizon because he is ethnically "other" to both the Bentleys and the Anglo-Canadian townspeople. Judith's baby, on the other hand, though born of an unwed mother, can become a figure of hope—however misguided, however ironic—because he is legitimized by his biological (or adoptive?) Anglo-Canadian father, Philip.

Reading *As For Me and My House* alongside *The Foreigner*, what becomes obvious is that Ross does not as explicitly rely on the Slavic character's ethnicity to carry forward his narrative. Unlike *The Foreigner*, in which the "Canadianization" of the Slavic "other" is overtly thematized,

As For Me and My House is only peripherally, if at all, concerned with the assimilation of Slavic characters to Anglo-Canadian society. But as a work of realist fiction—one that, by definition, "mirrors the attitudes of the dominant culture through its inscription of a particular set of norms validated by that culture" (Kirtz "'I am become a name'" 38)—*As For Me and My House* does rely on Steve's ethnicity (and the Anglo-Canadian characters' attitudes toward his ethnicity) to depict the realities of its time and place. Insofar as Ross's novel is a reflection of the social, cultural, and political milieus of small town Saskatchewan during the depression, its portrayal of Steve as "other" illustrates the persistence of Anglo-Canadian culture in shaping dominant definitions of the Canadian "self." The assimilationist ideology so explicitly and urgently articulated in *The Foreigner* may be absent from *As For Me and My House*, but through the character of Steve Kulanich, Ross's novel nonetheless illustrates that, thirty-odd years after the publication of Connor's novel, notions of Anglo-Canadian social and cultural superiority persist.

Margaret Laurence's *A Jest of God*

Published twenty-five years after *As For Me and My House* and set in a small prairie town roughly two decades after the depression, Margaret Laurence's *A Jest of God* (1966) picks up the story of the second-generation Slavic male through its portrayal of Nick Kazlik. Nick, unambiguously Ukrainian, belongs to the same generation as Steve Kulanich; both are sons of immigrants and both are marked as ethnically different from the other members of their predominantly Anglo-Canadian communities. Like *As For Me and My House*, *A Jest of God* is a work of realist fiction narrated in the first person by an Anglo-Canadian woman. As in Ross's novel, the Slavic character in *A Jest of God* serves a particular function in a narrative that includes but crucially is not about him. Just as Ross's novel focuses on Mrs. Bentley, Laurence's novel focuses on Rachel Cameron; just as Mrs. Bentley relies on Steve Kulanich to help solve her marital problems, so is Rachel drawn to Nick as a means to reinvent herself and help her through her personal crisis of identity. In these novels, the concerns and experiences of Steve and Nick are subordinate to those of Mrs. Bentley and Rachel. Yet, while neither *As For Me and My House* nor

A Jest of God focuses centrally on the Slavic/Ukrainian character, and while neither—like *The Foreigner*—is explicitly concerned with the situation of ethnic immigrants vis-à-vis Anglo-Canadian society, these texts illustrate Anglo-Canadians' perspectives on Ukrainian Canadians from the mid-1930s to the 1960s.

A Jest of God is the second novel in Laurence's Manawaka cycle, which comprises five texts in total, all set at least partly in Manawaka, a fictional town in Manitoba, not unlike Laurence's hometown of Neepawa. Each is centred on a strong female character, as these women grow up and—as in Hagar Shipley's case in *The Stone Angel* (1962)—grow old, in and sometimes beyond Manawaka, they all grapple with the town's complex hierarchy of social relations, trying to find their place within it.¹⁴ Many of Laurence's heroines strive to escape the restrictive patriarchal social structures upheld by their domineering fathers and husbands. Hagar, for example, struggles against her father, Jason Currie; Stacey MacAindra against her husband, Mac, in *The Fire-Dwellers* (1969); Vanessa MacLeod against her grandfather, Timothy Connor, in *A Bird in the House* (1970); and Morag Gunn against her husband, Brooke Skelton, in *The Diviners* (1974). Not a few heroines in Laurence's novels are drawn to men who openly defy the values and expectations of Manawaka's upright Anglo-Scots elite. Hagar marries Bram Shipley, Morag falls in love with Jules "Skinner" Tonnerre, and Rachel has an affair with Nick Kazlik. In *A Jest of God*, specifically, Rachel finds herself trapped by the social expectations of her family and community—at thirty-four, she is a spinster schoolmarm who shares a home with her controlling elderly mother, May Cameron. Not unlike Mrs. Bentley in *As For Me and My House*, Rachel craves a new start, a new life, and a new identity. Unlike Mrs. Bentley, however, whose future at the close of Ross's novel is uncertain, Rachel is transformed over the course of *A Jest of God*—at the end of the text, she quits her job, stands up to her mother, and prepares to move to Vancouver. And Nick is the unmistakable catalyst for Rachel's positive transformation. After her affair with Nick—after she mistakenly assumes that she is pregnant and the imagined pregnancy, the "non-life" (187), is removed—Rachel is figuratively reborn.

In her discussion of *A Jest of God*, Mary Kirtz outlines the ways in which Laurence, like Ross, constructs the Ukrainian as "other." In both novels, she says, "the emphasis on the 'oriental' cast of Steve and Nick's faces, particularly their black hair and slanted eyes, make the Ukrainians 'not quite white' and therefore even more suspect as 'Other,' representing the dark and dangerous side of life" ("'I am become a name'" 39). Indeed, in her descriptions of Nick, Rachel frequently focuses on his physical appearance, his physical "otherness." Nick's eyes are "rather Slavic, slightly slanted" (68); he has "[p]rominent cheekbones" and "black straight hair" (92); and his "hidden Caucasian face" is like the faces of the "hawkish and long-ago riders of the Steppes" (92). Rachel's descriptions of Nick are strikingly similar to Hagar's descriptions of Bram's "hawk-faced" farm hands (*Stone Angel* 114); to Vanessa's descriptions of Piquette Tonnerre's "dark and slightly slanted eyes" (*Bird* 116); and to Morag's descriptions of Skinner Tonnerre's "dark dark slanted eyes (*Diviners* 69), "brown hawkish face" (126), and "[l]ank black hair" (263). Because Bram's farm hands and the Tonnerres are Manawaka's "half-breeds"—because they are racially "other" to the "white" residents of Manawaka—their strong physical resemblance to Nick and to his father, Nestor, suggests that Ukrainians, too, function in Laurence's fiction as racialized "others" to the Anglo-Celtic "self." Rachel, in fact, directly links Nick's father to the Native people who live in and around Manawaka: Nestor's "wide hard bony face," she says, is "high-cheekboned as a Cree's" (194).

Of course, as Kirtz also points out, the "otherness" physically embodied by Laurence's Ukrainian characters is presented as "something to be embraced, not obliterated" ("'I am become a name'" 39). If, in *As For Me and My House*, Steve's ethnic difference marks him as inferior and undesirable to Horizon's Anglo-Canadian community, Nick's ethnic difference is valued—at least by Rachel—for its romantic appeal. Shortly after she begins seeing Nick, Rachel discusses with him her perceptions of Ukrainian culture. Recalling her childhood experiences with Nick's father, the town milkman, she says, "I used to get rides in winter on your dad's sleigh, and I remember the great bellowing voice he had, and how emotional he used to get—cursing at the horses, or else almost crooning to them" (94). In her own family, Rachel explains, "you didn't get emotional. It was frowned upon" (94). Attracted to the emotional expressiveness and freedom of Nick's family, she views Ukrainians as "more resistant…more free" (93) than her own Scots family. "I don't know how to express it," she says. "Not so boxed-in, maybe. More outspoken. More able to speak out. More allowed to—both by your family and by yourself. Something like that" (94). Rachel is no less drawn to the Ukrainian folk arts and family photos on display in the Kazlik home:

> a gilt-bordered ikon, and an embroidered tablecloth with some mythical tree nestled in by a fantasy of birds, and on the wall a framed photograph of long-dead relatives in the old country, the heavily moustached men sitting with hands on knees, wearing their serge suits and rigid smiles, the women aproned elaborately and wearing on their head black-fringed *babushkas* patterned with poppies or roses. (108–9)

Rachel's idealization of Nick's Ukrainian heritage—a legacy of the "hawkish and long-ago riders of the Steppes" (92)—provides an alternative to her emotionally restrained, morally upright Scots background. Nick's colourful family dynamics and equally colourful family home are attractive—if not seductive—to Rachel because they fulfill her desire for exoticism, romance, and adventure. Nick's cultural heritage represents, in Kirtz's words, the "submerged," "passionate," and "unrestrained" qualities that Rachel seeks to unleash within herself ("'I am become a name'" 39).

The seeds of Rachel's rebellion against her old way of life are planted, then, when she initially meets Nick as an adult and when she begins for the first time to question some of the values and assumptions that she has inherited from her mother. Upon meeting Nick, she recalls her mother's poor opinion of the town's Ukrainians (as well as her own uncritical acceptance of this opinion): "Mother used to say, 'Don't play with those Galician youngsters.' How odd that seems now. They weren't Galicians—they were Ukrainian, but that didn't trouble my mother. She said Galician or Bohunk. So did I, I suppose" (69). Later, as Rachel discusses Nick with her mother, May Cameron's pointed remarks about Nick again bring Rachel back to her childhood in Manawaka. After Rachel tells her mother that Nick is a high school teacher—and after May asks, "Really? How did he manage that?" (71)—Rachel reminds herself that "[h]alf the town is Scots descent and the other half is Ukrainian. Oil, as they say, and water. Both came for the same reasons, because they had nothing where they were before. That was a long way away and a long time ago. The Ukrainians knew how to be the better grain farmers, but the Scots knew how to be almightier than anyone but God" (71).

According to Kirtz, through Rachel's new-found sympathy for and interest in the town's Ukrainians, "the Ukrainian experience is given greater validity"—greater, that is, than in *As For Me and My House*—"but only as a counterweight by which one can criticize the dominant culture's mores rather than as a legitimate center of power itself" ("'I am become a name'" 38). In other words, Rachel's relationship with Nick and her romanticization of Ukrainian culture reveal her desire to react against her Scots upbringing rather than her genuine interest in understanding Ukrainians' experiences in Canada. Nick, as a Ukrainian Canadian, is important to the narrative only insofar as he helps Rachel redefine herself within Anglo-Canadian society. As Kirtz rightly points out, "this story is not Nick's but Rachel's." Like Steve Kulanich, Nick "simply disappears" ("'I am become a name'" 40) from the narrative when he has fulfilled his function. So while Rachel's attitudes toward Ukrainian Canadians seem to suggest that she is more open to and accepting of ethnic difference than her mother, her idealized notions of Ukrainian Canadian culture are no less essentialist than her mother's negative stereotypes of Ukrainians: Rachel, too, is fundamentally complicit in perpetuating Ukrainian Canadians' construction as "other" to the Anglo-Canadian "self."

To be fair, though, when *A Jest of God* is placed in the broader context of Laurence's Manawaka cycle, the strict binary opposition of (Anglo-Canadian) "self" and (non-Anglo-Canadian) "other" begins to break down. In the first place, Anglo-Celtic ethnicity does not guarantee high social status. Jason Currie and Timothy Connor, two of Manawaka's founding Anglo-Celtic fathers (Currie is Scots, Connor is Irish), both begin their lives in Manawaka with nothing: Currie comes to the town "without a hope or a ha'penny" (*Stone Angel* 15) and Connor "walk[s] the hundred miles from Winnipeg to Manawaka with hardly a cent in his pockets" (*Bird* 190). By espousing the Protestant work ethic, both become veritable pillars of Manawaka society. But Christie and Prin Logan—of Scots and English origins, respectively—occupy one of the lowest positions in the community's social hierarchy as keepers of the nuisance grounds. Their home on Hill Street in the North End of the town is more similar to the Tonnerre place on the outskirts of town than it is to the South End of Manawaka—the Logans' home is surrounded by "old car axles, a decrepit black buggy with one wheel missing, pieces of iron and battered saucepans...a broken baby carriage and two ruined armchairs with the springs hanging out" (*Diviners* 28–29) and the Tonnerre place is a "collection of shacks" around which lie "old tires, a roll of chickenwire, the chassis of a rusted car, and an assortment of discarded farm machinery" (136–37). Similarly, Hagar Shipley's husband Bram, though of English ancestry, bears resemblance—both in his physical appearance and in his behavior—to the Métis people of the town; that Hagar, daughter of Jason Currie, descends the social ladder by marrying Bram is further evidence that one's membership to the town's Anglo-Celtic elite is not immutable.

And as the trajectory of Nick's life illustrates, just as the category of (Anglo-Canadian) "self" is fluid, so too is the category of "other"—at least to some extent. Even as Rachel projects onto Nick romanticized aspects of physical and cultural "otherness," Nick's willingness to assimilate to Anglo-Canadian society and, more importantly, his success in advancing socially and economically within Anglo-Canadian society, demonstrate that Ukrainian Canadians' actual status as "other" to the Anglo-Canadian "self" is neither fixed nor absolute. In fact, over the course of the five Manawaka texts, as Laurence narrates the town's history from the arrival of its founding fathers in the late nineteenth century to the departure of its sons and daughters in the 1960s and 1970s, Ukrainian Canadians' ability to escape categorization as "other"—through assimilation to Anglo-Canadian society—becomes increasingly apparent. "Race" remains the only absolute signifier of difference. Unlike Laurence's Métis characters, who, by virtue of their racial difference, cannot escape the social and economic margins of Manawaka society, her Ukrainian Canadian characters can—and indeed do—transcend the category of "other." Although Hagar, as a young married woman, feeds a "bunch of breeds and ne'er-do-wells and Galicians" (*Stone Angel* 114), over the course of several decades and three generations, the Galicians rise above their half-breed brethren and find themselves, like the Kazliks, living in a "big house with real lace curtains and piles of delicious food" (*Diviners* 120). But as Laurence follows the Tonnerres over three generations, their family history is marked by a pattern of persistent poverty and recurrent tragedy. So, while Nick—once chastised in the community as a Galician and a Bohunk—is able to go to university and establish a successful career as a high school English teacher, the Tonnerres are unable to enter the ranks of white middle-class society. In fact, Ukrainian Canadians' assimilation to Anglo-Canadian society—their shift from "other" to "self"—is nowhere more clearly dramatized than in *The Diviners*, when Nick's sister Julie meets Morag in Vancouver. Morag has recently given birth to Pique, Jules's child, and Pique has apparently inherited her father's racial attributes because, upon seeing the baby, Julie says, "*[m]y gosh*" (original emphasis). A moment later, having collected herself, she adds, "[i]t's okay...I was only a little surprised, is all" (305). Only a generation ago Julie's people were discriminated against; now, having made the transition to Anglo-Canadian society, Julie herself takes on its discriminatory attitudes.

A number of critics read the Manawaka cycle as a broad narrative of positive social change. Karin Beeler sees Pique, specifically—the daughter of Morag Gunn and Jules Tonnerre, who appears in *The Diviners*—as a culturally hybrid character who "offset[s] antagonistic binary oppositions between superior/inferior, white/native categories of experience" (32); through Pique, Laurence "stresses ethnic diversity and mutual appreciation instead of the politics of exclusion" and works toward dismantling "cultural hegemony by affirming cross-cultural interaction within Canadian society" (33). W. H. New, in "*The Stone Angel* and the Manawaka Cycle" (1981), makes a similar point, not only about the relationship between Morag and Jules, but also about other relationships that figure centrally in Laurence's writing. New reads Rachel's involvement with Nick, and her attitude toward him, as a step—however tentative—toward genuine understanding of cultural difference. He says that Rachel's relationship with Nick (like Hagar's with Bram, and Morag's with Jules) reflects a shift toward "a kind of core understanding about the shaping elements within a culture" (26). In illustrating that her Anglo-Celtic characters have much to learn from her "other" Ukrainian and Métis characters, Laurence begins to articulate a nascent discourse of multiculturalism.

This, at least, is one way of reading Laurence's Manawaka fiction, as a commentary, that is, on the increasingly inclusive nature of Canadian society. But it's a reading that needs to be made cautiously, and with qualification. Nick Kazlik—and, more specifically, Rachel's relationship with Nick—may well represent a positive step toward the acceptance of Ukrainian Canadians as a vital part of the Canadian cultural landscape. But readers need to remind themselves that the man to whom Rachel is attracted—the lover she believes to be emotionally uninhibited and physically exotic, with intimate ties to the "old country" (108-9)—is more a figment of her imagination than a real person, and Nick knows this. When Rachel explains to Nick that she is envious of Ukrainian Canadians' emotional freedom—they "always seemed...more free" (93) to her—he challenges her romanticized assumptions about his culture. "More free?" he asks, "How did you think we spent our time? Laying girls and doing gay Slavic dances?" (94). Nick proceeds then to outline the uneasy, politically charged dynamics of his family. While his uncle "was never actually a Communist...he was pretty far left...and the chief tenet of his belief was that it was a good thing for the Ukraine to be part of the USSR" (94). His father Nestor, on the other hand, "held the opposite view" and "still believes the Ukraine should be a separate country" (94). And Nick recalls telling his father that he "couldn't care less what the Ukraine did" (95).

As he goes on to discuss his troubled relationship with his father, the gap between Rachel's ideas about what being Ukrainian Canadian means and Nick's actual experiences as a Ukrainian Canadian becomes obvious—and his actual experiences have been heavily influenced by Anglo-Canadian assimilationist ideologies and practices. Tensions between father and son stem from Nestor's fervent desire to pass on his Ukrainian heritage to Nick and Nick's staunch resistance to this inheritance. That Nick as a young boy internalized Anglo-Canadians' derogatory attitudes toward Ukrainian Canadians is evidenced by his desire to slough all signs of ethnic difference in order to "pass" as an Anglo-Canadian. He only speaks English—his father "couldn't ever accept the fact that [he] never learned to speak Ukrainian" (95)—and he has little interest in his father's stories of immigration (112). When Rachel asks Nick if he ever liked his family home, he replies, "I guess before I started school I did. Not after that. Historical irony—it took my father fifteen years to build up that herd of his, and I used to wish every goddamn cow would drop dead" (108). In school—the "greatest of all Canadianising influences," according to Connor (158)—Nick learned to loathe his father's attempts to perpetuate the Ukrainian cultural and political heritage in Canada. His decision to become an English teacher makes clear the distance that he has sought to establish between himself and his Ukrainian roots, as well as the extent to which he has been willing to embrace Anglo-Canadian culture. Tellingly, while Rachel seems distressed by the fact that Nick's parents "have an icon" but "no samovar," he is flippant about the loss of the artifact. His grandmother, Nick explains, "traded it to somebody on the boat, and no one knows what she got for it. She used to claim it went for medicine for my dad…. Personally, I think it probably went for vodka to make the trip endurable" (111–12). His indifference toward the lost samovar becomes symbolic of his indifference toward his lost ethnic culture.

Ultimately, then, in *A Jest of God* Anglo-Canadians finally move away from assimilation and begin to recognize the contributions of Ukrainian Canadians. The novel offers a much more positive perspective on Ukrainian Canadians than either *The Foreigner* or *As For Me and My House*. But we need to keep in mind one crucial fact: Rachel's embrace of Nick—and, by allegorical extension, Anglo-Canada's embrace of Ukrainian Canadians—happens precisely because Nick has been almost fully "Canadianized." With the exception of his surname, virtually all aspects of his Ukrainian heritage have been erased: he cannot speak Ukrainian; he speaks English without an accent; and he has no interest in Ukrainian politics or Ukrainian culture. Nick illustrates that the threatening "undigested foreign mass" of Connor's novel (255) has been successfully tamed, neutralized, and controlled. Ukrainian Canadians of Nick's generation no longer occupy the position of "other" vis-à-vis the Anglo-Canadian "self." They have paid, though, an enormous price—however willingly—for the chance to ascend the social and economic hierarchies of Canadian society. Whether or not it is too high a price to pay is the question we need to ask of Vera Lysenko's *Yellow Boots*.

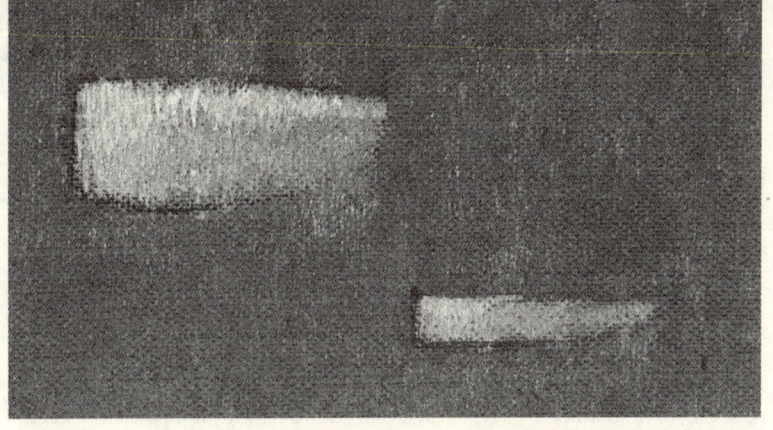

Re-reading the Female Ethnic Subject
Vera Lysenko's *Yellow Boots*

THE STARTING POINT of English-language Ukrainian Canadian literature is *Yellow Boots*, by Vera Lysenko, the first writer to "write back" to Anglo-Canadian representations of Ukrainian Canadians. For almost forty years, her novel—first published in 1954 by the Ryerson Press in Toronto—was largely ignored within the Canadian literary institution. Until its re-release in 1992 by the Canadian Institute of Ukrainian Studies and NeWest Press in Edmonton, the novel was rarely written about, taught or studied outside of the Ukrainian Canadian community.[1] The daughter of working-class Ukrainian immigrants, Vera Lesik—who went by the pseudonym of Vera Lysenko—was born in Winnipeg in 1910 and died in 1975. Over the course of her life she published, in addition to *Yellow Boots*, *Men in Sheepskin Coats: A Study in Assimilation* (1947) and a second novel, *Westerly Wild* (1956). As a Ukrainian Canadian woman who endeavoured to live by her pen at a time when women's roles were more conventionally defined in domestic terms, Lysenko was in many ways a pioneering literary figure. She was, however, subjected to "McCarthy-like treatment" as a result of her leftist political views.[2] Pushed to the margins of a literary canon that for many years has privileged Anglo-Canadian voices over those of ethnic minority writers, Lysenko would have slipped through the cracks of Canadian literary history entirely were it not for several scholars of Ukrainian Canadian literature who have recently pointed out the reasons why *Yellow Boots* merits serious scholarly attention.[3] Beverly Rasporich, Alexandra Kruchka Glynn, Sonia Mycak, and Tamara Palmer Seiler have all drawn attention to Lysenko's perspectives on ethnicity and gender—suggesting that *Yellow Boots* anticipated the emergence of both multiculturalism and feminism, years before either movement became firmly entrenched in public discourse on identity in Canada. That the book needs to be recuperated and carefully examined is obvious, not least of all because Lysenko deliberately scripted the novel as a response to Anglo-Canadian writers whose depictions of Ukrainian Canadian characters were, in her opinion, misguided. Exactly *how* Lysenko's work should be talked about—or, put another way, what the book actually says to us about Ukrainian Canadians at a particular place and time—is less clear. Does this novel achieve its authors objectives? Does it successfully challenge the "other" representations of Ukrainian Canadians that are present in such novels as *The Foreigner*, *As For Me and My House*, and *A Jest of God*?[4]

What Lysenko attempts to offer in *Yellow Boots* is the story of a Ukrainian Canadian girl who, in the process of growing up and leaving her family's rural home, makes a successful transition and a rich contribution to Canadian culture. The arc of the story is, broadly speaking, in line with Lysenko's notion that assimilation is a "two-way street," which she articulated in *Men in Sheepskin Coats*. Her belief was that, in the process of becoming "Canadianized," ethnic immigrants both influence and are influenced by their new society. Hence, Lysenko portrays—or tries to portray—a heroine who ascends the social and economic hierarchies of Canadian society while preserving meaningful ties to her ethnic heritage. What *Yellow Boots* actually presents is a decidedly more complicated—albeit largely unconscious—portrait of the extent to which assimilation resulted in profound linguistic and cultural loss for Ukrainian immigrants and their descendants. Contrary to other scholars' readings of Lysenko's work, I think the real value of this novel lies not in its illustration of the tenacity and resilience of Ukrainian Canadian culture but rather in the commentary she provides on the insurmountable societal constraints placed on Ukrainian Canadians during the first half of the twentieth century. While we might expect Lysenko's representations of Ukrainian Canadians to challenge those of Anglo-Canadian writers—and while the author herself *felt* that she was doing so—*Yellow Boots* in fact tells a story with unmistakable parallels to the novels I have discussed by Connor, Ross, and Laurence. The notable difference is that Lysenko's central character is female and ethnic. What we discover in her story, then, are the troubling ways in which Ukrainian Canadian women are doubly-marginalized in the decades preceding the advent of either multiculturalism or feminism.

Set in the small Manitoba town of Prairie Dawn, and in Winnipeg, between 1929 and 1941, *Yellow Boots* focuses on Lilli Landash, a young girl whose parents immigrated to Canada from Ukraine in order to escape the oppression of their Austrian overlords.[5] Lilli's childhood in rural Manitoba is a dismal one: at the age of six, she is "lent out" to her uncle by her abusive father, Anton; after five years of hard physical labour on her uncle's farm, she becomes frail and weak. At the outset of the novel, Lilli, deathly ill, is returned to her father. But nothing is more precious to Anton than land and sons, so Lilli's imminent death means little to him. In fact, as Lilli lies on her deathbed, neither her father *nor* her mother grieves for the dying child. Although Lilli's sisters—and certainly her brother Petey—are treated lovingly by their parents, Lilli herself is, for reasons never explicitly outlined in the narrative, treated as an outcast. Telling, if somewhat unbelievable, is the fact that during her five-year absence from the family, all have forgotten her real name—they refer to her pejoratively as "Gypsy." When Lilli miraculously survives her illness, no one rejoices. Indeed, throughout Lilli's childhood and adolescence, local schoolmaster Ian MacTavish is the only person who sees that she is an exceptional girl who has been given the gift of song. When Lilli turns sixteen and her father arranges her marriage to a loathsome brute, it is MacTavish who helps her escape to the city.

In Winnipeg, Lilli meets a number of other men who help her establish her new identity: the pianist Sam, the choir singer Tim, and the choirmaster Matthew Reiner. She joins a multi-ethnic choir, goes to night school, and eventually embarks upon a successful career as a concert singer. Ultimately, Lilli rejects a concert career, but she continues to express her artistic passion by singing the folk songs of her people and by establishing her own dressmaking shop. She also becomes engaged to her choirmaster. The novel concludes with Lilli's visit home to the Landash farm after a seven-year absence where she is dismayed to find that her family has embraced all-things-Anglo-Canadian and rejected all-things-Ukrainian. At the close of the novel, Lilli alone is left to preserve the traditions of her people through her gift of song. And there is little doubt that she will succeed in doing so, for, near the novel's conclusion, her mother gives Lilli her yellow boots, potent symbols—in the novel, at least—of Ukrainian culture.

In their readings of *Yellow Boots*, Alexandra Kruchka Glynn, Beverly Rasporich, and Tamara Palmer Seiler argue that Lysenko explicitly challenges Anglo-Canadians'—and, more specifically, Anglo-Canadian writers'—attitudes toward and perceptions of Ukrainian Canadians. In her introduction to the 1992 edition of the novel, for example, Glynn says that *Yellow Boots* "[does] not conform to the attitudes and images of the dominant Anglo presence in Canadian literature" (xi); in "Retelling Vera Lysenko: A Feminist and Ethnic Writer" (1989), Rasporich refers to Lysenko's text as "a tribute to Ukrainian settlement on the prairies," and "a progressive challenge to official Anglo-Canadian history" (40); and Seiler, in "Including the Female Immigrant Story: A Comparative Look at Narrative Strategies" (1996), suggests that Lysenko "asserts the beauty and value of Ukrainian culture" (55). These same scholars emphasize the notion, moreover, that *Yellow Boots* celebrates both the "beauty and value of Ukrainian culture" *and* the Ukrainian Canadian woman's crucial role in preserving Ukrainian culture. According to Glynn, the novel underscores the fact that "the retention of Ukrainian culture is carried out by the women" (xxi).

Scholars read *Yellow Boots* as a novel in which the Ukrainian Canadian woman becomes a champion of her own ethnic group *and* other ethnic minority groups. "By having Lilli sing not only Ukrainian folk songs, but also songs produced by a variety of immigrants," Seiler argues, "Lysenko subverts the imperial insistence on a unitary vision of Canadian culture and nationality"(56). Some critics, pointing to the text's mythologization of the prairie landscape, describe Lysenko's heroine as "a new world embodiment of the ancient female earth goddess, a female creator who can link old and new and synthesize diversity through the power of a nurturing and holistic female vision" (Seiler 56). Rasporich argues that the novel is a "fertility myth" in which Lilli "replants" herself in the "New World" and, "with feminine accommodation, assimilat[es] into the new mother culture, accepting all of its hybrid children in all of their ethnic diversity, and becoming their female artist" ("Engendering" 257). Generally speaking, critics' readings of *Yellow Boots* rely on three assumptions: first, that in leaving her father's home, Lilli successfully challenges patriarchal social structures; second, that in becoming a singer of Ukrainian songs, she retains her Ukrainian culture; and, third, that by singing the songs of numerous other ethnic groups as well, she helps preserve their cultures.

Yet Lysenko's attempts to "asser[t] the beauty and value of Ukrainian culture" (Seiler 55) are thwarted by her decidedly negative depictions of Ukrainian Canadians in portions of *Yellow Boots*. In the first paragraphs of the novel, as Lilli is being transported home to her father by railway worker Mike O'Donovan and schoolteacher Ian MacTavish, these two Anglo-Canadian characters establish the binary opposition upon which this narrative relies—modern, civilized Anglo-Canadian society versus backward, primitive Ukrainian culture. As O'Donovan and MacTavish talk, they struggle to "reconcile the evidences of modern civilization—telephone wires, grain elevators, railways—with the primitive character of the [Ukrainian] people" (12). Approaching the Landash farm, O'Donovan and MacTavish witness a group of Ukrainians on their way to church—four or five wagons "filled with men in sheepskin coats and women in leather boleros, long coloured skirts and white turbans" (10). MacTavish, who is new to the community, is intrigued by the Ukrainians' ethnic clothing and their old-fashioned mode of transportation. To him, they are "like something out of a history book" (19). And O'Donovan, who has spent many years in Prairie Dawn, agrees with MacTavish, explaining that the Ukrainians are "still pioneering, when pioneering days are over for most of the other settlers" (13). O'Donovan, in fact, says that he has seen the Ukrainians "plough the land as people used to in England in the time of Alfred the Great" (13). Neither O'Donovan nor MacTavish can "believe that this [is] the year 1929 in the new world" (11).

The conversation between O'Donovan and MacTavish, of course, reflects the (then dominant) attitudes of Anglo-Canadians toward ethnic minority groups; members of dominant Anglo-Canadian society, the two men see Ukrainians as strange and inferior—as "other" to the Canadian "self." As the narrative unfolds, Lysenko counters their negative perceptions of the Ukrainian settler community with positive descriptions of the Landash family's customs and traditions. Divided into six parts—the first five of which focus on Lilli's years at home—*Yellow Boots* offers countless detailed depictions of the family's cultural and religious practices. In "Rites of Spring," the first part of the novel, Lysenko dramatizes Ukrainian funeral rites (when Lilli is ill, her parents prepare for her funeral), folk stories and arts (her grandmother spins tapestries and tales), and folk dances (the children frolic and play en route to school). In "Songs of the Seasons," Lysenko traces a full year in the lives of the Landash family, drawing attention to the ways in which they worship the soil and the seasons. In "The Wreath Plaiting," she focuses on birth, matchmaking, and marriage rituals. "Dancing Boots, Peasant Boots," moreover, centres on Easter rites and Midsummer celebrations, and "The Grandparents" explores the rich Ukrainian musical heritage passed on from grandfather and grandmother to Lilli. Really, until Lilli faces the crisis of her arranged marriage—until she leaves her family home in the sixth and final part of the novel, "In Search of a Lost Legend"—the narrative meanders along with no apparent purpose, save to highlight the complexity and vitality of Ukrainian Canadian culture. Frances Swyripa's notion that *Yellow Boots* is a "valuable...record of Ukrainian peasant customs and beliefs as they were practiced by first-generation Ukrainians in Canada" (*Ukrainian Canadians: A Survey* 83) and Rasporich's notion that it is a "celebratory record of customs" ("Retelling" 43) are certainly grounded in the first five parts of the novel.

Without a doubt, *Yellow Boots* represents Lysenko's conscious attempt to combat many Anglo-Canadians' negative perceptions of Ukrainians and their way of life. As her concluding chapter to *Men in Sheepskin Coats: A Study in Assimilation* illustrates, she was conscious of—and disturbed by—the ways in which Anglo-Canadian writers had misrepresented Ukrainians in their work:

> [i]n the writings of our novelists and short story writers little or no cognizance has been taken of the fact that one-quarter of Canada's entire population is of non-Anglo-Saxon, non-French descent. Seldom indeed does one encounter a character of, let us say, Slavic origin, in Canadian fiction, except in the role of an illiterate, a clown, a villain or a domestic servant.... The magnificent drama of migration and assimilation to Canada's western lands of a polyglot population has not appealed to Canadian writers, mainly for the reason that consciously or unconsciously they still prefer to think of the non-Anglo-Saxon as a comic or uncouth personage, unworthy of elevation to the dignity of literary subject-material. (293–94)

To bolster her argument in *Men in Sheepskin Coats*, Lysenko refers to Morley Callaghan's *They Shall Inherit the Earth* (1935),⁶ which features a heroine of Ukrainian origin, Anna Prychoda, who regrettably "possesses no distinctively Ukrainian traits." According to Lysenko, Callaghan's protagonist "might as well have been of French, Irish or Icelandic ancestry" (293). Foreshadowing her own enterprise with *Yellow Boots*, Lysenko suggests that Canadian literature should represent the "particular characteristics and problems" of the multiple ethnic groups that it comprises (293). After pointing out that "much…was noble in the lives of the common folk who did the arduous work of pioneering in our western lands"—that "beneath the rough exterior and foreign tongue were concealed worthy motives"—she calls for Ukrainian Canadian writers of the second- and third-generation to "seize upon the opportunities for fresh and original expression in literary and artistic forms by exploiting their lives and the lives of their parents and grandparents as subject material" (294).

Yet as noble as her intentions were, Lysenko offers a decidedly ambivalent portrait of Ukrainians in *Yellow Boots*. The negative perceptions of Ukrainian Canadians articulated by O'Donovan and MacTavish in the first paragraphs of the novel are never entirely absent from Lysenko's later depictions of Ukrainian Canadians. Thus, not unlike the character of Nick Kazlik in Laurence's *A Jest of God*, she internalized, to some extent at least, many Anglo-Canadians' derogatory attitudes toward Ukrainian immigrants. Stereotypes of the Ukrainian community as barbaric and ignorant resonate throughout the text, undermining the novel's positive representation of Ukrainian Canadian culture. O'Donovan and MacTavish—and eventually Matthew Reiner—explicitly state that Ukrainians are "primitive" (12, 30), that their social and cultural practices spring from the "childhood of the human race" (292), and Lysenko implicitly affirms the accuracy of these observations. From the outset of the text, primarily through the character of Anton Landash, Lysenko foregrounds Ukrainian Canadians' inhumanity. Anton sends Lilli to work at the tender age of six; and, when Lilli is sent home, too ill to be of use to her uncle, her father chooses to use an old tool box for her coffin. Once Lilli recovers, he forces her to perform the work of a man, beating her after she has collapsed from exhaustion.

Importantly, too, Anton's wife Zenobia fails to defend Lilli against her husband's cruelty, and she similarly fails to intervene when Anton arranges Lilli's marriage to Simon Zachary in exchange for land. Both Anton and Zenobia are indifferent to the fact that Zachary "beat his last wife when she was carrying a child" and "as a result, the girl died in childbirth" (220). Neither her father nor her mother listens to Lilli as she pleads for her life. "That's my life you're trading for your fields," she says. "As long as I live, I'll be paying for those acres. That's too high a price" (219). Moreover, after a family photograph has been taken—after Anton cuts Lilli out of the picture with a pair of scissors and her "tiny piece" falls to the ground—his cruelty is *"not noticed by anyone except Lilli"* (76 emphasis added). In fact, the novel illustrates that not only Anton but Zenobia—not only the Landashes but the entire Ukrainian Canadian community—view women as subordinate to men. That the Ukrainian Canadians of Prairie Dawn clearly disapprove of unmarried, independent women is further evidenced by their treatment of the old eccentric widow Tamara. Tamara is a strong-willed woman who lives alone and is irrationally accused of casting evil spells on members of the community. One evening, as members of the community gather to discuss Tamara's witchcraft, their "voices swell in a crescendo of fury" (176). Acting on their superstitious suspicions that she has caused cows to stop giving milk and tomato plants to shrivel, they undertake a veritable witch-hunt and drive Tamara to her death.

Indeed, Ukrainian Canadians' barbarity in *Yellow Boots* is particularly evident in their treatment of women. Lilli's escape from her father, and hence from the unhappy marriage he has arranged, is as much an act of survival as it is an act of independence. She leaves home in order to emancipate and save herself from her father. Given that she leaves one patriarchal social structure only to enter into another, however, Lilli's status as a "practical feminist heroine" (Rasporich, "Engendering" 250) is questionable. Her transition from the farm to the city—from an abused farm girl to an independent city woman—is made possible less through her own actions than through the interventions of a series of men: her schoolteacher, Ian MacTavish; her pianist friend, Sam; her suitor, Tim; and her choirmaster-cum-fiancé, Matthew Reiner. With the "new" men in her life, Lilli is safe from the brutality of her father, but she is never free from domination by male figures. That many of the men (MacTavish, Tim, Reiner) who meet Lilli are sexually attracted to her points rather unambiguously to their ulterior motives in helping Lilli and invalidates a feminist reading of her movement into the world.

Ian MacTavish's initial interest in Lilli when she is still a child grows out of both his personal and professional ambitions. MacTavish originally comes to the country school in order to fulfill his aspirations as an anthropologist. He seeks to observe and record the transformation of primitive Ukrainian culture to modern Canadian culture, and Lilli becomes his prime specimen. "Without her," he wonders, "how many months it would have taken [me] to understand the [Ukrainians]!" (233). On Lilli's first day of school, MacTavish bestows upon her a new name, "Lilli," then proceeds to teach her to speak proper English and to sing British songs, all the while filling notebooks with ethnographic data regarding the state of Ukrainian culture in transition (41, 43, 56). Near the conclusion of *Yellow Boots*, schoolteacher Ian MacTavish is re-introduced as "Dr. Ian MacTavish, eminent anthropologist." The diaries that he keeps during his stint in Prairie Dawn become the "basis of his lifetime work" (351). As MacTavish studies Lilli, moreover, he becomes emotionally and physically attracted to her:

> as she stood in the brilliant sunshine, dressed shabbily in men's clothing too large for her, defensive yet secret, she had a feminine allure, the beginning of womanhood. MacTavish could not look at her without a stirring of emotion, compounded of pity and something akin to excitement, a consciousness that here was something rare and undeveloped. (59)

At once an object of "pity" and a source of "excitement," Lilli becomes MacTavish's project—something (not someone) "rare" that he can "develop" according to his own blueprints and designs. Instrumental in ensuring her escape from her father, he instructs her "in the business of leaving the village and obtaining employment in the city" (228). And while, years later, he marvels at her progress, MacTavish nonetheless regrets that he has had to "share [her] with so many others!" (353). He pines for his early days as a schoolteacher in Prairie Dawn when, as he says, "she was mine—my discovery" (353).

Tim, the young man who courts Lilli when she first arrives in the city, shares MacTavish's interest in Lilli. Like MacTavish, Tim is drawn to Lilli's innocence and naiveté; like MacTavish, he helps to facilitate Lilli's integration into Anglo-Canadian society. Though both men are attracted by Lilli's wild, untamed nature, they seek to educate her in the ways of the modern world by playing the part of father/lover. For Lilli, each meeting with Tim becomes a "voyage of discovery, a step forward in life" (274). After Tim discovers that Lilli knows neither her birthday nor her real name, he makes inquiries with the Manitoba government and eventually produces her birth certificate—"you see," he explains to Lilli, condescendingly, "everybody is born, that is how we get into the world" (275). Not unlike MacTavish, who transformed "Gypsy" into "Lilli," Tim, too, endeavours to rename her. "Oksana" is, according to Tim, Lilli's "real" name. In the act of renaming, Tim—like MacTavish before him—becomes a sort of father figure to Lilli; his tendency is to treat Lilli less like a woman than a child. After he renames her, he throws a birthday party for her, lavishing her with gifts—seventeen presents, one for each year of her life. Childlike, Lilli opens the gifts, treasuring the knickknacks that Tim has given her. Not surprisingly, his final gift is a diamond ring, which introduces the topic of marriage into their conversation. And while Lilli turns down his marriage proposal, Tim's sexual attraction to her and his desire to make her his wife are ever-present in their interactions.

Much like MacTavish and Tim, Matthew Reiner, Lilli's choirmaster, bases his relationship with Lilli on his double-edged desire to transform her in dress, mannerism, and speech, and to possess her physically and sexually. Reiner, a classically trained musician from Austria,[7] directs a multicultural choir that comprises ethnic immigrant factory workers. Like MacTavish, Reiner is interested in studying the assimilation of working class ethnic immigrants to Anglo-Canadian society. In fact, with unmistakable parallels to MacTavish, Reiner harbours a secret dream to conduct an experiment—"what could be done to develop a human being of great ability," he wonders, "but of almost absolute ignorance?" (273). In Lilli, Reiner finds the ideal specimen. She is "young," "naïve," "wild," and filled with "primitive passion" (267, 305). Upon meeting her, Reiner immediately recognizes that the perfect experimental subject stands before him—"here she is. What she may become depends on us" (280). As with MacTavish and Tim, Lilli's role in her own coming-of-age is muted by Reiner's domineering role in her life. He removes her from her position as a domestic servant and finds her a job in a factory, arranging for her to go to night school in the evenings. For her calluses, he suggests hand lotion, and exercises to give her hands "grace and pliability" (271).

Interestingly, when Lilli makes her own decisions—when she, for example, appears at choir practice in elegant evening attire—Reiner steps in, criticizing her choices. "We can wait a few years for this suit," he says, "next time, wear the green angora dress" (280). Lilli thrives, of course, under Reiner's tutelage; she establishes herself as a successful concert singer, then opens her own dressmaking shop. And she freely admits her debt to Reiner, stating "I studied hard to please you, to speak well, to dress properly.... All for you" (347). It is, though, only after Lilli's transformation from naïve country girl to mature modern woman that Reiner decides to make her his wife. Near the close of the novel, he announces that he has "waited long enough for [Lilli] to grow up" (347). Reiner has waited, yes, but not passively. He has actively directed her "growing up," molding her according to the precise specifications that he always has had in mind. For Reiner, the experiment is a success.

Is Reiner's experiment a success, however, for Lilli? In the process of growing up and leaving her father's home, Lilli must negotiate her way between not only two cultures but also two patriarchal systems. When she escapes from her parents' farm to the city, Lilli leaves both her abusive father and her traditional Ukrainian way of life. But she is only able to leave her abusive father with the help of MacTavish, an Anglo-Canadian man with decidedly imperial interests; she is only able to make a new life for herself by assimilating to Anglo-Canadian society under the insidiously controlling guidance of Tim and, especially, Reiner. To resist Ukrainian patriarchy, Lilli must become complicit with both Anglo-Canadian cultural imperialism *and* Anglo-Canadian patriarchy. In the end, hers appears to be a "lose–lose" situation.

Although *Yellow Boots* suggests that Lilli's movement to the city does not result in the total loss of her culture—moving to the city, after all, enables Lilli to take her Ukrainian part in the city's festive multicultural hubbub—one of the most curious aspects of the text is its insistence that, unlike the other members of the Landash family, Lilli alone has the potential to preserve their Ukrainian heritage. Upon returning to her home near the conclusion of the novel, she observes the changes that have taken place in the Landash household: "the phone, the radio and refrigerator. Everything [is] hygienic. One could not imagine any spirits, evil or benign living here" (329). In her first act of kindness toward Lilli, Zenobia laments the loss of the old ways:

if I could tell you, how shameful what the girls did with those carpets, embroideries, dress up and laugh! Costumes wear out and new ones not made. Girl will not spend time to embroider when she can order from mail order catalogue, so cheap, so fine!... No more kilims on wall, all, all, taken off and instead put on wallpaper, curtains from mail order, range where was old stove, so good to bake bread! (331)

Apparently—and this seems to me an unbelievable development in the story—seven years after Lilli leaves for the city, all Ukrainian customs and traditions have entirely disappeared from the Landash home, giving way to the modern, Anglo-Canadian way of life.[8] Somehow Lilli—who no longer lives in her ethnic community; who no longer speaks Ukrainian or eats Ukrainian food; who dresses in modern "Canadian" clothing—somehow *Lilli* becomes the symbol of her community's cultural preservation and is therefore able to comfort her mother by telling her that she "has one daughter still who loves the old" (331). Lysenko's logic here anticipates discourses of multiculturalism in the sense that she presents ethnic performance, the performance of song, as a valid means for maintaining and transmitting cultural traditions. This, at least, is Glynn's and Seiler's reading of the novel: *Yellow Boots* is the "first piece of Canadian fiction to advance the vision of a multicultural Canadian society" (Glynn xi) and that, "[b]y having Lilli champion the vanishing folk culture of her people, particularly music, Lysenko works to de-colonize Ukrainian ethnicity" (Seiler 56).

But a positive reading of *Yellow Boots* and its multicultural politics requires a leap of faith on the part of the reader. To accept that multiculturalism resolves the tensions between Lilli's status as a Ukrainian and as a Canadian, readers must overlook the irony of the novel's pat conclusion. Near the end of Lysenko's book, Zenobia gives her yellow boots to Lilli. These boots are rich in symbolic meaning because they are the very boots Zenobia wore as a girl in the Old Country; when mother passes them on to daughter, she passes on the matrilineal responsibility to protect and preserve the family's traditional way of life. Lilli, then, inherits more than a simple pair of boots; she becomes, in the exchange, the guardian of her family's culture. While the boots carry the symbolic weight of the Ukrainian cultural legacy, however, they also figure centrally in a final scene of the novel, the scene in which Lilli and Reiner at last unite. When Reiner sees Lilli pull on her yellow dancing boots before her last performance in the novel—when he has proof that her Ukrainian heritage is now simply a costume she will wear on stage—only then is he ready to claim her as his wife. The price that Lilli pays for escaping her father's patriarchal home is the reduction of her ethnic heritage to fetishized performance. Over the course of the novel, Lilli negotiates herself into a corner. While Lilli's father, Anton, was able to flee from his Austrian master in the Old Country, and while his son Petey is able to find freedom and opportunity in Canada, Lilli is never without a master. Her husband-to-be, after all, is Austrian. So readers are left to wonder how far Lilli's yellow boots really take her.

Yellow Boots may suggest that multiculturalism represents a viable alternative to Anglo-Canadian cultural hegemony, but in doing so it simultaneously reveals the ways in which multiculturalism is grounded in discourses of British imperialism, as Lysenko's treatment of language in the novel makes especially clear. Briefly, near the beginning of the novel, during language lessons with MacTavish, Lilli struggles with English grammar and pronunciations. "My tongue lame like old horse," she says. "I am so stupid!.... All the time, mistakes!" (56–57). But, determined to speak proper English, she announces her commitment to learning her new language—"all the time I will speak like this" (57), she tells MacTavish. And, for the rest of the novel, she does indeed continue to "speak like this"—in impeccably grammatical English, with no traces of a Ukrainian accent. Even if we suspend our disbelief and accept that Lilli is able to participate in Canadian society without losing touch with her Ukrainian culture, what are we to make of Lysenko's apparent desire to eradicate all traces of Ukrainian-ness from her heroine's voice—and, more importantly, from her own narrative voice? The medium—or the language—of the novel is, in a sense, the message: Lysenko's conscious motivation for writing *Yellow Boots* may be to illustrate what Canadian society stands to gain from Ukrainians but what she inadvertently demonstrates is how much heroine and author alike are willing to give up in order to become Canadians. The scene in which MacTavish teaches Lilli to speak English is a crucial moment in the novel because, as it dramatizes the superiority of Anglo-Canadian culture over the Ukrainian Canadian culture—not to mention the ubiquity of patriarchal social structures—

it reveals Lysenko's underlying attitude toward her ethnic group: Ukrainian Canadians are backward and ignorant; Anglo-Canadians, progressive and educated. Like her protagonist, Lysenko ultimately rejects her ethnic language, and by extension her ethnic culture, in order to make a successful transition to the dominant culture of Canadian society. Insofar as worlds are created through language,[9] the world that Lysenko creates is one in which Ukrainian Canadian culture is erased and replaced by Anglo-Canadian culture.

In the end, the story Lysenko wants to tell in *Yellow Boots* is undermined by the ideologies and practices of assimilation that were pervasive during the first half of the twentieth century in Canada. If we are to succeed in recuperating *Yellow Boots* from the margins of the Canadian literary canon and if we are to fully incorporate this novel into ongoing debates and discussions about the relation between ethnic and national identity, then we need to re-examine the reasons for which Lysenko could not tell a different story. By (mis)reading the novel as an unmitigated testament to the resilience Ukrainian culture, scholars overlook Lysenko's valuable, if unintended, commentary on the intense assimilationist pressures placed on Canadians of Ukrainian descent in the decades preceding the advent of official multiculturalism. The danger of interpreting Lilli's performance of folk songs as evidence of her resistance to Anglo-Canadian cultural hegemony is that such an interpretation enables Canadian readers to congratulate themselves on striking a balance between unity and diversity. Given that Lilli's performances become a superficial mimicry of the rich and complex Old World culture to which she once belonged, readers must question the underlying message of this novel. We must ask what the future holds in multicultural Canada for subsequent generations of Ukrainian Canadians whose only legacies, according to Lysenko, are folk songs and dancing boots.

PART TWO

RE-CLAIMING IDENTITY

Ukrainian Canadian Writers
and Multiculturalism

1971 to 1984

FOUR

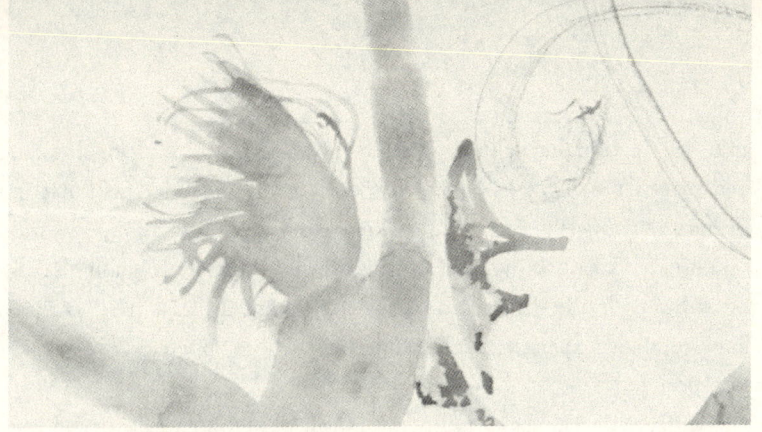

Ethnic Revival versus Historical Revision
Ukrainian Canadians and Multiculturalism

IN HIS INTRODUCTION to *Yarmarok: Ukrainian Writing in Canada Since the Second World War* (1987), an anthology of English- and Ukrainian-language literature by Canadian-born and émigré Ukrainian Canadian authors, Jars Balan declares that "it was not until the Second World War that the Ukrainian Canadian community produced its first successful writer in English" (xviii). The writer to whom Balan refers, of course, is Vera Lysenko. "After Lysenko," he continues, "a growing number of Ukrainian Canadian writers won recognition for books written in English" (xviii). The English-language selections in *Yarmarok* represent literary works by "nationally known" Ukrainian Canadian writers, such as George Ryga, Maara Haas, Myrna Kostash, and Andrew Suknaski. It also includes authors who are "firmly established in their careers but are just starting to win wider recognition for their work"—Dennis Gruending, Michael John Nimchuk, Ray Serwylo, Larry Zacharko, and Helen Potrebenko, for example—and "a few beginners with little or no publishing experience," among them, Ruth Andrishak and Bob Wakulich (xviii).

Without a doubt, "after Lysenko," a large number of second- and third-generation Ukrainian Canadians began writing and publishing in a variety of genres. But following the publication of Lysenko's *Yellow Boots* (1954) and *Westerly Wild* (1956), almost two decades passed before other English-language literature by Ukrainian Canadian writers began to appear on publishers' lists. Why the lengthy hiatus in English-language Ukrainian Canadian literary production, followed by the sudden increase in its production during the 1970s and 1980s? What cultural, ideological, and material changes in Canadian society made possible this burst in literary writing by and about Ukrainian Canadians? And how did Ukrainian Canadian writers of this period—some of whom Balan describes as "quite distant from their immigrant forbears [sic]" (xix)—explore their experiences of ethnicity in prose, poetry, drama, and non-fiction?

Official discourses of multiculturalism played no small part in the development of Ukrainian Canadian and other ethnic minority writing. "Since adopting in 1972 its official policy of pursuing 'multiculturalism within a bilingual framework,'" writes Mary Kirtz, "Canada has witnessed a great proliferation of work—literary, dramatic, artistic, communal—by and about the various immigrant groups which have shaped its demographic profile" ("Old World Traditions" 8). In the decades preceding the advent of official multiculturalism, few English-language Ukrainian Canadian authors wrote about their experiences as members of an ethnic minority group because they experienced intense pressure to reject their ethnic heritage and assimilate to Anglo-Canadian society. But as ideologies and practices of assimilation gave way to general public awareness and increasing acceptance of a "mosaic" model of Canadian nationhood—as Anglo-Canadian society began to recognize the value of ethnic minority groups within the new multicultural model of nationhood—second- and third-generation Ukrainian Canadians began to take pride in Ukrainian folk music, dance, and art. As Frances Swyripa points out "[m]ulticulturalism grants to Ukrainian community organizations and the activities they sponsor...facilitated the expression of a Ukrainian element and identity in Canada" ("From Sheepskin Coat" 24). Ukrainian Canadian writers benefited both directly and indirectly from Anglo-Canadian society's openness to cultural diversity.[1] According to Kirtz,

> [h]ad Canada not adopted a completely new approach to the heterogeneous makeup of its people, it is even doubtful that many of the works presently enjoying considerable acclaim would have been produced: much of the impetus for the production has come in the form of monetary grants and other kinds of official support provided by both federal and provincial governments. ("Old World Traditions" 9)

Multiculturalism created funding and audiences for Ukrainian Canadian literary works, so Ukrainian Canadian writers were able to acknowledge and explore their Ukrainian backgrounds for the first time with the officially-sanctioned support of Canadian governments, and with the more general approval of Canadian society.[2]

The appearance of Ukrainian Canadian literature on the Canadian literary scene, however, needs to be understood not only in relation to the advent of multiculturalism but also in relation to the development of the Canadian literary institution. While Ukrainian Canadian authors were encouraged by discourses of multiculturalism, these authors were also almost certainly bolstered by significant changes in the production and reception of Canadian literature. As W.H. New explains in *A History of Canadian Literature*, between 1960 and 1985, the landscape of Canadian literature changed dramatically with the creation of "new agencies of support for writing, research and publication"; "creative writing and writer-in-residence programmes"; and "Canadian literature courses in schools" (203). During this twenty-five year period, "some four hundred new serious writers appeared" (204), including numerous ethnic, female, and regional writers who challenged the established socio-political structures that had traditionally ignored or marginalized their experiences and their voices. "Ethnicity, region, gender: these three issues," New writes, "stood behind many a resistance movement" (204) in the latter part of the twentieth century. Furthermore, as a result of technological changes in the publishing industry, numerous publishing houses were established across the country—including Oberon, Ragweed, NeWest,[3] Talonbooks, Oolichan, Turnstone, Thistledown, Anansi, and Coach House—providing authors with more venues for their writing (214).

Beginning in the 1970s, then, influenced by more inclusive definitions of Canadian nationhood and by the burgeoning of the Canadian literary institution, a number of second- and third-generation Ukrainian Canadians started to write. What they wrote, and how they wrote it, however, often revealed their ambivalence toward the language, institutions, and values of their ethnic and national communities. Ironically, while multiculturalism empowered Ukrainian Canadian writers to explore and even celebrate their ethnic subjectivity, the experience of assimilation had profoundly affected them. Many had adopted English as their mother tongue, and most had accepted that the immigrant generation's traditional way of life must necessarily give way to the modernity of Anglo-Canadian society. Suddenly able to write and publish texts about being Ukrainian, these writers ironically tended to expose the mixture of anger, grief, and guilt they felt about not only losing their culture but also turning their backs on it. Much of the Ukrainian Canadian literature produced between 1971 and 1984 was shaped by the writers' desire to retrieve and record memories of the Ukrainian way of life that, in their minds, had come to pass.

While Ukrainian Canadian writers were grappling with the urgent need to document what had been lost through the process of assimilation, so too were other members of Ukrainian Canadian communities working toward reviving their cultural customs and traditions. In fact, as Swyripa points out in her essay "From Sheepskin Coat to Blue Jeans: A Brief History of Ukrainians in Canada" (1991), from the outset of their history in Canada, "Ukrainians supported a myriad of community organizations and their activities, combining politics with culture, education and entertainment" (24). Assimilation was not wholesale. Many Ukrainian Canadians, from the turn of the century onward, actively worked toward retaining aspects of their cultural heritage. Jars Balan's essays on pre-Second World War Ukrainian Canadian theatre, Alexandra Pritz's study of Ukrainian dance in Canada from 1924 to 1974, and Bohdan Rubchak's work on Ukrainian émigré poets of all three immigrant waves provide examples of the ways in which Ukrainian immigrants transplanted and nurtured their traditions of cultural expression in Canada.[4] The large number of Ukrainian newspapers in Canada that published poetry and short fiction by Ukrainian Canadian writers further attests to Ukrainian Canadians' interest in retaining their ethnic identity.[5] But because Canadian-born Ukrainians tended to reject the culture of their ethnic group in order to participate in Anglo-Canadian society, Ukrainian Canadian cultural traditions largely remained the provenance of immigrants. And it was not until the decades immediately preceding the introduction of official multiculturalism that both immigrant and Canadian-born Ukrainians, led by third-wave émigrés—pro-nationalistic dissident intellectuals who came to Canada in the late 1940s and early 1950s—became fully organized and mobilized to preserve and promote their culture in this country.

Indeed, as Robert Klymasz argues in "Culture Maintenance and the Ukrainian Experience in Western Canada" (1983), immigrants of the third wave significantly altered the cultural life of Ukrainian Canadians. The émigrés' "large and sudden dose of professional cultural know-how," Klymasz argues, made an "enormous, far-reaching and indelible" impact on Ukrainian Canadian cultural life (175). When these Ukrainians arrived in Canada, they found that the "downtrodden and often illiterate" immigrants of the first and second wave had largely accepted the dominant assimilationist ideology of Anglo-Canadian society. But unlike established Ukrainian Canadians, the émigrés staunchly resisted assimilationist pressures. "[M]ore educated, more sophisticated, and more aware" (175) than immigrants of the two previous waves, they were determined to preserve their culture in Canada. Following their arrival in Canada, then, they initiated a Ukrainian cultural revival by nurturing Ukrainian music, dance, and literary traditions. According to Klymasz, "[q]uiet denouement and a leisurely paced dissolution would have possibly transformed the Ukrainian community into what is nowadays euphemistically labeled, in multicultural circles, a 'dormant' ethnocultural group, were it not for the hypertrophic impact of thousands of Ukrainian war refugees" (175). Their "conscientious attention to, and formulation of, an aesthetic dimension for the Ukrainian ethnic experience in Canada" resulted in intellectually rigorous approaches to Ukrainian Canadian culture:

> [t]he printed and spoken word, for example, was not merely a means of communication and pamphleteering but an art form that demanded cultivation, careful study and an appreciation of a rich legacy of poetry, prose and drama. Scholars, artists and assorted literati embodied in their very mannerisms, lifestyle, decorum, and comportment the exalted values of a cultural configuration that was almost completely inconspicuous before their arrival in Canada. (Klymasz 175–76)

In other words, a distinct Ukrainian Canadian culture was self-consciously fostered for the first time by post-Second World War émigré intellectuals and artists who saw elevated modes of cultural production as an extension of their Ukrainian nationalist politics.[6] In seeking to retain their Ukrainian identity in Canada, they emphasized ethnic "purity" in the form and content of artistic and literary works (176).

For many years, "acute tensions" characterized the relation between established Ukrainian Canadians and the third-wave émigré community (Gerus and Rea 18); eventually, however, the two factions of the community reconciled their differences. By the 1970s, the émigrés' "cultural maintenance" had come to mean "conformity and uniformity in the interests of consolidating a package of instantly recognizable ethnocultural symbols, ranging from onion-shaped domes for Ukrainian churches to acrobatic hopaks for the national television network" (Klymasz 176). In response to multicultural Canadian society's demand for "crisp, well-packaged, snazzy, and eye-catching" ethnic culture, and in order to establish a place for themselves within the national mosaic, established and third-wave Ukrainian Canadians together turned their heritage into a commodity-like product, a staple developed

> and offered ... for all to appreciate and consume. In the interest of codifying the product, the national costume, the national instrument (the bandura), and even language norms came to be based solely on those traditions that originated in the Poltava region in central Ukraine. Sunflowers and red poppies, cross-stitch embroidery, traditional cookery, and religious festivities (twelve meatless dishes for Christmas Eve and ornamented consecrated eggs at Easter) filled out the list of ethnocultural symbols that were on call, so to speak, at a moment's notice. (176)

Ukrainian Canadians—united for the first time by common symbols and expressions of their ethnicity—began to take public pride in their cultural heritage.

And so throughout the 1970s and early 1980s, Ukrainian Canadian communities revived numerous, primarily folkloric, cultural traditions, often adapting these traditions to fit the unique context of multicultural Canada. Ukrainian dance became, arguably, the most visible aspect of the Ukrainian Canadian cultural revival as countless professional, semi-professional, and amateur groups were organized across the country: *Shumka* (1960) and *Cheremosh* (1969) in Edmonton, for example; *Vesnianka* (1958) and *Desna* (1974) in Toronto; *Zirka* in Dauphin,

Manitoba (1977); and *Yevshan* in Saskatoon (1960).⁷ These and many other dance ensembles performed and competed at annual Ukrainian festivals in Dauphin and Vegreville, Alberta.⁸ At the same time, Ukrainian Canadians published collections of folk songs, like Yurko Foty and Sviatoslaw Chepyha's *Let's Sing Out in Ukrainian* (1977), a songbook that contains the music and words—in the Cyrillic alphabet and in English transliterations—to over one hundred popular Ukrainian songs, including Christmas carols, love songs, children's songs, and Cossack ballads. Numerous Ukrainian Canadian dance bands, including "Bill Boychuk and His Easy Aces," "Ron Lakusta and the Hi-Lites," "The Ernie Zaozirny Band," "The Billey Family Band," and "The Female Beat," produced and sold studio recordings of folk songs that they frequently performed at weddings and other community gatherings.⁹

Musicians in these bands played Ukrainian folk songs in the style of country and western music, using a broad range of contemporary and traditional musical instruments: drums, piano, saxophone, and trumpet, as well as violin, dulcimer, and accordion.¹⁰ Some Ukrainian Canadians translated traditional folk tales into English for both children and adults, such as Victoria Symchych and Olga Vesey's *The Flying Ship and Other Ukrainian Folk Tales* (1975); Bohdan Melnyk's *Fox Mykyta* (1978); Lena Gulutsan's *The Mosquito's Wedding* (1980); and *Snow Folks* (1982).¹¹ Others brought together Ukrainian and non-Ukrainian recipes in cookbooks. Examples included Savella Stechishin's *Traditional Ukrainian Cookery* (1976); Emily Linkiewich's *Baba's Cookbook* (1979); the Ukrainian Women's Association of Canada's *Ukrainian Daughter's Cookbook* (1984).¹² *The Ukrainian Canadiana* (1976), *Visible Symbols: Cultural Expression Among Canada's Ukrainians* (1984), and *Art and Ethnicity: The Ukrainian Tradition in Canada* (1991) provide detailed information about Ukrainian Canadians' interest in dance, music, and folk tales, as well as embroidery, woodwork, and *pysanky* (Easter egg) making.¹³

Reflecting on Ukrainian Canadian folk culture in 1991, some twenty years after Ukrainian Canadians began taking a serious interest in reviving this culture, a number of Ukrainian Canadian scholars articulate positive perspectives on folk symbols and expressions of Ukrainian Canadian ethnicity. In "From Sheepskin Coat to Blue Jeans: A Brief History of Ukrainians in Canada" (1991), for example, Swyripa argues that a "cultural ethnic consciousness" rather than a "politicized national consciousness" best defines Ukrainian Canadian identity. She says that "politically inoffensive" symbols of Ukrainian Canadian ethnicity such as food, embroidery, and Easter eggs create a sense of community among Ukrainian Canadians. At the same time, Ukrainian Canadians are able to use these symbols to showcase their culture to non-Ukrainian Canadians because folk culture is "compatible with what is apparently a satisfactory grassroots definition of multiculturalism" (26). Wsevolod W. Isajiw, in "Ethnic Art and the Ukrainian-Canadian Experience" (1991), concurs. He divides folk culture into four categories—folk, naïve, professional, and souvenir art[14]—suggesting that all of these art forms enabled Ukrainian Canadians to revive and celebrate their cultural traditions. Isajiw sees souvenir art, in particular, as an "inexpensive way of representing the community's ethnic identity to the wider society" by providing "a visitor with a token that symbolizes the community and its culture" (36). Similarly, in "A Folklorist's Viewpoint on Ukrainian Canadian Art" (1991), Michael Owen Jones argues that Ukrainian Canadian folk culture, in general, and *pysanky*, in particular, contribute to Ukrainian Canadians' sense of pride in their ethnic heritage (57), as well as their "increased visibility" in Canadian society (55).

Yet, writing in the 1970s and early 1980s, a number of Ukrainian Canadian scholars express their concerns about the extent to which Ukrainian Canadians can preserve their ethnic identity through folk symbology. In "Museums and Ukrainian Canadian Material Culture" (1983), Steve Prystupa argues that ethnic customs and traditions must be re-placed in their historical contexts in order to facilitate a genuine understanding of Ukrainian Canadian culture (17).[15] Roman Onifrijchuk, in "Ukrainian Canadian Cultural-Experience-As-Text: Toward a New Strategy" (1983), argues that symbols of Ukrainian Canadian folk culture are problematic precisely because they are focused exclusively on the past and because they are detached from the contemporary experiences of Ukrainian Canadians (160). In "Ukrainian Cultural and Political Symbols in Canada: An Anthropological Selection" (1983), Zenon Pohorecky suggests that the popularization of Ukrainian Canadian folk culture in the form of "T-shirts showing Campbell's borshch or gag-buttons" is "good fun" (139) but he insists that "the future lies most securely in the Ukrainian textbooks and workbooks being produced in Canada to teach youngsters their ancestral language, always the best gateway to the rich Ukrainian heritage" (140).[16]

Interestingly, many Ukrainian Canadian artists who produced work during the 1970s and 1980s agree with Prystupa's argument that folkloric expressions of ethnicity fail as a means for preserving ethnic identity because—or, better, when—they are divorced from the complex historical and social realities of Ukrainian Canadians. Ukrainian Canadian painters William Kurelek and Peter Shostak, for example, draw upon their ethnic experiences in their realist renderings of prairie farm life. In their paintings, folk symbols—food, embroidery, or *pysanky*—are contextualized in the day-to-day activities of Ukrainian Canadians.[17] Artist Natalka Husar uses folk symbols in her work in order to draw attention to the ways in which Ukrainian Canadian folk culture, when removed from the lived experiences of Ukrainian Canadians, is simplified and trivialized.[18] With her sculpture *The TV Dinner Sviat Vechir* (1977), for example, Husar confronts the conflation of Ukrainian Canadian ethnicity with Ukrainian Canadian food. Her TV dinner includes the twelve traditional Christmas Eve (*Sviat Vechir*) dishes, but this conveniently pre-prepared meal, according to Husar, "eliminates more than just labour. It eliminates tradition, ritual, religion—all that is truly important— leaving only food" ("The Relevance of Ethnicity" n.p.). A second sculpture by Husar, *After all that, supper or Sex and the single Ukrainian girl* (1977), explores the objectification of women within Ukrainian Canadian folk culture. She arranges several items of women's folk costume on a plate so that red dancing boots and a white brassiere become meat and potatoes; coral beads resemble carrots; and a green ribbon, parsley. In Husar's words, "it is a Ukrainian girl on a platter" (n.p.). For her, folk culture is hardly "politically inoffensive" (Swyripa, "From Sheepskin Coat" 26). By delving beneath the surface of seemingly innocuous folk symbols, Husar exposes the troubling ways in which they actually circulate.

Not unlike Husar, a number of Ukrainian Canadian writers also openly object to the ways in which folkloric constructions of Ukrainian Canadian ethnicity fail to account for the multiple, complex dimensions of Ukrainian Canadians' experiences. Both published in 1977, *All of Baba's Children* and *No Streets of Gold: A Social History of Ukrainians in Alberta*, by Myrna Kostash and Helen Potrebenko respectively, react to the Ukrainian Canadian ethnic revival by undertaking historical studies of Ukrainians in Canada. Kostash primarily focuses on the Ukrainian Canadian community of Two Hills in northeastern Alberta, whereas Potrebenko looks more generally at the history of Ukrainian Canadians in Alberta. Insofar as Kostash and Potrebenko share with other Ukrainian Canadians the desire to "publicize ethnic history" (Kostash 8), and to legitimize Ukrainian Canadians' contributions to the nation by recording their experiences in the space of the scholarly printed text, their works are similar to other Ukrainian Canadian histories published during the 1970s and early 1980s. In terms of thematic structure and research methodology, too, *All of Baba's Children* and *No Streets of Gold* closely resemble numerous other Ukrainian Canadian history books. Not unlike, for example, Vera Lysenko's *Men in Sheepskin Coats* (1947), Kostash's and Potrebenko's texts examine the economic, political, social, and cultural lives of Ukrainian Canadians by reflecting on key moments in Canadian history—the large influx of Ukrainian immigrants at the turn of the twentieth century; the First World War; the depression; the Second World War—as well as on important material developments in Ukrainian Canadian communities such as the building of homesteads, churches, and schools. Just as scholars such as Michael Marunchak, Jars Balan, O.W. Gerus and J.E. Rea rely on newspapers, magazines, government documents, and scholarly books to understand the historical realities of Ukrainian Canadians, so too do Kostash and Potrebenko draw upon print sources in their research. Similar to Zonia Keywan's *Greater Than Kings* (1977), Harry Piniuta's *Land of Pain Land of Promise: First Person Accounts by Ukrainian Pioneers, 1891-1914* (1978), and William Czumer's *Recollections About the Life of the First Ukrainian Settlers in Canada* (1981), *All of Baba's Children* and *No Streets of Gold* also substantially draw upon the first person, oral testimonials of Ukrainian Canadians.

Many Ukrainian Canadian scholars, though, particularly in the 1970s and 1980s, construct narratives of Ukrainian Canadian history that follow a common pattern: they begin by tracing the history of Ukrainian immigration to Canada; next, they examine the ways in which Ukrainian immigrants and their descendants strove to overcome poverty and resist Anglo-Canadian society's assimilationist pressures; and, finally, by foregrounding the stories of individuals within the Ukrainian Canadian community who achieved success in professional, political, and artistic spheres, these scholars provide evidence of Ukrainian Canadians' success in maintaining their ethnic identity while ascending the social and economic hierarchies of Canadian society.[19] Implicitly or explicitly, they applaud Canadian society for embracing ethnic diversity, however belatedly. They also congratulate Ukrainian Canadians on developing a distinct, unified ethnic community, despite their historical differences.

Kostash and Potrebenko, by contrast, reject this narrative of progress. In *All of Baba's Children*, Kostash acknowledges that among Ukrainian Canadian historians and storytellers "[t]here is a tendency...to ascribe to an often miserable and thankless way of life a dimension of glory and to the people enduring it a prophetic vision, or at least a nobility of character, as though the unedited reality of their experiences is somehow vulgar or banal or even shameful" (31). To accept this "hackneyed" version of the "Canadian myth of the pursuit of happiness" is, in Kostash's words, to ignore the fact that Ukrainian Canadians'

> financial security was tenuous in the extreme, that their labour was far from remunerative, that their "freedom" to an education was to an anglicized one; the law was discriminatory, their non-Ukrainian neighbours were racists, their leftist political activities were persecuted; and the admonitions to "work" and "thrift" applied precisely and only to the working people—the resident elite had neither to work nor be thrifty. (31)

While, according to Kostash, "the 'official' histories demand that we see [Ukrainian Canadians'] lives as heroic or nothing at all" (31), she proposes a third option, an alternative approach to understanding and recording the experiences of Ukrainian Canadians. By focusing on the experiences of Ukrainian Canadians who cannot be included among the "success stories" of Ukrainian Canadian doctors, lawyers, politicians, and entrepreneurs (30), she undertakes a critical reading and writing of history that recognizes the "pain and loss and even failure of so many...lives" (31). Potrebenko provides a similar, if less nuanced, perspective on Ukrainian Canadian history: "I offer no heroes," she writes. "There were no heroes, there were only ordinary women and men" (302).

By drawing attention to the ways in which these ordinary Ukrainian Canadians are excluded from the Ukrainian Canadian "ethnic establishment" (Kostash 9) and marginalized within Canadian society, Kostash and Potrebenko adopt a critical stance vis-à-vis both their ethnic and national communities. As women, feminists, and proponents of socialism,²⁰ they strongly identify with Ukrainian Canadians whose experiences are under-represented in "official" versions of Canadian and Ukrainian Canadian history, so they write candidly about the gendered, religious, political, and class tensions within their ethnic group, as well as the conflicts between Ukrainian Canadians and Anglo-Canadian society (particularly during the years preceding the advent of multiculturalism). That Kostash and Potrebenko are sympathetic toward socialist and communist Ukrainian Canadians is unsurprising; nor is it unexpected that they expose the oppressive patriarchal social structures that characterize Ukrainian Canadian communities, as well as the prevalence of anti-Semitism within these communities. These writers refuse the notion that, in Kostash's words, "the only way to be a 'real' Ukrainian-Canadian [is] to accept romanticization of our history, trivialization of our culture and piece-meal demands for restitution" (9). They illustrate that an attentiveness to the complexities of Ukrainian Canadian history requires an acknowledgement of the uneasy realities of Ukrainian Canadians' experiences. The outrage expressed by members of the Ukrainian Canadian community in response to *All of Baba's Children* and *No Streets of Gold* attests to many Ukrainian Canadians' resistance to such an acknowledgement.²¹

My brief discussion of Kostash's and Potrebenko's texts brings us back, then, full-circle, to the question of how Ukrainian Canadian writers responded to the rise of multiculturalism and the concomitant revival of Ukrainian folk culture. Turning to Maara Haas's novel *The Street Where I Live* (1976), George Ryga's play *A Letter to My Son* (1981), and selections of poetry from Andrew Suknaski's *Wood Mountain Poems* (1976), *the ghosts call you poor* (1978), and *In the Name of Narid* (1981), the point I wish to underscore is that these writers, though almost certainly encouraged by the rise of multiculturalism to write about their experiences as members of an ethnic minority group, simultaneously reject officially-sanctioned folkloric expressions of their ethnicity. Although they—like other Ukrainian Canadians—are motivated by a desire to declare their presence in the nation's cultural landscape, Haas, Ryga, and Suknaski refuse the assumption that "song and dance" adequately reflects what it means to be Ukrainian and Canadian. These writers want to explore instead the complex realities of day-to-day life in Ukrainian Canadian communities —the hardship and humour, the conflicts that developed between generations, and between Ukrainians and non-Ukrainians. They insist, in their writing, that an understanding of their ethnic group's past is essential to maintaining ethnic identity in the present and future. This is not to say that the idea of multiculturalism is absent from their writing. A distinction, however, needs to be made between "official" multiculturalism, which promotes ethnicity diversity through the performance of folk culture, and what might be termed "grassroots" multiculturalism, which acknowledges the myriad, day-to-day realities of multi-ethnic communities. Whereas, in *Yellow Boots*, Lysenko espouses the former, Haas, Ryga, and Suknaski are more interested in the latter. This is especially true of Haas's novel, which takes place in the culturally heterogeneous world of North End Winnipeg during the late 1930s, and Suknaski's poetry, much of which explores his experiences growing up in the multi-ethnic community of Wood Mountain, Saskatchewan.

Most importantly, however, what we see in Haas's novel, Ryga's play, and Suknaski's poems are three writers whose commitment to reclaiming and proclaiming their identity as Ukrainian Canadians comes through not only in the stories that they tell but also in the languages and genres that they use to tell them. Just as Lysenko's unconscious rejection of Ukrainian culture is encoded in the language of her text—in standard English, that is—and in the form of the text, which is, at its core, a conventional fairy-tale romance, so too are Haas's, Ryga's, and Suknaski's perspectives on their ethnic group reflected in the linguistic and stylistic choices they make. *The Street Where I Live* is rife with ethnic characters who speak English with heavy accents and who incorporate words and phrases from their ethnic languages; the main character in *A Letter to My Son* speaks imperfect English with a Ukrainian accent as he struggles to express himself in a language that is foreign to him; and in many of his poems Suknaski records the voices of old Ukrainian homesteaders (and other ethnic immigrants, as well as First Nations and Métis people) with a faithfulness to their prairie vernacular. By writing about the past in languages that were used in the past, these authors supplement "official" versions of history that exclude the voices of ordinary, working-class ethnic communities. All three writers, moreover, experiment with form by blurring multiple genres, including autobiography, biography, drama, fiction, and documentary history. As a result, their texts pose implicit challenges to established literary conventions and, by extension, Anglo-Canadian cultural hegemony.

As I make clear, however, in my discussions of Haas's novel and Ryga's play, caution is needed when valorizing the politics of resistance that form the foundations of these texts. The stories that Haas and Ryga tell take place at particular places and times when resistance to Anglo-Canadian cultural dominance is possible, but both stories come to an end, and they end as ambivalently as Lysenko's *Yellow Boots*. Suknaski's poetry, I argue—focused as it is on the second-generation Ukrainian Canadian *writer's* perpetual struggle to maintain ties to the past—implicitly proposes a more positive strategy for keeping the idea of ethnicity alive. As a poet who self-consciously reflects on the ways in which the process of writing enables him to foster ties between the past and the present, Suknaski suggests that the preservation of ethnicity in the future requires an active imagination—that Ukrainian Canadian-ness resides in ongoing *acts* of imagination.

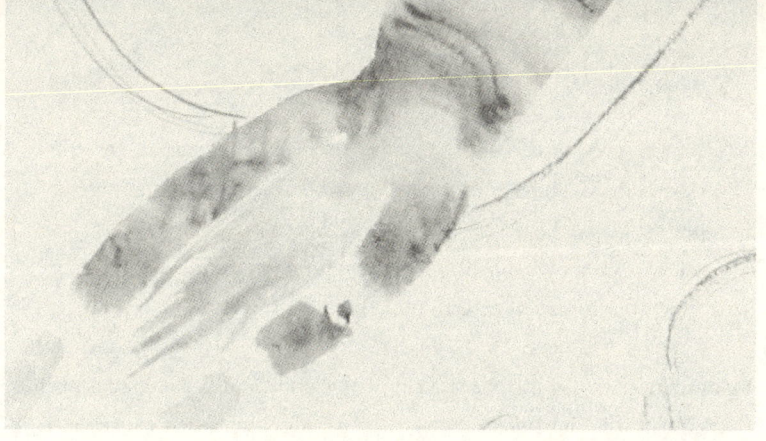

FIVE

"We aren't buying black oxfords"
The Ambivalent Politics of Hybridity in Maara Haas's *The Street Where I Live*

IN HER NOVEL *The Street Where I Live* (1976), published one year before *All of Baba's Children* and *No Streets of Gold,* Maara Haas addresses many of Kostash's and Potrebenko's concerns about the relation between ethnicity and multiculturalism. Like Kostash and Potrebenko, who write about their ethnic communities in order to come to terms with their own ethnic and national identities, Haas, too, sees the process of writing as an opportunity to revisit and make sense of her past. Just as Kostash and Potrebenko respond critically to the Ukrainian Canadian ethnic revival of the 1970s and 1980s, so too does Maara Haas criticize this revival as an inadequate strategy for Ukrainian Canadians to maintain ties with their cultural heritage. In much of her poetry and short fiction, collected in *On Stage with Maara Haas* (1986), Haas is critical of the ways in which official discourses of multiculturalism encourage Canadians to perform their ethnicity through folk song, dance, costume, and art. But her short story "folklorama" best exemplifies her attitudes toward superficial expressions of ethnic identity. Set during "Folklorama '77," a multicultural festival during which "[a]t least 60,000 people...will be visiting 30 pavilions in a mutual exchange of cultural ideas and traditions" (150), the story narrates Haas's participation in the festival. She appears as the ideal multicultural subject. "Stubbornly mosaic," she writes,

> I won't be hard to identify at Folklorama '77, but on the chance you might miss me in the crowd, I'll be wearing a handloomed

british wool skirt, hand-beaded, personally chewed indian hide moccasins, a hand-embroidered ukrainian blouse, a hand-strung phillipine necklace, a hand-blocked scandinavian kerchief, a flurry of handwoven dutch lace petticoats and an east indian emerald, the size of an onion, pierced through my nose. (151)

By drawing attention to the ways in which culture is reduced to costume, Haas illustrates the superficiality of officially-sanctioned expressions of ethnicity. Does ethnic costume, she asks, express an individual's complex experience of ethnic identity?

All three writers are frustrated with the ways in which official discourses of multiculturalism reduce Ukrainian Canadian ethnicity to fossilized and dehistoricized expressions of folk culture. All three are critical of the extent to which many Ukrainian Canadians, including some Ukrainian Canadian scholars, embrace folk culture as an expression of their ethnic identity. And, in seeking to subvert folkloric constructions of ethnicity, all three find themselves reconstructing the complex histories of their ethnic communities. But while Kostash and Potrebenko primarily draw upon the conventions of traditional history to explore their Ukrainian Canadian roots, Haas turns to fiction in order to recreate and reflect upon her experiences as a second-generation Ukrainian Canadian. She playfully reconstructs the past in order to understand and come to terms with it.

At once a written text meant for oral performance, a novel that brings together loosely connected selections of short fiction, and an autobiographical work that fictionalizes both the tragic and comic realities of a particular time and place, *The Street Where I Live* belongs to no single generic category. Set in the multi-ethnic community of Winnipeg's North End during the late 1930s—and narrated by an adolescent girl whose name and background are strikingly similar to those of the author[1]—the novel, broadly speaking, depicts the ethnic community in which Haas was raised. Although she refers to the text as a novel (its full title is *The Street Where I Live: A Novel*), and not as an autobiography, the book's genre is further complicated by its origin as thirty-eight discrete "episodes" or "scripts" for broadcast on the CBC radio programme "This Country in the Morning" (*On Stage* 34). *The Street Where I Live* could also be read as a collection of short fiction or a short story cycle—and the short sentences of Haas's prose suggest, moreover, that she may even be experimenting with the long poem. In "Including the Female Immigrant Story: A Comparative Look at Narrative Strategies" (1996), Tamara Palmer Seiler suggests that, collectively, the multiple stories in *The Street Where I Live* become the single coming-of-age story of Haas's narrator, Maara Lazpoesky, an aspiring young writer (59). The novel, then, might be seen as a female *bildungsroman* or *kunstlerroman*.

While Maara's voice shapes the text, however, her growth as a character is not the central focus of *The Street Where I Live*, since Haas gives as much or more attention to narrating the lives of the numerous other characters who share Maara's world. In a sense, the novel focuses less on a single character than on the character of the community as a whole. And its hybrid genre parallels the multicultural nature of this community. The multi-ethnic residents of North End Winnipeg, as Haas depicts them, are in the process of establishing the terms of their new, multicultural society—to use Benedict Anderson's term, they are imagining their community—by retaining some aspects of Old Country customs, by rejecting others, and by inventing many cultural and social practices that reflect the heterogeneous make-up of their world. *The Street Where I Live*, then, itself a hybrid reinvention of the novel genre, mirrors the nascent state of North End Winnipeg. Haas enables readers to engage with a new form of writing that seeks to capture, formally, the spirit of a new kind of community.

The Street Where I Live is inhabited by a lively, eclectic group of working-class immigrants and their children whose names humorously reflect their diverse ethnic backgrounds and, in some cases, their professions or outstanding personality traits. Haas introduces, for example, Mrs. Regina Brittannia, an English newcomer to the street; Mrs. Weinstein, wife of the local Jewish junk collector; and the Fransciosas, a family of Italian immigrants. The narrator's father is Meexash the Druggist, but Maara encounters numerous other men, including Orest the Undertaker, Herman the Laughing Butcher, Samuel Made-to-Measure Rothstein, Mr. Ph.D. Shumansky, and Beelay the Presser. Throughout the novel, countless characters appear with such names as Moishe the Manipulator, Josef the Bachelor, Aaron the Widower, and Horbaty the Hunchback. Seiler refers to the characters as "laughable but lovable caricatures of stereotypical ethnic characters" ("Including the Female Immigrant" 58), but Haas's motivations for presenting a collection of seemingly one-dimensional characters are complex. On the one hand, because Maara, the narrator, is a child, the names that she comes up with for the people in her community reflect the innocence and simplicity of her perspective on the world around her. At the same time, Maara, the author, even as she takes on the child's voice, is able to parody the conventions of the medieval morality play by ascribing single attributes to her characters. Her choice of nomenclature re-places the morality play in the context of working-class Winnipeg, borrowing from while subversively reinventing an archaic genre. Unlike characters in traditional morality plays, her characters personify neither good nor evil. Rather, their dominant characteristics illustrate that absolute binary oppositions ill-reflect the ways in which ordinary people conduct themselves. By drawing attention to individuals' professions, social roles, or physical attributes, Haas constructs a world in which no one character is superior to another—each is portrayed as comically one-dimensional; collectively, they form a colourful and complex community.

Over the course of the novel, then, as Haas examines all facets of her characters' day-to-day lives, *The Street Where I Live* becomes a text in which everything and nothing happens. Mrs. Kolosky and Mrs. Weinstein fight, make up, and fight again; Xenia Holub marries, leaves her mother's home, and returns with her husband; the Widow Siboolka outlives five husbands, only to be courted by four suitors; and the Beelays save their hard-earned money to bring over a relative from Ukraine who, upon arriving in Winnipeg, makes it her goal to do the same. Even Maara, the character closest to a protagonist, undergoes little change or development over the course of the novel—her observations of the street where she lives leave no dramatic impression on her. Numerous incidents in the novel, however, foreground the ways in which the seemingly ordinary, even mundane, lives of the residents of North End Winnipeg are enriched by a grassroots form of multiculturalism that emerges within their community.[2] Their street is the place, for example, where a Scottish man, Harry McDuff, marries a Ukrainian woman, Annie, and raises five sons—Bruce, Angus, Harry, Borislav, and Michaylo—to play "The Maple Leaf Forever" on the bagpipes, recite Robbie Burns poetry, and worship in the Ukrainian Catholic church. In this community, women like Mrs. Kolosky and Mrs. Weinstein come together, however briefly, to prepare nourishing Ukrainian dishes for the recent immigrant family from England. Schoolchildren from different cultural backgrounds are excused from school on British holidays as well as on their own ethnic holidays, such as Ukrainian Christmas, Passover, and St. Patrick's Day. Similar examples of the community's hybrid culture abound in *The Street Where I Live*. At the Shevchenko Hall, a meeting place for Ukrainian and non-Ukrainian Canadians alike, a "glossy calendar portrait of King George VI and Queen Elizabeth" hangs beside "the lithographed patriot-poet, Taras Shevchenko" (77). Members of the local baseball team, "The Star of David Ukrainian-Canadians," wear blue and yellow satin uniforms with "a Ukrainian Trident on the chest and a Star of David on the sleeve" (199). Catholics and Jews attend the Easter Monday supper at the Blessed Virgin Mary Parish (137–43), and everyone goes to the weekly cockroach races at the Cockroach Café where they bet on such competitors as "MacKenzie King," "Rasputin," and "Humphrey Bogart" (88–91). The world of North End Winnipeg becomes, in a sense, proof positive of the paradoxical notion that Canadian society is defined by "unity in diversity."

The Ukrainian Catholic wedding ceremony of Krisla and Xenia epitomizes the ways in which the residents of North End Winnipeg collectively reinvent Old Country customs in Canada. While Krisla and Xenia, two second-generation Ukrainian Canadians, prepare for their traditional Ukrainian Catholic wedding ceremony, their friends Orest the Undertaker and Moishe the Manipulator (a Ukrainian Canadian Jew) realize that many of the traditional marriage customs have lost their meaning in the context of Canada. As Moishe reads from "the book of Ukrainian Wedding Rituals," Orest prompts him to skip through much of the text:

De two betrotheds bind each udder's arms wit embroidered linen scarfs.

Skip that, says Orest.

De fodder takes de wheat to de mill. De mudder whitewashes de cottage.

De goil sews her princess shoit.

Skip that.

> De mudder gives de goil a needle and silk tred to sew a reet from de ever-green leaves of de periwinkle barweenok on de last night of her goilhood?
> Skip that. (18–19)

Moishe eventually questions Orest's instructions. "Skip dat, skip dat, skip dat," he repeats. "So what's left?" (19). What's left, Haas reveals, is a modified version of the wedding ritual in which three unlikely matchmakers "go see Xenia's old man," get his permission to take her to church, and then join the wedding party in the bridal car, a Model T Ford with a row of tin cans attached to its bumper (19–20).

But Haas's satiric description of the community's Ukrainian Canadian intelligentsia—those who ardently attempt to preserve the purity of Ukrainian Canadian culture by building Ukrainian Canadian community halls and organizing Ukrainian Canadian organizations—perhaps most pointedly illustrates that, like it or not, the residents of North End Winnipeg cannot distance or detach themselves from their multi-ethnic neighbours. To begin, she points out that

> [i]n our district there are twenty-three halls names after Shevchenko.
> The names of the buildings vary:
> Shevchenko Reading Hall
> Shevchenko Cultural Hall
> Shevchenko National Hall
> Shevchenko's Shevchenko Hall. (77)

Next, in her description of a political gathering in "Shevchenko Hall No. 18" hosted by the "Free Fraternity of Ukrainian Intelligentsia," Maara provides the credentials of the group's five members. They are:

> Ancient Grandfather Hetman Slovoda, archivist, linguist from the Free Academy of Obsolete Languages, now on C.P.R. pension, Professor Yakim Golombioski, graduate Gymnast, the University of Chernowitz and first-class bricklayer, Igor Kapusta, world famous Bandurist, composer, musician, ditchdigger. And last but not least, Wasyl Skrypnyk, graduate

Come Laddie from the University of Kiev, landlord-author of the brilliant thesis on twelfth century Onomastic Apostasy, a private collection. (79)

Haas's portrayal of the Ukrainian Canadian intelligentsia and their activities in Winnipeg is layered with irony. On the one hand, the educated elite's involvement in establishing some twenty-three Shevchenko halls illustrates their commitment to preserving Ukrainian culture in Canada—Shevchenko, after all, the "People's Poet" of Ukraine, is a ubiquitous symbol of Ukrainian nationalism.[3] The nationalistic purposes of the halls, however, are undermined by the fact that these halls become meeting places for individuals from diverse cultural backgrounds, united in their status as working-class immigrants. Furthermore, while the educated men of the "Free Fraternity of Ukrainian Intelligentsia" once enjoyed positions of prestige in their home country, they become, in Canada, ordinary members of the working class. Yet their loss of status is oddly appropriate, given that Shevchenko was born a serf and became the champion of the downtrodden peasant.

Haas's characters do not express their ethnic identities, then, by performing folk songs and dances, or by producing folk art; rather, they experience ethnicity in the hybrid social and cultural practices that become a part of their daily lives. As significant, however, as the multicultural practices Haas describes are the languages she uses in her descriptions. Few of the individuals in *The Street Where I Live* speak standard English. Some speak dialects of English—Harry McDuff refers to his wife as "Annive uv Afton, Annie ma' wee wife, Annie ma' dearrie, ma' luv" (14)—others, including many Ukrainian immigrants, speak broken English with heavy accents—before performing his first wedding ceremony in the city, Father Mashik says to himself, "God is vatchink, Bishop is vatchink…. Whole parish, she is vatchink poor village priest, greenhorn in new country" (17). Many of Haas's characters use words and phrases from their ethnic languages when they are speaking English—after finishing her wash one Saturday, Mrs. Fransciosa says, "[f]inire, perfezionare…. The sheets iss-ssa cook" (156). Haas's decision to incorporate the variations of standard English spoken by her characters is deliberate and strategic. The hybridization of language in her novel becomes a process through which individuals from multiple cultural backgrounds challenge (however unconsciously) the supposed superiority of standard English in Canadian society and, by extension, enduring discourses of imperialism that privilege Anglo-Canadian culture over the cultures of other ethnic groups. When Percival Pshawkraw, the English politician, addresses an audience of Ukrainian Canadian voters, he does so in Ukrainian (81) because he understands that if he uses English, he will alienate members of the Ukrainian Canadian community.

As Bill Ashcroft, Gareth Griffiths, and Helen Tiffin argue in *The Empire Writes Back: Theory and Practice in Post-colonial Literatures* (1989), language is "the medium through which a hierarchical structure of power is perpetuated, and the medium through which conceptions of 'truth,' 'order,' and 'reality' become established" (7), but the "syncretic and hybridized nature of post-colonial experience refutes the privileged position of a standard code in the language and any monocentric view of human experience" (41). Indeed, as Haas makes clear in *The Street Where I Live*, none of her characters actually speaks standard English—not even Regina Brittannia, the English woman who lives in North End Winnipeg. Regina speaks a Cockney dialect; commenting on a Ukrainian play, she says, "Blimey…[a]yn't it a pyle one. No bleedin' 'eads, no stabbin'. It tykes Shykespeare to do th' bit rye-t" (52). Ashcroft, Griffiths, and Tiffin—distinguishing between the standard "English" of the imperium and "english," the hybridized variants of the standard, suggest that the latter "abrogates the privileged centrality" of the former because it "signif[ies] difference while employing a sameness which allows it to be understood" (51). The "english" languages spoken in *The Street Where I Live* serve a political function in the text because they simultaneously draw upon and decentre the linguistic norms of Canadian culture. So when Haas's characters speak broken English or dialects of English with heavy accents, and when they use untranslated words from the ethnic languages in their speech, they not only reveal their status as newcomers and outsiders vis-à-vis Anglo-Canadian society, they also implicitly announce their refusal to embrace wholeheartedly the dominant language or the dominant culture of their new society. Interestingly, by including a number of untranslated Ukrainian words, phrases, and names into her novel, Haas makes outsiders of her English-speaking readers.[4] Readers who are not familiar with Ukrainian are excluded from "inside jokes" between the author and her Ukrainian-speaking audience. Translated into English, the gentle Mrs. Holub becomes Mrs. Dove; the Widow Siboolka, who makes her rejected suitors weep, becomes the Widow Onion; and the sniveling Shmarkaty Kapusta becomes Snot-nosed Cabbage Head.

Inside jokes aside, however, Haas illustrates the important contributions that members of ethnic minority groups can—and do—make to Anglo-Canadian culture by foregrounding the hybrid languages spoken by the residents of North End Winnipeg. Over the course of the novel, as various characters exchange words from each other's ethnic languages, they invent a common language appropriate to their multi-ethnic community. During the performance of a play at the Shevchenko Hall, for example, Mrs. Golombioski "offers to translate" for Mrs. Brittannia who, in turn, attempts to pronounce some Ukrainian words (48). After Mrs. Le Vert Frelon finishes measuring Mrs. Vloshkin for a new dress, the two women say their farewells, however imperfectly, in each other's languages: Mrs. Vloshkin says, "Bon Jor to you Mon Amee" and Mrs. Frelon replies, "Slolum" (195). Differences, and even conflicts or tensions, between members of diverse ethnic groups dissipate as individuals, in talking to one another, begin to speak the same hybrid language. Vloshkin, for instance, the Jewish tailor, makes his transition to Canadian society by sending a Christmas package home to his family in Ukraine. At the post office, in English peppered with Yiddish words, he says, "[n]u, I tell myself...don't be a schlemiel. Send a peckl of goods to your sister at Christmas and be Canadian" (60). "Worlds," Ashcroft, Griffiths, and Tiffin write, "exist by means of languages" (44), and the hybrid world that Haas creates in *The Street Where I Live* is coming into being through the "english" language spoken by the characters in her novel.

In terms of its hybrid genre and language, then, *The Street Where I Live* represents a dramatic departure from texts such as Vera Lysenko's *Yellow Boots*, Helen Potrebenko's *No Streets of Gold*, and Myrna Kostash's *All of Baba's Children*, all three of which are also concerned with exploring the ways in which Ukrainian Canadians reconcile their ethnic and national identity, but none of which challenges the boundaries of genre and language. Thematically, however, *The Street Where I Live* concludes as ambivalently as the texts by Lysenko, Potrebenko, and Kostash. If Haas seems to idealize the interactions between her characters by drawing attention to the ways in which they collectively and successfully resist assimilation to Anglo-Canadian society, the ongoing financial struggles of her characters simultaneously undercut the notion that these individuals' lives are without hardship. In other words, the immigrant community's hybrid linguistic, social, and cultural practices ultimately offer little in the way of practical relief from social and economic marginalization within Canadian society. Mr. Peekoosh and Mr. Hinkel must exchange vegetables for medicine—"Rose-Hip medicinal tea" and "a bottle of Sex-All," respectively—because they cannot pay the druggist with money (33); Moishe the Manipulator collects and re-sells stray buttons to make his living, though he often spends his earnings on crap games and "girlie" shows (6); and Mr. Weinstein is the local collector for his junkyard, "Half-Moon Paradise Palladium" (7).

Insofar as many, if not all, of the stories in Haas's text are at once comic and tragic—insofar as she reveals both the humour and the pathos in the daily lives of her characters—*The Street Where I Live* becomes a bittersweet portrayal of ethnic immigrants in Canada. The scene in which Annie McDuff returns to her home from the government relief office illustrates that the McDuff family wants to undermine the authority of the Canadian government. The McDuffs should not receive relief because Harry McDuff is perfectly capable of finding work and because, ostensibly, the family can afford precious commodities such as Annie's prized second-hand persian-lamb coat. From the point of view of the "Spy from Relief" who plagues the McDuffs with her frequent visits and her "nose like a gopher" (14), Harry is lazy. During one visit, she reminds him that, since coming to Canada in 1912, he has spent

> 1 hr. laying C.N.R. railroad ties
> 2 hrs. 12 minutes in the freight shed
> 35 minutes, 4 seconds—employed as a ditch digger
> 7 minutes—Canada Packers, in the slaughterhouse…
> 1 month in a bush camp 20¢ a day, at the generous expense of the Bennett government. (15)

According to the Spy from Relief, Harry has "taken no advantage of the golden opportunities this country has to offer" (15). She fails to understand that Harry is not indifferent to the so-called "golden opportunities" available to him; he deliberately chooses not to seize upon these opportunities because he refuses to accept the role of the exploited immigrant, under-paid for his backbreaking labour. But the McDuffs' apparent success in outwitting the Spy from Relief and, by extension, the government—Annie scrambles to hide her persian-lamb coat in the chicken coop, and Harry, feigning consumption in their brass bed, calls for the priest to deliver the Last Rites—becomes only a partial victory over the Canadian government, for the family lives in poverty and in constant fear of being caught. Harry is forced to spend much of his time in bed, and his wife cannot ever wear her persian-lamb coat.

So, in the end, the unofficial, grassroots form of multiculturalism that characterizes the ethnic community in *The Street Where I Live* becomes a decidedly ambivalent and arguably short-term strategy for challenging the ethnically-inflected social and economic hierarchies of Anglo-Canadian society. Seiler, who sees the dominance of Anglo-Canadian culture in Canadian society as a legacy of British imperialism, argues that "the nature of the post-colonial space Haas creates...is so profoundly ambivalent as to be an interesting but not altogether convincing challenge to imperial centres" ("Including the Female Immigrant" 59). Haas portrays the community in which she lived as a hub of linguistic and cultural exchange between multiple ethnic groups, and the resultant hybrid culture of North End Winnipeg attests to the community's success in resisting assimilation. Importantly, however, the characters in her novel do not consciously choose to construct a multicultural community in Winnipeg: they initially come together not because they are actively interested in each other's cultures but because, as ethnic immigrants, they are outsiders in relation to Anglo-Canadian society. Their ethnic identities and class status mark them as different from and marginal to the Anglo-Canadian mainstream. So the immigrants' hybrid linguistic, social, and cultural practices are less a deliberate strategy for resisting assimilation than an inadvertent by-product of their shared experience of marginalization. In a sense, the multicultural community in Haas's novel is an ethnic ghetto, a temporary stopping place for immigrants to gradually orient themselves to a new culture before inevitably joining mainstream Anglo-Canadian society. Haas's ambivalent portrayal of the hybrid, multicultural community of North End Winnipeg foreshadows the tenuous nature of her characters' resistance to assimilation.

Importantly, because *The Street Where I Live* focuses on the discrete and brief historical moment during which her characters begin the process of Canadianization, Haas does not explore the immigrants' and/or their children's inevitable movement away from the street where they currently live. But in the final scene of the novel, the scene in which Maara and her best friend Magda buy a new pair of shoes at Oiving Monahan's general store, Haas hints at the immigrant community's future—and in so doing, she alerts readers, however unconsciously, to the limits of the text's subversive potential. Enamoured with the glamorous lifestyles of Hollywood film stars such as Gloria Swanson and Jean Harlow, Maara and Magda buy not two practical, inexpensive pairs of black oxfords but a single pair of "Joan Crawford glamour shoes, black patent leather with an ankle strap and four-inch heels" (213). Just as Lysenko's *Yellow Boots* concludes with her heroine putting on a pair of dancing boots, symbols of her ethnic heritage that ironically signal the extent to which her ethnic identity has been reduced to the performance of folk culture, *The Street Where I Live* ends with Maara and Magda putting on their shoes—Maara wears the right shoe, Magda wears the left—and strutting out of the store. The destination to which they are headed, while unformed, is far from the street where they live; far from the immigrant community they presently call home; far from the culture in which they have been raised. Monahan understands that the "glamour shoes" foreshadow the girls' movement away from their ethnic roots, and so he weeps over their decision not to buy the black oxfords.

The problem is that, ironically, the elements of the narrative which enable Haas to criticize discourses of assimilation—her colourful depiction of an immigrant community through the eyes of a child narrator, and her decision to draw upon her own experiences growing up in multi-ethnic North Winnipeg—are the same elements which ultimately undermine the potency of the social critique that the novel offers. As playful as *The Street Where I Live* may seem, it is, at its core, a realist novel. Just as North End Winnipeg is a temporary stopping-place for ethnic immigrants on their journey toward Canadianization, so too is Maara's lighthearted commentary on her community representative of a provisional worldview. Her delight in the street where she lives can and will last only as long as her childhood—which is, as Monahan observes, on the cusp of ending in the final pages of the novel. Bound by a fundamental faithfulness to what life was like in Winnipeg during the 1930s—restricted, in other words, by the realist underpinnings of the text—

Haas cannot trace her narrator's transition from childhood to adulthood and simultaneously sustain her novel's anti-assimilationist politics because Maara's assimilation is unavoidable. So the story ends on a necessarily ambivalent note, with Maara on the threshold of growing up and growing away from her community. As Monahan weeps, he becomes an embodiment of Haas's inability to imagine a different ending for the inhabitants of *The Street Where I Live*. Hybridity may offer hope in this novel but historical realism has the final word.

SIX

"We laugh, but we are sad"

Oral History in George Ryga's *A Letter to My Son*

IN ITS EXPLORATION OF THE DIFFERENT WAYS in which first- and second-generation ethnic Canadians struggle to make sense of their role and identity in Anglo-Canadian society, George Ryga's *A Letter to My Son* (1981) picks up where *The Street Where I Live* leaves off. One of the final, fleeting images in Haas's novel—the image of an elderly immigrant weeping as he watches the world change before him—becomes, in a sense, the starting point of Ryga's play. Like Haas, Ryga attempts to retrieve ordinary, working-class Ukrainian Canadians from the margins of Ukrainian Canadian, and indeed Canadian, history. Both writers seek to challenge the ways in which "official" history excludes the stories of the ethnic immigrant "everyman" by focusing their texts on the social realities of Ukrainian immigrants and their children in Canada. In comparison to *The Street Where I Live*, *A Letter to My Son* is a more complex depiction of a Ukrainian pioneer who struggles—with his family, with the institutional structures of Canadian society, and with the secrets of his past—to come to terms with his ethnic and national identity in the present. At the same time—and largely because Ryga chooses drama, as opposed to fiction, to tell his story—Ryga's play is a simpler, starker, and more stylized portrayal of a specific aspect of Ukrainian Canadian history. Whereas Haas's novel takes place in the colourful, multi-faceted urban context of North End Winnipeg during the 1930s, Ryga's play, set in the late 1970s, unfolds against the sparse rural backdrop of the Manitoba prairies. While

Haas, from a child's perspective, examines the relationships between numerous immigrants from multiple ethnic backgrounds who are united in their similar experiences as newcomers to Canada, Ryga, from the point of view of an old man, focuses on the relation between one Ukrainian immigrant and his son—two men divided by their very different experiences as first- and second-generation Ukrainian Canadians. The main difference, however, between *The Street Where I Live* and *A Letter to My Son* is that the latter explicitly addresses the intergenerational conflict between immigrants and their children.

A Letter to My Son is not the first of Ryga's works to feature Ukrainian Canadian characters, nor is it unique in its focus on the condition of the peasant/working-class man. Although best known for *The Ecstasy of Rita Joe* (1967), a play that draws attention to the plight of First Nations people in Canada, Ryga wrote numerous poems, short stories, novels, screenplays and radio dramas that narrate or dramatize the stories of farmers and manual labourers, including Ukrainian pioneers and their descendants.[1] As Jars Balan explains in "'A Word in a Foreign Language': Ukrainian Influences in George Ryga's Work" (1982), Ukrainian Canadian characters appear in numerous novels and plays by Ryga. "In addition to the Bayracks, Ruptashs, Zaharchuks, Sadowniks, Makars and Burlas of *Ballad of a Stone-Picker*, and Joe Skrypka and his friend Nick in *Hungry Hills*," Balan writes, "we encounter a Michael J. Tomaschuk in *Sunrise on Sarah* (1973), a Grace Stefanyk in *Portrait of Angelica* (1984), and a…character named Romeo Kuchmir in the novel *Night Desk* (1976)" (39). According to Christopher Innes, moreover, in *Politics and the Playwright: George Ryga* (1985), Ryga's texts frequently thematize "the positive values of manual work and the individual who defines himself in opposition to an alien and alienating social structure, which imposes an inner exile on its citizens and turns all into displaced persons" (14). His texts often examine, too, the "distorting emptiness of official history that presents the achievements of the governed masses as the acts of the governing few" (14). In much of his writing, he implicitly calls for a "unifying cultural myth drawn from the unarticulated experience of the immigrants and outcasts, the subculture of the working classes who built the country" (14). Ryga seeks to both dismantle national metanarratives that exclude the voices and experiences of ethnic immigrants and refashion a version of the past that acknowledges both the hardships and the triumphs of those who have been forgotten.

As critics such as Balan, Innes, E. David Gregory, and James Hoffman suggest, Ryga's lived experiences explain to a large extent his identification with peasant and working-class people, especially Ukrainian Canadians, and his desire to explore their way of life in his writing.[2] Born in 1932, the son of second-wave Ukrainian immigrants, Ryga grew up on his parents' homestead near Athabasca, Alberta. As an adult, however, he left the farm and worked as "a carpenter, cook, waiter, dry cleaner, furniture remover, and, naturally enough, farm-hand" (Gregory 47) while pursuing his career as a playwright and novelist. Certainly Ryga's background—as a second-generation Ukrainian Canadian who rejected his father's way of life by leaving the farm and becoming a writer—sheds light on his motivations for examining the complex and conflicted relationship between one Ukrainian immigrant and his son in *A Letter to My Son*. In part an (auto)biographical exploration of his vexed relationship with his father, the play becomes Ryga's attempt not only to retrieve the immigrant everyman from the margins of official history but also to come to terms with a particular man in his own private history. In an essay on the play written in 1985 and published posthumously in *The Athabasca Ryga*, Ryga insists that *A Letter to My Son* is not a fictionalized rendering of his relationship with his father, George Ryga Sr.: "this is not the story of my father," he writes, "it is the story of many mythical fathers" (78). Yet, in describing his father's reaction to the play when he first saw it performed, Ryga reveals the extent to which both he and his father were emotionally affected by *A Letter to My Son*. "When my father first encountered this drama," Ryga writes, "he wept, and we both achieved a reconciliation we had never had before" (78).

A short, two-act play first produced in 1981 at the Kam Theatre Lab in Thunder Bay, Ontario, *A Letter to My Son* comprises a small cast of characters in comparison to *The Street Where I Live*, and it unfolds against a relatively bare set. The play focuses on Old Man Lepa, an aging Ukrainian immigrant who lives alone in his sparsely-furnished farmhouse, and the main action of the play revolves around two problems with which he grapples in his old age. In the first place, Lepa wants to write a letter to his estranged son, Stephan, and in so doing reconcile their differences. Stephan, a schoolteacher in the city, has no interest in his father's way of life; and Lepa sees his son's movement to the city as a betrayal of both his ethnic heritage and his peasant roots. Each time he sits down at his kitchen table to write to his son, however, Lepa becomes tongue-tied and his mind wanders back to moments from his past, for Lepa is preoccupied with a second, though not unrelated, matter. Although he has worked hard all his life, and although he has applied for the old age pension, he has not yet received his first pension cheque. Lepa, then, has two problems to contend with. He wants Stephan to acknowledge the role he has played in making a better life for his son, and he wants the government to recognize the contributions he has made to the building of the nation. Lepa's letter writing is frequently interrupted by the appearance of Nancy Dean, a young social worker—a third-generation Ukrainian Canadian Jew, roughly the same age as Stephan—who has been assigned to help Lepa with his application for pension. Frequently, though not consciously, Lepa detaches himself from his conversations with Nancy by revisiting incidents from his younger days: much of the play, in fact, unfolds as a kind of monologue in which Lepa talks to himself as he recreates scenes from his past.

As Lepa revisits his past, he comes face to face with an incident that he would rather, but cannot, forget. While he was working away from the farm, and while Hanya was left alone—pregnant with Stephan—to tend to the homestead, she accepted help from a wandering religious fanatic. Lepa, upon arriving home and seeing a strange man in his yard, wrongfully accused Hanya of adultery. He drove the fanatic from his yard, only to learn several days later that the man was hit by a train during a blinding snowstorm. In effect, Lepa killed an innocent man—a man who wanted only to help a poor immigrant woman—and, in his own words, he contributed to Hanya's untimely death as well. In a draft of his letter to Stephan, Lepa explains that "something in her health and spirit died that day" (89): "[i]t was my fault that I had broken her spirit" (90). So *A Letter to My Son* thematizes not only one man's refusal to be forgotten by his son and his country but also one man's struggle to come to terms with how he will be remembered.³

Unlike the characters in Haas's novel, who share a sense of belonging to their multi-ethnic community, Lepa is a loner and an outcast in relation to his ethnic community.⁴ Although he is not without family, his son Stephan, sister Marina, and brother-in-law Dmitro live in the city, and they have little in common with Lepa. Marina and Dmitro are prosperous clothing merchants and active members of the organized Ukrainian Canadian community; they have successfully entered the Anglo-Canadian middle class while retaining aspects of their ethnic heritage. When Stephan was a child, they ensured that he attended Ukrainian language classes in their basement of their church; when he graduated from high school, they encouraged him to go to university. They are, in Lepa's words, the "ones who did good"—the "ones the Angliki call 'them good Ukrainians'" (74). Lepa, by contrast, has no affiliations with the Ukrainian Canadian community. He is a pro-nationalist Ukrainian who also believes in socialism, but—save for one incident during the depression in which he was accidentally drawn into a political rally—he has never been involved directly in politics, and he is outspoken in his criticisms of the church: "I came to Canada," he says, "so I would never bend my knee to another man. For me the road to God was always blocked by a priest" (100). Lepa's loyalties are to the uneducated peasant and working-class Ukrainian, for he has devoted his life to farming and migrant labour. Lepa lives alone in his empty farmhouse, the last remaining trace of his lifelong labour, and a poignant metaphor for the lonely life he has built for himself.

But insofar as Lepa is an outsider in relation to the Ukrainian Canadian community, he is also marginalized within Canadian society. In contrast to the characters in *The Street Where I Live* who rarely, if ever, leave the borders of their ethnic community, Lepa has spent much of his life living and working among Canadians. He has long been conscious of his low economic and social status as a working-class Ukrainian immigrant. In fact, at the outset of *A Letter to My Son*, when Lepa learns for the first time that, because the Canadian government has no record of his existence, he in fact has no status at all, he is neither surprised nor outraged. As Nancy Dean explains, Lepa cannot receive his old age pension because he was killed in 1934 while working in a northern Ontario coal mine. In the eyes of the government, he must have died, for a newspaper article about the accident listed Lepa as one of the two men who were killed. Seemingly unaffected by Nancy's information, Lepa says, "So?" before he *"moves wearily away from her, almost into gloom in periphery of set"* (78). Lepa's movement to the margins of the set, upon hearing that he is officially dead, dramatizes his feelings of helplessness and resignation—and it dramatizes, too, his exclusion from the official public record. In an ironic commentary on the ways in which an individual's existence is validated through official documents and records, Nancy's personal encounters with the living, breathing Lepa—not to mention his own testimony that he did indeed survive the accident—do not constitute proof that he is alive. Over the course of the play, Nancy makes numerous attempts to solicit from Lepa appropriate documents or records that will legitimize his existence: she asks to see his land title (82); a passport or immigration papers (97); Canadian citizenship documents (97); a bill of sale (98); bank or hospital records; and a social insurance number (112). More anguished than angry that he cannot produce the required papers, Lepa offers matter-of-fact explanations for why he has no official proof of his existence. He strategically placed his farm in Hanya's name, in case something were to happen to him. "To be a widow immigrant is bad," he tells Nancy. "To be a widow with nothing is like being blind and deaf and having nothing to eat" (83). Hanya then willed the farm to Stephan, who subsequently sold it; and before she died, she also mistakenly burned Lepa's landing card and immigration documents. Lepa could have applied—and almost did apply—for reissued documents. But, with his limited literacy in English, he could not understand the application forms.

Old Man Lepa's problem, simply put, is that he is suspended between the past and the present, and his inability to come to terms with either—foregrounded by the structure of the stage, as well as the background music and sound effects that Ryga calls for in his stage directions—is what haunts Lepa throughout *A Letter to My Son*. Lepa's psychological movement between the present to the past is dramatized by his literal movement between the two levels of the stage. While he writes to his son and talks with Nancy in his kitchen, on the lower front level of the stage, Lepa's flashbacks to his younger days are enacted on an elevated portion of the stage behind the kitchen. As Ryga suggests in his stage directions, Lepa should struggle to ascend the raised part of the stage, foregrounding not only his physical frailties but also his psychological difficulties in coping with the past (71). Given that, while elevated, Lepa periodically imagines conversations that he has had with his son—conversations that never actually took place—the bi-level stage structure dramatizes, too, the extent to which Lepa is unable to distinguish between reality and fantasy.

Although mournful Ukrainian folk songs become the background music in much of *A Letter to My Son*, drawing attention to the extent to which Lepa lives in the past, the opening scene of the play begins with a musical collage—or, better, clash—of songs that reflect his divided sense of loyalty to his ethnic and national communities, as well as the tensions between his socialist politics and his nationalistic sentiments toward Ukraine. At the outset of the play, as Lepa sits at his kitchen table, drafting the letter to his son, he—and the audience—hears strains of Ukrainian folk music that segue into the opening bars of "Solidarity Forever," followed by abrupt shifts between portions of "O Canada," "Land of Hope and Glory," the Soviet national anthem, "God Save the Queen," "The Internationale," and "Battle Hymn of the Republic" (72).

But it is language, ultimately, that both prohibits Lepa from leaving the past behind and offers him a means through which he can live, fully, in the present. Lepa's inability to read and write English well, after all, is what prevents him from either re-establishing a relationship with his son or asserting his identity to the government. Lepa speaks a hybrid "english"—to use Ashcroft, Tiffin, and Griffith's term—that is both similar to and different from standard English. While he is clearly fluent in English, he often makes grammatical errors—"I don't know how to read English too good," he says to Nancy (77). And while he uses few Ukrainian words, he speaks with a Ukrainian accent, frequently incorporating common Ukrainian expressions, translated into English, in his speech. As he struggles to write to his son at the start of the play, he says, "[w]hy is it when I write a letter, I am making a wallet out of wood?" (72); and, in describing Marina and Dmitro to Nancy, he explains that "the devil wore his way through a pair of boots finding them for one another" (76). On the one hand, Lepa seems to subtly refuse wholesale assimilation to Anglo-Canadian culture by retaining aspects of his ethnic language. He is certainly, at moments, stubborn, angry, and agitated—raising his voice, for example, when he speaks about Marina and Dmitro. At the same time, however, his speech, like that of the characters in *The Street Where I Live*, is a constant reminder of his "otherness" within Anglo-Canadian society—exacerbated by his low economic status and socialist politics. Often, then—and especially when he fights to find words to write to Stephan—he becomes sad, soft-spoken, and defeated.

If Haas's characters, however, are playfully unaware of the ways in which their hybrid languages will hinder their chances of advancing within the social and economic hierarchies of Canadian society, Lepa is painfully conscious that his speech marks him as inferior to educated, middle-class Anglo-Canadians—and inferior, as well, to second- and third-generation ethnic Canadians like Stephan and Nancy. Embarrassed that he is unfamiliar with some of the vocabulary Nancy uses, he admits, "I don't understand them big words" (85); ashamed that he cannot write a simple letter to Stephan, he says, "[m]y son is an educated man and would laugh at this foolishness" (72). Lepa believes that, in Stephan's eyes, he is an ignorant man. In several conversations between father and son—imaginary conversations that take place between Lepa and Stephan on the elevated portion of the stage—Stephan admonishes Lepa for his inarticulate way of expressing himself. "Be precise and to the point," says Stephan, speaking to Lepa as a schoolteacher would speak to a student, "I have no time for animal grunts from the ignorant!" (89). Lepa, of course, is not ignorant. He is literate in Ukrainian, as well as in Polish. But in order to re-establish a relationship with his son, and in order to receive his pension, he must learn to use "English," the dominant language of Canadian society. He must, more specifically, learn to read and write "English." Just as Lepa is suspended between the past and the present, so too is he caught between two languages—he is able to speak oral "english," but writing in "English," for Lepa, is "the labour of the damned!" (74).

Given that Lepa cannot write his way out of his identity crisis, speaking becomes the only viable means through which he might tell his story and, in so doing, come to terms with the life he has led and the man he has become. The resolution to Lepa's situation, then, hinges on Nancy—or, rather, Lepa's relationship with Nancy. If the government is unwilling to accept Lepa's word, and if Stephan is uninterested in reading Lepa's words, perhaps Nancy is willing to listen to Lepa talk; perhaps she is interested in his stories. If Nancy, in listening to him narrate his life, were to acknowledge him as a man worthy of her attention and affection—if she were to become, in a sense, the daughter he never had (or a female incarnation of the son he wished he had)—Lepa might be able to accept his exclusion from the official public record as well as his uneasy relationship with his son. Nancy could teach him, albeit unintentionally, that his informal, oral way of expressing himself and asserting his identity is no less valid than formal, written texts; that his life can be narrated and legitimized beyond the boundaries of the written word. Symbolically, moreover, the development of a relationship between Lepa and Nancy could resolve a number of underlying tensions in the play: tensions not only between different generations of Ukrainian Canadian but also between Ukrainian Canadian men and women, as well as Jewish and non-Jewish Ukrainian Canadians.

Ryga, then, offers a resolution to Old Man Lepa's situation not through his application for old age pension, or through the letter to his son, but through his relationship with Nancy. At the outset of *A Letter to My Son*, Lepa and Nancy are divided by their experiences as first- and third-generation Ukrainian Canadians, respectively. Lepa's conversations with Nancy are often characterized by his stubborn refusal to listen or talk to her; when he does respond to her, he is usually angry. Lepa cannot accept the rules of the government that Nancy represents, and she cannot understand his unwillingness to cooperate with her. During her first visit to his home, Lepa is suspicious, unfriendly, and outspokenly sexist. He greets her with a series of questions, insinuating that she is incompetent because she is a woman. "What's the matter?" he asks. "They afraid to send a man to talk to a man?" (76). On several other occasions, Lepa raises his voice to Nancy, unleashing his frustrations on her through sarcasm. At one point in the play, he goes so far as to accuse Nancy of betraying her ethnic heritage by changing her name from Odinsky to Dean (84). Though she would rather not discuss her personal life with Lepa, he presses her to reveal her origins: "What's your name?" he says. "Nancy? Nancy?... Gimme the rest.... What's your name?... I want to know your real name!" (84). And, later in the play, when she insists that she needs "something more substantial than [his] word" to prove his identity, Lepa "*fumbles in his pants pocket and takes out a closed pocketknife, which he opens and swings under her nose*": "[a]llright," he says, "get the jar by the stove!... I cut that vein there and fill the sonofabitch to the brim...you can take that to your boss—a present from Ivan Lepa!" (97-98).

These two moments in the play—when Lepa asks Nancy about her name, and when he pulls out his pocketknife—are crucial in the development of the relationship between the two characters. For much of the play, Nancy resists the temptation to lash out at Lepa by remaining professionally aloof, refusing to divulge personal information when they talk. When, however, Lepa demands that she tell him her name, Nancy becomes angry for the first time; and when Lepa pulls out his pocketknife to draw his own blood as proof of his existence, Nancy lets down her guard entirely, calling him an "obstinate peasant who has no need of a pension" (98). "There should be no pensions for people like you!" she roars. "I think the government should give you a few carrot and turnip seeds. You can plant them…watch them grow…harvest them and make yourself soup. And as you eat your soup, you can pontificate to your four walls as to how you did right, while the rest of the world is skidding down to hell!" (98). Nancy's outburst marks a turning point in their relationship and, indeed, in the play itself. After she speaks her mind, Nancy and Lepa glare at one another across the kitchen table, but their anger is soon transformed into laughter as the two wordlessly acknowledge that they are equally stubborn, and can be equally childish in their interactions with each other. By standing up to Lepa (in a way that Hanya never could) and by challenging him without the condescending tone that Stephan often takes with his father, Nancy breaks through the emotional walls that the old man has built around himself. Tellingly, after their argument, Nancy "*reaches out to pat [Lepa's] hand reassuringly*" as a daughter might and "*[t]hey each pick up their coffee cups and toast each other silently*," like two old friends (98). The two have connected at last. To break the silence between them, then, Nancy begins to ask Lepa about his past: "[w]hen you were first married," she says, "what was it like?…how difficult was it to live?" (98-99). Rather than ignoring or circumventing each other's questions, Nancy and Lepa begin to engage in a two-way conversation, listening and speaking to each other—a dramatic change from Lepa's monologues. After laughing and toasting each other with their coffee cups, Nancy and Lepa chat about the different worlds from which they come. She tells him about growing up "with all the food [she] wanted…television, cooks, records…a car"; he, in turn, talks about watching "men cut fields with scythes, and women beat grain on the threshing floor…like they did a thousand years before" (99).

In the final scene, Lepa sits alone again at his kitchen table, trying once more to write a letter to his son. But upbeat country and western music now plays in the background—heralding, in its tempo, the start of a new and brighter day for Lepa, and in its style, Lepa's successful transition from the past, his Ukrainian roots, to the present, contemporary Canadian society.⁵ Midway through this draft of his letter to Stephan, Lepa "*[b]reaks his pencil and throws the pieces across the room*"; as the music "*rises in volume slightly*," he then "*slaps the table with his hands, his expression elated*" (117). Lepa chooses to speak—rather than write—about his life because he has learned from Nancy that, orally, he can author his own life story. While Stephan is not present to hear his father speak, Lepa addresses him nonetheless. "Ah!" he says. "It should go like this—Stefan…a man wants to be remembered for the good things he made possible…not the stupid things, but the good things" (117). As the light fades and the curtain closes on him, Lepa proceeds to tell stories about his experiences as a young man, chuckling at some of the individuals and incidents he describes. The figure of the aging immigrant, weeping for the past, becomes the figure of an old man laughing as he celebrates it—laughing, that is, as he reinvents the past, remembering some events and forgetting others, in his own words and in his own voice.

Yet the conclusion of *A Letter to My Son* is as poignant as it is triumphant. Earlier in the play, commenting on the ways in which official history excludes ordinary peasant and working-class immigrants, Lepa suggests to Nancy that the government "make a big monument of stone" in Halifax to commemorate all the nameless, faceless immigrants who built the country—a monument "of a man standing looking into the country…he's got hands, feet—everything. But no face. And we put that up in Halifax to remind us how we got a fresh start, no?" (86). Although they laugh together at the irony of Lepa's suggestion, Lepa quickly becomes serious. "We laugh," he says to himself, "but we are sad" (86). By forgiving himself for his mistakes and finding humour in his hardships, he comes to terms with the life he has led; by becoming the oral teller of his own history, and by choosing the aspects of his history that he wishes to be remembered, he challenges the ways in which official history is recorded. But if Lepa's history, left unrecorded, can only be told by him, what will happen when he is no longer around to tell it? The oral history that Lepa embraces is not without its limitations. Nancy has heard his history, but will she pass it on? While lively country and western music promises the start of a new life for Lepa at the end of the play, the sun setting on the fields outside his window foreshadows the fact that his life is simultaneously coming to a close. In describing his inevitable passing,

Lepa says, "I feel like a dying man who has closed the big book on his life" (117). The phrase he uses, however, is sadly figurative: no book exists in which his history is included.

The obstacle that Lepa faces as a character is ultimately the same obstacle that Ryga comes up against as a writer—how to imagine an alternative conclusion to the story of a father and son divided, how to take the "big book" of the ethnic minority experience and write a happy ending, not only for the immigrant generation but for the next generation as well. Just as Lepa returns in his dream-like memory sequences to the past, so too does Ryga revisit his own past in this play. But while both attempt to use their imaginations to come to terms with vexed father-son relationships—with inter-generational rifts brought about by assimilation—they are able to dream up or to script scenarios that deviate from reality. The problem is, at its core, a generic one. As with Haas in *The Street Where I Live*, the over-arching realism of *A Letter to My Son* is what prevents Ryga from moving beyond the boundaries of his own observations and experiences to explore what might be possible, in the realm of fantasy at least, for first- and second-generation Ukrainian Canadians. Lepa never dreams of reconciliation with his son because he cannot envision it anymore than Ryga can, within the realist logic of his play. The old man's tentative connection with Nancy—which is, tellingly, never fully explored and extended into the future—is the most that the playwright can manage. Insofar as the ambivalent conclusion of the play becomes, like the final pages of Haas's novel, a mirror to the author's world, it illustrates the extent to which Ryga is unable to imagine himself out of his social reality. In the end, then, as accurate as both authors' representations of reality may seem—and as valuable as they may be as forms of history that record the lives of ordinary ethnic immigrants and their children—these texts model for readers a troubling acquiescence of the imagination. Marked less by a refusal than by an inability to re-invent the experience of ethnicity in texts that transcend the generic limitations of realism, Haas's and Ryga's attitudes toward writing about Ukrainian Canadians become reminiscent of Vera Lysenko's. Wanting to "write back" to dominant discourses of identity but constrained by the dominant literary conventions of their time, all three writers to some extent close the "big book" on Ukrainian Canadian-ness, leaving little room for fluidity and negotiation. It would take another kind of writer to open it up again.

SEVEN

"easter bread and clouds"
The Poetry of Andrew Suknaski

FOR READERS WHO ARE FAMILIAR with Canadian poetry published in the 1960s and 1970s—and for those who are familiar, more specifically, with the work of such avant-garde poets as Al Purdy, Robert Kroetsch, Eli Mandel, and John Newlove—Andrew Suknaski needs little introduction. Suknaski, a second-generation Ukrainian Canadian, belonged to this loose fraternity of writers who are well known and have been well received within the Canadian literary institution for their experimentation with language and genre. These poets—all from the prairies, some from ethnic minority backgrounds[1]—began publishing at a time when public discourse on Canadian identity was changing to reflect an increasing openness in Canadian society to ethnic and regional diversity. The simultaneous rise of both regionalism and multiculturalism created a space for the voices of writers whose self-conscious aims were to develop new literary forms that would fully and accurately reflect the ways in which their experiences as prairie-dwellers—the distinct cultures, histories, languages, and politics of their region—had shaped their identities.

To be sure, a similar impulse lies behind the work of such writers as Haas and Ryga, who draw attention to the experiences of ordinary ethnic immigrants and their children—individuals who might otherwise be forgotten—in texts that blur the distinctions between autobiography, history, and fiction. Ryga, in particular, invites comparison to the prairie poets who came to voice in the 1960s—and to Suknaski, especially[2]— because, in broad thematic terms, these writers were all interested in creating a new prairie mythology that would pay tribute to the cultural, political, and socioeconomic uniqueness of the region. A crucial aspect of this mythologization involved examining the ways in which First Nations peoples have affected the literal and figurative or cultural landscapes of the prairies—acknowledging, that is, the indigenous status of aboriginal groups, exploring their mistreatment by the government and by settlers, including ethnic immigrants, and simultaneously, albeit paradoxically, drawing parallels between the experiences of First Nations peoples and those of ethnic minority groups.[3] The play that Ryga is best known for—*The Ecstasy of Rita Joe*, which explores the devastating long-term effects of colonialism on aboriginal people—has much in common, thematically, with many poems by Purdy, Kroetsch, and Suknaski that thematize Native history and culture.[4] These writers' shared fascination with the conflicts as well as the common ground between aboriginal and non-aboriginal communities on the prairies marks a turning point in Canadian literature—specifically, the emergence of postcolonial consciousness among western Canadian writers.

Importantly, however, despite the similarities between Ryga's work and that of such poets as Purdy, Kroetsch, Newlove, and Suknaski—despite the fact that these writers all played key roles in orienting Canadian literature toward discourses of regionalism, multiculturalism, and postcolonialism—contemporary scholars of Canadian literature tend to place less importance on Ryga's contributions to reshaping the field. The problem is not that Ryga was any less prolific than his contemporaries but rather that his writing is seen by critics as, formally speaking, less experimental, less innovative, and, hence, less provocative. The same can be said of Maara Haas's work. Ryga's fundamental adherence to realist aesthetics means that, in contrast to the edgier counter-cultural poetics of other prairie writers, his work is perceived as less subversive than conventional, regardless of the fact he was as forward-thinking in his sensitivity to First Nations issues. Suknaski, by contrast, as a member of the avant-garde prairie poetry scene, has been more outspokenly embraced by critics for the crucial part he played in ushering in a new chapter of Canadian literary history. His impressive body of work,[5] says Stephen Scobie, and his approaches to producing it, had an "immense influence upon the development of Prairie poetry" in the 1970s.[6]

The son of second-wave immigrants who arrived in Canada and homesteaded near Wood Mountain in 1914—his father came from Ukraine, his mother from Poland—Suknaski was born in 1942. After Andrew Sr. left the family, in 1948, Suknaski was raised by his mother, and at the age of sixteen, he "ran away from home" (Abraham 25), beginning a seventeen-year period of "wandering around Canada and various parts of the world as an itinerate [sic] labourer, occasional student, and apprentice poet" (Balan, "Voices from the Ukrainian Steppes" 121). He studied both writing and art at various institutions in British Columbia and Québec,[7] and his first published poetry—visual poems collected and self-published in *Rose Way in the East* (1971), *In Mind Ov Xcrossroads Ov Mythologies* (1971), and *Y th Evolution into Ruenz* (1972)—reflect his interest in blurring the boundaries between image and text. As Jars Balan explains, Suknaski's early poetry is "characterized by a markedly avant-garde and counter-cultural spirit" ("Voices from the Canadian Steppes" 121). In 1969, he founded *Elfin Plot*, an underground literary magazine and, on one occasion, he floated issues of the magazine "down the North Saskatchewan River in poet Al Purdy's empty cigar tubes" (122). Around the same time, he established the Elfin Plot Press and self-published numerous pamphlets and hand-bound books with "drawings and handstitched text, which he reproduced in editions of three on cardboard, rice and mulberry paper and gave away without recording or remembering the titles" (121). Suknaski also "inscribed poems on clay pots and candles," constructed "poem-kites," and had a friend drop paper airplane poems from an airplane (Balan, "Voices from the Canadian Steppes" 121). Clearly, he was experimenting with radical new ways of writing and disseminating poetry in order to escape—both literally and metaphorically—the confines of the modernist poetic tradition.

Eventually, after moving back the prairies in the 1970s and attempting to "re-establish himself as a resident of Wood Mountain" ("Voices from the Canadian Steppes" 121), Suknaski moved away from visual and concrete poetry, turning instead to more realist narrative and documentary poems. As numerous critics point out, however, his later poems reflect his ongoing experimentation with language and form, as well as image and text. According to Harvey Spak, who produced a National Film Board documentary about Suknaski in 1978, entitled

Wood Mountain Poems, Suknaski's writing process has never been conventional. When Spak first met Suknaski, in 1976, the poet was "typing up long poems on blue foolscap sheets or brown grocery bags" that he would subsequently hang on a nail above his table (3). Suknaski apparently said to Spak that "he liked the feel of type on thick brown kraft paper" (3). But insofar as he was particular about the texture of the paper on which he wrote his poems, he was also particularly interested in texturing his published collections of these poems with photographs, images, and artwork related to his writing. *Wood Mountain Poems*, for example, is framed by photographs taken in and around Suknaski's hometown. *In the Name of Narid* includes not only photographs of Suknaski and his parents but also fragments of Ukrainian prayer books. And *East of Myloona* incorporates Suknaski's sketches of the First Nations people he met while travelling through the Northwest Territories.

Scholars who have worked on Suknaski's poetry are quick to point out his adeptness at authentically transcribing the voices of ordinary prairie people. Spak says that Suknaski gives the "otherwise forgotten people [of Wood Mountain] a voice" (Spak 4). Scobie, in his review of *the ghosts call you poor*, argues that Suknaski's poetic method is "deliberately unobtrusive"; his language is "casual, flowing, colloquial" (4). The rhythms of Suknaski's poems, Scobie writes, "are those of speech, and the line divisions are used as a kind of loose notation for the speaking voice rather than as formal devices" (4). And, as Anne Munton repeats throughout her discussion of Suknaski's poetry, his accurate transcription of dialect is "a particular achievement" because it authentically captures the voices of the prairies: Suknaski "clings to the authenticity," she writes, "the veracity of the voices of real people"; "always the voices sound authentically"; his poems are characterized by "uncompromising authenticity" (81–82).

In terms of his interest in faithfully "chronicl[ing] the consciousness of a people most of us would dismiss as unimportant" (Spak 4), Suknaski has much in common with both Haas and Ryga. As with these other two writers, he documents the history he shares with the still living and long dead inhabitants of the prairies—individuals whose way of life has been or will be forgotten within the annals of official history—in order to legitimize their status as historical subjects. Very much in keeping with *The Street Where I Live* and *A Letter to My Son*,

Suknaski's poems are characterized by an attentiveness to seemingly insignificant moments of human tenderness and humour—moments that have no place in or relevance to macro-narratives of prairie or Canadian history but that are crucial in defining the micro-history of a community like Wood Mountain. In such poems as "Vasile Tonita" (*WMP* 85–87), for example, and "Sat" (*ghosts* 65–67), Suknaski looks back with fondness on the times he spent with his friends and father figures Vasile Tonita and Tonita's son-in-law Lee Soparlo. Wood Mountain is a world in which individuals develop tightly-knit bonds through their everyday experiences on the prairies, and they nurture these bonds in the ordinary pubs and pool halls where they gather to swap stories over pints of beer. Indeed, beer parlours become the central meeting places in which the history of Wood Mountain—much of it lighthearted—unfolds. While spending time in the community watering holes, Suknaski hears about local store-owner Charlie Blouin's casual handling of a holdup by a well-known neighbour—"*pete*," Charlie says, "*you better put that gun down / before you hurt yourself*" (*WMP* 29, original emphasis)—and he hears James Lethbridge talk about being torn between the "buckin broncos" of the Calgary Stampede and his "good woman" in Wood Mountain (92). In the pub, too, an upstart Suknaski, ruminating on the philosophy he has learned at university, is challenged by a local who asks him, "*where the fuck did you get your education?*" (*WMP* 77, original emphasis). Not unlike Haas's novel, Suknaski's poems narrate the day-to-day goings-on of a multi-ethnic community where everything and nothing happens.

Yet, at the same time, the cafés and taverns of Wood Mountain are the places where Suknaski remembers, or hears for the first time about, dark moments in the history of the town. At Hoy's place, the poet learns about the elevator agent who shot himself after imagining that his wife had taken a lover (*WMP* 29). Drinking beer with friends in Assiniboia's Franklin Pub, he recalls Leila Hordenchuk's fatal fall from a runaway horse (*WMP* 36). And, sitting at the West Central, he hears the story of Bill Brown, a regular at the bar who froze to death during a blizzard, drunk outside his own front door (*WMP* 91). As Suknaski illustrates in his poems, many residents of Wood Mountain have experienced extreme tragedy and hardship. Philip Well, a man who homesteaded near Suknaski's father, shot himself with his "rusty .22" (*WMP* 39). Johnny Nicholson, a local farmer, died of a heart attack in his son's arms while the two were fixing fence (*WMP* 95). Summer-fallowing one afternoon, Jim Lovenzanna was crushed under a tractor (*WMP* 32). Insofar as Wood Mountain is layered with history, it is likewise layered with sadness. The starving Nez Percés, driven from Montana to Saskatchewan with little more than the rags on their backs, are a "walking graveyard" (*WMP* 57)— their way of life has ended. But so, too, has the pioneer way of life ended for the immigrant settlers who displaced the First Nations people from their land. Aging immigrants such as Soren Caswell, Eli Lycenko, and Louis Leveille have nowhere to go save for the local pub, where they meet with other retired farmers. The last remaining residents of the ghost town, these men, not unlike Old Man Lepa in *A Letter to My Son*, live within their stories of the past.[8]

Insofar as Suknaski seeks, then, to reconstruct an authentic portrait of the community in which he grew up, recording both the positive and the negative aspects of its past, he takes on the role of historian. He too writes his versions of history in the "english" languages that he heard spoken in and around his hometown. Many of Suknaski's poems draw upon the vernacular dialects spoken by the oldtimers he meets on his visits home—like the unnamed old man in "Shugmanitou II" who, in giving advice to Suknaski about killing coyotes, says, "i tellya *boy* / them skidoo's kind / compared to that strychnine / they useta use" (*ghosts* 28, original emphasis). Numerous characters who appear in *Wood Mountain Poems*, *the ghosts call you poor*, and *In the Name of Narid* speak in heavily-accented, broken, and/or pidgin English, and Suknaski transcribes these characters' speech phonetically, implicitly foregrounding the limitations of standard spellings in reconstructing the hybrid "english" languages spoken in Wood Mountain and in other, nearby prairie communities. In "Jimmy Hoy's Place," for instance, Suknaski recalls Hoy's reaction to an obnoxious drunk who is making trouble in the café: "*gee clyz / all time slem ting hoy would say /...all time takkie to much / makkie trouble sunna bitch / wadda hell madder wid you?*" (*WMP* 28, original emphasis). And, in "Suknatskyj Taking a Greyhound North," the poet remembers his *baba* talking about a conflict between family members. She says, "*vhat ees to say now? / dhat sohn een law / on heez brrahderr / dido vahz alvays call dhem / tasyhany! geepsiez!*" (*Narid* 58, original emphasis). Some of the phonetically transcribed words in Suknaski's poems must be orally reproduced if the reader is to understand the story being told. But even reading some poems aloud is not enough to make sense of the language because he occasionally incorporates untranslated words from languages other than English, Ukrainian and Dakota especially. Readers are drawn into a world where multiple languages are spoken and where words are not always easily understood.

Without a doubt, the business of writing, or rewriting, history is an important feature of Suknaski's poems, as is his authentic rendering of language. By focusing, however, on the ways in which he gives the "otherwise forgotten" people of Wood Mountain a voice (Spak 4), and by emphasizing his "deliberately unobtrusive" poetic method (Scobie 4), readers run the risk of overlooking the complex—and in many ways pioneering—commentary on ethnic and national identity that is embedded in Suknaski's work. In choosing to see his poetry simply as renderings of history, and the poet himself as a poet-historian, we miss the extent to which Suknaski self-consciously reflects on the role that his imagination plays in continuously interpreting and reinterpreting history. The enterprise of recording history involves, or at the very least suggests, fixedness. In their attempts to objectively document the past, historians set down fixed, linear perspectives on it. Even writers like Haas and Ryga who challenge official versions of history nonetheless make it their goal to mirror reality in their writing. Suknaski's poetry, by contrast, is less about writing true narratives of history than it is about examining the process of writing itself and exploring the ways in which the creative process can be used to be transform reality, past and present. Scholars who have studied Suknaski in the context of experimental prairie writing of the 1960s and 1970s are interested in precisely this—his privileging of process over product in poems that eschew beginnings and endings, present history as spatial rather than temporal, and refuse "fixed" interpretations. To date, however, scholars have not considered the ways in which Suknaski's ruminations on the process of writing reveal his attitudes toward negotiating identity.

And yet poems drawn from *Wood Mountain Poems, the ghosts call you poor*, and *In the Name of Narid* clearly illustrate that, as he explores the complex relation between the past and the present of the prairie space in which he was raised, Suknaski repeatedly confronts questions of identity—who he is, where he belongs, how his writing informs his sense of self and community. As these collections of poetry document his perpetual return, both literally and figuratively, to Wood Mountain, they simultaneously narrate his coming of age in the world outside of his hometown. *Wood Mountain Poems* reflects his interest in recording the past authentically: he is, in this collection, predominantly the poet trying out his role as historian. What he discovers, however, is that, in the process of transcribing history, he cannot help but alter it because the process of writing is necessarily selective and subjective. Increasingly conscious of the fact that the process of writing history is less about replicating than reinventing the past, Suknaski takes on a new role in *the ghosts call you poor*—that of the poet-shaman, deliberately searching for ties to First Nations history in a self-conscious attempt to rewrite his own. By borrowing aspects of Native culture, he seeks to claim indigeneity—consolidate, that is, his sense of belonging to the prairies. Ironically, however, even as Suknaski discovers that the past and his relation to it is constructed—which enables him to recreate himself as a kind of "new Indian"[9]—he must also acknowledge that he cannot fully and accurately translate First Nations culture into English and onto the page. As an outsider vis-à-vis Native communities, he is unable to bridge the gap between their culture and his representation of it. *In the Name of Narid* narrates another step in his development as a writer, as Suknaski's turns away from his fascination with aboriginal people and returns to his Ukrainian roots. In this collection, he finally comes to terms with the fact that translation—both the translation of non-English words into English, and the translation of reality into language—is never exact. At the same time, he learns that while language can act as a barrier between people—between cultures, between the past and the present—it can also be used, creatively, to forge new connections. What Suknaski becomes, ultimately, is not the poet as historian or the poet as shaman but the poet simply as poet. And arriving at this understanding of himself means that, paradoxically, he has not arrived at all. The poet as poet recognizes that negotiating identity is an ongoing process inextricably connected to the continuous mobilization of the imagination in and through the process of writing.

In many ways typical of the poems in *Wood Mountain Poems*, "In Memory of Alfred A. Lecaine" (*WMP* 34-35) pays tribute to an oldtimer of Suknaski's hometown who has passed away while commemorating a way of life—the pioneers' way of life—that has also come to pass.

By remembering Lecaine, who both belongs to and comes to stand in for Suknaski's bygone childhood in Wood Mountain, the poet at once rediscovers and reconnects with his past. With his old friend Lee Soparlo and two of Lee's sons, Suknaski travels to Lecaine's grave, at once returning to the prairie landscape in which he was raised, re-establishing his relationship with the Soparlos, and revisiting the history of Wood Mountain. The poet's description of his trip to "the lecaine cemetery" is marked by the mingling of the past and the present, the voices of the people who live, or lived, in the prairies, and the sounds of the prairies themselves. As he listens to Lee talk about Lecaine's funeral—"*there were cars all over the hills and in the coulees / must have been over 200 people at least*" (34, original emphasis)—Suknaski takes note of the "poplars and willows" (34), and the gopher that "whistles" in the distance (35). As he gazes on the "sioux indian cemetery visible on the next hill," he hears the weather report on the radio. He waves at Chief Billy Goodtrack stacking hay bales with his sons and recalls a hockey game, years ago, in which Billy scored the winning goal against Lecaine's team—and after which Lecaine joked, "*if those indians don't take it a bit easier / I'll pull out my telescopic tomahawk / then we'll show em*" (35, original emphasis). In fact, as the poem unfolds, it becomes less a specific meditation on Lecaine—for Suknaski says surprisingly little about Lecaine—than a more general exploration of the world of Wood Mountain. He draws upon Lee's storytelling voice, the radio voice of the weather reporter, and Lecaine's teasing voice in order to paint a seemingly realistic portrait of his community.

But "In Memory of Alfred A. Lecaine" is by no means a sort of "found" poem, unshaped or even minimally shaped by the poet. Suknaski's voice is prominent throughout the poem, and it is a voice that asserts, more indirectly than directly, its ability to bridge the gap between reality and representations of reality—indeed, the central theme of the poem is the relation between the two. In the telling first two stanzas of the poem, Suknaski reveals that Fred Lecaine was a painter. Two of Lecaine's faded paintings of the prairies hang on one of the outside walls of Charlie Blouin's general store. Before leaving Wood Mountain, Suknaski decides to retrace Lecaine's brushstrokes and, in so doing, bring to life again Lecaine's depictions of the area around Wood Mountain. The parallel between Lecaine's paintings and Suknaski's poetry is subtle, yet unmistakable: one man seeks to capture the spirit of the land on canvas, the other, on the page. In a sense, Suknaski becomes Lecaine as he retouches the original artist's work. He "sign[s] *fred lecaine* over his faded signature in a corner" (34, original emphasis). Determined to preserve Lecaine's paintings, moreover, he applies "a clear varnish to protect everything" (34). The task of the artist/poet, he suggests, is to preserve and protect the past from the forces of social change. Suknaski's confidence in the artist's and the poet's ability to replicate the past is reflected in his descriptions of Lecaine's work—descriptions that draw no distinctions between Lecaine's paintings, the landscape that Lecaine painted, and the images that surround Suknaski as he examines Lecaine's work. In the first four lines of the poem, Suknaski makes clear the fact that he is observing the land around his home, both unchanged and at rest: "wood mountain and indian summer /," he writes, "still here / where my childhood ghosts move in the tall grass / taking over the half-abandoned village" (34). But as the poet shifts from his description of the land to his description of Lecaine's paintings, the line between reality and the artist's depiction of reality is blurred.

> i repaint two of fred's faded paintings:
> a pair of brown horses rearing against high green hills
> in the reserve
> in the distance beneath the horses
> cattle peacefully gaze in coulee (34)

Is Suknaski talking about Lecaine's painting here? Or is he observing his immediate surroundings as he retouches Lecaine's paintings?

What Suknaski seems to suggest, in the first stanzas of the poem—and what he attempts to underscore in the remaining stanzas—is that the "still here" prairie landscape can be, and indeed must be, recorded for posterity. As caretakers of the past, the artist and the poet become partners in recording and preserving history. Lecaine's paintings, though faded, and the pioneers' way of life, though fading, can be recuperated by the poet who reanimates both through language. Yet, "In Memory of Alfred A. Lecaine" hints, in a single phrase, at the constructedness of the artist's and poet's representations of the prairies and prairie history. After Suknaski finishes his work on Lecaine's paintings, he nails the paintings back up "on the false front of charlie blouin's old store" (34). Is it not possible that the paintings themselves are also a kind of "false front"—not because they necessarily idealize, or, conversely, demonize, Wood Mountain but because they are representations of reality, rather than reality itself? In writing about his repainting of Lecaine's paintings of the prairies, Suknaski is thrice removed from the actual landscape. How "authentic," then, is the poet's depiction of his world?

In subsequent poems, Suknaski—still focused on documenting the history of the prairies, and increasingly interested in staking his claim to the prairies—explores the notion that, because his world is invented (or reinvented) in language, he can use language to define (or redefine) his relation to the past and to the place in which he was raised. A number of his poems, in both *Wood Mountain Poems* and *the ghosts call you poor*, narrate the process through which Suknaski attempts to claim First Nations language, history, and mythology as his own, and in so doing proclaim his indigenous relation to the land.[10] In part, Suknaski's fascination with First Nations language and culture is an extension of his interest in documenting the history of Wood Mountain, specifically, and the prairies, more generally. He is drawn to the Sioux people, their culture, and their language in particular because their history intersects with the history of Wood Mountain.[11] The history of Sitting Bull and his tribe is a recurrent concern for Suknaski in such poems as "The Teton Sioux and 1879 Prairie Fire" (*WMP* 62-63), "The Sun Dance at Wood Mountain" (*WMP* 64-65), "Poem to Sitting Bull and his Son Crowfoot" (*WMP* 66-67), and "The Bitter Word" (69-70).[12] Acutely aware of the ways in which the Sioux were displaced from their land and forced to give up their traditional way of life, Suknaski seeks to "right" history by writing frankly about their mistreatment by both Americans and Canadians. In "Poem to Sitting Bull and His Son Crowfoot," Suknaski alludes to the "lying faces of men who betrayed [Sitting Bull] / giving him an ultimatum: / *starve or surrender to the enemy*" (*WMP* 67, original emphasis), and in the concluding stanza of "The Bitter Word," the poet imagines that Sitting Bull, unable to return to the U.S. but unwelcome in Canada, "must have sensed the hunger to follow / which was exactly what the authorities hopes for / on both sides of the border" (*WMP* 70). To some extent, though, Sitting Bull and his tribe come to stand in for all First Nations people in Suknaski's poems. In recording the specific history of this group, Suknaski draws attention to the general plight of all aboriginal groups in Canada. Importantly, too, he seeks not only to document the history of First Nations people but also to recuperate some aspects of their lost way of life by using their language, at least in part, to narrate their histories and by focusing on some of their cultural and spiritual practices. Hence, in poems such as "Neehhreson" (*WMP* 74) and "Soongeedawn" (*WMP* 75), he implicitly reveals the close connection between First Nations culture and the natural world; and in "The Sun Dance at Wood Mountain" (*WMP* 64–65) and "The First People" (*ghosts* 20–25), he writes explicitly about important Sioux customs and rituals. As he explores First Nations history and mythology, Suknaski implicitly situates himself as more than a sympathetic outsider—he presents himself as someone who understands the Sioux people intimately enough to be a member of their community.

By claiming Sioux culture and language as his own, Suknaski makes a transition from the poet as historian to the poet as shaman, a transition illustrated emphatically by "The First People" (*ghosts* 20–25). Like "In Memory of Alfred A. Lecaine," "The First People" is focused on an individual from Suknaski's past: the "you" to whom the poet speaks throughout the poem is Nelson Small Legs Jr., a First Nations political activist from Wood Mountain who committed suicide at the age of twenty-three.[13] Just as Suknaski sees Lecaine as both belonging to and representative of the pioneer way of life, so too does he see Small Legs as at once a participant in and a symbol of First Nations history. Small Legs's tragic death mirrors the dying culture of his people, but by remembering Small Legs, Suknaski seeks to resurrect the Native man and, by extension, his culture. "Resurrect" might seem too strong a word, except that Suknaski incorporates Small Legs into his nascent prairie mythology, a fusion of Biblical and First Nations mythologies.

Divided into six sections, "The First People" begins by rewriting the Biblical Book of Genesis: the world, in the opening lines of the poem, is created not by the Christian God but by "unktehi," the "feminine creator" of Sioux mythology (20). In fact, in the first part of the poem ("*genesis*"), Suknaski provides a long list of the Sioux gods or spirits who help "unktehi" bring the world into being: she is helped by tunkan the "stone god", takuskanska the "moving spirit", wakinyan the "thunder spirit" and wakan tanka or manitou the "great spirit" (20). As Suknaski explains in the second part of the poem ("*the first people*"), "the first people of the plains were humble / knew they were not worthy enough / to speak directly to manitou / and therefore appealed in prayer or song / to intermediators" (21). The third part of the poem ("*prayer*") then serves as a guide for re-enacting the Sioux practice of speaking to manitou through animal "intermediators" such as shoonkawaka, the "holy wild horse," good sister ookjekeehaw, the "magpie," and uncle khaahxree, the "crow" (21). "[P]ray to shugmanitou [coyote] for endurance," Suknaski writes, in the imperative: "pray for courage"; "pray with care" (21). In the fourth part of the poem ("*failure*"), Suknaski turns his attention to Small Legs's death, after which the young man returns to his ancestors—"the broken hoop" is "made *one* again" as Small Legs joins his people on "the other side," "more real and lasting" than the world he has left (23, original emphasis). Small Legs has not failed his people by giving up the will to live. Rather, he has been failed by "'the white man' betrayer," "'the green frog skin world' of money lenders," and the "'fattakers' bloated on the blood / of the first people" (23–24). Small Legs becomes, in the fifth and sixth parts of the poem ("*ascent*" and "*descent*"), a Christ-figure who has given his life for his people: he has become an "intermediating" spirit, promising in a suicide note to "always help...from the other side" (23), but never leaving the prairie space to which he belonged. Though he has passed into the spirit world, he is ever-present among the living.

Neither unique nor unproblematic, Suknaski's references to aboriginal culture squarely place him in a long tradition of Canadian writers who have used this culture as "literary material" (Fee 15).[14] As Margery Fee argues in "Romantic Nationalism and the Image of Native People in Contemporary English-Canadian Literature" (1987), writers who thematize aboriginal culture—and she names Suknaski in her long list of examples[15] —do so to confess their complicity in the mistreatment of aboriginal peoples, but they simultaneously, if unintentionally, perpetuate the marginalization of Native groups through a form of cultural theft that is "analogous to this historical territorial take-over" (Fee 15–17). Indeed, while Suknaski was never explicitly singled-out in the appropriation debates that raged in Canadian literary circles during the 1990s,[16] he might well have been, given the extent to which he—to use Lenore Keeshig-Tobias's phrase—"steals" Native stories. As politically incorrect as his use of Native culture may seem now, however, Suknaski's identification with aboriginal people offers telling commentary on his predicament as a second-generation Ukrainian Canadian, and the "poet as shaman" phase of his writing life becomes a crucial turning point in his understanding of himself and his place in the world—a point at which he is forced to confront his ambivalent position vis-à-vis multiple communities in Canada. Being the son of ethnic immigrants means that he is marginalized within Anglo-Canadian society. Though born and raised in—with strong emotional attachments to—the prairies, he is not, as aboriginal peoples are, indigenous to the land. And despite his genealogy, as an assimilated second-generation Ukrainian Canadian, he is simultaneously alienated from his ethnic group.

In his "in between" status, Suknaski is not unique. His position closely resembles that of the "settler subject" theorized by postcolonial scholars Stephen Slemon and Alan Lawson, who argue that newcomers to a settler colony like Canada are "suspended between 'mother' and 'other,' simultaneously colonized and colonizing" (Lawson 25). Although Slemon and Lawson have in mind British colonial subjects, their thinking can be generalized to describe the situation of more recent immigrants from other ethnic groups, as well as their descendants. The point is that, by settling in the colony, immigrants participate in the colonial enterprise, serving the British imperial "mother." At the same time, even as they permanently move to the colony, they become separate from the imperium, seeking instead the indigenous status of the First Nations or aboriginal "other." Mimicry, Lawson writes, is "a necessary and unavoidable part of the repertoire of the settler." The settler subject "represents, but also mimics, the authentic imperial culture from which he—and more problematically, she—is separated" while he simultaneously "mimics, appropriates, and desires the authority of the Indigene" (26). Because the settler is "caught between two First Worlds, two origins of authority and authenticity"—because he "has colonized and has been colonized"—he "must speak of and against both [his] own oppressiveness and [his] own oppression" (28-29). As such, the settler subject "emerges from the material and textual enactments and enunciations of imperial power as a central site of investigation of the actual operations of colonial power" (32). The situation for a writer like Suknaski is even more complex because he is suspended between more than two "origins of authority and authenticity." Like many ethnic immigrants, he is suspended between mainstream, Anglo-Canadian society, aboriginal groups, and his Ukrainian people. Suknaski's attempt to overcome his ambivalence, moreover, by aligning himself with Native culture is not a solitary move. As George Melnyk argued in "The Indian as Ethnic" (1981)—and as Robert Klymasz has more recently suggested in a talk delivered at the 2004 conference of the Ukrainian Academy of Arts and Sciences in Winnipeg—a close relationship exists between ethnic groups and aboriginal peoples, born of their shared experience of marginalization.[17]

The fundamental problem for Suknaski—and it is a problem that he does not overcome until he shirks the role of poet as shaman in *In the Name of Narid*—hinges on the fact that, despite his best intentions, he cannot become the "Indian" he aspires to be. By taking on the role of poet as shaman, Suknaski clearly shifts writerly gears—from objectively documenting history to subjectively rewriting his own past as well as his future. History, he seems to learn, is a product of language. So when, for example, in a poem like "The First People," he rewrites foundational Christian myths by incorporating First Nations figures and stories in these myths, he is conscious of the ways in which language can be used to reconstruct the past because history is always mediated by words, by the writer's imagination. Yet, in "The First People," as well as in other poems about First Nations culture, Suknaski seems *un*conscious of the possible gaps between this culture and the language in which he writes about it. Rife with English translations of Sioux words and phrases, his poems implicitly suggest that First Nations culture and mythology can be fully experienced and known in English—that nothing is lost or gained in the process of translation.[18] In such poems as "The First People," Suknaski attempts to construct a new, hybrid prairie mythology, but he leaves unexplored—at the level of language—its newness and hybridity. He never actually confronts or reflects upon the nature of its constructedness. Just as animals serve, in his representation of First Nations mythology, as "intermediators" between the human and the spirit world, so too does language mediate between First Nations culture and Suknaski's understanding of it. But while Suknaski seems to understand the extent to which history is mediated by language, he does not reflect on the ways in which his words affect the meaning of the culture that he writes about it. "[P]ray as the young sioux boy prayed to become a man," he writes,

through the four day fast
ending with his first holy vision
"*tunkashila*

       tunkashila

            tunkashila

grandfather...grandfather spirit...help me!" (22 original emphasis) The poet as shaman is thrice removed from the prayer he describes: he hears the Sioux boy's words, transcribes them in Sioux, and then translates them into English. Does the prayer change with each remove? Does it mean something different to the Sioux boy and to the poet (not to mention his readers)? Are "*tunkashila*" and "*grandfather spirit*" really one and the same thing, as Suknaski implicitly asserts, or does the meaning of "*tunkashila*" change when the word is lifted out of its original cultural context?

Not surprisingly, coming to terms with his ambivalent identity—his simultaneous sense of belonging to and alienation from Anglo-Canadian, aboriginal, and Ukrainian communities—requires Suknaski to confront his familial and ethnic roots. He does this, finally, in the poems collected in *In the Name of Narid*, in which he does not focus on his multi-ethnic hometown or on his fascination with First Nations groups but specifically on his Ukrainian heritage. "Paska I Khmary" (*Narid* 60), emblematic of the poems in this book, narrates Suknaski's return to his ethnic roots. The poet, who, geographically, has travelled back to the prairies, and who, temporally, has revisited the history of the prairies, now explores his most intimate, familial connection to both. More importantly, he explores the ways in which he can (re)connect with family members through language.

In comparison to some of Suknaski's earlier poems in *Wood Mountain Poems* and *the ghosts call you poor*, "Paska I Khmary" represents a crucial shift in his attitude toward language. In "In Memory of Alfred A. Lecaine," for example, Suknaski is confident in his ability to document history in and through his poetry. Similarly, in "The First People," he assumes that he can translate First Nations culture into English and onto the page—that translation is not only possible but also a possible strategy for forging links between different ethnic communities. In "Paska I Khmary," by contrast, Suknaski confronts the notion that language can drive a wedge between people—specifically between first-generation Ukrainian Canadians who speak Ukrainian, and their second-generation children who speak English. Focused on the poet's relationship with his mother, this poem reflects on the ways in which the two are separated by the different languages that they speak. As the poem reveals, coming home requires that Suknaski come to terms with his inability to speak the language of his ancestors. Translation, he learns now, as he did not learn in his poems about Sioux culture, is uneasy, and sometimes impossible, because the meanings of words—and, by extension, the complex nuances of culture—are often lost in the movement between languages. What Suknaski discovers over the course of the poem is that language—the very barrier that stands between him and his mother—can also be used in creative ways to bring them together. Translation, he comes to realize, is a creative process. The poet as poet not only acknowledges his active role in (re)creating the world as he moves within and between languages, he is also empowered by his ability to re-establish personal relationships through language.

Not unlike "In Memory of Alfred A. Lecaine," "Paska I Khmary" centres on a painting of the prairies—a linocut by Suknaski's friend George Melnyk.[19] On one level, the poem is about Suknaski's and his mother's impressions of the print: the poem describes the two drinking black current wine together as they talk about Melnyk's picture. On another level, however, "Paska I Khmary" is about the ways in which mother and son—native Ukrainian- and English-speakers, respectively—manipulate languages in order to speak to one another. In the opening lines of the poem, Suknaski's mother "gazes at the print / on his shack's wall" and "asks what it is" (60). The title of Melnyk's work, the poet explains, is "*the land also rises*," but "too long from home / and unable to speak ukrainian," Suknaski "cannot translate his friend's title" (60). Unable to come up with a literal translation, Suknaski is nonetheless determined to bridge the linguistic distance between him and his mother, and so he comes up with a translation that enables his mother to relate to the print: "*paska i khmary*," he says, "*easter bread and clouds*" (60 original emphasis). Less abstract than Melnyk's original title, and more rooted in the concrete world with which his mother is familiar, Suknaski's translation enables his mother to relate to the picture. For the remainder of the poem, mother and son study Melnyk's depiction of the prairies, giving voice—in Ukrainian and English—to their impressions. Suknaski's mother asks, "'vhat be dhat underr clouds?'" (60). With his limited knowledge of Ukrainian, Suknaski answers, translating his Ukrainian words into English.

> '*polia*
>
> ... fields'
>
> he murmurs
>
> '*navit polia*
> *v nebi*
> even fields in
> heaven' (60, original emphasis)

Broken by pauses and hesitations, Suknaski's description of Melnyk's print reveals his struggle to find words in which to speak to his mother. After Suknaski says "*navit polia*," he pauses, trying to remember "*nebi*," the Ukrainian word for heaven. Unsure of his choice of Ukrainian words, and his ability to accurately translate these words, he speaks softly. As Suknaski's mother offers an alternate interpretation of Melnyk's work, she, too, struggles to find words that her son will understand, pausing and hesitating as she speaks: "orr myte be rrayz ov sohn," she says, "ahbofh cloudz brroken / by geese koming norrt" (60). Like the sky in Melnyk's painting that Suknaski's mother describes as "brroken / by geese," Suknaski's language and his mother's language are "broken." He speaks imperfect Ukrainian; she speaks imperfect English. What matters, however, is not the imperfection of Suknaski's Ukrainian or his mother's English; what matters is that they are able to experience a rare moment of closeness and intimacy by meeting each other halfway. Despite the different languages that they speak, they make themselves understood.

Ultimately, Suknaski's transformation over the course of *Wood Mountain Poems*, *the ghosts call you poor*, and *In the Name of Narid*—from poet as historian to poet as shaman to poet as, simply, *poet*—foregrounds the important position he occupies in the Ukrainian Canadian literary tradition. Like such writers as Maara Haas and George Ryga, and, before them, Vera Lysenko—indeed, like second-generation Canadians—Suknaski's struggle to come to terms with his ethnic and national identity is defined by a profound sense of ambivalence toward his ethnic inheritance and the society in which he lives. That his efforts to come to terms with this ambivalence by recording the history of Wood Mountain, specifically, and the prairies, more generally, are unsuccessful is not surprising. Nor is it surprising that his attempts at adopting the culture of Native communities fail to provide him with a resolution to his conflicted feelings about who he is and where he belongs. Taking on the role of historian requires the poet to document history without engaging with it—something that Suknaski finds he cannot do. Performing the role of shaman similarly means that he must overlook the ways in which he is implicated in the vexed historical relations between aboriginal and non-aboriginal people in Canada. Here again, Suknaski discovers that glossing over this history—by assuming that he can translate First Nations culture onto the page—is not possible. Whether playing at historian or playing at shaman, the poet implicitly seeks a role that will free him from the "in between" position he occupies. Such writers are Maara Haas and George Ryga experience similar ambivalences and they draw attention to them in their writing. But even as *The Street Where I Live* and *A Letter To My Son* describe the predicament of ethnic immigrants and their descendants, neither text proposes a solution to the problems their characters—or they themselves—encounter. What distinguishes Suknaski from both writers is not that he offers clear-cut, "easy" answers to questions about identity, history, and belonging. What he offers, instead, is self-conscious reflection on the fact that these questions must be confronted and engaged with in and through the process of writing. The poet as poet arrives at the paradoxical conclusion that the search for identity is necessarily ongoing and open-ended, never fixed or absolute, subject to constant re-invention. While Haas and Ryga use language to tell stories, Suknaski uses stories to narrate his ongoing engagement with language. Embracing his role as a poet, he discovers that he is at home less in the literal landscape of the prairies—the backdrop against which history, mythology, and community take shape—than in the figurative landscape of language itself.

In one of his poems, collected in *In the Name of Narid*, Suknaski reflects on one of his many departures from Wood Mountain. "Leaving home again," he writes,

>   suknatskyj knows
>   it will not be easy
>   in the darkening avenue
>   of memory
>   is fully aware
>   there'll be no
>   absolute forgetting
>   ("Leaving Home Again," *Narid* 61)

But Suknaski is not really leaving Wood Mountain. Just as his words move across the page and back again in this poem, so too does he continually depart from, and return to, his home in his other poems. "Suknatskyj knows" that there will be no absolute remembering, but he also knows that there will be "no / absolute forgetting"—what there will be, in his writing, is a constant exploration of the space between. At once located in, and defined by, that "space between," the poet finds room for the words that make possible remembering *and* re-inventing.

PART THREE

RE-IMAGINED COMMUNITIES

Transcultural Ukrainian Canadian Literature

1985 to 2005

EIGHT

From Multiculturalism to Transculturalism
Shifting Paradigms in the Search for Identity

IN HER 1991 ESSAY "From Mosaic to Kaleidoscope," published in *Books in Canada*, Janice Kulyk Keefer offered a new perspective on trends in Canadian ethnic minority writing that was—for its time, and especially in relation to Ukrainian Canadian literature—groundbreaking. According to her, discourses of multiculturalism were no longer sufficient for defining the experiences of ethnic minorities in Canada—multiculturalism, in her opinion, placed too little emphasis on the countries and cultures from which ethnic minority groups originated. Transculturalism, she argued, more accurately reflected the day-to-day realities of individuals from ethnic minority backgrounds, many of whom harbour strong material and/or emotional attachments to their ancestral homelands.

Prefaced by an autobiographical overview of her experiences as a second-generation Ukrainian Canadian and a writer, Kulyk Keefer's essay—subtitled "Out of the multicultural past comes a vision of a transcultural future"—begins by tracing the historical changes in dominant attitudes toward ethnic minorities and their literatures in Canada. "In the Canada in which I grew up," she writes, "that is, the Toronto of the 1950s and 60s, there was no such thing as multiculturalism." Belonging to a "non-British ethnocultural group" was "definitely not an asset in the school system of the day.... There was no question in my school of our studying or even being apprised of the value of languages, literatures, and cultures other than English" (13). As a university student in the 1970s, Kulyk Keefer explains, "there was a sudden flurry of interest around the term 'ethnic'"—a flurry that she attributes, retrospectively, to "the Trudeau government's creation of something called 'multiculturalism' in 1971" (14). The popularity of "doing the ethnic thing" in the 1970s, however, had "no impact on [her] sense of what [she] could do as a writer" (14). In her words, "I grew up convinced that only people with names like Smith or MacPherson could be published and read in this country—a belief that led me to think and write, for the most part, in what I understood to be the manner of a Smith or a MacPherson" (14). Kulyk Keefer admits that "for all my attempts to put my linguistic, cultural, and I suppose one might say racial 'otherness' behind me, I continued to be haunted by the stories my family told of a country that didn't exist anymore." But, she says, "it is only now, some 20 years after I first started to write with any seriousness, that I feel it's possible for me to address that other 'where' in a Canadian writer's life...that other country by which immigrants' children are so often obsessed" (14).

Why was Kulyk Keefer unable to address her feelings toward Ukraine until the early 1990s? What was it about this historical moment that enabled her to confront her sense of allegiance to the "other 'where'" in her life? The uneasy feelings that she expressed in 1991 about both her ethnic heritage and discourses of multiculturalism were not unique: in their writing, published long before "From Mosaic to Kaleidoscope," such writers as Myrna Kostash, Helen Potrebenko, Maara Haas, George Ryga, and Andrew Suknaski had articulated very similar ambivalences about their ethnicity, and about Canadian society's attitudes toward ethnic minorities. Unlike previous Ukrainian Canadian writers, however, who identified problems associated with multiculturalism but who stopped short of offering solutions, Kulyk Keefer went one step further by presenting an alternative. Adopting a transcultural vision of Canadian society would, she felt, better describe the unique predicament faced by members of ethnic minority groups in Canada—especially those individuals caught between ethnic and national identity, belonging to both and neither—and it would ultimately help them come to terms with their divided sense of self.

For Kulyk Keefer, the Roman deity Janus—god of "new beginnings" who "presides over doors, thresholds, and gateways, his two heads looking out in opposite directions"—symbolically captures the meaning of transculturalism. Janus, she says, is a "particularly appropriate *daimon*" for writers who "find themselves compelled to look back to their ancestral country of origin, and also ahead to the possibilities of their actual homeland, Canada" (15). In "From Mosaic to Kaleidoscope," as she outlines her definition of transculturalism, Kulyk Keefer quotes Ven Begamudré's notion that while multiculturalism "seeks to preserve and succeeds in paralysing cultures," transculturalism "brings out the dynamic potential of cultural diversity, the possibility of exchange and change among and within ethnocultural groups" (14). What Canada needs, she says, is a "change in Canadian iconography" from the mosaic, or multicultural, model of nationhood to a kaleidoscope, or transcultural, model. She argues that, as a metaphor for transculturalism, the kaleidoscope "suggests ongoing process rather than fixed and finished product" (16); it reflects the continual, fluid exchange of culture both within and between different nations. Whereas the mosaic promotes cultural "separation and rigidity," the kaleidoscope emphasizes "interconnection, mobility, and transformation" (16).

Transculturalism was not a new term in the early 1990s: Cuban sociological Fernando Ortiz introduced it in his studies of Afro-Cuban culture during the 1940s, and Uraguayan literary critic Angel Rama first drew the word into literary studies in the 1970s (Ashcroft, Griffiths, and Tiffin, *Key Concepts* 233). And while over the past fifteen-odd years a number of scholars across disciplines have nuanced and complicated the relevance of transculturalism to various debates within cultural studies—debates, for example, about the politics of migration, immigration, globalization, hybridity, and metissage—Kulyk Keefer's work has never risen to the forefront of scholarship related to these phenomena. Mary Louise Pratt's *Imperial Eyes: Travel Writing and Transculturation* (1992) is widely regarded as a core text in understanding how cultural practices evolve in "contact zones" where "disparate cultures meet, clash and grapple with each other, often in highly assymetircal relations of dominance and subordination" (Pratt 4). Homi Bhabha, Robert Young, and Aijaz Ahmad have emerged as equally important figures in scholarly dialogue about whether transculturalism suggests mutuality or oppositionality in the exchange of culture that takes place in contact zones (Ashcroft, Griffiths, and Tiffin 119).[1] And such scholars as Smaro Kamboureli, Rey Chow, Ien Ang, Rajagopalan Radhakrishnan, Amy Kaminsky, and Pico Iyer are well known for their work on the ways in which diasporic writers from Latino, East Asian, South Asian, and African backgrounds negotiate their hybrid identities within and between local and global spaces.[2]

Kulyk Keefer, by contrast, has not figured prominently in international literary criticism or theory about transculturalism. The definition of transculturalism that she introduced in 1991 was relatively straightforward: it emphasizes cultural exchange between home country and host country without critically analyzing or theorizing the dynamics of that exchange. But in the context of ethnic minority literary studies in Canada, Kulyk Keefer's "From Mosaic to Kaleidoscope" was—and in some ways still is—exceptional. Whereas most work that has been done on transcultural or diasporic writing focuses on "racial" minority groups,[3] Kulyk Keefer placed her emphasis on the transcultural aspects of *ethnic* minority writing. And while most scholars who work on ethnicity and ethnic minority writing have tended to focus on the experiences of ethnic minority groups in *Canada*, Kulyk Keefer placed emphasis on the movement, real or imagined, of ethnic minority groups between their ancestral homelands and their adopted country. "From Mosaic to Kaleidoscope" is noteworthy, in other words, not because it "invented" transculturalism or ethnic minority literary criticism but because in this essay Kulyk Keefer synthesizes the two, suggesting for the first time that scholars focus their scholarly attention on the bi-focal, Janus-faced nature of ethnic minority writing.

Daphne Winland has bolstered the innovation of Kulyk Keefer's approach. In "'Our Home and Native Land'?: Canadian Ethnic Scholarship and the Challenge of Transnationalism" (1998), she argues that the dominant view of ethnic minorities assumes that "an immigrant simply uproots from her country of origin to settle in a new land" (557); as a result, "Canadian studies have, by and large, overlooked those factors that enmesh ethnic groups in global processes, and have focused instead mainly on the internal dynamics of ethnic communities and intergroup relations" (562). Referring to the work of such sociologists as Wsevolod Isajiw and Leo Driedger, Winland suggests that "[a]pproaches to the issue of ethnic identity are usually framed by pluralist frameworks that routinely stress the cultural vitality and contributions of immigrant/minority groups in a multicultural society" (563). Ethnic minority scholars often rely upon a definition of community that is static and homogeneous; their studies "concentrate largely on familiar themes of ethnic persistence/retention and incorporation" (563). And the underlying assumption of most ethnic minority scholars is that all ethnic immigrants eventually undergo assimilation in their new country. Immigrants' experiences are characterized by a shift "from culturally coherent and homogeneous settings in the country/region of origin, to the host country, where [they] either assimilate to the dominant way of life or selectively appropriate new patterns and symbols in efforts to accommodate to their next context" (563). According to Winland, "few ethnic researchers have investigated the powerful attachment of homeland ties for ethnic group identities in Canada" (562). Despite the "plethora of both historical and contemporary Canadian examples of sentimental, political, or material links between immigrant groups and homelands," she writes, "there has been little if any systematic effort to problematize this dimension of ethnic group experience" (564). In other words, by focusing on the experiences of ethnic minority groups in Canada, scholars have left unexplored the extent to which, the ways in which, and the reasons for which these groups remain connected, literally or figuratively, to their ancestral homelands.

Literary scholars have good reason for making Canada the locus of their work on ethnic minority literatures. Most ethnic minority writing, Kulyk Keefer argues, falls into three categories: "Getting There"—accounts of immigration; "Being Here"—literature of "acculturation and accommodation"; and "Turning Back"—narratives about return to the homeland. Because two of these categories privilege immigrants' and their descendants' host country over their country of origin, scholars have tended to focus more substantially on the ethnic minority experience in Canada ("From Mosaic to Kaleidoscope" 16). Careful to point out that "the enormous upheaval involved in changing cultures is not something that can be 'worked out' in one generation," Kulyk Keefer notes that the three dominant themes within ethnic minority literatures are "often conflated in literary texts" (16). Nonetheless, if critics have tended to under-emphasize the relation between ethnic minority groups and their ethnic homelands, they have done so at least in part because ethnic minority writers often foreground their characters' experiences "here" rather than "there."

Certainly the development of literature by Canadians of Ukrainian descent, from the beginning to the end of the twentieth century, attests to the extent to which Ukrainian Canadian writers have been preoccupied with their ethnic group's history in Canada. In what Winland calls the "increasingly globalized world" (557) of the late twentieth century—a world characterized by the "deterritorialization of the borders and boundaries of nations" (556)—many Ukrainian Canadian writers continue to focus their texts on the experiences of Ukrainian immigrants and their descendants in Canada. Much like Illia Kiriak's *Sons of the Soil* (1939-45) and Vera Lysenko's *Yellow Boots* (1954), a number of works published by Ukrainian Canadian writers after 1985 are historical narratives that sentimentalize or romanticize the bygone days of early immigration and settlement. Novelists Yuri Kupchenko (*The Horseman of Shandro Crossing*, 1989), Gloria Kupchenko Frolick (*The Chicken Man*, 1989; *Anna Veryna*, 1992), and Larry Warwaruk (*The Ukrainian Wedding*, 1998) all revisit the pioneer past with an underlying, but unmistakable, sense of nostalgia for what they see as a simpler time and place, a nobler way of life. Kupchenko Frolick's collection of short fiction, *The Green Tomato Years* (1985), and Ted Galay's play *Tsymbaly!* (1987) are similarly sentimental in their portrayals of first-wave immigrants' experiences in Canada.

In "'A Different Story' by Helen Potrebenko: The Prairie-Pioneer Myth Re-Visited" (1996), Sonia Mycak astutely reads these relatively recent Ukrainian Canadian texts as "part of an entire genre of Ukrainian-Canadian pioneer stories" (68). Central to the genre, she argues, is the "readily identifiable" prairie pioneer myth that, by the 1970s, had come to define the image of Ukrainian Canadians in popular culture (68). Mycak goes on to list no less than seven "significant and identifiable aspects" of the prairie pioneer myth which is built upon (1) the "undeniable hardship" that Ukrainian pioneers endured, and (2) the "toil, blood, and sweat" they invested in their homesteads. The Ukrainian farmer, specifically, is (3) "imbued with a certain nobility of character": he is "stoical, hard-working, honest, trustworthy, and morally upright, albeit at times mischievous and decidedly rough around the edges." And Ukrainian pioneers, more generally, are (4) "presented as being responsible not only for the future generations of their own off-spring, but for helping to build a strong and healthy country from which all Canadians now benefit." Central to the prairie pioneer myth is the depiction of Ukrainian immigrants as a "founding people of the Canadian nation."

Frequently, in writing about Ukrainian pioneers, writers rely on (5) "biographical material and alleged socio-historical truth" with the "conscious aim of documenting the history of a particular area or era in the history of Canada." They are encouraged to do so by (6) the "multicultural ethic" and their goal, in part, is to provide (7) "positive models with which today's Ukrainian-Canadians can identify" (68–69). To my list of literary texts that focus on the pioneer era of Ukrainian Canadian history, Mycak adds several titles: Susan Woywitka and Randy Mueller's play *Kyla's Christmas Concert*, for example, first performed in Edmonton in 1994; Danny Evanishen's short stories collected in *Vuiko Yurko* (1994); and Yar Slavutych's bilingual poetry collected in *The Conquerors of the Prairies* (1984). By identifying the ways in which the prairie pioneer myth circulates—not only in literary texts but also in Ukrainian Canadian "scholarship, media, official material, and cultural artifacts" (69)—Mycak draws attention to the ways in which a particular narrative of Ukrainian Canadian history has become dominant within Ukrainian Canadian communities.⁴ The myth is predicated on and simultaneously perpetuates a narrative of progress that constructs Ukrainian immigrants and their children as innately amenable to hard work; as willing to assimilate to Canadian culture while retaining some aspects of their ethnic identity; and as successful, ultimately, in ascending the social and economic hierarchies of the multicultural society they helped build.

In her reading, then, of Helen Potrebenko's "A Different Story" (from *Hey Waitress and Other Stories*, 1989), Mycak outlines the ways in which Potrebenko tries to rewrite this narrative of Ukrainian Canadian history. Like such writers as Maara Haas, George Ryga, and Andrew Suknaski, Potrebenko attempts to subvert the prairie pioneer myth by exploring the complex and uneasy aspects of Ukrainian Canadian history. While, Mycak argues, "A Different Story" incorporates many of the "significant and identifiable aspects" (68) of the prairie pioneer myth, the text "functions as a parody of the myth of the glorified pioneer" (71). According to Mycak, Potrebenko's satirical approach to narrating the experiences of Ukrainian Canadian pioneers undermines the "stereotypes" and the "syrupy nostalgia" of the prairie pioneer myth by foregrounding the darker sides of Ukrainian Canadian history (82). "A Different Story" criticizes the "capitalist exploitation of farmers, labourers, and immigrants alike" as well as the "subordinate position of Ukrainian women" within the patriarchal structures of Ukrainian Canadian communities (82). The problem with Potrebenko's story is that, even as the text exposes the harsh realities of Ukrainian pioneers' experiences, it simultaneously reaffirms the centrality of the pioneer era in the Ukrainian Canadian imaginary. And the problem with Mycak's reading of "A Different Story" is that, in heralding the text as a provocative re-telling of and successful challenge to the hackneyed prairie pioneer myth, Mycak fails to consider the possibility that Potrebenko's criticisms of the pioneer era are themselves hackneyed. By the late 1980s, and in the wake of such texts as Potrebenko's *No Streets of Gold* and Myrna Kostash's *All of Baba's Children* —not to mention Maara Haas's *The Street Where I Live*, George Ryga's *A Letter to My Son*, and Andrew Suknaski's poetry—Potrebenko's interest in exploring the negative aspects of Ukrainian Canadian history seems less provocative than predictable.

Beginning in the 1990s, in theme and form, the more innovative challenges to the prairie pioneer myth have come from those authors who, to use Kulyk Keefer's terminology, write about "Turning Back" to their ancestral homeland. In fact, although Kulyk Keefer made only passing reference to Ukrainian Canadian literature in "From Mosaic to Kaleidoscope"[5]—and although she explicitly called for literary *scholars* to emphasize the transcultural, rather than the multicultural, nature of ethnic minority writing in Canada—she also, albeit implicitly, argued as a Ukrainian Canadian *writer* for a shift in the Ukrainian Canadian literary tradition. Unsurprisingly, perhaps, in the years following the appearance of "From Mosaic to Kaleidoscope," Kulyk Keefer began to explore her own "Turning Back" experiences as the daughter of Ukrainian immigrants. In her novel *The Green Library* (1996) and in her family history *Honey and Ashes: A Story of Family* (1998), Kulyk Keefer narrates her belated interest in, and rediscovery of, her ethnic roots as she writes about her journeys to the "Old Place" from which her family immigrated. In several essays, moreover, and in her introduction to *Two Lands, New Visions: Stories From Canada and Ukraine* (1998), co-edited with Solomea Pavlychko, Kulyk Keefer continues to make the case for transcultural approaches to the writing and study of ethnic minority literature.[6] Kulyk Keefer, however, is neither the first nor the only Ukrainian Canadian writer to travel "back" to Ukraine—"back," that is, for the first time to the country she heard about from her parents while growing up in Canada. Myrna Kostash, in *Bloodlines: A Journey Into Eastern Europe* (1993) and *The Doomed Bridegroom: A Memoir* (1998), also returns to Ukraine in order to explore the meaning of her ethnic and national identity as a third-generation Ukrainian Canadian. In fact, *Bloodlines* and *The Doomed Bridegroom* narrate Kostash's long-term engagement with the politics and the people of not only Ukraine but also other countries in Eastern and Central Europe, including Czechoslovakia, Poland, Yugoslavia, and Greece.

Why, exactly, do Kulyk Keefer and Kostash travel to Ukraine—and, in Kostash's case, throughout Eastern and Central Europe? Their return to the ancestral homeland is not unlike Haas's, Ryga's, and Suknaski's return to their roots: all of these writers view history as a crucial component of ethnicity. But whereas such writers as Haas, Ryga, and Suknaski revisit their childhood experiences on the prairies, Kulyk Keefer and Kostash travel further back, temporally, and further away, geographically. Kulyk Keefer does so in part because the newly-opened borders of Eastern Europe made travel to this part of the world easier. Visiting Eastern Europe was not impossible before the fall of Soviet-style communism. Kostash, after all, made her first trip to Eastern Europe in 1982. Beginning in the late 1980s, however, dramatic changes began to take place throughout Eastern Europe, changes that would significantly alter day-to-day life within Eastern bloc countries and that would also ease the tense relations between these countries and the rest of the world.

In 1986, after Gorbachev, the newly-appointed leader of the USSR,[7] announced his policies of "glasnost" and "perestroika,"[8] state control over the economic, social, and political institutions of the USSR gradually decreased. The Gorbachev government began to allow elections to take place, and to introduce freedoms of press, speech, and assembly. Without a doubt, Gorbachev's initiatives promised democratic reform and increased economic prosperity, accompanied by unprecedented openness in social, political, and cultural spheres. And, at least from the perspective of individuals living outside of Eastern Europe, Gorbachev seems to have succeeded in initiating positive social change in this part of the world.[9] By the time he resigned from the leadership of the Soviet Union in 1991, Soviet-style communist rule had come to an end. In 1989, the Berlin Wall came down; the Warsaw Pact was dissolved in 1991; and by the mid-1990s, the Cold War was drawing to a close. Most importantly, perhaps, the Soviet Union itself had collapsed under the pressure of independence movements in virtually all of its member states. When, in 1991, eleven of these states joined together to form the Commonwealth of Independent States, they did so as sovereign nations.[10] For the first time in decades, the borders of Eastern Europe were open to economic trade and cultural exchange with the rest of the world, and people living within these borders were able to take an active role in determining the future of their nations.

The collapse of communism meant that countless political prisoners were freed and that some were able to take on leadership roles in their nations. Following the "Velvet Revolution" in 1989, for example, Vaclav Havel became president of Czechoslovakia, and Solidarity leader Lech Walesa was elected president of Poland in 1991. Artists, writers, and intellectuals were able to express their political and social views openly, without fear of recrimination and ordinary people were given a voice in democratic elections, as well as new opportunities for social and economic advancement. But the people of Eastern Europe paid, and continue to pay, a high price for the promise of economic, social, and political freedom. Economic hardship, social upheaval, and political unrest have characterized many Eastern European societies since the late 1980s as newly-independent nations scrambled to establish new systems of government and to reform existing economic infrastructures. Beginning in 1989, a series of violent street demonstrations and strikes took place in Czechoslovakia, Romania, Poland, Ukraine, and Lithuania. At times, conflict erupted between the Soviet army and pro-independence groups—this was the case in Lithuania, where, in 1991, Soviet troops killed fourteen people who were peacefully demonstrating against Soviet control of the country. Violent encounters also occurred between communist regimes and pro-democracy agitators. In 1989, for instance, the Romanian army staged an uprising against Nicolae Ceausescu, dictatorial leader of Romania for almost twenty-five years, which culminated with the trial and execution of Ceausescu and his wife Elena in December, 1989. At times, too, in the vacuum of power left by the retreat of Soviet troops and the collapse of communist governments, hostilities increased between groups vying for territory within or control over former communist states. In the Balkans, most notably, ethnic tensions between Serbians, Bosnians, Croatians, Albanians, Macedonians, and Slovenians escalated into a full-scale, decade-long war—a war in which NATO countries repeatedly intervened, sparking debate and controversy about the role of "peacekeepers" in the former Yugoslavia.[11]

For many Eastern Europeans—even those who have not experienced bloodshed—the beginning of a "new era" in Eastern European history has had little positive impact on day-to-day life. Devalued currencies, food shortages, and low wages persist in many former Soviet states, despite moves toward free trade and economic privatization. In these politically and economically unstable societies, widespread unemployment and high crime rates remain constant; a good deal of political power, moreover, rests in the hands of Mafia-style organizations that control strong black market economies. Certainly the circumstances surrounding the 2004–2005 elections in Ukraine—a period referred to as the "Orange Revolution"—suggest that the struggle for democracy in this part of the world is ongoing.[12]

Broadly speaking, the changes that have taken place in Eastern Europe since the 1980s raise a number of questions about the ways in which nation-states, and international relations between them, have been reconfigured. Does the collapse of the Soviet Union signal the decline, or the triumph, of the modern nation-state as the politically unifying force of the twentieth century? Does it reflect, or challenge, worldwide trends toward globalization, transnationalism, and transculturalism? One the one hand, the opening of the borders of Eastern Europe seems to privilege the global over the local—individuals' relation to the world takes precedence over their relation to the nation. At the same time, the increasing insularity of ethnic communities in Eastern Europe—witness, for example, the fracturing of Yugoslavia in the 1990s—suggests that nationhood and nationalism remain central to the ways in which people define their individual and group identity.

According to Masao Miyoshi, in "A Borderless World?: From Colonialism to Transnationalism and the Decline of the Nation-State" (1996), the radical changes that took place in Eastern Europe during the 1980s and 1990s—the effects of which are still being felt—signal the demise of the nation-state in an increasingly globalized world. But rather than embracing globalization as a positive phenomenon, he points out the fact that it too closely resembles the "historical metropolitan-colonial paradigm" (79), primarily benefiting multinational and transnational corporations based in or headed by individuals from industrialized nations. While the nation-state "did, and still does, perform certain functions, for which there is as of now no substitute agency"—it, for instance, "defines citizenship, controls currency, imposes law, protects public health, provides general education, maintains security, and guides the national economy"—transnational corporations are becoming increasingly powerful and influential in the spheres of economics, politics, and culture (92). "Against the effective operation of [multinational and transnational corporations]," he says, "the nation-states more and more look undefined and inoperable" (92). For Miyoshi, the splitting of such countries as the USSR and Yugoslavia into numerous, often ethnically-homogeneous, nations says less about the viability of nationhood and nationalism as a politically unifying force than it does about the "rapidly altering" and "bewilderingly complex" network of transnational power relations. Separatist movements in Eastern Europe—in the Balkans, for example—are "expressions of ethnicism," he argues, "not nationalism" (92). "As globalization intensifies," Miyoshi says, "neoethnicism is appealing because of its brute simplicity": "[i]t is as if the inadequacy of the nation-state is now fully realized, and the provincial strongmen are all trying to grab a piece of real estate for keeps before all is incorporated and appropriated by transnational corporations" (92). Ethnically-based nations that hearken back to tribal-like structures of community become "local" defense mechanisms against the encroachment of the "global."

Miyoshi's discussion of globalization and its implications for Eastern Europe is important because it draws attention to the ways in which transculturalism—the phenomenon that Kulyk Keefer celebrates in "From Mosaic to Kaleidoscope"—is predicated on a troublingly uneven network of international economic and political relations. As Max Pensky argues, in his introduction to Jürgen Habermas's *The Postnational Constellation* (2001), globalization may be a term that has become "indispensable" and "unavoidable" in discussions "from political economy and democracy, law and human rights to cultural controversies over identity and difference" (vii), but it is a term that seems "destined to provoke only ambiguous reactions" (vii). For some—like Kulyk Keefer—globalization evokes a "utopian vision" of the world, an image of "proliferating interconnections and interrelationship, of better communication between the most far-flung regions of the world, challenging old prejudices and pointing toward a future where the cultural, geographical, and political sources of social conflicts have become antiques" (vii). For others, however, globalization hints at "the dystopian specter of forced cultural homogenization either by decrees of a centralized administration or by market fiat" (vii). Developing countries, in particular, face the "eradication of the sources of any cultural identities unconducive to the mandatory, market-drive adaptation to Western-style modes of life" (vii). It is precisely this ambivalence that Eastern Europeans have had to contend with over the past two decades: how to negotiate between the promise of an increasingly inter-connected and inter-related world, and the reality of neo-colonial global hierarchies of power.

In their relatively broad and abstract approaches to the ambivalent phenomenon of globalization, of course, both Miyoshi and Pensky necessarily leave unexamined the ways in which individuals are affected by increasingly globalized networks of social and cultural exchange. What impact have the changes in Eastern Europe had on relations between individuals living in former Eastern bloc countries and those who have familial and/or cultural ties to these countries? Evidence abounds of the extent to which Canadians of Eastern European descent, including Ukrainian Canadians, have been able to travel back to, and reconnect with, their ethnic homelands following the collapse of communism in the early 1990s. Over the past few years, for example, numerous writers have returned to Eastern European and published accounts of their travels. In *Blood and Belonging: Journeys into the New Nationalism* (1993), Michael Ignatieff writes about his travels in Russia; Eva Hoffman (*Lost in Translation: A Life in a New Language*, 1989; *Exit into History: A Journey Through the New Eastern Europe*, 1993; *Shtetl: The Life and Death of a Small Town and the World of Polish Jews*, 1997), Lisa Appignanesi (*Losing the Dead*, 1999), and Irena Karafilly (*Ashes and Miracles: A Polish Journey*, 1998) write about their experiences in Poland; Anna Porter, in *The Storyteller: Memory, Secrets, Magic and Lies* (2000), narrates her return to Hungary; and Tony Fabijančić, in *Croatia: Travels in Undiscovered Country* (2003), revisits his homeland, the former Yugoslavia. Since the independence of Ukraine in 1991, more specifically, Ukrainian Canadian writers and artists have been particularly active in developing connections with Ukraine.[13] In addition to Kulyk Keefer and Kostash,[14] filmmaker John Paskievich documents his return to Ukraine in *My Mother's Village* (2001); and Natalka Husar draws upon her travels to Ukraine during the early 1990s in many of her paintings, including her series *Black Sea Blue* (1995).[15] But Ukrainian Canadian scholars have been, arguably, most tireless in their ongoing efforts to maintain intellectual, social, and cultural links with Ukraine and Ukrainians. The Canadian Institute of Ukrainian Studies (CIUS) at the University of Alberta and the University of Toronto sponsor numerous projects focused on Ukrainian history, culture, and politics—some of them based jointly in Canada and Ukraine—as well as exchange programs that promote cross-cultural contact and dialogue between Ukrainian and Ukrainian Canadian scholars.[16]

Ultimately, however, the formal and informal transnational or transcultural connections between Eastern Europeans and Canadians of Eastern Europe descent—between Ukrainians and Ukrainian Canadians, especially—should be interpreted with caution. Transnational networks of social and cultural exchange seem to transcend national borders, challenging nation-based notions of identity and community by bringing individuals from different countries but ostensibly similar cultural backgrounds in contact with one another. But how exactly do these networks operate? Who actually travels between Canada and Eastern Europe, and why? Who benefits from the increasingly open borders of Eastern Europe, and how? In the specific context of transnational relations between Ukrainians and Ukrainian Canadians, the socioeconomic inequalities between the two groups seem to me impossible to ignore. How often do Ukrainians travel to Canada? Do Ukrainians write about their travels to Canada? Are Ukrainian scholars able to visit Canada without the support of exchange programs funded by Canadian organizations?

The reality is that, because Ukrainian Canadians are decidedly better off than the majority of people in Ukraine, transcultural exchanges between Canada and Ukraine most often take the form of Ukrainian Canadians traveling to Ukraine and Ukrainian Canadian scholars implementing cross-cultural programs. Without a doubt, many Ukrainian Canadians travel to Ukraine and/or nurture ongoing relationships with Ukrainians in order to help improve the situation in their homeland— witness, for example, the 500 Ukrainian Canadians who visited Ukraine in January, 2005, to help monitor the elections there. Before the Orange Revolution, many Ukrainian Canadians participated in charity projects, often church-sponsored, that send clothing and household items to families in Ukraine. And, on a broader scale, such initiatives as the Canada Ukraine Legislative and Intergovernmental Project, established by the CIUS in 1996, have worked toward strengthening the economy in Ukraine. Despite their best intentions, however, Ukrainian Canadians cannot escape their economic superiority over Ukrainians. Living in Canada, they have access to better health care and food, and a wider variety of household commodities and consumer goods. Even Ukrainian Canadians with modest incomes by Canadian standards are, by Ukrainian standards, wealthy—not only because Ukrainians are poorly paid but because the exchange rate between Canadian dollars and Ukrainian *hryvnia* heavily favours the former. As a result, Ukrainian Canadians who return to Ukraine have the best of both worlds: by traveling back to Ukraine, they satisfy their desire to strengthen their bonds with the ethnic homeland, and, in the process, may help to improve the living conditions of their family, friends, or colleagues, while never actually having to face the hardships of day-to-day life in Ukraine. They travel, after all, as tourists with Canadian passports—with the security, that is, of knowing that they can and will return to Canada.

My analysis of the relation between Ukrainian Canadians and Ukrainians may seem unduly critical but it points to the ways in which terms such as globalization, transnationalism, and transculturalism take on different meanings for people living in different parts of the world.[17] In her examination of the ways in which "global-local intersections" produce new forms of culture ("In Whose Interest?: Transnational Capital and the Production of Multiculturalism in Canada" [1996]), Katharyne Mitchell identifies many scholars' tendency to "celebrate the positive implications of transnationalism" by focusing on "notions of hybridity and pluralism" (219–20). She notes that "[c]ulture-workers interested in questions of identity and the constitution of subjectivity herald the ways in which new cross-border movements have facilitated the production and reworking of multiple identities, dialogic communications, syncretic cultural forms, and seemingly emancipatory multicultural ideologies" (220). But as Mitchell suggests, "this kind of abstract celebration of travel, hybridity, and multiculturalism" is premature (220). The problem with "numerous celebratory representations of these 'new' transnational cultures and hybrid subject positions" is that the "powerfully oppressive socioeconomic forces underlying the changes are neglected" (220). The luxury of exploring the exciting spaces between the global and the local is simply not available to many individuals from former Eastern bloc countries who are necessarily preoccupied with negotiating the daily demands of life in the midst of political and economic instability. Individuals who have the privilege of living in relatively stable, developed nations such as Canada are more likely to be able to afford to travel beyond the borders of their nations—and, of course, back again.

Turning my attention in the following chapters to Kulyk Keefer's and Kostash's books, I want to emphasize that neither writer is unaware of her relative privilege as a middle-class Canadian. As both self-consciously attempt—in their travels and in their writing—to close the gaps between their actual status as Canadians and their emotional ties to the fraught "other" world of Eastern Europe, they have no choice but to confront the material as well as the cultural differences between Canadian society and that of Ukraine. Reading through their texts, however, what becomes obvious is that as similar as their enterprises may seem—broadly speaking, these writers have in common a desire to connect with their ethnic homeland—their respective approaches to building cross-cultural, transnational relationships with people in Ukraine are markedly different. Genealogy is Kulyk Keefer's prime motivation for visiting Ukraine. She travels to rediscover and consolidate her familial ties to this part of Eastern Europe. And, as *The Green Library and Honey and Ashes* suggest, her trips "home" prove what she suspected before she set out: her family's bridge of blood between Canada and Ukraine is as real as she imagined it to be. Kostash, by contrast, travels to Eastern Europe with a view to developing professional and personal relationships that transcend borders and bloodlines. Although she spends some time with relatives in Ukraine, her primary goal is not to re-establish links to family in the Old Country but rather to create new bonds with individuals who share her political beliefs and writerly interests. But, unlike Kulyk Keefer, Kostash comes to see that she cannot change her status as an outsider vis-à-vis the multiple communities she visits. In the process of writing *Bloodlines* and *The Doomed Bridegroom*, she comes to realize that only by blurring the boundaries between fiction and non-fiction can she overcome the reality of the alienation she feels in Eastern Europe. Despite the obvious parallels, then, between Kulyk Keefer and Kostash, their work in fact invites comparison to that of other Ukrainian Canadian writers. Kulyk Keefer's interest in scripting narratives that adhere as closely as possible to the reality of her family's and her own experiences mirrors in many ways Maara Haas's and George Ryga's approaches to setting down their stories. Writing, for all of these authors, is less about exploring new possibilities in theme or in form than it is about realistically depicting the world around them in relatively conventional genres. But as Kostash—like Suknaski before her—self-consciously engages with the process of writing and with her identity as a writer, she is empowered to re-imagine her sense of self, community, history, and home. Language, Kostash illustrates, has the potential to transform reality in the space of the literary text.

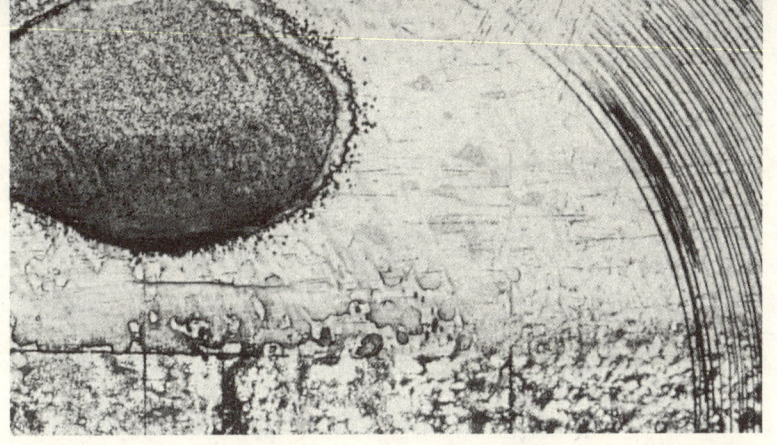

NINE

From Canada to Ukraine—and Back
Janice Kulyk Keefer's *The Green Library* and *Honey and Ashes*

The Green Library

In "'Coming Across Bones': Historiographic Ethnofiction" (1996), Janice Kulyk Keefer reflects on her reasons for writing her recently-completed *The Green Library*. Referring to her protagonist as a woman who "having grown up as a WASP Canadian, suddenly discovers that she is half-Ukrainian"—and whose identity is, consequently, "multiply fractured along familial, ethnic, and even national lines"—Kulyk Keefer could be describing herself (84). Unlike Eva Chown, the central character in *The Green Library*, of course, Kulyk Keefer grew up knowing that she was, and is, Ukrainian; yet, for many years, and particularly as an adult, she deliberately distanced herself from her ethnic roots. In order to "remove [herself] as far as possible from the claustrophobia and painfully split subjectivity induced by [her] experience of ethnicity" (87), she moved to England, married an "*Anglik*," and, for a time, even developed an English accent. She became, in her own words, an "arch-Anglophile" (88). Although Kulyk Keefer insists that she neither wanted to nor could "shake off" (88) her grandmother's, mother's, and aunt's stories about Ukraine, she established herself as a writer largely without drawing upon this family history.[1] She explains her "recalcitrance vis-à-vis 'writing ethnicity'" by admitting her reluctance, "even in the heyday of multiculturalism in the 1980s, when it was suddenly 'fun to be ethnic,'" to be "pigeonholed as an ethnic writer, someone whose work would only be of interest to a small community of 'like-blooded' readers" (89). But she confesses, as well, to feeling ashamed of her ethnic background—ashamed of "being tied, despite the fact of [her] Canadian birth and citizenship, to a country that some said did not exist, or was a mere colony of vastly more important, culturally more imposing states"; and ashamed of "being marked...by an ethnicity whose visible signs were the butt of ethnic jokes about hunkies in sheepskin coats eating perogies" (89).

Why did Kulyk Keefer suddenly, in the 1990s, decide to explore her ethnicity in her writing? In part, she says, her interest in "writing ethnicity" (as she terms it) was sparked by "the collapse of the USSR and the emergence of an independent Ukrainian state," developments which "made it imperative for [her]...to visit Ukraine for the first time" (89).[2] Outspokenly critical of the ways in which officially-sanctioned, folkloric models of ethnicity trivialize the social and historical realities of Ukrainian Canadians' experiences, she set out in search of "the true site of [her] ethnicity" (89). To "authentically" reconnect with her ethnic heritage, she felt that she needed to travel, both literally and figuratively, to the Old Country, the place where "familial stories" and "collective history" intersect (89). As Kulyk Keefer explains, however, she travelled to Ukraine with her eye on the future as well as on the past. "[I]n terms of descent or biological affiliation," she says, "ethnicity has reached a dead end with me" (89). Because her children "consider themselves to be Canadians, unhyphenated, *tout court*," she felt an obligation and a responsibility to record her family's history—a history that she believed would be otherwise lost or forgotten—for future generations (89).

That Ukrainian and Ukrainian Canadian history becomes a central theme, then, in *The Green Library* is unsurprising. Rather more surprising—given Kulyk Keefer's notion that ethnicity in her family will reach a "dead end" with the third or fourth generation—is the fact that *The Green Library* implicitly affirms the centrality of genealogy in defining identity. On the surface, Kulyk Keefer's novel illustrates that ethnicity "has nothing to do with religious rituals, social customs, cultural traditions, national costume, and cuisine." Her heroine's "newly discovered" Ukrainian-ness, instead, "has to do with history," at once "personal and public, private and collective" (84). But the underlying theme of the novel—underscored by recurrent references to, and images of, blood— is that ethnicity has "to do," most of all, with bloodlines. In fact, Kulyk

Keefer structures her text around two assumptions. First, that individuals are connected to particular histories through genealogy; and, second, that they can reconstruct and lay claim to these histories by returning to the "true sites" from which they originated.

Set in Canada and Ukraine, and spanning a period of sixty years—1933 to 1993—*The Green Library* focuses on Eva Chown, a forty-three-year-old woman living in Toronto. As complex as it is convoluted, Eva's story—or, rather, the story of her family—is narrated in multiple voices that constantly shift in time and space, often disorienting the reader. The novel's collage-like structure, however, effectively mirrors Eva's struggle to piece together the details of her past. Eva is a daycare worker with an eleven-year-old son, Ben. She lives with her partner of nine years, Dan, who runs a travel agency. All is well in Eva's life until, one day, she receives a puzzling photograph from a strange man who has been watching her and her son. Troubled by the photograph—obviously taken decades ago—of a woman and a boy who bears a striking resemblance to Ben, Eva begins to doubt everything she knows, or thought she knew, about her past. She embarks, then, on a quest to find out the truth about her family history. Who are the people in the photograph? How is she connected to them? Seeking answers to these questions, Eva travels to Porcupine Creek in northern Ontario where her parents, Holly and Garth Chown, lived before Eva was born and where, she discovers, her mother had a brief affair with Ivan Kotelko, a "DP" from Ukraine. Eva suspects—quite rightly—that Kotelko is her biological father. He was the little boy in the photograph, and the stranger who gave her the photograph in the first place.

Having discovered that she is actually half-Ukrainian, Eva is unable to stop thinking about her father: who is he, exactly, and what is his story? How is he related to the woman in the photograph? Why has he suddenly appeared in her life? At the same time, she is overwhelmed by a flood of long-repressed memories of other Ukrainian "DPs" she knew, briefly, during her childhood and adolescence in Toronto—Olya Moroz, the Chowns' cleaning woman, and her two children, Oksanna and Alex. Determined to know more about her father, Eva enlists the help of Oksanna and Olya, who still live in Toronto. Alex, the boy with whom Eva was infatuated as a girl, returned to Ukraine with his father in 1963. Olya is particularly helpful. She provides Eva with information about the mysterious photograph—the woman in the photograph is Kotelko's mother—and she also urges Eva to visit her grandmother's grave in Ukraine. Eva does indeed travel to Ukraine, but her motivations for doing so become confused once she contacts Alex in Kiev, for he becomes more than her tour guide and translator—he also becomes her lover. Distracted by her involvement with Alex, Eva spends little time thinking about her family's past experiences in Ukraine—and rather more time grappling with her ambivalent attitudes toward the current state of affairs in the country. She is at once fascinated with, and appalled by, Alex's life in Kiev. After returning to Canada, Eva's relationship with Dan ends; and, though she and Ben, with the help of Oksanna, are reunited with Kotelko—at Porcupine Creek, the very place where Eva was conceived—her story concludes on a bittersweet note. Kotelko, who is dying, wants to develop a relationship with his grandson, not with his daughter. Eva, who wants to make a life with Alex, is unable to bridge the distance between them. In the final scene of the novel, she tentatively reaches out to Alex by telephone, but their connection is poor.

In terms of its commentary on ethnicity, *The Green Library* foregrounds the notion that, in order for Canadian-born Ukrainians to understand the meaning of their heritage, they must come to terms with their ethnic group's history in both Canada and Ukraine. This perspective marks a shift from Haas's, Ryga's, and Suknaski's exclusive emphasis on the history of Ukrainians in Canada, and on the prairies, more specifically. Like these previous writers, however, Kulyk Keefer clearly posits history as an alternative to folkloric expressions of culture that trivialize the complexities of Ukrainian Canadian identity. Before finding out that she is half-Ukrainian, Eva pays little attention to the ethnic "kitsch" displayed by stores and restaurants in Bloor West Village, the predominantly East European neighbourhood in Toronto where Dan's travel agency—Janus Travel, "specializing in trips back to the Old Country" (12)—is located. And Dan, who is Jewish, balks at "embroidered appliqué on duck-shaped ceramic ashtrays" and "identical busts of some national hero wearing an astrakhan hat, a walrus moustache and sad, small eyes" (51). Dan, in fact, is the character who first introduces the importance of privileging history over folklore, and his opinions of Ukrainian history are not favorable. He, after all, has "grown up on cossack-shaped bogeyman; for him, borscht suggests something saltier and far darker than mere beets" (51). In fact, when Eva comes to Dan, excited about the discoveries she has made about her past, he is quick to point out that "[i]t's not just Easter eggs and perogies, being Ukrainian. It also happens to be things like pogroms" (112). By telling Eva about Bohdan Khmelnitsky, a national hero of Ukraine who was "one of the great pogrom-makers of all time," and by mentioning the "little matter of Babi Yar," the "Old Women's Ravine" outside Kiev where seventy thousand Jews were murdered by Nazis and their Ukrainian collaborators in 1941, Dan draws attention to the fact that these unsettling moments in Ukrainian history are also a part of her ethnic inheritance (113).

But Eva is willing to acknowledge both the positive and the negative aspects of Ukrainian and Ukrainian Canadian history. Compelled to know more about people like her father and the Moroz family—her people—she starts by going to the local library, poring over books about so-called "Displaced Persons," the "people she grew up calling, when she thought of them at all, Dee-Pees" (75). Slowly, Eva begins to understand what brought these immigrants to Canada, and how they suffered in exile from their homelands. She reads stories about the "hundreds of thousands" from Eastern Europe who, having fled to Germany when the Soviets invaded their countries or having been shipped to Germany by the Nazis, were left with nothing at the end of the war: "[n]ot just without a roof over their heads, and no family to return to, but without a country" (76). Once in Canada, she learns, women worked long hours for poor, sometimes "starvation," wages as "domestics in private homes, cleaners in hospitals, workers in textile mills"; and men, trained in their home countries as teachers, writers, and doctors, were forced into mining and lumber camps (76). Thinking back to her experiences with the Moroz family—with Oksanna Moroz, especially, who was in Eva's class at school—Eva realizes that she was more than insensitive to their situation. As a girl, she was particularly cruel to Oksanna, telling their classmates that Oksanna's mother scrubbed toilets for a living (84). Aware for the first time of the ways in which the Moroz family struggled during their early years in Canada, Eva sees, too, that, some fifty years later, they continue to grapple with the aftermath of the Second World War. Olya, no longer a housekeeper, now works as a translator for a professor from the Department of Slavic Studies, but she has had no contact with her son, Alex, since his father took him back to Ukraine in 1963. And, although Oksanna is a successful doctor, a dermatologist with a thriving practice, she is a cold woman, embittered by years of discrimination. Fittingly, her Ukrainian surname, "Moroz," translates as "frost." No longer interested in her Ukrainian language or culture, in fact, she has adopted the anglicized version of her name.

And Eva's own family history, as she discovers, is no less marked by hardship and tragedy. From Olya Moroz, who recognizes the woman in the photograph given to Eva by her father, Eva learns that Kotelko was born in an artists' colony—"Soloveyko" or "Nightingale"—near Kiev. His mother, Lesia Levkovych, was a well-known poet, and his father, Pavlo Bozhyk, an artist (98–99).[3] Olya explains that, for a period of ten years before Stalin came to power, in 1929, the painters, writers, actors, and musicians who formed Soloveyko were able to work in their own language, keeping their Ukrainian culture alive. "Publishing houses, newspapers, journals, theatres—everything was allowed, everything that would keep the language alive and open and growing" (100). A student then, Olya witnessed this renaissance of Ukrainian culture. But she witnessed, too, Stalin's aggressive moves toward wiping out all things Ukrainian: "[b]ooks were hauled off library shelves," she says, "plays banned, theatres closed. Even the museums were ordered to dispose of pottery, embroidery—anything identifiable as Ukrainian. To be Ukrainian was to be anti-Bolshevik; to use our language was to commit counter-revolution" (100–101). Executions followed, often without trial. Nearly all of the Soloveyko artists and intellectuals "died before their time," either in Stalin's purges or in the Second World War, and everything they worked for was "wiped out" (99). From an excerpt that Olya finds in *The Literary History of Ukraine*—one that chillingly echoes Dan's reference to Babi Yar—Eva discovers that Lesia, her grandmother, was among "those executed in 1941 for political activities deemed subversive by the Nazi occupiers of Kiev": she was "taken to Babi Yar and shot, her body thrown in the ravine" (120). While some Ukrainians may well have perpetuated injustice—at Babi Yar, for example, where they collaborated with the Nazis—others, even non-Jews such as Lesia, suffered unspeakable violence and terror.

But insofar as *The Green Library* illustrates that second-generation Ukrainian Canadians must learn their history if they are to understand the meaning of their ethnicity, the novel also suggests that they must return to the original site of this history—to Ukraine—in order to claim their ethnic inheritance. Eva visits the country in which her grandparents lived and died because she feels connected to it by blood; by virtue of her newly-discovered ethnicity, Ukraine has become her homeland. From the outset of her story, Eva's thoughts turn again and again to "[b]lood ties" and "family ties" (41). Paddling a canoe, for example, through the waters of Porcupine Creek—where she first learns about her mother's affair with Kotelko, and where, in a sense, she is reborn as the daughter of a Ukrainian—she tries to imagine "what it must feel like in the womb, its blood-warm waters" (54). And, listening to Olya Moroz talk about Lesia Levkovych, Pavlo Bozhyk, and Ivan Kotelko, she visualizes a "bloodline," a "thin, tough line of blood linking her, now, in this glass and concrete library, with these doomed people" (99). "Suddenly," she sees that "the impossible distance between this young, scowling boy in the photograph and her own son has been bridged, and by nothing more than a line of blood" (99).

The problem is that, when Eva actually traces this bloodline back to Ukraine, she discovers that her connection to the country is less real than imagined. Her status as a middle-class Canadian marks her, indelibly, as a foreigner in Ukraine. While making plans to meet Alex Moroz in Kiev, she asks if she should "wear a rose in [her] lapel" to identify herself; he replies, "I'll have no trouble finding you, Miss Chown. I'm afraid it's still all too easy to spot the Westerners in any crowd" (130). Although Dan warns her about the standard of living in Ukraine—"[y]ou'll pay first-class hotel rates for a place where you wouldn't want to leave your dog," he says, and "you'll get sick of potatoes and cabbage after your first two days" (110)— Eva is ill-equipped for the stark poverty she encounters there. In fact, she is bewildered and frightened by everything in Kiev—telephones and elevators that don't work, subway stations and apartments that are over-crowded. Because she cannot speak Ukrainian, the simplest tasks become impossible. She "can't flip through a newspaper, buy an apple from a sidewalk vendor, ask for directions" (158). But her inability to speak Ukrainian is not the only obstacle she faces in Ukraine. Local "customs" and "survival tactics" mystify her as well (158). Without the help of Alex, her "eyes and ears, her guide, interpreter, bodyguard," she is as "clueless" and as "helpless" as a "baby wet from the womb" (158).

In some ways, Eva is powerless in Kiev without Alex. As a naïve tourist, she relies upon him, the savvy native, to guide and protect her. But even as she seemingly surrenders to him sexually, she holds all the cards, so to speak, in their relationship. Both Eva and Alex are painfully aware of the differences—the dramatic inequalities—between them. To Eva, Alex's apartment "seems almost as small as the playhouse she had as a child, and just as bare" (155); and Alex, who has lived in Canada, is embarrassed by his meager lodgings—by the poor restaurants in Kiev, too, and the sparsely-stocked markets, and the general lack that characterizes his day-to-day life. When Eva offers to buy him dinner at a "good restaurant"—an "expensive one"—Alex obliges, knowing full well that she will be disappointed, if not shocked, during their evening out (141). She anticipates a meal of "sturgeon, cucumber salad, meringues, and berries in cream"; "[w]ine from Georgia and Crimean champagne"; and a "small string orchestra" playing in the background (142). What she actually experiences is "more dreadful than she'd ever imagined," for the "expensive" restaurant offers no variety in its menu, and neither wine nor vodka. Rather than choke down her meal, Eva "pushes a chicken leg across her plate, hiding lumps of gristle under the potatoes" (142-43). Eva is more impressed by, and at home in, the market to which Alex takes her—until she learns that "ordinarily, he never shops here; only rich people, those in government and business," can patronize the place (156). Tellingly, when Alex exorbitantly spends half a week's salary on a shawl for Eva, his sacrifice goes unnoticed by her. He wants her to impress her with a gift that she can take home, but she spreads it across his kitchen table. For her, the shawl is nothing more than a tablecloth.

Clearly, in becoming involved with Alex, Eva wants to become a part of his world, to make his world her own. Once, while making love, she attempts to stake her claim to both Alex and his country by "baring her teeth, nipping him until she tast[es] his blood on her tongue" and "[s]wallowing the blood as if it were some red bead she could lodge inside herself forever" (166). But the words "as if" are key. Eva's desire to bridge the differences between herself and Alex is unrealizable because, while they may be physically intimate, Eva knows little about Alex—about his failed marriage; his daughter who has developed bone cancer as a result of the Chernobyl nuclear disaster; and his daily struggle to survive as a professor at the Academy of Sciences who earns a mere seventeen dollars a month. After Eva insists that they visit Babi Yar, moreover, and makes a series of flippantly critical comments about Ukrainians' involvement in the massacre, Alex also begins to see that she knows little about the complexities of Ukrainian history. He sees her as an insolent foreigner, breezing in and out of Ukraine, presuming to "judge him, his country, [and] its history" (188) with neither sensitivity nor compassion. As she prepares to leave Ukraine, the simmering tensions between Eva and Alex erupt into a heated argument precisely because she has the luxury of leaving Ukraine and returning to the stability and comfort of Canada. Flaunting both her arrogance and her ignorance with regard to Alex's situation, Eva says, "[w]hen are you coming back to Canada?" (204). After explaining that he cannot travel on his salary, Alex turns her question around. "What about you, Eva?" he asks. "When are you moving to Kiev?" (204). And then, giving voice to his belief that "[t]hey will always be playing the swineherd and the princess" (188), he says, "[w]hy don't you stay home if you can't live without pizza and Coca-Cola? Why don't all you Westerners, with your big money that you spend like water over here, for Christ's sake just stay home?" (204). Oddly enough, on the day of her departure, while strolling through a museum in Ukraine—wearing, for the first time, the shawl that Alex bought for her—Eva is reminded of the reason for which she could not "just stay home." Quite accidentally, she comes face to face with a painting by her grandfather, Pavlo Bozhyk—a portrait of Lesia Levkovych, her grandmother—and, as she gazes at the painting, an old woman tenderly but wordlessly links arms with her. Suddenly, despite the tumultuous few days she has spent with Alex, her trip seems worthwhile. The old woman, standing in for Eva's grandmother, becomes her living link to Ukraine.

Eva's chance discovery of Pavlo Bozhyk's painting at the museum in Kiev and her unexpected encounter with the old woman are troubling in that this entire scene rather too conveniently redeems her trip to Ukraine—as if a moment of symbolic connection with her long-dead grandparents can cancel out her actual detachment from Ukraine. Eva's experience in the museum—just one of several accidents or coincidences around which *The Green Library* is structured—undermines the realism of the text because it reveals Kulyk Keefer's authorial presence in the novel, making apparent her desire to drive home the notion that individuals' destinies are pre-determined by blood. To some extent, as with all works of fiction, readers must suspend their disbelief when they approach this novel. One of the most important and, arguably, one of the most coincidental turn of events in Eva's life comes near the end of the novel, during her visit to Ukraine. After venturing out of Alex's apartment one day, she meets Mykola Savchuk, an old friend of Kotelko's—the "one person in [Kiev] who can tell her what she needs to know" about her father (192)—who happens to live next door to Alex. From Savchuk, Eva learns that her father was a soldier in the underground Ukrainian nationalist army.

For several reasons, Eva's meeting with Savchuk becomes a crucial moment—the turning point, really—in *The Green Library*. For Eva, the meeting, not unlike her chance discovery of Bozhyk's painting, affirms what she has always suspected about Ukraine and her relation to it—she can neither ignore nor escape her blood connection to the country and its history. Clearly, she was meant to come to Kiev. For readers of *The Green Library*, too, Eva's meeting with Savchuk provides important insight into the narrative structure of the text. From the outset of the novel, Kulyk Keefer leaves a trail of puzzling clues about Eva's family history. Eva's story, narrated in the third person, is interrupted by her grandmother's story, also narrated in the third person. In addition, italicized portions of text, narrated in the first person by an unknown scribe, appear to be telling Lesia Levkovych's story. Who is the unknown scribe? He is Savchuk, Kotelko's old friend-cum-historian, a man determined to record Kotelko's family history for posterity. However, Eva never learns the full truth about Kotelko's past from Savchuk. Unlike readers of the novel, she is not privy to Savchuk's thoughts, so she never discovers that Kotelko was a revolutionary who, caught up in an internal conflict between two factions of the nationalist underground, sided with the German army in order to oust the Bolsheviks from Ukraine. Eva never learns that her father turned over his own mother, Eva's grandmother, to the Nazis, ensuring her death at Babi Yar. In an attempt to hide the truth about his friend's past—to protect Kotelko, in the present—Savchuk chooses not to tell Eva about her father's complicity in Lesia Levkovych's murder. He also chooses not to *write* about Kotelko's act of betrayal. Although Savchuk knows that his friend moved to Canada after the war, he insists to Eva that Kotelko died in the war. "It is best for Ivan to be dead in the war," he thinks. "Dead men court no dangers" (201). While Eva necessarily questions Savchuk's story, for she knows that her father is alive, her meeting with Savchuk "adds up to the same thing." Eva is "no longer the stranger, the permanently foreign visitor [Alex has] taken her to be, but a prodigal, like him. Someone who's had to return to the place where she came from, however little she belongs to it" (197).

Kulyk Keefer seems to suggest that, although Eva is connected by blood to Ukraine, she will never really belong in Ukraine, because she is Canadian. She will never learn the full truth of her family's history there. Structurally, *The Green Library* illustrates the inherent gaps between history and historiography and thematically, too, the novel ostensibly questions the assumption that blood is enough to connect Ukrainian Canadians to Ukraine and to Ukrainian history. Propelled as it is, however, by a series of fateful events and seemingly pre-destined occurrences, all related to Eva's newly-discovered ethnicity, the text repeatedly underscores the notion that individuals are powerless to ignore or deny their blood ties to family and to history. "Blood ties," thinks Eva, "family ties. You're born with family like a chain around your neck: metal rings, each one kissing, biting into the next. And even if you break the links, the chain doesn't dissolve. It just sinks under your skin, you wear it without knowing" (41). So the explicit message of the novel, ultimately, is that bloodlines *do* constitute an absolute link between Ukrainian Canadians and Ukraine, between Ukrainian Canadians and their history in both Ukraine and Canada. As Kulyk Keefer makes clear in the final chapters of the novel, while Eva may never know the truth about her family's—especially her father's—history, her son Ben will, precisely because he is related to Kotelko by blood.

Indeed, the conclusion to *The Green Library* hinges less on Eva than on Ben, the boy who unwittingly set in motion her quest to uncover the truth about her past. When Eva returns to Toronto from Kiev, her quest—not to mention her relationships with both Dan and Alex—appears to come to an end, leaving her with a bittersweet sense of belonging to, and separation from, Ukraine, and only a partial understanding of her family's history. But in a final twist of fate—the last in a long series of unusual events and occurrences—Oksanna Moroz appears out of nowhere, whisking Eva and Ben off to Porcupine Creek, against Eva's will, to meet Ivan Kotelko. Throughout the novel, Eva has been careful to shield her son from the truth about her—or, rather, their—ethnicity because she wants neither to confuse nor to frighten Ben with this information. Yet Oksanna, Eva learns, has been meeting with Ben in secret, telling him about his grandfather. "Hungry" from the start of his friendship with Oksanna for stories about his *dyido*, Ben is now eager to meet Kotelko (243)—and Kotelko is equally, if not more, eager to meet his grandson. At first, Eva resents the fact that Kotelko wants little to do with her; that he is only interested in his grandson. To Kotelko, she is "not a daughter but the woman who has given him his grandson" (252). Eventually, however, Eva comes to recognize the importance of her role as a link between generations. She is part of the past as well as the future because "the womb which tipped her out is linked to that other womb, the one that harboured the man who is her father" (261). Arriving at a curiously gendered understanding of genealogy, she sees herself as one in a "series of connecting rings: her mother, her grandmother, herself" (261). Whereas her son is connected to his grandfather and great-grandfather—he looks like Kotelko, and he is naturally artistic, like Pavlo Bozhyk—Eva is connected to her mother and grandmother. "Holly," Kulyk Keefer writes, "Lesia: their lives, their stories—[Eva] carries them in her bones" (261). But regardless of the gendered ways in which the past, from Eva's perspective, seems to live on in her and her son, what matters most, from the reader's perspective, is that Ben inherits more than his grandfather's genes. Kotelko is determined to meet his grandson because he wants to tell Ben about his past—"tell it to the boy alone, and make him promise to keep it secret, even from his mother" (255). Clearly too young to take in all of the details of his grandfather's experiences in Ukraine and in Canada, Ben will hear "a story, one with a great deal of weaving and folding and hiding in its lines." Kotelko will tell him everything, though, trusting that "the child, remembering the story as a grown man, will undo the folds and see what he's meant to find" (254).

Ironically, then, given in its fragmented narrative structure, seemingly rife with gaps and fissures, *The Green Library* leaves no questions unanswered, no mysteries unsolved, and it articulates, in the end, a relatively straightforward and conventional understanding of both ethnicity and history. Bloodlines become the bottom line in Eva's quest to understand the meaning of her ethnic identity. Just as ethnicity is passed on through blood, so too is history: Ben inherits both. But Kulyk Keefer's notion that bloodlines transcend national borders, connecting Ukrainian Canadians to Ukraine despite their Canadian citizenship, too easily glosses over the actual differences between Ukrainian Canadians and Ukrainians.

The narrative never fully reconciles the inherent material inequalities between Eva and Alex. When, near the end of the novel, she tries to reach him by phone, the "connection is poor," and they have trouble making out each other's voices (267). After Eva hears Alex say her name—signaling a tentatively hopeful new beginning to their relationship—she thinks that, "[f]or the moment, this is enough" (267). But is it enough? Little has changed between them. Eva initiates contact with Alex from the relative luxury and comfort of her house in Toronto, "a mansion, a palace compared to the apartments in Kiev" (253). If she returns to Kiev, she will go back only for a visit—for "two or three weeks a year" (265)—certainly not to stay. And Alex has said, in a letter, "*the sum total of what I am is just this: where I am, where I have to stay. A place that turns out to be as far away from you as if I lived on a star*" (264). Beyond her relationship with Ben—a boy who knows little about, and has never seen, Ukraine—what real connection to the country does she have? What real connection is she willing to make? Readers must suspend their disbelief once more if they are to accept that Eva's and Ben's lives have been altered in any concrete way as a result of their newly-discovered ethnicity and history. Eva's notions that "[y]ou're born with family like a chain around your neck" and that "even if you break the links, the chain doesn't dissolve" are convenient precisely because, as she explains, the chain "sinks under your skin" and "you wear it *without knowing*" (41, emphasis added). At the close of the novel, mother and son alike are left with the best of both worlds, the luxury of claiming Ukraine as their imagined homeland "without knowing" the hardships of day-to-day life in this country; without giving up the relative safety and comfort of their actual home in Canada.

Honey and Ashes: A Story of Family

Structured as it is around Kulyk Keefer's quest to piece together the multiple stories that comprise her family's history in both Canada and Ukraine, *Honey and Ashes: A Story of Family*, like *The Green Library*, illustrates that the experience of being Ukrainian Canadian has little to do with folkloric expressions of culture. If second-generation Ukrainian Canadians are to understand the meaning of their ethnic identity, they must come to terms with their history—preferably, moreover, by returning to Ukraine, the original site of this history. "For me," Kulyk Keefer writes, in the prologue to *Honey and Ashes*, "ethnicity has been no voluntary affair of food and dress but a mesh of old place and new, of personal and public history—a mesh that cuts deep into the skin" (7). But, she explains, "as I wrote down the stories my family had told me of their lost home," and "as I pored over maps and encyclopedia entries and history books, I realized that I would have to make another kind of journey to the Old Place" (5). At the same time, *Honey and Ashes* seems to question the notion that Ukrainian Canadians can uncover the "truth" about their pasts through oral stories, written histories, and/or first-hand observations of Ukraine—historical "facts" are, after all, always selectively recorded and subjectively remembered. Yet, as with *The Green Library*, even as *Honey and Ashes* explicitly draws attention to the inherent gaps between history and representations of history—including official historical documents and records, written works of history, and family stories—the structure of the text provides a seamless sense of resolution to her quest, implicitly contradicting Kulyk Keefer's skepticism about what can and cannot be known about the past.

Given that she draws upon the conventions of fiction and non-fiction, biography and autobiography, history and travelogue, the genre of Kulyk Keefer's text is difficult to define. Broadly speaking, however, the text narrates Kulyk Keefer's family history—the history, that is, of her maternal grandparents, Tomasz Solowski and Olena Solowska; her mother, Natalia; and her aunt, Vira. In many ways, *Honey and Ashes* resembles a standard work of history. It is prefaced by maps of Eastern Europe, illustrating the changes that took place in Ukraine and Poland between 1936 and 1997, and the Solowski family tree. At its halfway-point, Kulyk Keefer interrupts her narrative with a collection of family photographs, complete with explanatory captions. And she concludes with a series of scholarly footnotes as well as a bibliography of the historical works she consulted while writing the book. But the narrative itself, as she suggests in "Personal and Public and Public Records: Story and History in the Narration of Ethnicity" (2000), follows a "tripartite" structure (7). The first two sections of *Honey and Ashes*, "The Old Place" and "Departures, Arrivals: Staromischyna—Toronto," are primarily devoted to family stories related to the Solowskis' experiences in Ukraine and in Canada. Tomasz, Kulyk Keefer explains, first came to Canada in 1927; his wife and daughters followed in 1936. Second-wave immigrants who settled in Toronto, Tomasz and Olena struggled during the depression trying to make ends meet while becoming accustomed to a new language and a new culture. Natalia and Vira, who were fourteen and twelve respectively when they immigrated, have vivid memories of the hardships they endured in Ukraine and in Canada, and Kulyk Keefer substantially draws on their memories and stories, as well as Olena's, in narrating the first two sections of *Honey and Ashes*.[4] In the third, relatively brief, section of the text, "Journeying Out," Kulyk Keefer turns to official historical records and scholarly works of Ukrainian and Ukrainian Canadian history in order to place her family's personal stories in the context of public history. She begins by outlining the ways in which the borders—and indeed the very name—of the Solowskis' home province have continually shifted over the years.[5] After providing an overview of the harsh conditions under which Ukrainian peasants lived for centuries, she devotes some attention to the tense sociopolitical climate in Ukraine and Poland around the time of her grandfather's first trip to Canada. In this part of the book, noting the historical conflicts and tensions between Ukrainians and Poles, as well as Ukrainians and Jews, Kulyk Keefer reflects on Ukrainians' historical roles as perpetrators as well as victims of violence and oppression. In the fourth section of *Honey and Ashes*, "Journeying Out," having explored her family's past through personal stories and public history, Kulyk Keefer offers a third and final perspective on this past. This final portion of the book focuses on her actual observations of, and experiences in, Staromischyna as she narrates her return, in 1997, to the village from which her family emigrated.

But while *Honey and Ashes* seems rather neatly organized around the three sources of information that Kulyk Keefer relies upon to piece together her family's history—her family members' memories and stories of their experiences in Canada and Ukraine; official, written records and historiographical works related to these experiences; and her first-hand experiences in Ukraine—the narrative structure of the text is neither as simple nor as straightforward as it seems. Although, at times, Kulyk Keefer attempts to focus on her family's stories about their day-to-day life in Staromischyna, she is unable to separate these stories from what she knows about the broader realities of Ukrainian and Polish history.[6] Nor can she document Ukrainian/Polish history without simultaneously considering the ways in which her family members were personally affected by, or involved in shaping, this history. So when, for example, in the portion of *Honey and Ashes* ostensibly focused on family stories, she writes about her grandmother's friendship with Helka, a Jewish woman who ran a store near Staromischyna, Kulyk Keefer finds herself half-doubting the friendship, given the "traditional hostility" between Ukrainians and Jews (79). Even if she believes the story of their friendship, she cannot write about it without also writing about the historical tensions between Olena's and Helka's people. Similarly, in the midst of her discussion of Ukrainian and Polish history, when she mentions the Polish-Ukrainian war that took place from 1918 to 1919, Kulyk Keefer begins speculating about her grandfather's actions during the war. She knows that Tomasz was a soldier in the Ukrainian Galician army; though half-Polish, he fought against the Poles. Did he also march into Kiev in July, 1919? Was he among the troops responsible for the massacre of "between 35,000 and 50,000 Jews" (177) believed to be Bolsheviks? Not surprisingly, *Honey and Ashes* is rife with these sorts of questions because, while she wants to know the truth about her family's history in the Old Place, she knows that memory is fallible, history is selective. Neither family stories nor official history can provide her with a full, objective account of what really happened in the past.

Conscious that "there's no such thing as a true story, just the echoes between different versions, and the desire to know" (62), she structures *Honey and Ashes* around precisely such "echoes." From beginning to end, as Kulyk Keefer suggests, the text is "interrupted and traversed by breaks and complications in both narrative method and the 'story line' itself," so that the structure of the book mirrors the complex and uneasy nature of her quest to uncover the "truth" about her family's past ("Personal and

Public" 8). And Kulyk Keefer explicitly states, moreover, she can never know the truth about her family's history. "I do not claim to know or tell The Truth about my family," she says in her prologue, "what I am doing is sieving memory and retelling stories that make memory material, and public. The difference between what I was told and what I heard; what memory hides and what imagination discloses—all this is part of the book I have written" (*Honey and Ashes* 5).

Interestingly, Kulyk Keefer's approach to collecting fragments of stories, reordering them, and filling in the gaps between them results in a highly romanticized family history. In describing her grandmother's family, for instance, she depicts her grandmother as the heroine of a fairy tale—although she is treated like Cinderella by her miserly stepfather, cruel sister, and heartless mother, Olena never loses her Snow White-like "goodness" and "largeness of heart" (35). Fairy tale romance, moreover, forms the foundation of Olena's and Tomasz's marriage—as Kulyk Keefer sees it, at least. Despite their parents' opposition to a union based on love rather than on land, Olena and Tomasz married for love. "It's love she married for, not bread," says Kulyk Keefer of her grandmother, in a passage near the beginning of the book. "[W]hat I'm about to tell you is a love story from a world where bread is hard and sour, honey rare as amber" (30). Of course, as the title of the text suggests, *Honey and Ashes* is characterized as much by tragedy and loss as it is by romance and love. Kulyk Keefer writes about the children her grandparents lost early in their marriage, and about Olena's unnamed sister who, at the age of fifteen, chose death over the amputation of an injured and infected leg. Haunted by dark secrets and tantalizing mysteries related to the Solowskis's family members and friends who never left Ukraine, the overall tenor of the text is one of high drama and intense romance. What became of Helka, Olena's Jewish friend? What happened to Volodko and Adela, Tomasz's half-brother and half-sister, and Hannia, Tomasz's sister? As Kulyk Keefer narrates her trip to Ukraine in search of answers to these and other questions, she places herself in the centre of a theatrical story that she deliberately constructs as such.

Kulyk Keefer's romanticization of her family's history may well be a choice she makes because her experiences in Ukraine are marked by disappointment. The actual village of Staromischyna is nothing like the Old Place of her family's stories, and the relatives she meets in and around

Staromischyna are neither as warm nor as welcoming as she had hoped. Although, before going to Ukraine, she tells herself that six decades of social change and political and economic upheaval will have dramatically altered the landscape her family left behind, Kulyk Keefer is nonetheless shocked by present-day Staromischyna. She and her husband prepare well for the physical difficulties of travelling in Eastern Europe—they secure the appropriate travel documents, buy a car sufficiently modest and second-hand to take into Eastern Europe without fear of theft, and carry with them a host of household and personal items unavailable in Poland or, especially, Ukraine. They fully expect delays at border crossings, poor roads, low standard hotel rooms, and heavy pollution. But nothing, it seems, could have prepared Kulyk Keefer for the differences between her family's stories about their homeland and the realities of contemporary life in Ukraine. As she scours the landscape around Staromischyna for traces of her family's lives, seeking the lush orchards and quaint thatched houses she has heard about from her mother and aunt, she finds only potato fields and homes "roofed with corrugated iron...all of them built after the war" (245). The "outdoor cafés, where people sit at white plastic tables," and the "parks with statues of Shevchenko"—none of these, she says, "could have existed in [her] mother's time" (245). Where, Kulyk Keefer wonders, are the schoolhouse, marketplace, and store that she knows from her mother's stories? When, at last, she locates a building from her mother's childhood—the gloriously modern new schoolhouse that her mother described—Kulyk Keefer is dismayed by its appearance. "The school's tin roof looks rusted through; great pieces of stucco have peeled from the walls, leaving turquoise scars" (276). Unsurprisingly, perhaps, Kulyk Keefer finds what she is looking for in the L'viv ethnographic museum: "a small house with whitewashed walls, its thatch crowned with a row of crossed sticks...my grandmother's house, the very room where my mother was born. What I've always longed for" (255). Walking barefoot around the museum, she proclaims—with self-conscious irony—that she is at last "in the Old Place" (256), acknowledging that the idealized Old Place of her family's stories and her own imagining no longer exists, if indeed it ever really did.

But just as Kulyk Keefer is disappointed by what she finds in Staromischyna, so too is she frustrated by her inability to communicate and establish relationships with her relatives in Ukraine. In

Staromischyna, for example, she meets Evhen Pokotylo, the son of her grandfather's stepbrother, who greets her with thinly-veiled hostility. "[H]is thoughts," says Kulyk Keefer, "are as clear as if he'd spoken them: 'These people who breeze into the village, showing off their good fortune like too many rings on their fingers—what do they want out of me?'" (281). Evhen, naturally enough, is unable to see her as she sees herself—a "native of this place" (257)—for she cannot speak Ukrainian and has never lived in Ukraine. She believes that she is an "envoy" for her mother and aunt, her "absent sons," and her "dead grandparents" (244), but Evhen knows the truth—she is a tourist; she doesn't belong. In a sense, the inequalities between Kulyk Keefer and Evhen are not simply defined by her relative economic prosperity as a Canadian and his relative poverty as a Ukrainian. True, she has the luxury of travelling to Ukraine in a car that she and her husband bought specifically for the trip and Evhen's modest home lacks the most basic amenities, such as indoor plumbing. As a result, Evhen, to be sure, envies Kulyk Keefer's wealth. She, however, envies his first-hand knowledge of family history. That he reluctantly answers her questions about family members, providing few of the details she craves, and that she awkwardly offers him a gift of money before parting, which will make little impact on his circumstances, underscores their inability to connect on equal terms. In Skarszewy, Kulyk Keefer is more warmly welcomed by Adela Wolanik, her grandfather's half-sister, and Adela's children, but similar tensions characterize their time together. Adela and Kulyk Keefer struggle to communicate because they are separated by language. Adela's son translates Adela's words into German for Kulyk Keefer who understands them imperfectly. And, as with Evhen, Kulyk Keefer's relative wealth creates an awkward dynamic. Because Adela has no space in her home for guests, Kulyk Keefer and her husband stay in a hotel room that is opulent by Ukrainian standards, wondering if they should offer it to Adela. Although Kulyk Keefer wants Adela to talk about what happened to Helka, Hannia, Hannia's sons, and Volodko, her questions "go badly" (314), for Adela is not a storyteller and, more importantly, she is reluctant to relive the horrors that she has experienced.

In narrating her encounters with both Evhen and Adela, however—and even as she understands that they see her as a wealthy foreigner, breezing in and out of their lives, "showing off" her "good fortune" (281)—Kulyk Keefer sees herself as wronged by history. While she feels guilty about her relative privilege as a Canadian, and while she is sympathetic toward her Ukrainian relatives' plight, she nonetheless constructs herself as a victim of historical circumstance. Near the conclusion to *Honey and Ashes*, she becomes a figure in another fairy-tale-like story: a princess with peasant roots who is unjustly misunderstood by those who should see past her outward trappings of superiority and recognize her as a kindred spirit with an open heart. She wants to hear stories, but her family members refuse to share them. History, for her relatives in Ukraine, is real, heart-wrenchingly personal, and viscerally painful; being denied access to that history, for Kulyk Keefer, is no less agonizing.[7] Forced to leave both Staromischyna and Skarszewy earlier than she planned, she becomes frustrated by "[a]ll that [she] didn't ask, all that [she] couldn't say" (324), and when she arrives home, she wonders if she has found what she was looking for in the Old Place.

On the one hand, the suggestion of this book seems to be that, even after travelling to Staromischyna, Kulyk Keefer is no closer to uncovering "The Truth" about her family history. In fact, her failure to learn "The Truth" about one family member, in particular—Volodko, whose mysterious past particularly fascinates her—becomes emblematic of her failure to fully reconstruct her family history by reconnecting with family members in Ukraine. Volodko, Tomasz's half-brother, is a recurring figure in *Honey and Ashes* who haunts the text with his simultaneous presence and absence. "Of all the family left behind in the Old Place," Kulyk Keefer explains, early in the text, "he was the most mysterious, the most seductive" (26). An "artist of sorts," Volodko made furniture in Staromischyna, including the miniature cupboard that Kulyk Keefer's grandmother brought with her from Ukraine to Canada. Both the cupboard and its maker carry a great deal of symbolic weight throughout *Honey and Ashes*. Kulyk Keefer describes the cupboard—one of Olena's few keepsakes from Ukraine—as "the seed for the dining room suite that furnished the happy ending of her fairy tale." It "[h]olds the memory of everything [Olena had] had to leave behind" (26); and passed on, over time, like family stories, from Olena to Natalia to Kulyk Keefer, it comes to stand in for Kulyk Keefer's ethnic inheritance. At the same time, the vertical lines that divide the mirror on the cupboard symbolize Kulyk Keefer's split identity. When she gazes into the mirror, she sees a fractured reflection of her self. The lines "seem to divide [her] reflection, making it shift and blur, as if it were crossing border after border" (327).[8]

What, she wonders, is the story behind the cupboard? How did Olena come to own it? What became of its maker? Although she meets individuals in Ukraine who have information about Volodko, Kulyk Keefer is unable to solve the mystery of Volodko's past. From a woman named Varvara who she meets in Staromischyna, Kulyk Keefer learns that Volodko was killed "by the Fascists—or the Soviets—at the start of the war" (277); Evhen says that Volodko, taken by the Red Army in 1944, died sometime later in an unspecified gulag (283); and Adela, hinting at Volodko's anti-Semitism, suggests that he was captured in 1944 by the Russians, though she gives no specific reason for his arrest (319). After hearing these conflicting stories, Kulyk Keefer continues to wonder about what really happened to Volodko. His cupboard, the only physical trace left of him, becomes a tangible reminder of the ways in which individuals and "The Truth" about them fall through the cracks of history, both personal and public.

Yet Volodko's story simultaneously reveals Kulyk Keefer's refusal to construct her search for "The Truth" about her family's past as a failed quest. Near the end of the text, writing once more about the mysterious man, Kulyk Keefer discloses a secret that she has been "carrying with [her] like a jewel sewn up in the hem of a coat," a secret contained in a story that her mother, Natalka, told her long ago about Olena (321). Volodko and Olena were lovers, while Olena's husband was away in Canada and before he sent for his wife and daughters. Why does Kulyk Keefer choose to share this story at the end of *Honey and Ashes*, rather than at the beginning? Why does she withhold this information—this secret that was told to her long before she set out to explore her family's history—until the final pages of the text? As deliberate as it is strategic, Kulyk Keefer's decision to conclude *Honey and Ashes* with Olena's and Volodko's love story implicitly illustrates her desire to provide not only an ending but a happy ending to the text. True or not—and Kulyk Keefer suspects that it is true—this story suggests that, despite her apparent inability to arrive at any definite conclusions about her family history, the author wants to leave her readers with a sense of resolution and closure— as though she *has*, after all, succeeded in understanding the past.

But Kulyk Keefer's belated disclosure of her grandmother's secret is not the only narrative strategy she uses to tidy the loose ends of her narrative. At the outset of *Honey and Ashes*, Kulyk Keefer sets a task for herself: to "build a bridge out of words" between the past and the present, Canada and Ukraine (8). Yet, as she insists again and again throughout this text (as in *The Green Library*), a figurative bridge of blood already exists between herself and her family's history. This imagined bridge is made visible and real in the "genetic repetitions" that give Kulyk Keefer her grandmother's "near-sighted eyes" and her grandfather's "height and temperament" (15): "I have them in my bones," she says of her grandparents (47). Family, she argues, is what "we carry...inside our very cells" (15); history is a "burden you carry in your bones" (300).

Not surprisingly, rivers—at once real and figurative—become recurrent motifs in *Honey and Ashes*. Staromischyna lies on the river Zbruch; Kulyk Keefer's home in Ontario is located near a river. And these literal rivers become constant reminders of the figurative "river of the past" (4) that flows in her veins. Indeed, as she leaves Eastern Europe, driving toward Szczecin in western Poland, and as she witnesses floods in the region, Kulyk Keefer draws an implicit parallel between the swollen rivers and her family bloodlines—in both she sees the "[p]ast and present awash," with "nothing to stand between them and the future" (325). Just as Kulyk Keefer has long carried the secret of Volodko and Olena, so too has she always maintained the belief that the past is in her blood. So *Honey and Ashes*, though explicitly concerned with Kulyk Keefer's inability to uncover "The Truth" about her family's history, implicitly reaffirms "The Truths" she has always known.

From the outset of *Honey and Ashes*, moreover, Kulyk Keefer takes for granted that, however bewildering and fraught she may discover her family's past to be, it will have no material bearing on her in the present. Her literal and figurative journeys "back" to Ukraine may be disorienting and painful, but she knows, long before she departs, that she will return, and that her life in Canada will continue, unchanged. In the epilogue, Kulyk Keefer says "what [she] really want[s] is...to be at home" (328). She regrets, though, that—unlike individuals such as Sofia, her tour guide in Ukraine, who "know, infallibly, where home is" (327)—she has no clear sense of where she belongs. And so she concludes that "[p]erhaps home is only this: inhabiting uncertainty, the arguments desire picks with fear. Not belonging, but longing—that we may live in the present, without craving the past or forcing the future" (328). But does Kulyk Keefer not know—and has she not always known, "infallibly"—where her own home is? While she wants to believe, and wants her readers to believe, that her understanding of home is marked by "uncertainty" and "longing," her attempts at complicating notions of home are undermined precisely because, in the final pages of *Honey and Ashes*, she comes full circle back to the place at which she began: to her comfortable, middle-class home in Canada; to the river that runs outside the window of her study, a quaint reminder of the stories that have always run in her blood.

Readers are left to wonder, in the end, what a different text *Honey and Ashes* would be if it had concluded differently—if, that is, Kulyk Keefer had decided not to narrate the text self-consciously from her "stone house by a river" in Ontario (328); if she had instead dramatized her ambivalence vis-à-vis Canada and Ukraine, belonging to both and neither, by scripting a conclusion that takes place in Ukraine or perhaps in the air, literally suspended between both worlds. Not unlike Olena's and Volodko's love story, the details of which she knew before she set out on her quest, the symmetry of her return to the place at which her quest began illustrates that Kulyk Keefer has always known how her story would end. In other words, the "uncertainty" she ostensibly feels about home is undercut by a firm conclusion that ultimately tells a different story. Harkening back to the final scene in George Ryga's *A Letter to My Son*, in which the main character of the play feels like "a dying man who has closed the big book on his life" (117), *Honey and Ashes* enacts another form of closure that runs the risk of shutting down dialogue about the ways in which ethnicity might be re-imagined by future generations of Ukrainian Canadians. And, as with both *A Letter to My Son* and Maara Haas's *The Street Where I Live*, it is not only the theme but also the form of Kulyk Keefer's text that prevents her from exploring new strategies for reconciling her ethnic and national identity. In the process of documenting her genealogical ties to Ukraine in the form of non-fiction—an enterprise she explicitly undertakes for her sons who, she assumes, will not engage in their own literal or figurative journeys "back" to Ukraine—she implicitly constructs *Honey and Ashes* as the final, definitive chapter in the story of her family's connection to the Old Country. Insofar as the "big book" that she writes leaves no room for imaginative "re-visions" of the ethnic minority experience, it offers troubling commentary on the future of Ukrainians in Canada.

TEN

Between Borders, Beyond Bloodlines
Myrna Kostash's Creative Non-fiction

Bloodlines: A Journey Into Eastern Europe

THE TEMPTATION IS STRONG, I think—certainly at first glance—to draw parallels between Janice Kulyk Keefer and Myrna Kostash. Between the writers, that is, as well as their writing. Both Ukrainian Canadian women, relatively close in age,[1] Kulyk Keefer and Kostash have enjoyed long and successful careers as writers and, in the 1990s, each published two books about her travels to and within Eastern Europe.[2] Broadly speaking, in their thinking about ethnicity, neither writer accepts that officially-sanctioned, folkloric expressions of Ukrainian Canadian culture accurately or authentically reflect the complex nature of their ethnic identity. They focus their writing on re-placing Ukrainian Canadian ethnicity in the context of Ukrainian and Ukrainian Canadian history. In order to understand more fully the meaning of their ethnicity, they explore and document the intersections between personal and public history, acknowledging both the positive and negative aspects of their ethnic group's past.

But, looking closely at their texts, substantial differences emerge between Kulyk Keefer's and Kostash's perspectives on, as well as their specific approaches to writing about, Ukrainian Canadian ethnicity and history. In *The Green Library* and *Honey and Ashes*, Kulyk Keefer draws attention to the inherent gaps between history and historiography—between, that is, historical realities and representations of these realities—and she seeks to complicate her understanding of home by drawing attention to the tensions between her real and imagined sense of belonging to two countries. Implicitly, however, as Kulyk Keefer closes the gaps and resolves the tensions in both texts, she undermines her own attempts to challenge conventional understandings of history and identity. A second-generation Ukrainian Canadian whose mother was a second-wave immigrant from Ukraine—and who is herself, crucially, the mother of two sons—Kulyk Keefer takes for granted her genealogical ties to her family's past and to their ethnic homeland. Her writing affirms the assumption that bloodlines define ethnic identity and that they constitute definitive links to Ukraine and Ukrainian history. Writing from the comfort of her middle-class Canadian home, she has the best of both worlds—the right to claim Ukraine as her imagined homeland without giving up her actual home in Canada. For Kostash, by contrast, who is less concerned with family stories and genealogies, the process of traveling to Eastern Europe and writing about her journeys is bound up with her desire to redefine her identity and sense of community by exploring allegiances that transcend family bloodlines and national borders.

In part autobiography, in part history, *Bloodlines* is, first and foremost, an account of Kostash's travels to and within Eastern Europe during the 1980s and 1990s. Over the course of nine years, beginning in 1982 with her initial travels to Rumania, Hungary, and Yugoslavia, Kostash made no less than six separate trips to Eastern Europe. In 1984, two years after traveling for the first time to Bucharest, Budapest, and Belgrade, she visited Ukraine, Poland, and Czechoslovakia, and she revisited Yugoslavia—Croatia, more specifically, Bosnia, and Serbia. In 1986, she made her third trip to Yugoslavia, and in 1987, she returned to Poland, Czechoslovakia, and Yugoslavia—this time to Slovenia and Serbia. In 1988, she went again to Poland, Czechoslovakia, Yugoslavia—including Kosovo and Macedonia—and Ukraine. Finally, in 1991, she returned once more to Serbia and Ukraine.

As Kostash explains in the introduction to *Bloodlines*, she "did not travel haphazardly" (1). Her plan, at least initially, was to "interview writers of [her] generation, bred by the events of the 1960s, who were writing from within the opposition in their respective societies" (1). In her own words, "I was most interested in how they coped, as creative people, with the *political* demands of their situation" (1). At the same time, she admits to limiting her travels to "Slavic Central and Eastern Europe (excluding, therefore, Rumania, Hungary and Bulgaria)" (1) because her project was also "in some still unformulated way" shaped by her sense of "solidarity," as a Ukrainian Canadian, not only with Ukrainians, specifically, but with Slavs, more generally (1-2). And she notes, too, that her "third traveller's hat was that of the New Leftist socialist" (2). After struggling to come to terms with "the nature of the Soviet Union" by reading books and speaking casually with dissident exiles, she was eager to see for herself "how 'actually existing socialism' looked" and "how this might affect [her] own political beliefs" (2). Conscious that her plans and motivations might sound relatively "neat and tidy," Kostash underscores the fact that her actual experiences traveling in Eastern Europe were "turbulent" and "very upsetting" (2). "I lost control of my plan," she confesses, "as I met more and more people who took me further and further afield in my inquiries," and as, moreover, "I realized that much of the solidarity I felt with them—political, generational and ethnic—was illusory, or at least ambiguous" (2). Reflecting on the research she conducted into the history and politics of Eastern Europe before setting out, and on her first-hand experiences of Eastern Europe, she says, "[m]y travels and my reading threw into question all the assumptions I had leaned on, on the basis of my limited awareness in Canada, to interpret events in Eastern and Central Europe" (2). Fittingly, Kostash summarizes the reasons for which she chose to travel to Eastern Europe and to write about her experiences there with a question rather than a "neat and tidy" assertion. "Take a second-generation Ukrainian Canadian," she writes, "a feminist, a writer, an alumna of the 1960s, and put her on a train in Belgrade heading north. What exactly is her business?" (2)

Certainly Kostash's "business" in writing *Bloodlines* is to make sense, retrospectively, of her travels, and the form of the text reflects her desire to create order and meaning out of her "turbulent" experiences in Eastern Europe. Not unlike *Honey and Ashes*, *Bloodlines* is prefaced by a map of Eastern Europe, and, in an appendix to the text, Kostash provides an extensively annotated bibliography of works related to the history and politics of Eastern Europe—books that she read before, during, and after her trips—adding scholarly credibility to her project. Less a linear or chronological account of her travels than a collage of narrative snapshots, *Bloodlines* is not without structure. The book is divided into four chapters, each centred on a single country to which she made repeat visits—Czechoslovakia,[3] Yugoslavia, Poland, and Ukraine; and these chapters are further broken down into distinct sections similar to diary entries with date, place, and subject headings that focus on specific individuals Kostash met or events she witnessed. But despite its semblance of order, the narrative structure of *Bloodlines* in many ways mirrors Kostash's loss of "control" over her plans while traveling in Eastern Europe. While she introduces her chapters with brief outlines of historical events related to the specific countries to which she traveled, these ostensibly objective "facts" immediately give way to her subjective interpretations of them which are then frequently undercut by her first-hand encounters with people who live in Eastern Europe—and whose perspectives are often very different from her own.

In part, the turbulent nature of Kostash's narrative reflects the tensions that she perceives between history—what actually happened in the past—and historiography—what is selectively and subjectively recorded in history books. At the same time, insofar as *Bloodlines*, narrated in the perpetual present tense, is characterized by uncertainty and instability, the text implicitly illustrates her desire—and simultaneous inability—to become a part of the present and the future of the communities she visits. From the outset of her travels, Kostash is unable to maintain the detachment and journalistic objectivity of an "outsider" because of her strong sense of belonging to, and solidarity with, multiple communities in Eastern Europe. If a single story emerges from the multiple narratives that Kostash includes in *Bloodlines*, it is the story of her repeated attempts to make real her imagined sense of belonging to this part of the world. Though constantly reminded of the distances, both cultural and geographical, that separate her from the people she meets, as well as their politics and their histories, she refuses to give up on her quest to connect with them and, in so doing, to redefine her sense of self and community. That *Bloodlines* ends without a clear sense that she has succeeded in her quest—but, rather, with a gesture toward a future in which she will do so—is fitting, for this is a text shaped, from beginning to end, by Kostash's self-conscious optimism about the ways in which cross-cultural communities are formed.

Throughout her travels, then, Kostash's objective is to seek out kindred spirits in Eastern Europe—writers, intellectuals, and political activists who share her interests and ideals. Her agenda, however, is routinely disrupted by encounters with individuals who should but do not see eye to eye with her—individuals, that is, who challenge, rather than affirm, her personal and political beliefs. In Czechoslovakia, for example—in Prague, more specifically, 1984—she meets with Jiri, a Jew whose "generation had hit the streets" (19) of Prague during the spring and summer of 1968 in support of Alexander Dubcek's "experiments with socialist pluralism" (5). Wearing her "New Leftist socialist" traveller's hat (2), and thinking back to her own involvement during the 1960s in student protests against the war in Vietnam, Kostash announces her solidarity with Jiri and his generation. "There was a time," she says, "when I considered myself to be a citizen of Prague, in the spring of 1968" (17). Though Jiri scoffs at her statement, calling it "an illusion" (17), Kostash persists in drawing parallels between their experiences in Czechoslovakia and Canada. "We thought *you* were magnificent," she says. "You took on Stalinism, we took on Yankee terror" (19). But, again, Jiri's response is cool: "if you'll pardon me," he says, "what exactly did you have to protest about?" (19). In pointing out the inherent contradiction in Kostash's politics—her tacit support for the communists in Vietnam and her simultaneous support for the anti-communist movement in Czechoslovakia—Jiri deflates Kostash's hopes of building a cross-cultural bridge between her and him. When Kostash attempts to explain herself— when she insists that members of the New Left in Canada were critical of "Marxism-Leninism" but open to "socialism with a human face" (19)— Jiri counters once more with thinly-veiled hostility: "[y]ou want socialism? Look around" (19). Though Kostash tries to defend her position— "[n]o," she says, "[n]ot *that* kind of socialism"—the sarcasm in his voice is unmistakable as he has the final word: "[w]e call this the real one" (19).

Everywhere she travels in Eastern Europe, Kostash wears the hat of the political idealist and, wherever she goes, her political naiveté is called into question. In Belgrade, 1991, as in Czechoslovakia, her pro-socialist/anti-capitalist ideals come under fire again, albeit indirectly this time, from her friend Sonja. A Serbian sociologist and peace activist, Sonja has long supported democratic socialism; frustrated, however, by the "nightmare of murderous nationalisms" (108) surfacing within Yugoslavia, she decides that capitalism is the only answer to her country's problems. Capitalism, she argues, produces the idea of the "inherent dignity of the individual citizen" without which "it is very difficult for [the individual] to emerge from the tribe" (108). Kostash, in this encounter, is encouraged to see that, from the perspective of those who have lived under oppressive communist rule, capitalism's emphasis on individual freedom is attractive in the extreme.

Yet, even as her beliefs are routinely called into question, and even as she gradually becomes aware of her naiveté, Kostash has a difficult time accepting that her understanding of Eastern European politics and history is idealistic. Jiri may have the last word in their conversation but Kostash has the last word in her account of it. "[L]ooking back to 1968," after talking with Jiri, she refuses to "see the ghosts of the victims of power": she sees, instead, the ghosts of "our own youth" (19). Despite Jiri's insistence on the acute differences between North American and Czech protest movements during the late 1960s, Kostash still draws parallels between the two. In her view, the young people of her and Jiri's generation, in both North America and Czechoslovakia, bid farewell to their adolescence as they came of age as politically-savvy adults. Similarly unwilling to wholeheartedly accept Sonja's rejection of socialism, Kostash concludes her chapter on Yugoslavia by questioning her friend's embrace of capitalism. According to Kostash, and here again she has the final word, the benefits of capitalism are "difficult to see, amid the blood" (108).

Kostash's struggles to find a common ground with the people she meets are most apparent in her observations that some of the political movements she supports as a socialist are decidedly patriarchal in structure and, hence, offend her feminist sensibilities. In Poland, for example, Kostash sympathizes with the free trade movement led by Lech Walesa because Solidarity stands in opposition to the economically and politically repressive, pro-communist Polish United Workers' Party. When she discovers, however, that Solidarity also stands in opposition to women's rights—their right to abortion, for example—Kostash faces a dilemma. In Canada, her New Leftist and feminist political activism has always gone hand-in-hand; her political coming-of-age in the 1960s involved simultaneously embracing both. Women in Eastern Europe, by contrast—even women who are active in opposition movements against repressive governmental power structures—have a difficult time pushing gender issues to the forefront of their political agendas. As Julia—one of the "rare" women activists within Freedom and Peace, a pro-democracy organization in Poland—explains to Kostash, women most often participate in Polish politics by "applauding their darling boyfriends and offering to make coffee and sandwiches" (149). Indeed, Kostash notices that Julia herself is little more than a glorified secretary: "is there no Polish male capable of doing his own typing?" she wonders (149). Faced with overwhelming evidence of the pervasive sexism in Poland—the roots of which can be found in the male-dominated structure of the Catholic church[4]— Kostash is troubled by the ways in which women, and especially feminist women, are viewed by men in Poland. In Warsaw, 1987, for example, she meets Teresa, a self-avowed feminist who has been married for fifteen years and whose husband used to see their marriage as a relationship defined by "absolute equality" (133). Now, "feeling the pressure of the social and economic crisis," Teresa's husband "renounces such egalitarian notions of marriage and demands that his wife be at home to cook his suppers, wash his socks, [and] stroke his poor, embattled head" (133). He sees his wife's "feminist buddies" as "frigid," "disappointed," and "unattractive"; "no longer really women," according to him, they are "deeply unhappy in their repression of a woman's real desires (marriage, motherhood)" (133). Talking with a small group of Teresa's friends and fellow feminists, Kostash learns that women in Poland have three "female destinies" to choose from: "the devoted wife and mother, selfless and speechless in the family"; "the nun, likewise effaced in the church"; and the "streetwalker" who spends her time "near the socialist train stations, fucking for vodka" (134).

But while Kostash assumes that gender issues represent a promising point of connection between her and the women she meets in Eastern Europe, many of these women refuse to align themselves with Kostash and her "western" ideas about gender roles. Marketa, a member of the anti-communist "Charter 77" organization in Czechoslovakia, eschews the "women's movement in the West," along with "its ideas concerning the patriarchal family and the struggle of women for equality in the workplace" (39). Having endured years of police surveillance and interrogation as a result of her involvement in "Charter 77," Marketa craves the simple, "humanizing" pleasures of home and family (38–39). "I've never understood women in the West," she says, "why you would choose a dull and stuffy office job doing stupid work all day when you could be at home with your children!" (39). Even Julia, the outspoken Warsaw feminist, is "fed up to here with kowtowing to western feminists who have big houses and refrigerators stuffed with meat, and who dash about in their cute Japanese cars, bringing enlightenment to their oppressed Polish sisters": "[w]hat the hell do *they* know about oppression?" (150). Expected to "play the role of the jackbooted feminist from the West" (149), and simultaneously criticized for doing so, Kostash finds herself in a no-win situation. How is she to reconcile her "western" feminist ideals—and her relatively privileged "western" lifestyle—with the day-to-day material realities of the women she comes to know in Eastern Europe? Firm in her assumption that women everywhere share the same goals and desires—the ability to choose a career over marriage and motherhood—Kostash is bewildered by, and alienated from, the women she meets who embrace traditional gender roles.

Kostash becomes most vulnerable to criticism, however, when she interacts with intellectuals and writers in Eastern Europe. That she holds a special place in her heart for her colleagues from Eastern Europe is obvious from the outset of the text, as she lays out her mission to "interview writers of [her] generation" (1). Because her own writing is politically motivated, and because she tends to conflate the roles of the writer and the political dissident, she believes that she has much in common with writers and intellectuals in this part of the world. At the very least—even if they differ in the specific issues they address in their writing—she assumes that they share similar philosophical perspectives on the relation between politics and art. Again, however, Kostash's intellectual ideals and political beliefs are challenged as she comes face to face with writers who refuse to use their writing as either a platform for political commentary or a vehicle for social change. In Belgrade, 1988, for example, Kostash meets David, a short fiction writer who criticizes her tendency to valorize the figure of the writer as political dissident. Conscious of the ways in which people from "the West" require East European writers to be "persecuted and disreputable" (98), David knows that he fails to live up to the stereotype of the dissident writer. He is "not disreputable. He's boring. He says so. Writing stories about family life and private conscience and domestic memory. Trying to find a place as a 'Yugoslav' writer—not as a persecuted Jew, not as an insulted Serb, not as a dissident" (98). Not unlike Marketa in Czechoslovakia, David wants to experience ordinary human life, free from the burden of history and politics. Disgusted by the "spurious, self-appointed vocation of the writer as the people's voice on issues of public import," he believes that "the only free territory for poetry is to be found in poetic creativity itself" (99).⁵

David, importantly, is not the first writer who challenges Kostash's thinking about the relation between politics and writing. In Warsaw, 1984, four years before meeting David, she talks with Ryszard who is similarly critical of her assumptions about the role of the writer in society. "How could a writer in our times," Kostash asks Ryszard, "refuse the subjects provided by violent social change? What a gift!" (123). But violent social change is, for Ryszard, no gift. Like David, he too dreams of living in an "ordinary" country; the realities of the country in which he lives are both a "burden" and a "curse" (122–23). According to Ryszard, writers in Eastern Europe have three options available to them: they can choose "speechlessness" within their totalitarian states in order to protect themselves from persecution; they can find "refuge" in "art for art's sake," also protecting themselves from persecution; or they can "go underground," putting their writing "in the service of the revolution," albeit clandestinely (124).⁶ Unlike David, who clearly chooses the second option, seeking "refuge" in the apolitical act of writing "the perfect sentence" (124), Ryszard "has made none of these 'pure' choices"—he opts instead to live and work "in the interstices between them" (124). Sympathetic toward those writers who choose "art for art's sake," and skeptical of the notion that his political writing deserves "special credit" for its ostensibly revolutionary content—he suggests that "sympathizers from the West make too much of such modest gestures" (125)—Ryszard only sometimes, and even then reluctantly, plays the role of the dissident writer. Working as an editor at an "uncontroversial literary magazine that specializes in translations from world literature" (124), he wants what Kostash has— the luxury of living in a part of the world where writers are not "socially necessary" (126). And this troubles Kostash precisely because, in her words, "I *want* to be necessary" (126). Although she is not unconscious of her tendency to romanticize the realities of "violent social change" (123), she nonetheless struggles to see the "ordinariness" of her life in Canada as desirable. The "brouhaha of History" upon which Ryszard "gags" is what she has always wanted to experience and write about (127).⁷

Though flippant in her reference to the "brouhaha of History" (127), and though sometimes guilty of seeing the historical as well as the contemporary realities of life in Eastern Europe as romantic, Kostash does confront the complex and uneasy nature of these realities—not only from her point of view as a New Leftist socialist, a feminist, and a writer but also, and always, from her perspective as a Ukrainian Canadian. Indeed, while she devotes only one chapter of *Bloodlines* to Ukraine, her relation to Ukraine and Ukrainian history is a central concern throughout the text. Over the course of her travels—even when she is in other countries, and even when she seems to focus on issues or events that are not directly related to her ethnicity—Kostash finds herself unable, and at times unwilling, to ignore the ways in which her ethnicity shapes her observations of, and experiences in, Eastern Europe. Long before she reaches Ukraine in her narrative, she is forced to grapple with the ambivalent nature of her ethnic inheritance. On the one hand, her ethnic identity forms the basis for her broad sense of identification with the people of Eastern Europe—with Ukrainians, specifically, but also with Slavs, more generally. At the same time, her ethnicity simultaneously, and ironically, complicates her attempts at establishing relationships with many of the people she meets. Simply put, her ties to Ukraine—however distant they may be—implicate her in enduring conflicts and tensions between Ukrainians and other ethnic groups in Eastern Europe.

At times eager to claim Ukrainian history as her own, at times distressed by her inability to separate herself from this history, Kostash discovers that her ethnicity is at once a gift and a curse. To be Ukrainian, she acknowledges, is to confront both the positive and negative aspects of her ethnic group's past, but the business of coming to terms with how this past actually lives on into the present is no easy task. In Prague, for example, 1987, Kostash befriends Zdenek, a literary scholar and a member of "Charter 77" whose professional and political interests coincide with her own. Their friendship becomes strained, however, when Zdenek points out several troubling facts about her people's historical relations with his. As a child, Zdenek explains, he and his family used to holiday in Uzhhorod, "[c]ool and bucolic on the western slopes of the Carpathians" (30). Now part of Ukraine, Uzhhorod is "lost" to him; it was taken over by the same people who were recruited by the Nazis to decimate villages in Slovakia (30). That Kostash has never been to Uzhhorod—that she has no connection to this part of Ukraine and, in fact, cannot get there, even after enlisting the help of a travel agent in Edmonton—matters little: she is, in Zdenek's mind, linked to the place and hence to Ukraine's aggression toward Czechoslovakia.

And if Kostash is unable to escape history during her conversations with Zdenek in Czechoslovakia, she is no more able to ignore history in her encounters with writers and political activists in Poland—though in Poland she is the one who, like Zdenek, cannot separate the Poles she meets from their people's long history of conflict with Ukrainians. Indeed, Kostash's feelings about Poland—Polish people and Polish history—are overwhelmingly mixed because, while she sympathizes with Poland's struggle for democracy, she cannot forget that, for centuries, Poles systematically oppressed Ukrainians. In 1984, for example, after visiting a Ukrainian family living in Przemysl—a Polish village that was once part of Galicia in Ukraine—Kostash recalls the Polish government's "Pacificacija" campaign: "in the fall of 1930," she writes, "armed units of the Polish Army and the police terrorized some eight hundred Ukrainian villages in Polish-held Galicia," destroying "community halls and reading rooms, putting books and newspapers to the torch, confiscating property and arresting more than two thousand 'nationalist' troublemakers" (121). Unprepared for "how witheringly the Poles hate the Ukrainians in their midst," Kostash learns that Ukrainians throughout southeast Poland have never recovered from Pacificacija (140). They have been "sentenced to endure the loss of public memory," she says. "Nothing that belongs to public discourse as a whole—monuments, names, liturgies, nomenclature—refers to them or their view of things" (140). How is she to reconcile her pro-Polish and pro-Ukrainian sentiments when the Polish "freedom fighters" she admires are descended from the "landlords and rapists" who oppressed her people—and, when, moreover, the historical oppressor/oppressed relation between Poles and Ukrainians still, to some extent, exists (143)?

Constructed within *Bloodlines* as her final destination, Ukraine becomes the climax of Kostash's narrative, the most crucial stop in her narrative journey because, after a long series of failures and disappointments, it represents her last—and arguably best—chance to consolidate her sense of belonging to Eastern Europe. In a sense, her writing about Czechoslovakia, Yugoslavia, and Poland serves as narrative build-up to the final portion of the text in which she at last addresses her most personal reasons for traveling to Eastern Europe. Writing about her experiences in Ukraine, Kostash returns to the series of questions she asked in her introduction to *Bloodlines*: "[h]ow does the 'old country' live on in the citizen of the new?"; "[h]ow may I understand these people and their extraordinary history—my blood relations, as it were, from whom I was separated by the accident of being born into the new family line in Canada?"; and "[w]hat is the source of my feelings—feelings I didn't even know I had—about their history, their landscape, their languages, their sites of collective memory?" (2). To be sure, Kostash's personal motivations for traveling to Ukraine—her desire, as a Ukrainian Canadian, to explore her ethnic or familial ties to the country—are also political; and her political and professional interests in Eastern Europe are personal. But Ukraine becomes the context in which Kostash is most sharply attuned to the intersection between the personal and political. "Quite simply," as she explains, "for a Ukrainian Canadian Ukraine is not a country like other countries. Everything about it is 'loaded,' freighted with meaning" (168).

Paradoxically, while Kostash is most familiar with, and most emotionally attached to, the culture and history of Ukraine, this country represents the most unfamiliar, disorienting stop in all her journeys. As she discovers over the course of her travels to Czechoslovakia, Poland, and Yugoslavia, the dividing line between "Eastern" and "Western" Europe is difficult to define: in these countries, "East" and "West" collide, collapsing the binary opposition between the two. Despite falling under Soviet-style communist rule after the Second World War, for example, Czechoslovakia bears the impress of its centuries-long cultural interaction with Western Europe. Prague, Kostash notes, is the "Paris of the East," a "feast at first sight" in comparison to the "unlovely Stalinist renovations of Kiev and Warsaw and ramshackle Belgrade" (6). Poland, also an Eastern bloc country, predominantly Roman Catholic rather than Eastern Orthodox, is similarly caught between "East" and "West." Among Serbians, her fellow Slavs who follow the Eastern Orthodox church and who use the Cyrillic alphabet, Kostash seems to find rather unambiguous evidence of their "Eastern-ness." But, as she repeatedly asks in her chapter on Yugoslavia, are the Balkans—the Kosovo region of which is "90 per cent Muslim" (75)—even part of Europe? In portions of this chapter narrated under headings such as "Where Does Europe End?" (72) and "Are We Still In Europe?" (81), Kostash wonders how far east one goes before Eastern Europe becomes Asia. True to its title—*Bloodlines: A Journey Into Eastern Europe*—Kostash's narrative moves roughly eastward, away from the western-most and most "westernized" country in Eastern Europe toward the eastern-most and least "westernized." Situated further east than Yugoslavia, "U-kraina"—meaning "[a]t the edge" or the "frontier" (210)—lies on the cusp of Europe itself.

Not surprisingly, then, despite her ostensible familiarity with Ukrainian culture, Kostash feels most bewildered in, and alienated by, Ukraine. The most politically repressive and economically backward country that she visits in Eastern Europe—the only Soviet country to which she travels, too—Ukraine shocks and enrages her. Though before going to Ukraine for the first time, in 1984, she expects "economic wreckage, social inertia, aesthetic vulgarity and administrative cruelty" (164), she is unprepared, much like Kulyk Keefer, for the "myriad manifestations" of these realities—the "livid exhaustion on the women's faces" who stand in long lines for poor-quality food; the countless crones, amputees, and cripples who beg on the streets; the "obligatory first-class prices" she must pay for "second- and third-class service and facilities" (165). Under constant surveillance by Intourist and the Ukraine Friendship Society, organizations that at once facilitate and control her movement within Ukraine, Kostash struggles against paranoia; knowing that cabbies and doormen are KGB informers, and that the lamp fixtures in her hotel rooms are bugged, she is forced to take precautions. She travels "under cover of night" from Kiev to L'viv, for example, in order to meet with a dissident journalist, and she waits until she is in Poland to "write up [her] notes of the entire Ukrainian visit" (167–68). Waiting to meet with family members for the first time in Chernivtsi, 1984, Kostash realizes that, despite their blood ties to one another, they are strangers. "How are we going to communicate?" she wonders. "My relatives and I have nothing in common—least of all language—except that my grandmother and their grandfather were sister and brother. Baba got away. End of shared history" (162–63). Certainly, to some extent during her travels to other countries in Eastern Europe, Kostash experiences similar difficulties—police surveillance; the inability to communicate with some of the people she meets; and a generally lower standard of living than she is accustomed to in Canada. These realities, however, in Soviet Ukraine, are not only more pervasive but also, from her perspective as a Ukrainian Canadian, more troubling. "Why was I," she asks, "not nearly so offended by the Stalinist features of rebuilt Warsaw, say, or the sullen brow-beatenness of the citizens of Prague, or the dilatory ways of business in Belgrade?" (168). In "those other capitals," she confesses, "I was to forgive and overlook much": "in Ukraine, 1984, I overlook and forgive nothing. What is this double standard of evaluation and emotion?" (168). The "double standard" derives from the fact that in Ukraine, more so than in any other part of Eastern Europe, she wants to belong. Yet Ukraine, more emphatically than any other Eastern European country, reminds her that she does not.

But while Kostash's narrative of her experiences in Ukraine—not unlike her writing about Czechoslovakia, Yugoslavia, and Poland—seems to dramatize her inability to connect with the people and places she visits, the final chapter of *Bloodlines* also exemplifies her tenacious refusal to remain an outsider and a foreigner in Eastern Europe. Just as she returns again and again to Czechoslovakia, Yugoslavia, and Poland, making repeat visits to individuals with whom she feels a sense of political and/or professional solidarity, so too does she travel again and again to Ukraine—in 1984, 1988, and 1991. In 1984, though, after returning to Canada from her first trip to Ukraine, she makes a crucial decision: she will not go back without first learning how to speak Ukrainian. Ashamed that she could not communicate with her relatives during her 1984 trip, and troubled by her inability to read the poetry of writers such as Taras Shevchenko, Volodymyr Ivasiuk, and Vasyl Stus—dissidents whose tragic lives are symbolic to her of the Ukrainian people's struggle for freedom—Kostash spends the next four years honing her Ukrainian language skills, beginning where she "left off thirty years earlier," in Ukrainian "Saturday School" (193). Her "forcible return to baby talk, to simple, declarative sentences and the present tense for all actions" becomes a "humbling," yet ultimately deeply rewarding, experience (195). As a writer, Kostash is keenly aware of the relation between language and culture: "never just a means of expression," she says, language is a "carrier, a veritable caravan of cultural and psychic and political import" (193). So when, finally, she is able to read Shevchenko's poems in Ukrainian—when she discovers that she is "*inside* the language, understanding it directly, the profoundly familiar sounds carrying a story, a voice, a personality where before there had been only babble" (195)—she is elated. Empowered with the ability to "open

[her] mouth and speak," she returns to Ukraine with a mission: to forge new connections to Ukraine with and through language. "Baba," she writes, "was the last person in a long line of generations who spoke only Ukrainian; I broke the chain, speaking it not at all. Now I pick it up, wanting to hammer back my link, so that Baba might live again in my broken, stammering syllables" (196). Kostash sees language as the link between generations and between communities. Unwilling to passively accept that her ethnic inheritance is defined by blood, she actively seeks to redefine her ethnic identity by learning to speak Ukrainian.

What Kostash learns in Ukraine—and this explains her decision to construct Ukraine as her final destination in *Bloodlines*—is that bloodlines alone are not enough to link her to the ethnic homeland: she cannot take for granted that her ethnic identity—any more than her identity as a socialist, a feminist, and a writer—guarantees her connection to Eastern Europe, its people, and its history. In fact, whether or not she shares common interests—political, professional, or cultural—with the individuals she meets during her travels matters little in the end: what matters is that she shares with them a common language. When Kostash returns to Ukraine in 1988, and again in 1991, she is not yet fluent in Ukrainian, and so she struggles to communicate with "broken, stammering syllables" (196). Still rudimentary, her language skills represent the first, not the final, steps toward building a genuine cross-cultural bridge between her real and her imagined homeland, and the conclusion to *Bloodlines*—less an ending, really, than a new beginning—reinforces the notion that Kostash's "business" in Eastern Europe is not yet complete. Absent from her text is the closure that Kulyk Keefer provides in *Honey and Ashes* by narrating her return to Canada. Kostash, in the conclusion to *Bloodlines*, remains in Ukraine. But precisely because she concludes her narrative in Ukraine, foregrounding her refusal to retreat to the comfort and familiarity of her life in Canada, *Bloodlines* offers the possibility, if not the promise, of a future in which she will succeed in bridging the gaps between Canada and Ukraine. While lacking a clear sense of resolution—a clear sense that she has succeeded in making real her imagined connection to Ukraine— the conclusion to *Bloodlines* is characterized by a distinct sense of hope, not only for Kostash and her quest to connect with the people of Ukraine but also for Ukraine itself and the Ukrainian people's struggle for political independence as well as economic prosperity.

Tellingly, in narrating her 1984 trip to Ukraine—just prior to the turning point in the text where she decides to learn Ukrainian—Kostash writes about the 1933 famine in Ukraine, one of the most terrible events in Ukrainian history. As a result of Stalin's high quotas for grain and livestock production, between seven and ten million Ukrainians died of starvation. Focused less on objective facts and statistics than on individual horror stories, her brief description of the famine is without question the most chilling portion of *Bloodlines*. Readers are left with the haunting images of people who bartered for bread with gold; of a woman who was tried for sabotage, her home destroyed, because she hid fourteen potatoes from the Soviets; of a wife and husband who, "[h]aving cut off their children's heads," then "salted them away for meat" (191-92). Situated as it is, however, near the conclusion of her 1984 trip to Ukraine, Kostash's discussion of the famine becomes more than a glimpse into the unspeakable horror of this moment in Ukrainian history. The famine represents her feelings toward Ukraine in 1984—her "hunger" for connection with the ethnic homeland—and it becomes symbolic, too, of the Ukrainian people's "hunger" for a better life. Her first observation of Ukraine, then, upon her return in 1988, is crucial: "[t]he Ukrainian lands seen from the air in June," Kostash writes, "are green, green and green again" (245). In the four years since her first trip to Ukraine, Kostash sees the beginnings of a "new," post-Soviet Ukraine. In the words of her friend Seriozha, the nation is "stirring to life" (201). She is still subject to intense scrutiny by Customs officials, food queues are still long, and Kiev is still dreary (197-200), but the *beginnings* of change are grounds enough for optimism with regard to the future. Just as she has been transformed in the process of learning Ukrainian, so too is the nation undergoing dramatic changes. In the final pages of *Bloodlines*, as Kostash draws attention to the centrality and sanctity of both wheat and bread in Ukrainian culture,[8] she suggests that the history of Ukraine may be marked by famine and war—the "Ukrainian lands" (245) may be fertilized by blood and bones—but the future of Ukraine springs from its rich black loam. Indeed, for her, the "green, green and green again" wheat fields of Ukraine, the literal "beginnings of bread" (245), become a symbol of hope, however tentative, for both the Ukrainian people and her ability to connect with them.

The Doomed Bridegroom: A Memoir

Although the last pages of *Bloodlines* appear to pave the way for a sequel to Kostash's first journeys into Eastern Europe, a sequel in which she finally succeeds in making real her imagined sense of belonging to this part of the world, *The Doomed Bridegroom* thwarts readers' expectations—at first glance, at least. Focused as it is on her doomed love affairs with men from Eastern Europe—and from Canada and Greece as well—Kostash's memoir appears to tell the familiar story of her failure to develop lasting cross-cultural, transnational relationships. Despite her discovery, near the end of *Bloodlines*, that language can offer her a way "into" Eastern Europe, Kostash chooses not to follow through with the "business" of using Ukrainian to forge links to the people, politics, and history of her homeland.

And yet Kostash *does*—albeit in unexpected ways—pick up in *The Doomed Bridegroom* where she left off in *Bloodlines*. In *The Doomed Bridegroom*, after all, as she narrates the real and imagined relationships she developed over a period of thirty years with men from within and beyond the borders of Eastern Europe, radically blurring the boundaries between fiction and non-fiction in the process, Kostash also implicitly narrates her career-long relationship with language. As much the story of her love affair with the process of writing as it is the story of her love affairs with various "rebel men," her memoir reveals the ways in which she becomes empowered as a writer to redefine her sense of self and community in and through language. Whereas, in *Bloodlines*, she learns a new language in order to forge links to Ukrainian, in *The Doomed Bridegroom* she finds a new way to use language that enables her to develop a new identity and, in turn, relationships that transcend borders and bloodlines. Over the course of this text, as she becomes a practitioner of creative non-fiction, moving away from the more objective, journalistic impulses that characterize her previous books, Kostash simultaneously reinvents herself as figurative mother to future generations of writers to whom she is connected by her new style of writing.

In *The Doomed Bridegroom* Kostash at once revisits her fascination with Eastern Europe and revises her thinking about this "other" part of the world. Like *Bloodlines*, *The Doomed Bridegroom* explores, in part, Kostash's interest in the history, politics, and people of Eastern Europe.

In both texts, Kostash's ethnicity represents one—but by no means the only—point of intersection between her identity and the identities of the individuals she meets over the course of her travels. Not unlike *Bloodlines*, *The Doomed Bridegroom* explores the multiple reasons Kostash is drawn to Eastern Europe—her sense of political and professional, as well as ethnic, solidarity with individuals from Eastern Europe. Just as *Bloodlines* narrates Kostash's attempts to redefine her sense of self and community by journeying "into" Eastern Europe—by trying to develop relationships that transcend family bloodlines and national borders—so too does *The Doomed Bridegroom* reflect upon her desire to bridge the gaps between her imagined sense of belonging to, and actual detachment from, this part of the world. Focused as it is, of course, on Kostash's career-long infatuation with "rebel men"—political activists, dissident poets, and freedom fighters, some of whom live within the borders of Eastern Europe, and others of whom live beyond these borders—*The Doomed Bridegroom* is at once broader and narrower in scope than *Bloodlines*. Whereas *Bloodlines* centres on Kostash's travels to Eastern Europe between 1982 and 1991, *The Doomed Bridegroom* addresses her experiences in Canada and the United States, as well as in Poland, Ukraine, and Serbia, over a period of more than thirty years, beginning in 1965, with Kostash's coming-of-age as a writer in Edmonton, and ending in 1997, with her mentoring of a young Serbian poet in Belgrade. So, temporally and geographically, *The Doomed Bridegroom* covers more territory than *Bloodlines*. At the same time, because Kostash strictly focuses *The Doomed Bridegroom* on the romantic and sexual relationships she developed with six men—as distinct from the larger number and wider variety of relationships she writes about in *Bloodlines*—her memoir offers more limited, though arguably more intimate, insight into her life.

Divided into six chapters, each focused on one of her lovers, *The Doomed Bridegroom* narrates—more or less chronologically—Kostash's "personal history of arousal by transgressive men, alive and dead" (vi). By acknowledging, in her preface to the text, that she "came simultaneously to politics and sexuality in the 1960s" (v-vi)—and by confessing that, since then, she has been drawn "over and over again, in sympathies of desire, to heroic figures in the extremity of resistance and sacrifice" (vi)—Kostash makes clear the extent to which both her private life and her career as a public intellectual have been shaped by her attraction, at once political and sexual, to "suffering and martyrdom, particularly as they were lived out in the political dramas of the Cold War and the New Left" (v). Her lovers include Lenny, an American draft-dodger she met in 1965 while both were university students in Edmonton; Kostas, a supposed communist freedom fighter from Greece; dissident Ukrainian poet Vasyl Stus, who died in a Russian gulag in 1985; K, an aging communist bureaucrat living in Warsaw; Canadian writer Patrick Friesen, whose Mennonite ancestors came from Ukraine; and, finally, a young, unnamed Serbian poet from Belgrade. But while all of these men are—or, in Stus's case, were—real, and while most are or were involved in very real "dramas of courage, despair, and failure in countries wracked by a certain complex of cultural and political history" (vi), Kostash's relationships with them are defined by her inability to distinguish reality and fantasy. At times, in fact, she deliberately chooses not to separate the two. Some of her actual relationships are predicated on fictions and, in a few cases, on lies; others are nuanced by the imagined, though ostensibly historically-determined, roles that she and her lovers find themselves enacting, either consciously or unconsciously; and at least one of Kostash's love affairs, her affair with Stus, is entirely made up. But all of her love affairs, real or imagined, are shaped by her tendencies to romanticize and idealize the "men of the 'other' Europe," their histories and their politics (vi). For her, these men are caught up in "huge swirls of historical narrative that threw Slavs down to the Adriatic, Tatars across the Black Sea, Cossacks into the steppes, Byzantine monks to Rus, Ottomans to Belgrade" (vi). In admitting that she is attracted to the "otherness" of her lovers—she associates them with "Bolshevik revolutionary songs, the Cyrillic alphabet scratched in clandestine poems, ruined Orthodox monasteries, doomed peasant insurgents, heroic labourers in the mines and mills of Soviet bosses" (vi)—Kostash reveals her desire to become a part of their romanticized "other" worlds. "Take me," she repeats again and again in the preface to *The Doomed Bridegroom*, as she addresses a lover from Prague, one of several "bridegrooms" she mentions only briefly in the introduction to the text: "tell me stories of Jan Hus and his uprisings, of the bands of men and women in possession of this countryside before they were defeated and perished, take me in cornfields, limbs flailing near the dead, take me in cobblestoned squares near the funeral pyres" (vii). To be physically or sexually "taken" by her lovers, "in an embrace of excited camaraderie," is to be taken, symbolically, into their worlds and into their histories.[9]

Thematically, then, in *The Doomed Bridegroom* Kostash confronts for the first time—and with unprecedented candor—the intensely personal ways in which she has been drawn to the people, politics, and history of Eastern and Southern Europe. In terms of its subject matter, her memoir represents a departure from *Bloodlines*, a text that leaves largely unexamined the romantic relationships she developed over the course of her travels. This is not to say that Kostash's romanticized perceptions of Eastern Europe are absent from *Bloodlines*; on the contrary, she travels repeatedly to and within this part of the world precisely because she longs to experience the romance of revolution, political upheaval, and social change. But in *Bloodlines*—and this is a point reinforced by the narrative structure of the text—as Kostash sets out to observe and experience the "real" Eastern Europe, she seeks to *make* real her imagined sense of belonging to, or solidarity with, multiple communities in Czechoslovakia, Yugoslavia, Poland, and Ukraine. While she blurs in *Bloodlines* the genres of autobiography and biography, history and travelogue, the text is, unquestionably, a work of non-fiction, for in it she seldom strays from her actual travels in Eastern Europe—except, of course, when she provides historical background on the places she visits.

In *The Doomed Bridegroom*, by contrast, Kostash allows herself the freedom to explore—formally as well as thematically—how her long-term obsession with Eastern and Southern Europe has been defined by the inextricability of reality and fantasy. By maintaining, in part, her characteristic role of the objective and impartial journalist keen on recording her actual observations and experiences—but embracing, at the same time, the role of the storyteller, whose imagination is as limitless as it is lively—she is able to draw upon the conventions of both non-fiction and fiction as she narrates her love affairs. Each chapter of *The Doomed Bridegroom* becomes a complex narrative montage in which Kostash moves in time and space, shifting narrative voices as she alternates between real and imagined scenarios. Alongside matter-of-fact descriptions of her actual encounters with her lovers, and historical accounts of her lovers' backgrounds, she provides poetic—sometimes erotic—renderings of her imaginary encounters with them. She frequently interrupts first-person confessions of her feelings with third-person analyses of her behaviour. Quoting from personal letters, and from published poetry, articles, and books, Kostash draws upon myriad "real" sources throughout *The Doomed Bridegroom*, but she also invents mock interviews between herself and an imaginary interviewer, mock love letters that she never actually sent to her lovers, as well as "probable" biographies of her lovers.

Sorting through and making sense of Kostash's fragmented, at times disjunctive, narrative style is no easy task, for she seems set against the business of constructing *The Doomed Bridegroom* as a unified or coherent narrative of her growth or development over the course of her relationships. And, though each chapter of the text appears to stand alone, so that *The Doomed Bridegroom* might be read as six distinct love stories, these stories rarely follow a discernible plot. Indeed, the question Kostash asks of her relationship with K—"[i]s there a narrative here [...]?" (79)—is a question readers might well ask of every chapter, as well as of the text as a whole. There is a narrative here—there is a story—but in order to understand its meaning readers must pay close attention to the complex ways in which Kostash tells it. While the text is divided into a series of separate love stories, each focused on a specific "doomed bridegroom," collectively they form a single story of the "doomed bride." In attempting to form lasting relationships with her lovers—and, by extension, their "other" parts of the world—Kostash takes on, or tries out, various different roles: friend, girlfriend, mistress, comrade, colleague.[10] Yet all of her relationships, real and imagined, come to an end because she never plays the role of wife. Insofar as her bridegrooms are doomed to live out their lives "trapped in long histories played out at the overlapping territories of East and West, formed by brutal events" (vi), Kostash is doomed to live outside of these histories. Despite her willingness to blur the boundaries of fiction and non-fiction, Kostash cannot imagine, and chooses not to construct, alternate—"happy"—endings to her doomed love affairs. Not unlike *Bloodlines*, *The Doomed Bridegroom* seems to narrate Kostash's failure to connect with the "other" worlds with which she is obsessed, but her memoir in fact concludes with a tentatively hopeful step toward such connection. For, even as she comes to terms with her intense attraction to, but simultaneous detachment from, her lovers, her writing itself becomes the key to her success in re-imagining her sense of self and community beyond borders and bloodlines.

In the first chapter of *The Doomed Bridegroom*, "Mississippi Dreaming," Kostash introduces herself as the blushing virgin—innocent, both sexually and politically, but eager, at the same time, to enter the erotic "other" world to which her boyfriend Lenny belongs. Both study at the University of Alberta; they meet in 1965 while taking a class in "Political Institutions of the Soviet Union" (2). Reliving her days as a student in Edmonton, before meeting Lenny, Kostash becomes a wide-eyed dreamer once more: as she "crunch[es]" her way to class "through the shocking whiteness of the Edmonton winter," she longs to be in Mississippi (1). "I wish to be in that hot, moist place," she writes, "tramping along the delta, my arms linked through black arms, on a freedom march" (1). As presumptuous as it is naïve, Kostash's language blatantly sexualizes the political climate of Mississippi. Without reflecting on the painful realities of racism and prejudice, she assumes that the racial politics of the American South are at once exotic and erotic. "Whiteness," for her, is humiliatingly ordinary and dull; "blackness," by contrast, sexually and politically exciting. Against the backdrop of the snowy campus, a constant reminder of her "white girl's humiliation in the middle class," Kostash dreams of being "elsewhere, in the drama of strangers in pain" (1). That she would be accepted into the black protest movement is a given in her mind. When she describes all the boys of the "NDY," she draws attention to the ways in which they "snap and sizzle, heating up the space around them...with the ardour of their ideas" (2). Tellingly, too, she likens her first encounters with these boys to the loss of her virginity; their talk of "oppression, class enemy, being and nothingness" effects the "defloration of [her] virginal vocabulary" (2).

But it is Lenny, an American draft dodger from the Bronx, active in the protest movement against the Vietnam War, and a member of the New Democrat Youth, who offers her a way out of the symbolic Edmonton winter and into the heat of another world. Lenny is particularly attractive to her because he is more exotic—more daring and dangerous—than the other "NDY" boys. He has an accent—"Gotta kwawtah foh a cuppa kawfee?" (2)—and he uses drugs to stay awake at night writing "articles for the student paper about Vietnam and the draft resistance in the United States, speeches for a rally in front of the legislature, not to mention letters to all his strung-out friends back in New York, each one of whom, it seems, is in deep shit" (2). Most importantly, perhaps, he is an experienced lover. That Kostash is attracted to both his physical body and his body of political ideals—that she cannot, in fact, separate the two—is obvious. While sitting cross-legged together on a gymnasium floor at an anti-Vietnam War teach-in, and talking about the situation in Vietnam, her eyes settle on the "bulky bulge of his crotch" (3).

Drawn to Lenny's otherness, Kostash eventually gives herself to him sexually, attempting to consummate the union of their political ideals, if not their love. But their relationship is doomed precisely because he is so different from her. Unsatisfied with their sexual relationship, Lenny criticizes Kostash for "being altogether too passive, too virginal, lying there *being made love to* rather than being a participant in a sharing process" (4). Underlying his criticism of her passivity in bed is a deeper—albeit unspoken—sense of disdain for her political passivity. In the years following their break up—years in which Kostash completes her Master's degree in Russian Literature at the University of Toronto and then begins her career as a freelance journalist—Lenny becomes more militant in his pro-communist, anti-capitalist political activism. She chooses a career in writing; he chooses a career in revolution. In fact, Lenny is eventually sent to a California prison for his revolutionary activities. And in letters to Kostash from prison, he gives voice to the reasons for which their relationship could not, and cannot, work. "[W]e were abstractions from each other's life," he writes, "figments of each other's imagination" (11). According to Lenny, their relationship was "not real. What was real was the killing in the yard two weeks ago and the stabbing last week, tension, aggravation, friends locked down. The three thousand pages of his files from the FBI. Cold coffee in styrofoam, cold tortillas from the canteen, a wet towel hanging from a nail" (11). Six months after his release from prison, Lenny marries his lawyer, leaving Kostash with little more than her memories of the time she spent with him. His references to "cold coffee" and "cold tortillas" hearken back to her winter days in Edmonton, before she knew the warmth of his embrace. Without him, she is once again "present at the scene of [her] own white girl's humiliation in the middle class" (1). In 1987, while staying at her cabin, Kostash reflects on her relationship with Lenny some twenty-two years after their love affair ended. "It's cool inside the cabin," she notes. "[T]he sheets are cool" (12). Thinking about Lenny, though, she "throw[s] open the windows" and "throw[s] off the covers" of the bed to "let in the heat" (12). Acknowledging that, realistically, she will "not be going to Mississippi"—she will "never go to Mississippi"—she draws upon the warmth of memory as her only defense (13).

In many ways more complicated than her relationship with Lenny, Kostash's love affair with Kostas—the subject of her second chapter, "The Collaborators"—seems to mark her transition from naïve girlhood to savvy womanhood. Kostash meets Kostas in 1981 while vacationing in Greece. Older now, more confident about the direction of her career and the nature of her politics, she carries herself with the self-assuredness of a maturing writer.[11] Fittingly, when Kostas meets her for the first time, she is sitting in a seaside taverna, writing. The first question he asks her is not "[w]here are you from?" but "[a]re you a writer?" (15). Insofar as his next question, "[w]hat do you write about?" (15), marks the point at which their love affair begins, the way in which Kostash answers this question comes to define the terms of their relationship. Her assumption, upon meeting Kostas, and before finding out anything about him, is that he will not be familiar with such words as "prairie, Ukrainian, Cree, counterculture, New Left, sisterhood" (15), words that describe her interests as a writer. The world in which he lives, after all, "[t]his Greek place," is "nothing like her homeplace" (16). "Here," she writes of Greece, "there were no hippies...and no free-for-alls in campus offices"; here instead were "students trapped in the searchlights beamed from the army tanks that rolled over the iron gates of the Polytechnic and into the forecourt, the machine guns following the beams of light" (16). In order to make herself understood, then, she tells Kostas simply, she writes about "oppression, exploitation, resistance, and struggle" (16). That she feels "imbecilic" as she makes these broad generalizations about her work is important (16). When she was younger, dating Lenny, such generalizations would have adequately reflected her largely unformed political ideals. In 1981, however, having learned from her experiences with Lenny about the harsh realities of specific resistance movements, and having focused her own work on ethnicity, feminism, and New Leftist socialism, she is no longer a political or sexual virgin; she has a clear sense of who she is and what she believes.

Yet, from the moment she meets Kostas, her sense of self-confidence with regard to both her politics and her sexuality is shaken. In the taverna, despite her attempts to busy herself with writing, playing the part of the independent woman traveller, she becomes self-conscious of the fact that she is alone—"[s]uddenly I was no longer a woman alone but a woman without a man" (15)—and she is unable to articulate her precise motivations for writing. In other words, with Kostas—who, like Lenny, represents the exotic and erotic "other"—Kostash becomes a virgin once more, unsure of herself and the terms of their relationship. In fact, Kostash is never sure of precisely who Kostas is. Although he tells her that he is a communist freedom fighter—an "organizer for the socialist party" in Greece (PASOK), and a member of an "underground" group of militant communists who meet "in secret to train for guerilla warfare" (18)—he gives her no details about what he does when he leaves their bed, where he goes or how he enacts his political ideals. And so she finds herself inventing, for the most part, the details of his life. She daydreams about clandestine, late-night gatherings of men "with moustaches…smoking suicidely, shouting and waving their arms in the chop-chop Greek manner." They are, she imagines, surrounded by "heavy wooden boxes holding AK-47's from Bulgaria" as they plot their "strategies for the defence of the Greek republic" (20). Uncertain, more generally, about the details of Greek history—when, for example, Kostas tells her about his involvement in a student uprising in 1973, she feels "ashamed" that she "did not know this story" and asks "[w]here the hell was I, and all my friends, on November 17, 1973, that this story should not be known?" (24)—Kostash imagines the Greeks as "a people abandoned to semi-literacy and cowed by generations of tyrants in the schools, the courts, the police stations, not to mention at home, in the family" (19). For her, their history is marked by "blood-soaked village squares, ghost armies, and unmarked graves" (19), but by few specific details. All Kostash knows for certain, really, is that she has been seduced by Kostas, and by the seemingly dangerous world to which he ostensibly belongs.

Should she know more? Or, rather—in retrospect—should she have known more? This question, ultimately, comes to define Kostash's purpose in writing about her relationship with Kostas, and the narrative structure of "The Collaborators" underscores her desire to find answers. Whereas Kostash narrates "Mississippi Dreaming" entirely in the first person, and in the present tense, reliving her love affair with Lenny as it unfolds, she approaches her relationship with Kostas from a different perspective—or, more accurately, from two different perspectives. Looking back on her experiences with Kostas as an outside observer, she narrates their story in the third person, past tense, but this narrative is frequently interrupted by segments of an imaginary interview (in which

Kostash speaks in the present tense with an imaginary interviewer about her relationship with Kostas). Distanced from the relationship itself, Kostash is able to analyze what she felt at the time of her affair; how she succumbed to Kostas's advances; and, most importantly, why he deceived her throughout their time together. Throughout the chapter—beginning with her "imbecilic" answers to Kostas's questions about her writing (16)—Kostash hints at the ways in which she played the fool in relation to him. She was too eager to accept his stories at face value: "he kept feeding me stories," she says to her interviewer (24). She was too passive to challenge him when he showed a decided lack of interest in her wide-ranging political and social concerns. Speaking to him of "Ukrainian weddings and the crisis in the Writers' Union, of a picket line and a study group, she could see on his face how risible these were compared to the project of the Greek revolution" (28). Reflecting on the truth about Kostas—that he sold "agricultural chemicals manufactured by an American multinational corporation" for a living; that he was married with two children; that he was never involved in political uprisings, as he claimed to be (31–33)—Kostash sees that she was in love with half-truths and lies. Just as she came to understand in "Mississippi Dreaming" that she and Lenny were "abstractions from each other's life, figments of each other's imagination" (11), so too does she come to realize in "The Collaborators" that she and Kostas invented each other. Near the conclusion to the chapter, Kostash acknowledges that they were both active in constructing the fictional terms of their affair: "[s]he wanted a lover who was leafletting the Greek countryside with revolutionary pamphlets. As for Kostas, he wanted someone who would see him, see him in the blue hills back of Pylos, stride manfully into the village square" (33). By admitting her willingness to see past Kostas's lies in order to play out her transgressive fantasies, Kostash comes to terms with her complicity in the affair. Perhaps, in the end, she was not the naïve virgin. Perhaps, from the start, she was an active participant—a "collaborator"—in shaping this doomed love story.

With Lenny and Kostas, then, Kostash begins to recognize the ways in which her imagination influences her perceptions of and behaviour toward her lovers. When, however, in 1990, she chances upon an article in a magazine about dissident Ukrainian poet Vasyl Stus (1938–1985), and soon finds herself imagining her romantic involvement with him, she arrives at a turning point in her thinking about the relation between reality and fantasy. In "Inside the Copper Mountain," one of the most stylistically complex chapters in *The Doomed Bridegroom*, she tests the boundaries of non-fiction by narrating her love affair with Stus, a man she came to know only through his writing and through others' writing about him. In part, this chapter narrates the process through which she became familiar with Stus. While studying Russian literature, she explains, in the mid-1960s, she began collecting books by and about dissident Russian poets. "I was not then," she says, "aware of dissident Ukrainian poets who were not in any case at the centre of my concern" (35). In time, however, as her "reading persisted"—as her library of books filled with the "excruciating stories of the men and women of the Gulag" (35) became a "harrowing archive of that archipelago of punishment called the Zone" (36)—she began to focus more and more on the "particularly relentless persecution of Ukrainian intellectuals" (36). Acknowledging her sense of ethnic solidarity with these intellectuals—many of them writers—she explains that she learned Ukrainian, the "language of [her] grandparents," in order to "understand better who these dissidents had been and what had happened to them" (36). Next, she "began subscribing to Ukrainian journals and magazines" (36). Eventually, she writes, "I noticed the repetition of certain names, made connections among events, stared at photographs" (36). A photograph of Stus—dark-haired and dark-eyed, wearing a black turtleneck sweater and looking like a "Ukrainian Marlon Brando" (34)—is what initially sparked her interest in his story.[12]

But as Kostash narrates her increasing obsession with Stus, the story of her research into the lives of persecuted Ukrainian intellectuals is almost immediately overtaken by his. Determined to piece together the facts surrounding Stus's life, as well as his death, Kostash provides an overview of his biography by drawing upon the memoirs of Stus's friend, Mykhailyna Kotsiubynska, published by the magazine *Ukraina* in 1990 as "In the Mirror of Memory." She also consults various historical works related to Stus, and his poems.[13] Yet, having learned through her relationships with Lenny and Kostas that what is real is always nuanced by what is imagined—and conscious, at the same time, of the gaps between what has been written about Stus and what he actually experienced over the course of his life—she cannot resist the temptation to insert herself into his story. Particularly "enchanted" by Kotsiubynska—with whom she shares the same initials—Kostash says, "[t]he temptation is huge: to enter her words here and join her voice contrapuntally as the woman who did not know Stus" (38). At this, one of the most compelling moments in *The Doomed Bridegroom*, Kostash makes the transition from narrator of, to character in, Stus's narrative by identifying with Kotsiubynska. While Kostash never knew Stus, "*she* [Kotsiubynska] did" and, by imagining herself as Kotsiubynska, Kostash becomes part of his story: "there I am," she writes, "she is, beside Vasyl Stus" (38). In subsequent portions of the chapter, under the deliberately ambiguous heading of "MK," Kostash merges her voice with that of Kotsiubynska, placing herself next to Stus in recreated scenarios originally narrated by Kotsiubynska in her memoirs. Writing, for example, about Stus's outburst in a Kiev cinema in 1965, the starting point of his protest against the Soviet regime, Kostash says, "we stood up together. He shouted something despairing— 'Whoever is against tyranny, stand up now!'—while trembling in every cell of his body. I could feel it through the arm I held around his shoulder as we left the hall" (38). And "here was Vasyl," she writes, narrating Kotsiubynska's encounter with him after she rescinded her communist party membership in 1966, "waving his arms about, shouting cheerfully at me" (42). Most importantly, perhaps, in numerous italicized passages, also under the heading of "MK," Kostash narrates entirely imagined and sometimes erotic scenarios involving "MK" and Stus—all written in the first person from "MK's" point of view, and many addressed to Stus. Collectively, these scenarios form the narrative of a love affair between "MK"—Kostash/Kotsiubynska—and Stus that never really took place.

In order to become closer to Stus, then, Kostash takes on the persona of "MK," and invents a romantic relationship between "MK" and Stus. Ironically, however, the doomed nature of this relationship serves less as a challenge to than a reminder of her distance from Stus. Despite her attempts at imagining a love affair with Stus by (re)imagining herself as Kotsiubynska, Kostash cannot "un-imagine" the fact that Kotsiubynska was never actually involved with Stus romantically and that he was, in reality, not only married to another woman but, by all accounts, intensely devoted to his wife and child. Doomed less by his anti-Soviet political activism than by his commitment to his family, "MK's" love affair with Stus is strained from the start because—even within the realm of fiction—Kostash is unable to ignore the very real presence of his wife.

Not surprisingly, within the italicized portions of text through which the love story between "MK" and Stus unfolds, Kostash frequently makes reference to Stus's wife, Valentyna Popeliukh. At one point, for example, early in "MK's" relationship with Stus, Kostash—addressing him—notes with thinly-veiled jealousy that "*[y]our wife sits curled up on the sofa and glares coldly at you. She has been looking at you like this for some time, while you and I have been talking. She is thin and beautiful. Her neck is fluted with grooves. She does not wear the look of a woman in love. Perhaps I do*" (41–42). Later in the chapter, after "MK" and Stus make love, Kostash, again addressing Stus, draws attention to his relationship with his wife: "*[y]ou slide from my bed to wash, for it is time for you to go home*," she writes. "*Ah, the marriage bed. And do you find your ardour there at three o'clock in the morning?*" (46).

That Kostash rarely refers to Valentyna by name is telling—"[h]e loved her," she writes, "[h]e chose her" and "[h]e bedded her" (42)—for Stus's wife is present as an absence in documents related to his life. Although he dedicates his poems to his wife, Kostash finds little information about Valentyna in her research: "[w]here is she?" Kostash wonders. "Where is the wife? No one mentions her" (67). "There is no bride here at all," Kostash suggests. "She has a name—Valentyna Popeliukh—but no figure, no face" (41). And yet, Valentyna—the ghostly absence/presence who haunts "MK's" imagined encounters with Stus—is never far from Kostash's thoughts as she writes. There is a bride here, in his story, who cannot be erased from history by Kostash any more than the Soviet regime could erase Stus. "*[F]ecund and child-bearing*," Valentyna shares a life with Stus that ultimately, Kostash admits, "*has nothing to do with me*" (54). Following a description of the day-to-day domestic activities of Stus and his family—"*[y]ou brush breadcrumbs off your lapel, check the contents of your briefcase*" while "*[y]our wife is distracted, thinking of the day ahead for herself—the grocery shopping*"—Kostash says, with a tinge of regret, "*I would bear books*" (54). Clearly, what Kostash longs for in "Inside the Copper Mountain"—and she underscores this in the title of, as well as the epigraph to, the chapter—is to become a part of Stus's world. The epigraph, an excerpt from one of his poems, reads,

> *A thunder of resurrection on the mountain*
> *is being announced for me.*
> *Smash your fists against despair,*
> *hiding within the copper mountain.* (34)

To imagine herself as Stus's lover is to raise her fist beside his in the fight against the metaphorical "mountain" of "despair." In the process of narrating her imagined relationship with Stus, however, Kostash learns as much about the limits of fantasy as she does about the constructed nature of reality. She is prohibited from joining Stus "Inside the Copper Mountain" because he already has a bride there, at his side.

In subsequent love affairs—and particularly in her relationship with K, her Polish lover—Kostash becomes increasingly conscious of the other women in her lovers' lives, as well as the role she plays as the "other" woman vis-à-vis these women. In "The Masked Man in Warsaw," for example, as she narrates her actual relationship with K, Kostash struggles to find a place for herself in his life because the mysterious K—whose politics are as ambiguous as his love life is complex—is not only married, he also already has a mistress. After meeting K at a "literary conference in Slovenia in May 1986" (71), Kostash remains in contact with him for the next few years. But aside from the time she spends with him in Warsaw, in 1987, their love affair takes place almost entirely through letters. Looking back on the beginning of their relationship, she explains that what first attracted her to K, a man who belonged to "the Communist Party *nomenklatura*," was his "public declaration in the conference hall in support of the heroic and persecuted Polish labour organization, Solidarity" (72). Poland, she says, "seemed to me...a place where it was unwise to speak too loudly, painful to breath too deeply," but "here was K, a bona fide Communist...proclaiming in clear English, his name tag pinned to his good suit, that Solidarity has been shamefully repressed" (72). Initially "aroused with admiration" (72) for K, Kostash corresponds with him for a year before travelling to Poland and seeing him again. Over the course of this year, however, she is unable to sustain the "near-frenzy of repressed erotic excitement" that K once inspired (72). K, she learns—from him, as well as from her friends who know him—is not the man she thought he was. In the first place, he is not, according to one of her friends, "a garden variety Communist"—he is "high-ranking" (78).

Immediately overcome by a feeling of "queasy shame that [she] had let his touch arouse [her] when [she] should have been more alert" (78), Kostash realizes that she "misrepresented" K in her "own imagination as a dissident" (72). "What I had really wanted," she says, "was a lover from my own generation, one who had fought the student battles of 1968, the Solidarity battles of 1980–81, and who had then gone to jail" (72). K, though, "belonged to an earlier generation who had joined the Party in its heady, reformist days of 1956 and then made endless little 'adjustments' as the Party reneged on all its promises" (72–73). Troubled by the discrepancies between his "public declaration" of support for Solidarity (72) and reports that he is a "leading Communist" (123), Kostash wonders "[j]ust who [is] K 'with'?" (81). Is he, as her friend Jan suggests, "one of those weaklings who went whichever way the wind blew"? (123).

But Kostash is equally, if not more troubled, by the complexities of K's personal life. At once the "unfaithful" and the "devoted" husband (72), he has been married for thirty-two years, and has kept a mistress (B) for nearly as long. Always, Kostash writes as she describes his letters, "there was news of his two women" (76). And so, just as Kostash questions K's political allegiances, so too does she wonder about his personal fidelities. "I was becoming afraid of Warsaw," she writes, "of the mask upon mask my lover donned to make his way through his obligations" (77). To whom is K faithful? The Community Party or Solidarity? His wife or B? "[W]hat really," as Kostash phrases it, "would he do with yet another woman clamouring in Warsaw for his attention?" (77). Clearly, to become a part of his life, Kostash must fight for K's affection, yet she feels more pity than rivalry toward the other women in his life—not simply because both are ill (K's wife with glaucoma, B with cancer) but because, in reading K's letters, Kostash realizes that both women, over the course of their long-term relationships with K, have become locked into the traditional, domestic role of the "wife." Even between K and his mistress "there was...a *nuptial* faithfulness" (80). In meeting K a second time, moreover, in 1987, she sees that his identity, too, has been subsumed by his role as "husband" to both women. From the moment of her arrival in Warsaw, Kostash knows that he is "neither going to seduce [her] nor be seduced"; exhausted from taking care of his wife and B, he is "frail, not virile, distraught, not self-possessed" (80). During their time together, she struggles to keep her "erotic energy" focused on K and "away from the young men in denim" who "sat in jails and swore revenge" (82) because the domesticity in which he is ensconced holds no attraction for her. She wants a rebel hero, not a cowed husband. "If I want a Polish lover," she concludes, after visiting K in Warsaw, "I will have to dream him up" (82).

As Kostash learns, however, again and again in *The Doomed Bridegroom*, the process of "dreaming up" a lover is never easy because she is never entirely able to divorce her imagined love affairs from reality. And K's domesticity is not the only reality she must face in her relationship with him. In "The Masked Man in Warsaw," even as—or precisely because—she seeks to reinvent K as her ideal *Polish* lover, Kostash cannot ignore his, and indeed her own, ethnicity. Given the historical tensions between Ukrainians and Poles, and given that both Kostash and K are acutely aware of the uneasy relation between their respective ethnic groups, their relationship—real or imagined—comes to represent more than a union of one man and one woman. But whereas K believes that, in forming their "own little Polish-Ukrainian Friendship Society" (113), they can undo the traditional enmity between Ukrainians and Poles, Kostash is less willing to either forget or forgive the ways in which, and the extent to which, Poles oppressed Ukrainians over the course of their shared history. From the outset of their relationship, K confesses that Kostash's Ukrainian-ness—like his wife's Jewishness—is "exciting to him" (75). He repeatedly refers to her as his "blue-blooded" (111) lover. He sees her as a "'Ukrainian lady' of Byzantine provenance" (110) whose "profile remind[s] him of the origin of the Ukrainian nation in the excursions of the Viking princes into Rus" (75). Kostash, however, is skeptical about what he finds "so glamorous in [her] Ukrainianness" (111). Recalling a different moment in history, when Ukrainians "had been bonded labour on the great Polish estates of Galicia" (111), she identifies not with the blue-blooded Byzantine princess but, rather, with "the Galician, wide-hipped, bawdy, sly" (111). If K is to "lust after the Ukrainian in [her]," she says, "it should be that wench, barefoot in his kitchen, heating up his bathwater" (111). On the one hand, Kostash wants to believe that, in speaking together in a "new language," English, she and K can transcend the roles assigned to them, ostensibly, by history (114). "English," she writes, enables her and K to "say things to each other impossible in our old languages. The landlord and serf girl, for example,

[have] been doomed to play their respective parts: in Polish, the rapist; in Ukrainian, the violated maiden. In the new language, however, we [are] freed into a new theatre together" (114). On the other hand, Kostash provides no specific examples of the "new theatre" that she and K are "freed into" by speaking to each other in English. The problem is that K gives little more than a passing glance to the historically uneven relation between Ukrainians and Poles. She may believe that they can enter a "new theatre" of dialogue in English about the injustices of the past, but his answer to the "Ukrainian question" is to not talk about it at all, in any language. Instead of confronting Poles' predominantly negative perceptions of Ukrainians—according to Kostash, "the Ukrainian has stood for a whole repertoire of brutes that terrorize the Polish imagination: shifty Asiatic, godless Orthodox, witless yokel, treacherous bandit" (112)—he clings to the idealized version of the Ukrainian lover that he has "dreamed up": the timeless Byzantine princess who transcends history.

Kostash, however, in "dreaming up" her Polish lover, is unable or perhaps unwilling to ignore the enduring tensions between Ukrainians and Poles, brought home to her by K's reluctance to acknowledge his people's oppression of hers. Gradually, in her imagination, K becomes the Polish lord. She draws unmistakable parallels between the *pan*, lord and master of his estate, and K, high-ranking Communist Party member, Kostash resolves her lingering ambivalence toward K by constructing herself as the figure of the Ukrainian handmaiden who is attracted not to the Polish gentleman with "his slim-ankled bay mare, his red velvet riding coat, [and] his golden braid looping his right shoulder" (115) but to the Ukrainian ploughman who "dreams of running away, far east of here, to the emptied lands of Rus scourged by the Mongols, to join the other runaways—the serfs, the defrocked peasants, the army deserters, the town adventurers on the lam—known as the Zaporozhian Cossack Host" (117). And, in fact, once Kostash realizes that she is aroused by neither the real K nor her "dreamed up" version of him—for both are complicit in perpetuating the uneven relation between Ukrainians and Poles—she stops corresponding with K; stops toying with the possibility of taking a Polish lover, literally or figuratively. Her "long unfulfilled desire" goes "stale" and she becomes "distracted, looking out for a more promising avatar of revolution" (119). Doomed from the start, in a sense, her love affair with

K ends not because they suddenly have "nothing more to say to each other" (122) but because they have never really been able to speak to one another outside their "pre-scripted" historically- and ethnically-determined roles.

In "Lord, History Falls Through the Cracks," then, the penultimate chapter of *The Doomed Bridegroom*, Kostash revisits—with mounting anger and frustration—the ways in which particular patterns of historical relations between Ukrainians and other ethnic groups prove difficult to break. As she writes about her relationship with Canadian poet Patrick Friesen, who is of Mennonite descent, Kostash turns her attention to the intersecting history of Mennonites and Ukrainians, devoting little of the chapter to her specific experiences with Friesen. The details of her relationship with Friesen are sketchy, at best. They come together, briefly, after he divorces his Mennonite wife; though Kostash is eager to become involved with him—she makes "plans, arrangements"—he rejects her and "[f]all[s] in love with somebody else" (141). Determined to understand the reasons for which their friendship is doomed never to evolve into a love affair, she embarks on a quest to learn about the historical relations between her people and his—a quest that takes her to Ukraine and into the archive of Mennonite Canadian literature. Drawing upon her experiences with K, she explores the ways in which she and Friesen are unwittingly re-enacting, in their personal relationship, a drama that was played out by their ethnic groups on the stage of history, against the backdrop of Ukraine, and that has since been recorded again and again—rather one-sidedly—in Mennonite literature.

Examining Mennonite versions of their shared history with Ukrainians, Kostash is troubled by a specific historical moment in 1775 when Mennonites took on the role of colonizer vis-à-vis the Ukrainian colonized at Khortytsia[14] and she is no less troubled by the ways in which contemporary Mennonite writers, including Friesen, perpetuate this binary opposition between the two groups in their writing. Given that Mennonites have in common with Ukrainians the historical experience of injustice and oppression—at Khortytsia both were eventually forced from their homes, albeit at different times—she expects contemporary Mennonite writers to approach Mennonite–Ukrainian history with a modicum of sensitivity, if not sympathy, for the ways in which Ukrainians were mistreated by Mennonites. What she finds, however, in works by

Rudy Wiebe, Al Reimer, and John Weier, is that Ukrainians appear in a limited number of roles, usually as houseservants or hired hands, inferior and/or subservient to Mennonite characters—virtuous landowners and their chaste wives.[15] Kostash believes that Friesen—who, as a writer, "belong[s] to The Word" (145)—has internalized the notion of the Ukrainian, and especially the Ukrainian woman, as "other." She becomes at once the object of his desire and disavowal; he will choose her for a night, but not for a mate. That she stubbornly refuses to accept this role, however, is evident from the outset of the chapter. In "Lord, History Falls Through the Cracks," sardonically addressed as a letter to Friesen—her "Dear Heart"—Kostash "writes back" to Mennonite versions of history by retrieving Ukrainians from the margins of these stories.

In some ways similar to her writing about K, Kostash's chapter on Friesen is primarily focused on "righting" history by drawing attention to the historical tensions between Mennonites and Ukrainians. If, however, she is resigned with K to play the Ukrainian handmaiden to his Polish *pan*, she stubbornly refuses with Friesen to re-enact the historically uneven relation between their ethnic groups. Throughout "Lord, History Falls Through the Cracks," her tone is aggressive and confrontational. Although Friesen insists that his people "have no homeland"—that it is "the Mennonite condition" to be "devoid of nationality, of country" (134-35)—Kostash reminds him that Mennonite settlers "on the Dnipro and the island of Khortytsia" stayed "long enough to become landlords" (128). By no means unaware that Mennonite history is, in part, a "story of flight"—"you have to be able to get up and go," she says to Friesen, "when you feel the pressure, the danger; you have to be able to shake off the dirt as though this earth were not beloved" (135)—Kostash acknowledges that, by the 1930s, the Mennonites living in Khortytsia were driven from Ukraine by Soviet authorities, not unlike the Cossacks before them who were driven out by the imperial army of Russia. But given that the Mennonites, despite their own experiences of injustice and oppression, embraced the role of colonizer/oppressor vis-à-vis their Ukrainian neighbours for well over a hundred years, she takes some delight in writing to Friesen while she travels in Ukraine about the ways in which the Mennonites' presence in Khortytsia has been erased. "Where are they now, those Menno villages of Khortytsia?" she asks. "Where are your names?" (129). And then, answering her own questions, she says, "[e]ffaced and relettered. There are Ukrainian villages here now" (129). With a sense of triumph, albeit belated, over the Mennonite settlers who displaced Ukrainians from their land, she says, "[y]ou left and we grew back. You are utterly gone. No one remembers you" (136). While Friesen's ancestors may have oppressed hers, the Ukrainians seem to have the final say in naming and claiming back their homeland.

And yet, the lingering problem for Kostash—a problem she seeks to rectify in and through her discussion of Nestor Makhno—is that, in Mennonite versions of history, Ukrainians have no say at all. Makhno (1889-1935), she explains, was a Ukrainian revolutionary, a political idealist and a guerilla fighter, who, between 1918 and 1921, led the "Revolutionary Insurgent Army, a force in the service of no government, no political party and no dictatorship" (152). To Friesen—who writes disparagingly of Makhno in one of his poems—and to many other Mennonites as well, Makhno was a "bandit, assassin, highway robber, [and] pogromist" (146). Upon meeting Kostash for the first time, Friesen's mother asks, "[s]o why did your people kill my people?" And she goes on to denounce Makhno for slaughtering "199 Mennonite farmers from God knows which and whose village" (144). From Kostash's point of view, however, Makhno, known as "*Batko*" or "Father" to his followers, is a man to be admired precisely because he and his army (the *makhnovtsi*) stood up for the Ukrainian people. They took an active role in reshaping their country, fighting for the ideals of freedom and justice for all. As a "real life" Ukrainian hero, Makhno challenges fictionalized notions of the Ukrainian man as "blockhead" that so pervasively circulate within Mennonite literature and he also offers the Ukrainian woman a way out of the Mennonite/Ukrainian "political economy of cross-cultural desire" (168). In imagining herself as his lover, Kostash rewrites the role of the Ukrainian woman—no longer the passive servant/slut who can be taken and rejected at any time by her Mennonite master or by Ukrainian men, she announces and acts upon *her* desire. By retrieving Makhno from the margins of Mennonite history, and by placing him "inside" a "Ukrainian story" (138) as her rebel lover, Kostash ensures that neither he—nor she— slips "through the cracks" of the Mennonite-Ukrainian past.

In a sense, really, of all her lovers, real or imagined, Nestor Makhno is the figure with whom Kostash identifies most strongly, not only because he was a Ukrainian who stood up for his oppressed and downtrodden people, but because Makhno's real struggle—which mirrors, in many ways, Kostash's own struggle throughout *The Doomed Bridegroom*—is to represent himself in and through the written word. Although she acknowledges that the success of Makhno's peasant movement in challenging the power of the "rich" in Ukraine was short-lived—the *makhnovtsi* revolt was quelled by Stalin's Red Army in the winter of 1920–21 (153)—Kostash believes that Makhno's actual defeat came years later. Forced to flee from Ukraine to France, in 1921, Makhno—less martyr to his cause than scapegoat for Mennonite bitterness toward Ukrainians—"eked out a miserable existence" for the next fourteen years in exile; he died a pauper in 1935 (154). In a telling commentary on the ways in which Makhno's historical agency was ultimately undermined, his "enemies [didn't] even bother to arrange his assassination; they just [stopped] talking about him" (154).

In the years before his death, frustrated by misleading accounts of his life—especially N. Herasymenko's *'Father' Makhno: Recollections of a White Guardist* (1923)—Makhno tried to write his own memoirs, but only one of the three volumes he wrote was published in his lifetime. The other two volumes were published posthumously by Makhno's friend, Victor Eichenbaum.[16] Sifting through the multiple existing biographies of Makhno, including Al Reimer's *My Harp is Turned to Mourning*, a fictionalized rendering of Makhno's life story,[17] and comparing these with Makhno's autobiography, edited and, importantly, "embellished" by Eichenbaum (149), Kostash begins to see his revolution as "a rage to find a language" (150). In her own attempts to separate his voice "from the clamour of those who spoke for him" (149), she discovers that Makhno, ironically, "could neither speak nor write Ukrainian with facility" (150); while he wrote in Russian, moreover, he "admits in his memoirs that he 'mutilated' the Russian language in a most shameful manner" (150). Kostash sees Makhno, in his final days, "sweating furiously for a language, any language, a system to hook him into a code of meaning that is neither cryptic nor provisional, but historic": she sees him as a "man trying to catapult himself into the universal language of cause-and-effect, into the company of the revolutionaries who preceded him and those who will come after" (156). "That he could act," Kostash writes, "we agree; that he had agency, well, history cut him off in the middle of a speech" (156). In his fight to make himself heard—to tell his own story, in his own words—Makhno's voice was silenced by those who misrepresented him in their accounts of his life story.

Yet if Kostash intimately understands Makhno's desire to "catapult himself into the universal language of cause-and-effect, into the company of the revolutionaries who preceded him and those who will come after," it is precisely because she is searching herself for a "language" or a "system" that will hook her into a "code of meaning that is neither cryptic nor provisional, but historic" (156). Although she explicitly focuses *The Doomed Bridegroom* on her relationships with various lovers, her text becomes, implicitly, the story of her love affair with language itself. On the one hand, in writing about her career-long obsession with "rebel men," Kostash reveals her attempts to become a part of their "other" worlds and fraught histories by developing relationships with them. What she seems to crave is a place in history beside the revolutionaries whose stories attract and arouse her; she seems to want to reinvent herself as an agent of social change, a "rebel woman" actively involved in the dramas that have characterized the histories of Eastern and Southern Europe. But even when she imagines herself as lover to the men who actually played a part in these dramas, she is doomed to play a passive, supporting role in relation to them—as girlfriend, comrade, or mistress, her identity is defined in relation to her lovers. By ultimately rejecting, then, the full repertoire of traditional female roles, and especially the conventional roles of wife and mother, Kostash carves out a new role for herself that is not defined by her relationship, real or imagined, with any man. She narrates her coming-of-age as a particular kind of "rebel woman," one whose constant companion is her pen; who commits herself to a lifelong relationship with words; who is married, in a sense, to her writing. The process of writing, after all, is what empowers her to transcend the limitations of reality, and what simultaneously enables her to accept the limitations of fantasy. By creating a textual world in which the boundaries between fiction and non-fiction are radically blurred, Kostash arrives at a new understanding of herself. In doing so, she at last succeeds in her quest to redefine her sense of community beyond borders and bloodlines—at least in her own eyes. In and through her writing, she comes to embrace her role as the bearer of books—"*I would bear books*"

(54), she announces—and as a mother-figure to the next generation of writers who will learn from her about the ways in which language can transform the realities of the past, the present, and the future.

In the brief final chapter of *The Doomed Bridegroom*, turning once more to her infatuation with the men of the "other" Europe, Kostash narrates a familiar story: "Belgrade," a kind of coda to the text, focuses on an unnamed Serbian boy she meets in 1997 and who reminds her, in different ways, of all her previous lovers. Boyish and lanky, like Lenny, he is a poet, like Stus, and he has another woman in his life, not unlike Kostas, K, and Stus. Most importantly, perhaps, he feels trapped in—or doomed by—the state of his country. "The truth is gone out of here," he tells Kostash, "out of this world. Only the enemy is telling the truth. I am losing ground under my feet. Everyday is the same. I get this terrible feeling that I am who I am now, and it will always be like this. Serbia is the worst place to live in the universe" (174). "Why," he asks, "are you so interested in us? Why do you keep coming here to Belgrade?" (174). Although Kostash never answers him directly, she has been scripting a reply, in a sense, from the beginning of *The Doomed Bridegroom*. A disillusioned neophyte poet who has yet to discover the transformative power of language, the Serbian boy needs to be guided and nurtured. Motherly toward him—she buys him dinner; lets him fall asleep on her breast as they watch a movie together (172)—Kostash sees the boy as inheritor of her literary legacy. She looks forward to a day when "[her] story will be his" (174). In time, she suggests, he too—learning from her example—will discover the ways in which he can use language to re-imagine his past as well as his future. Her "story" will become his when he recognizes as she has that he is not doomed by the brute facts of history but rather empowered, as a writer, to transcend them.

And so, in the end—with striking similarities to the realization Andrew Suknaski arrives at in his poetry—Kostash comes to see that what she has always been seeking in her travels and in her relationships with "rebel" men from "other" parts of the world is less an intimate connection to Eastern Europe than a deep understanding and acceptance of her identity as a writer. Just as Suknaski returns again and again to Wood Mountain, taking on different roles as he attempts to define his sense of community, history, and home, so too does Kostash make numerous journeys to Eastern Europe, determined to find a place where she belongs. In one way or another, really, all of the writers whose work I have focused on in the book—Vera Lysenko, Maara Haas, George Ryga, Andrew Suknaski, Janice Kulyk Keefer—are looking for a place and a way to belong, as Ukrainians and as Canadians. What such writers as Suknaski and Kostash illustrate, however, is that the feeling of belonging requires an ongoing negotiation of their multiple subject positions—not just their ethnic and national identities, but also their regional, gendered, generational, and, above all, professional identities. "Take a second-generation Ukrainian Canadian, a feminist, a writer, an alumna of the 1960s, and put her on a train in Belgrade heading north. What exactly is her business?" (2). Take a second-generation Ukrainian Canadian painter, a prairie boy, a poet, an alumna of the avant-garde poetry scene, and put him on a bus in Toronto heading west. What exactly is his business? Their business is to refuse to arrive, to keep exploring new avenues of language and genre in their writing, and, in doing so, to keep the dialogue on identity open-ended and alive. For these writers, identity is not contained in a "closed book" or a "stone house" but rather in words that are open to constant "re-vision."

Post-script

**Monumental Culture and the Future
of Ukrainian Canadian Literature**

SEVERAL SUMMERS AGO, in July, 2002, I made a trip home to northeastern Alberta. I had with me a friend who was visiting from New Zealand. Although Michael had been to Canada once before, he was seeing the prairies for the first time. My sister Jana drove us from Edmonton, where our plane landed, to St. Paul, two-and-a-half hours northeast of Edmonton. As we passed by various landmarks, and as Jana and I gave Michael a running commentary on our surroundings, I was struck by the feeling that we were travelling through history. Just after entering Elk Island National Park, we spotted a herd of buffalo grazing along the highway, remnants of the pre-settlement era of Canadian history. Then we passed by the Ukrainian Cultural Heritage Village, a perfectly-preserved turn-of-the-century pioneer settlement—here was evidence of the immigrant homesteaders who came to conquer the land. I pointed to the "Grekul House" on the edge of the Village, a reconstructed home that belonged to one of our ancestors. Michael was intrigued. We promised to come back and spend a day at the museum. Meanwhile, Jana and I told Michael that he would be seeing many more ancestral homes along the way—old farmhouses, granaries, and barns, long-abandoned and hardly standing. We would be driving past our great-grandparents' original homesteads around Two Hills and Hairy Hill, where some of our relatives still live, and eventually we would come to the Greek Orthodox church at Szypenitz where many of our people are buried. Michael had many questions about Ukrainian pioneers, Ukrainian history, and

Ukrainian culture. Our mom, we assured him, would prepare Ukrainian food for him—without being asked—and our dad would need little encouragement to narrate the entire family history. I suggested that we all take in the Vegreville *Pysanka* Festival. I wanted Michael to see Ukrainian dancers perform. His trip to the prairies was shaping up to be very Ukrainian.

But before reaching Two Hills, Hairy Hill, and Szypenitz—and before winding our way past Duvernay, Brosseau, and St. Brides, on the last stretch of road to St. Paul—we would first have to drive through Mundare, a small Ukrainian Canadian farming community situated roughly at the half-way point between Edmonton and St. Paul. Jana and I exchanged glances as we approached the Mundare turn-off. I wondered if it was too late to turn back, and take a different route to St. Paul. It was. I glanced back at Michael in the backseat, hoping that he might have fallen asleep. He hadn't.

Should we warn him? Could we distract him so that he would miss it?

For as long as I can remember, Mundare, Alberta—population 700—has been known for its award-winning Ukrainian sausage. Woytko Stawnichy founded Stawnichy's Meat Processing in 1959; his son Ed took over in 1971. Over the years, the Stawnichy operation doubled and then tripled in size. It has grown from a small family business to a large and immensely profitable sausage empire. In fact, using state-of-the-art food processing equipment, Ed Stawnichy has diversified his business, so the company now produces numerous meat products—pepperoni, beef jerky, wieners—as well as several traditional Ukrainian foods—*perohy*, *perishky*, *holuptsi*, and *nelysnyky*.

But *kolbasa* is what made Stawnichy's—and indeed Mundare—famous. So, in 2001, when *Mayor* Ed Stawnichy decided that the town needed a tourist attraction to give the local economy a boost, he, naturally enough, decided to build a giant *kolbasa*.

Anyone who is familiar with small-town, and even big-city, Canadian culture knows that countless communities across the country have built similar monuments. The list—which would include the Sudbury Nickel, the Wawa Goose, the Gimli Viking, and the Kamloops Trout—is actually too long to recount here.[1] Alberta, however, may well boast the most man-made giants. Fahler has a giant bee; Vilna, a cluster of giant mushrooms; Andrew, a giant duck. Smoky Lake is known for its giant pumpkin and Pincher Creek for its giant pincers. My hometown built a giant U.F.O. Landing Pad in 1967 for their centennial project; then, in 1995, Vulcan, now known as our sister-town, constructed a giant spaceship. And as far as ethnic communities go, Alberta's Ukrainian Canadians are far-and-away the leaders in leaving their unique cultural mark on the prairie landscape. In 1974, the town of Vegreville built a giant Ukrainian Easter egg to commemorate the RCMP centennial. The *Pysanka* is 31 feet high, 25.7 feet long, and 18 feet wide; it weighs over 5000 pounds. In 1991—in an attempt to draw tourists to their village—the people of Glendon, population 400, erected a giant *Perogy*, pierced by a giant silver fork. The *Perogy*, situated in "*Perogy* Park" just off "*Perogy* Drive," is 25 feet high and 12 feet wide, and it weighs over 6000 pounds.

The Mundare *Kolbasa*, then, wasn't the first—and may not be the last—Ukrainian Canadian prairie monument, though it is certainly the tallest and arguably the least attractive. Dark reddish-brown in colour, the *Kolbasa* has been the butt of endless jokes in our family. We laugh because it looks less like a coil of sausage than a coil of dog feces; because the thing could be read as a tribute to homo-erotic desire; because *who in the world* would erect a forty-two-foot ring of Ukrainian garlic sausage?

Michael demanded that we stop.

He forced Jana and me to pose in various spots around the base of the *Kolbasa* while he snapped pictures of it—and us—from every imaginable angle.

We ate lunch—Stawnichy's *kolbasa*-on-a-bun, of course—beside the *Kolbasa* while Michael stared, at once dumbfounded and delighted by the sheer audacity of it. After Jana and I gave him a quick history of the *Pysanka* and the *Perogy*, he asked if we could visit these monuments as well.

In the end, Michael didn't find the Ukrainian Cultural Heritage Village terribly interesting. He loved my mother's Ukrainian dishes, though; he thought that the Ukrainian dancing at the Vegreville *Pysanka* Festival was terrific; and, of course, he couldn't stop talking about the *Pysanka*, the *Perogy*, and, especially, the *Kolbasa*.

As for me, I saw home through new eyes during my trip back last summer. I hadn't been to the Ukrainian Cultural Heritage Village or to the Vegreville *Pysanka* Festival in years, and I remembered them differently. The Village that I remembered was magical—it was a place where history came alive. When I was young, I wanted to be a role-playing tour guide. I dreamed about living in the "Grekul House," hoeing the Grekul garden, feeding the Grekul chickens. Vegreville was even more exciting. I Ukrainian danced for ten years and the *Pysanka* Festival was an annual highlight for our whole dance club. Walking around the Festival grounds in our costumes and our stage make-up, wearing the medals that we'd won in competition, poking around the cultural exhibits and buying souvenirs at the marketplace—I don't ever recall feeling so proud to be Ukrainian. The *Pysanka* Festival was "cool"; there, being Ukrainian was "cool" too. So I was surprised in 2002 at how much the Village and the Festival had changed—or surprised, I suppose, at how much I had changed. Walking through the Village last summer, I thought the role-players looked bored and listless—just a group of university kids trying to get through the day, eager to get back to the city for the evening. My "people," the "Grekuls" seemed uninterested in the whole charade. In many ways more disappointing than the Village, the *Pysanka* Festival made me wish that I hadn't brought a guest along with me to Vegreville. I remembered a busy, bustling marketplace with dozens of merchants selling a wide variety of classy Ukrainian souvenirs. Had it really gone so down-hill? Or were there always just a handful of craftspeople hawking cheap pottery and kitschy T-shirts? Strolling through the cultural exhibits with Michael and my family, I paused for a moment at a dusty display of "Ukrainian Christmas Foods"—twelve dishes of real food that had been shellacked—and felt my stomach turn. The cabbage rolls and *perohy* were discoloured, the mushrooms black and shriveled. A violin player in an embroidered shirt strolled by playing "Danny Boy." We watched dancers at the Grandstand Show in the afternoon, and they *were* terrific—polished professionals; lively, energetic, full of life. Then the headliners "Mickey and Bunny" took to the stage. An aging couple who made it big in the 1960s and 1970s with their Ukrainian renditions of popular songs like "This Land is Your Land," Mickey and Bunny had lost their touch.[2] They sang off-key and forgot the words to their songs; their geriatric drummer couldn't keep a steady beat; and, perhaps worst of all, nobody else in the crowd seemed to notice. Mickey and Bunny received a standing ovation.

On our way home to St. Paul, we stopped at the outskirts of Vegreville to have one last look at the *Pysanka*—and, posing in front of it while my dad pulled out his camera, I wanted to cry. Are we doomed?

I wondered. *Click*. Is this all we are? *Click*. How do we drag ourselves out from the under the shadow of the giant egg? *Click*.

Just as my thinking, though, about Ukrainian Canadian literature and why it has slipped through the cracks of Canadian literary studies has changed over the past couple of years, so too have my attitudes toward Ukrainian Canadian culture. Writing this book has helped me understand where my disdain for hackneyed symbols and fossilized folklore has come from. It has come, I believe, from a fervent desire to see fresher, "sexier," and more innovative images of our culture circulate in Canadian society; and it has come from a simultaneous fear—passed on from my grandparents' generation to my parents' generation to mine—that such images simply do not, or cannot, exist. In *All of Baba's Great-grandchildren: Ethnicity in the Next Canada* (2000), Myrna Kostash addresses this exact problem. "[P]erformances of Ukrainian dancing are very popular with general audiences," she writes, "the giant *Pysanka* in Vegreville, Alberta, is a tourist attraction, and Sunshine Records of Winnipeg distributes over fifty titles in the category, 'Baba's Records.'" But even as these representations of Ukrainian Canadian ethnicity "increasingly disconcer[t] those born several generations down the line from the Galician pioneers of western Canada" (21–22), most Ukrainian Canadians "still generally go along with the popular view of themselves as colourful, dancing, *horilka*-tippling hunkies recently arrived from a wheat farm in Saskatchewan" (30). "There's no getting around the psychological *insecurity*," she says, "of a community that has periodically lived under a cloud in Canada as 'enemy aliens' in the Great War, 'Reds' in the 1930s, anti-Communist extremists in the 1950s, and aging, anti-Semitic alleged pro-Nazi collaborators in the 1980s and 1990s" (32). Who, Kostash wonders, *wouldn't* choose the image of the "fun-loving bumpkin" over these "stigmatizations" (32)?

In other words, little has changed since Kostash published *All of Baba's Children*. Ukrainian Canadians of the fourth- and fifth-generations are battling the same deeply-entrenched, song-and-dance stereotypes of their ethnic group that she railed against in the late 1970s. Turning her attention to *Zdorov*, a Toronto-based, English-language magazine that caters to "20-and-30-something" Ukrainian Canadians—and that was modeled on the "very cool *Eyetalian* magazine, also published in Toronto"—Kostash laments the "unvarnished folksiness" of the

Ukrainian publication (*All of Baba's Great-grandchildren* 29). Whereas *Eyetalian* is characterized by "hyper-urban design smarts and nuovo Tuscan chic" (29)—its contributors include *Globe & Mail* columnists and "a Governor General's Award-winning novelist" (24)—the layout of *Zdorov* is neither "snazzy" nor "sumptuous" (24). Not unaware of the ubiquitous image of Ukrainians as "colourful, dancing, *horilka*-tippling hunkies" (30), the editor of *Zdorov*, Nestor Gula, tells Kostash that his goal is to represent Ukrainians in his magazine as "[n]ormal. Even cool" (24). The problem, though, as he sees it, is that Ukrainian culture simply *isn't*. "Italians," he says, "think it's really cool being Italian and going to Italy and listening to opera, and the rest of the world thinks so too. For Canadians, Italy is the Roman Empire, the Renaissance, the source of civilization, while Ukraine?... They think of us as dancers" (24-25). In other words, while Gula wants to challenge stereotypes of Ukrainian Canadian culture, he has no alternative images upon which to draw. He could focus more substantially, perhaps, on "provocative issues" such as the "under-representation of Ukrainian-Canadians in the Canadian elites, and the pursuit of alleged war criminals by Canadian courts"—issues around which his magazine "walk[s] softly" (31). But according to Kostash, Gula "treads a fine line between what's 'interesting' about Ukrainian-Canadians and what's 'negative,'" keeping in mind that his targeted audience of Ukrainian Canadian "yuppies" wants to hear the "good news" of "Ukrainian Canadian achievement in the arts, science and business" (31). So even as *Zdorov* attempts to transform Ukrainian Canadian culture into something "cool," sexy, and fun—one issue provides "Ten reasons why *varenyky* are better than sex" (29)—the magazine is forced to *reinforce*, albeit playfully, the very stereotypes that it seeks to challenge. Gula seems to have no other choice.

Kostash's argument, ultimately, is that Ukrainian Canadians of the next generation face the same challenges as their parents', grandparents', and indeed great-grandparents' generations—how to retrieve their experiences from the margins of Canadian history; how to overcome enduring stereotypes of their ethnic culture; how to make their ethnicity meaningful in, and relevant to, their time and place. And she concludes *All of Baba's Great-grandchildren* by suggesting that, if Ukrainian Canadian ethnicity is to survive into—and beyond—the twenty-first century, then Ukrainian Canadians must continually re-invent themselves and re-imagine their place in Canadian society. "[E]ach new generation of Canadians," she say, "has to think through its own relationship to the past and to its own civic desires" (37) because uncertainties about "who we 'really' are" are "never resolved by any particular generation once and for all" (37).

Perhaps what matters, then, is not whether we find the "best" way to represent ourselves in Canadian society but rather that we continue trying to make our presence visible in the cultural landscape of this country. Perhaps the business of "getting it right"—promoting the "right" image of Ukrainian Canadians—is not as important as fostering ongoing dialogue about what it means to be Ukrainian and Canadian. Despite my initial reservations about monumental Ukrainian Canadian culture, I've come to appreciate the Mundare *Kolbasa*, the Glendon *Perogy*, and the Vegreville *Pysanka*, in part because all three have become conversation pieces. They have sparked lively debate among friends and family members, divided in their opinions about the monuments, but united by their interest in understanding what they mean. These days, in fact, my feeling is that the *Kolbasa*, the *Perogy*, and the *Pysanka* have less to do with Ukrainian Canadians promoting specific folk customs than with Ukrainian Canadians boldly refusing to be an "invisible" minority. In a sense, the Ukrainian Canadians who erected these giant symbols of our culture share my motivations for writing *Leaving Shadows*. What these monuments declare to the world is that we're here; that we've made "enormous" contributions to the nation; and that we will not be forgotten. Whether we choose to write literature, produce literary criticism, or build monuments, we all want to come out from the shadows of assimilation and leave new shadows, new marks on the nation.

What this book shows is that English-language Ukrainian Canadian writers have been "leaving shadows" for the past fifty-odd years, and that we—by which I mean Ukrainian and non-Ukrainian Canadians alike—need to listen to their voices, read those shadows, not only to understand where we have come from but also to help chart a map to where we are going.

To be sure, the writers whose texts I have examined struggle in their attempts to come to terms with being Ukrainian and Canadian. Each is forced to grapple with the constraints of his or her historical moment. Few are able to formulate a definitive, universal answer to the question of how Ukrainian Canadians might best negotiate their divided sense of self.

Indeed, most of the writers in this study illustrate the incommensurability of their dual identities. In *Yellow Boots*, Vera Lysenko puts forth a (pre)multicultural vision of the nation that ostensibly allows her heroine to retain her ethnic culture while ascending the social and economic hierarchies of Canadian society, but that vision is clouded by the actual comprises Lilli Landash is forced to make as a woman from an ethnic minority background. By the end of the novel, Lilli, twice-marginalized by virtue of her gender and ethnicity, has all but fully assimilated to patriarchal Anglo-Canadian culture; her Ukrainian culture has been reduced to folk songs and a pair of dancing boots. Such later writers as Maara Haas and George Ryga confront the dilemma of second-generation Ukrainian Canadians whose ties to their ethnic heritage have been severed by the policies and practices of assimilation. These writers want to reconnect with their ethnic roots but they reject officially-sanctioned song-and-dance expressions of ethnicity, choosing instead to explore the experiences of "ordinary" Ukrainian Canadians who have been excluded, under-represented, or misrepresented in the annals of Canadian history. In Haas's *The Street Where I Live* and Ryga's *A Letter to My Son*, genre and language become sites of resistance to Anglo-Canadian cultural hegemony as these authors begin to experiment with hybrid generic and linguistic forms that reinforce the Ukrainian Canadian past about which they write. Writing about the past, though, in texts that predominantly adhere to realist literary conventions is precisely what undermines the success of their enterprise because their stories ultimately narrate the dying culture of a bygone era. The underlying message of both texts is that Ukrainian Canadian ethnicity has come to pass. Neither Haas nor Ryga proposes a "plan" for how Ukrainian Canadians might actively nurture their ethnicity and keep it alive in the future. They are unable to imagine "endings" to Ukrainian Canadian narratives that deviate from their own experiences and observations.

Janice Kulyk Keefer's *The Green Library* and *Honey and Ashes: A Story of Family* suffer from a similar assumption that ethnicity and history are not actively negotiated and interpreted but rather passively inherited through genealogy. That Kulyk Keefer self-consciously documents her family history for her sons is key. On the one hand, by drawing attention to the fact that she has children, she establishes the continuance of her family bloodlines. At the same time, by scripting the family history *for them*—with a resolution that leaves no questions unanswered, no mysteries unsolved—she cripples their potential for playing an active role in (re)defining their identities as third-generation Ukrainian Canadians. The subtext of *Honey and Ashes* is that, should her sons re-discover their ethnicity someday and become interested in the Old Place, they need only read their mother's book to learn "The Truth" about their past—and "The Truth," according to Kulyk Keefer, is not that ethnicity is constantly redefined by the fluid exchange of culture between two worlds and two homes but that it is contained, rather, in her ready-made family history, as firmly rooted in Canada as the stone house in which she writes.

Andrew Suknaski and Myrna Kostash are the two writers who emerge from this book as the most promising avatars of the future of Ukrainian Canadian literature because they emphasize the notion that reinvention is the key to maintaining ties to their ethnic roots. Neither writer embraces a "pre-packaged" model of ethnicity—as do Lysenko, with song-and-dance; Haas and Ryga, with prairie history; and Kulyk Keefer, with bloodlines and family history in Ukraine. For Suknaski and Kostash, identity is not product but process played out in a constant, ongoing, imaginative engagement with language. In their texts, they are always departing, always setting out, always on the move. Their writing is less about coming home than about the open-ended, perpetual search for home. Suknaski's suggestion that language functions as a carrier of culture—his self-conscious interest in using language as a living link between the past and the present—and Kostash's deliberate decision to blur the boundaries between reality and fantasy point to the creative process as key to re-imagining their sense of self, community, history, and home.

But, as I argued in the Introduction to this book, creativity alone is not enough for people to take notice of the existence and value of an ethnic minority group's literary tradition. While working on this project and simultaneously witnessing the release of my novel, *Kalyna's Song*, I have often thought about Enoch Padolsky's observation that "many minority writers are still being published, individually or in anthologies, in group-specific journals or by group-run, small, or regional presses," and that production conditions on the margins, which is where much minority writing and criticism can be found, tend to entail 'marginal' problems: distribution of texts is often difficult, reviews are fewer and less prominent, libraries are less likely to carry texts, publishing houses are less able to reprint them, teachers less likely to teach them, students to write theses on them, critics less likely to find them, write on them, and be published. (375)

The problem is not that Ukrainian Canadian literature doesn't exist but that the collective body of publishers, editors, reviewers, scholars, critics, and teachers has allowed this literature—like that of other "invisible" minority groups—to remain in the margins of the Canadian literary institution, choosing instead to make "race" the locus of debate about identity. Ukrainian Canadian writers, and indeed other ethnic minority writers, have made substantial and relevant contributions to discussions about assimilation, multiculturalism, and transculturalism; about the intersecting issues of ethnicity, "class," gender, and sexuality; about nationalism, transnationalism, and diaspora. But if their voices aren't heard—if their texts aren't read, studied, written about, and taught—these contributions become meaningless.

My experiences with *Kalyna's Song* have driven home to me, again and again, the precarious state of ethnic minority literature in Canada. I wrote the novel with re-invention in mind. My goal was to write a Ukrainian Canadian story that hadn't been told before—a story set not in the distant pioneering days but in the multicultural heyday of the 1980s and early 1990s; a story shaped as much by humour as by hardship; a story that would explore ethnic "roots" without focusing on going "back" to Ukraine. I wanted to write a contemporary novel about how a fourth-generation Ukrainian Canadian girl experiences her ethnicity in part through the folkways she inherits from her family, in part through the history lessons she learns from her music teacher, a Holocaust survivor, and in part through her unique synthesis of the multiple languages and cultures she encounters in both Canada and her unlikely destination of Swaziland, in southern Africa. I wanted to show both Ukrainian and non-Ukrainian Canadian readers that ethnicity still matters to third- and fourth-generation Ukrainian Canadians. And I also wanted to inspire Ukrainian Canadians of my generation to set down their stories. I've seen first-hand, however, that writing a novel and having it published do not guarantee that it will circulate widely and attract a broad readership.

If I have learned anything over the course of writing this book and *Kalyna's Song*, it is that the future of Ukrainian Canadian literature lies as much in the hands of readers, critics, and scholars as it does in the hands of the writers themselves. The Ukrainian Canadian literary tradition simply will not survive if it is not included in classroom syllabi and drawn into ongoing debates in Canadian literary studies—and if readers take one lesson away from this book, I hope it will be that, while *Leaving Shadows* covers a good deal of territory, it provides a starting, rather than an end, point to discussion about how Ukrainian Canadian literature is relevant to Canadian literary studies. The challenge for Ukrainian Canadian literary scholars—which mirrors that of early feminist and postcolonial scholars—is how to incorporate this "marginal" body of literature into the mainstream without losing sight of the ways in which it challenges and subverts mainstream assumptions, values, and beliefs. Finding ways to talk about points of convergence and divergence—exploring sameness as well as difference—should be our goal. As Kostash suggests, we must not "confuse the ideal of commonality with the assumption that we therefore live in community, blissfully ignorant of the multiplicity and instability that complicate any given group's identity." We are all, she says, "being challenged to come up with a language that may be employed persuasively in the public sphere, which is where our *collective* if not common interests coincide" (*All of Baba's Great-grandchildren* 37).

My hope is that, by taking Ukrainian Canadian literature in new directions, we will succeed in making it visible in the "public sphere" Kostash talks about, where our collective, though not necessarily common, interests coincide. I hope that we can make this literature as visible in the Canadian cultural landscape as the Mundare *Kolbasa* or the Glendon *Perogy* are on the prairies. What I have come to believe is that, if we are indeed stranded under the shadow of a giant Easter egg, perhaps this isn't such a bad place to be. As Marusya Bociurkiw reminds us, after all, "*in Ukrainian, the word for writing is pysaty and...the word for Easter Egg is* pysanka: *literally, written object*" (*Woman Who Loved Airports* xi). Perhaps as writers and as scholars, we need to see the Vegreville *Pysanka* as a tribute to our literary past and as a guiding light for the future of Ukrainian Canadian literature, keeping in mind that "*[t]o write—because with the pysanka, each mark is a symbol with a specific meaning—is to continue history and to believe in eternal life*"(xi). We have the chance to write ourselves out of existing shadows and leave new ones, we just need to take it.

Notes

Listening to *All of Baba's Children*

1 The Canadian Institute of Ukrainian Studies at the University of Alberta and University of Toronto; the Ukrainian Folklore Program at the University of Alberta; the Centre for Ukrainian Canadian Studies at the University of Manitoba; the Prairie Centre for the Study of Ukrainian Heritage at the University of Saskatchewan.

2 Ryga and Haas were present at a conference called *Identifications: Ethnicity and the Writer in Canada*, held at the University of Alberta in 1979. In a panel discussion, Haas said, "it takes great discipline on my part not to vomit when I hear the word ethnic. My reflex action is to spit on the word that was spat on me in my formative years of the middle thirties. Dirty ethnic, rotten Slavic ethnic, ghetto freak ethnic. I was hyphenated, set apart by the English, Scottish, Irish factors outside the ghetto. Each time the word ethnic rears its hyphenated head, the odour of a clogged sewer smelling of racism poisons the air" (Balan, *Identifications* 136). Ryga, in the same panel discussion, said, "we're discussing Canadian literature in a Canadian context and everything that implies. As a contributor to that literature, I find it difficult to see myself as a so-called hyphenated Canadian.... When I wake up in the morning, I check myself out to see if I am still a man. Having determined that I am, I then face the world on its merits.... I do not live in the past. I do not live in my father's frame of reference" (140–42).

3 I borrow this phrase from Janice Kulyk Keefer who says, in "'Coming Across Bones': Historiographic Ethnofiction" (1995), "I know that in the eyes of the Ukrainian Canadian community, my emphasis on a history that cuts both ways, showing Ukrainians as both oppressed and oppressors, may be perceived as the attitude of someone so alienated from her ancestry that she has taken to fouling her own nest" (99).

4 The question of whether the study of "race" should be distinguished from the study of ethnicity has been the subject of debate among scholars (see, for example, Michael Banton's *Race Relations*, 1967; Pierre van den Berghe's "Class, Race and Ethnicity in Africa," 1983; and Thomas Hylland Eriksen's "Ethnicity, Race, and Nation," 1997). I draw a distinction between "racial" and "ethnic" minority writing because, as Winfried Siemerling suggests, "ethnicity has...been rejected sometimes as a serviceable category by those who feel that it might depoliticize issues by conflating them, for instance those concerning minorities in general with those concerning visible minorities" (11).

5 *Harvest: Anthology of Mennonite Writing in Canada 1874–1974* (1974); *Other Voices: Writings by Blacks in Canada* (1985); *Arab-Canadian Writing: Stories, Memoirs, and Reminiscences* (1989); *Transplanted Lives: Dutch-Canadian Stories and Poems* (1989); *Italian-Canadian Voices: An Anthology of Poetry and Prose (1946–1983)* (1984); *Chilean Literature in Canada/Literatura Chilena en Canada* (1982); *Yarmarok: Ukrainian Writing in Canada Since the Second World War* (1987); and *Voices: Canadian Writers of African Descent* (1992).

6 Canadian literature's dialogue about race began in the late 1980s, when Canadian literati engaged in heated discussions about white authors' right to depict cultures other than their own. As Marlene Nourbese Philip writes in "The Disappearing Debate; or, How the Discussion of Racism Has Been Taken Over by the Censorship Issue" (1997), discussions about cultural appropriation started in 1987 when the editors of the Women's Press in Toronto argued about whether or not to include three short stories (by white writers who had "drawn on and used the voices of characters from cultures and races other than their own" [97]) in their anthology *Imagining Women* (eventually published in 1988). In 1988, Lee Maracle (at the annual meeting of the Writers' Union of Canada) asked Anne Cameron to stop using Native stories in her writing; in 1989, the role of minority writers became an issue at the PEN conference in Toronto; in the 1992 newsletters of the Writers' Union of Canada "issues of censorship and the writer and voice" took centre stage (Philip 97); and in 1995, the Writing Thru Race Conference, held in Vancouver, aroused much media attention (the conference excluded white writers from most of its workshops; for a fuller description of the conference and the controversy that surrounded it, see Roy Miki's essay "Sliding the Scale of Elision: 'Race' Constructs / Cultural Praxis" [125–59] in *Broken Entries* [1998]). Myrna Kostash found herself at the centre of these debates, as she served as Chair of the Writers' Union of Canada from 1993 to 1994.

7 Diaspora has been defined as, for example, "a relational network, characteristically produced by forced dispersal and reluctant scattering" (Gilroy 207); a group characterized by "a history of dispersal, myths/memories of the homeland, alienation in the host... country, desire for eventual return, ongoing support of the homeland, and a collective identity importantly defined by this relationship" (Safran, paraphrased in Clifford 284); and a term that encompasses "a whole range of phenomena that encourage multi-locale attachments, and dwelling and travelling within and across nations" (Clifford 285).

ONE Ukrainian Canadians

1. According to Frances Swyripa, by 1941, Ukrainian Canadians were the fourth largest ethnic group in Canada (behind British, French, and German Canadians). By 1981, they had fallen to fifth place, supplanted by Italian Canadians (Swyripa, "From Sheepskin Coat" 18). In *Creating a Landscape: A Geography of Ukrainians in Canada* (1989), Lubomyr Luciuk and Bohdan Kordan suggest that in 1989 Ukrainians, with a population of 529,615, still ranked fifth in size of all ethnic groups in Canada. Over time, however, ethnicity becomes increasingly complex and difficult to track with accuracy, given multiple "mixed" ethnic origins. Statistics from the 1996 census regarding Ukrainian Canadian ethnicity, for example, are difficult to interpret because they include "single" and "multiple" responses. Statistics Canada states that in 1996 the population of Ukrainian Canadians was 1,026,475, making Ukrainian Canadians the ninth largest ethnic group in Canadian. But a significant number of these Ukrainian Canadians (694,790) reported multiple, unspecified ethnic ancestries as well (http://www.statcan.ca).
2. Ukrainians also immigrated to the United States and to South America (especially Brazil). See Orest Subtelny's *Ukrainians in North America* (1991).
3. Wasyl Eleniak and Ivan Pillipiw are generally acknowledged as the first Ukrainians who immigrated to Canada in 1891 and their "news" apparently spread quickly, causing a "sensation at home" (Gerus and Rea 5). Dr. Joseph Oleskiw also visited Canada in 1895 and wrote a pamphlet entitled "About Free Lands" that circulated widely among Ukrainians—Marunchak calls him "their Moses of a sort, leading them to a promised land" (29). Clifford Sifton's immigration policy is also frequently cited as crucial to encouraging Ukrainian migration to Canada (Woycenko 11; Gerus and Rea 7; Marunchak 71).
4. According to Marunchak, 94% of Ukrainian immigrants settled in the western prairie provinces (67).
5. *Chytalny* grew out of the *Prosvita* movement, established in Ukraine in 1868. *Prosvita*, according to Marunchak, "organized reading societies, co-operatives and credit unions" (161), and *chytalny* gave "even illiterate farmers access to a broad range of literature—technical, political, and creative—through the books, newspapers, and pamphlets that were read aloud for their benefit" (Balan, *Salt and Braided Bread* 7).
6. Some of the most prominent newspapers of this period (all published in Winnipeg) included *Kanadiiskyi Farmer/Canadian Farmer* (1903), founded by the Liberal party, and *Robochyi Narod/Working People* (1909), which provided a voice for the Ukrainian Social Democratic Party. *Ranok/Dawn* (1905) served proselytizing purposes on behalf of the Presbyterian Church; *Ukrainskyi Holos/Ukrainian Voice* (1910) was a pro-nationalist newspaper that also advocated for an independent Ukrainian Orthodox Church; and *Kanadiiskyi Rusyn/Canadian Ruthenian* (1911) reflected the views of the Ukrainian Catholic Church (Gerus and Rea 10). A large number of other newspapers "appeared and collapsed with startling rapidity" (Gerus and Rea 10): Marunchak discusses these at length (238-96).
7. In the early 1920s, the Polish government confiscated large Galician estates from wealthy individuals and the Orthodox Church. Although 91% of the region's population consisted of Ukrainian peasants "engaged in subsistence farming," 300,000 Polish

farmers were brought into the region and the confiscated land was then redistributed among them. The Polish authorities simultaneously embarked on a "relentless programme of enforced assimilation," closing down Ukrainian schools and arresting hundreds of Ukrainian students, soldiers, and political activists. In 1930, Marshal Pilsudski's military government formally initiated the "pacification" of western Ukraine which resulted in widespread atrocities toward Ukrainians (Balan, *Salt and Braided Bread* 8–10).

8 Again, see Marunchak for a detailed discussion of these and other groups (393–423). In *Creating a Landscape: A Geography of Ukrainians in Canada* (1991), Luciuk and Kordan provide a rather more concise overview of important Ukrainian Canadian political and religious organizations (17).

9 Marunchak (434–40) discusses Ukrainian Canadians' involvement in provincial and federal governments during this period. He also discusses the emergence of new newspapers—*Canadian Sitch*, *Truth and Liberty*, *Veterans News*, and *The Truth*, for example, all published in Winnipeg—as well as the continuity of existing newspapers, especially *Ukrainian Voice* and *Canadian Ukrainian* (470–98).

10 For a detailed look at the third wave of immigration, see Lubomyr Luciuk's *Searching for Place: Ukrainian Displaced Persons, Canada, and the Migration of Memory* (2000). Ukrainians continued, and continue, to immigrate to Canada, though in much smaller numbers. As Swyripa points out, restrictions placed on emigration by the former Soviet Union resulted in a "trickle of newcomers." She suggests that, by 1991, Ukrainian Canadians were "overwhelmingly Canadian born" ("From Sheepskin Coat" 18).

11 See Paul Yuzyk's *Ukrainian Canadians: Their Place and Role in Canadian Life* (1967), Ol'ha Woycenko's *The Ukrainians in Canada* (1968), Michael Marunchak's *Ukrainian Canadians: A History* (1982), and Ramon Hnatyshyn and Robert Klymasz's *Art and Ethnicity: The Ukrainian Tradition in Canada* (1991). Marunchak's text includes numerous photographs of prominent Ukrainian Canadians.

12 Lubomyr Luciuk and Bohdan Kordan, for example, write that, upon arrival in Canada, Ukrainians "no longer remained locked into the parochialism of village or regional loyalties and politics but became increasingly conscious of a national Ukrainian identity.... Ukrainians, living in bloc settlements of the Prairies or in inner city ghettos like North End Winnipeg, came to think of themselves as a group, bound together by religious, cultural, socio-economic, and political ties" (n.p.). See also Paul Yuzyk's *Ukrainian Canadians: Their Place and Role in Canadian Life* (1967), Ol'ha Woycenko's *The Ukrainians in Canada* (1968), and Michael Marunchak's *The Ukrainian Canadians: A History* (1982).

TWO   "Digesting" the "Foreign Mass"

1 Connor's writing was immensely popular during the first decades of the twentieth century. He is best known for his earlier romance novels *The Sky Pilot: A Tale of the Foothills*, 1899, and *The Man from Glengarry: A Tale of the Ottawa*, 1901. In "Ralph Connor's *The Foreigner: A Tale of Saskatchewan* and Paradigm Shifts" (1999), Walter Swayze argues that *The Foreigner* is "almost unknown" to readers, with the exception of "those who read it as outdated sociology and attack and ridicule it as racist, imperialist, and patronizing" (42).

2   Connor's description of Winnipeg as the "cosmopolitan capital of the last of the Anglo-Saxon Empires" (11) draws attention to the dramatic changes that took place in that city, and in the prairies more generally, after the turn of the century. As Alan F. J. Artibise explains, "[b]etween 1871 and 1901, the population of the prairies jumped from 70,000 to more than 400,000" (8). Agricultural advances, the construction of railways, and a large influx of immigrants contributed to the "expansion and consolidation of prairie settlement" (15). By 1913, Winnipeg became the third largest city in Canada, after Montreal and Toronto (16). This period of intense "growth and prosperity" ended, according to Artibise, with the onset of the depression (23).

3   Although the main Anglo-Canadian characters in *The Foreigner* are established Canadian citizens, Connor introduces several minor Anglo-Canadian characters who are new to the country and who therefore still retain aspects of their Anglo-Celtic ethnic heritages. For example, Mrs. Fitzpatrick speaks with a thick Irish accent and frequently includes Irish colloquialisms and idiomatic expressions in conversation. For example, she introduces herself as "Mishtress Timothy Fitzpatrick, Monaghan that was, the Monaghans o' Ballinghalereen, an owld family, poor as Job's turkey, but proud as the divil, an' wance the glory o' Mayo" (69). Similarly, Connor describes Sergeant Cameron of the Winnipeg City Police as "diligently endeavouring to shed his Highland accent and to take on the colloquialisms of the country" (85). But these characters' assimilation to Canadian society is not an urgent concern to Connor—in fact, Mrs. Fitzpatrick functions as a comic figure whose Irishness marks her as different from but not threatening to Anglo-Canadian society, and Cameron clearly functions as a upstanding citizen.

4   Swyripa convincingly argues that this portion of the novel reads like "a fictional supplement to the annual reports on work among Galicians and Ruthenians to the general assembly of the Presbyterian Church of Canada" (*Ukrainian Canadians: A Survey* 12).

5   In *Racial Attitudes in English-Canadian Fiction 1905–1980*, Terrence Craig says "Rosenblatt is identifiable as a Jew by appearance, behaviour, and name. He is beyond redemption, Gordon [Connor] apparently not considering it credible to extend the idea of conversion to Presbyterianism to include a Jew. His death is not mourned and provides a convenient climax as well as a moral lesson. There is no place for the old oppressive European ways in Gordon's Canada. It would seem, too, at this time at least, that there is no place for Jews" (34).

6   In "Immigration, Nation, and the Canadian Allegory of Manly Maturation" (84), Daniel Coleman argues that Kalman becomes an allegorical "test case of Canadian national maturity" (93).

7   Connor foregrounds the noble aspects of Kalmar's political activities early in the novel. When Kalmar meets Mrs. Fitzpatrick's husband, an immediate kinship develops between the two men—upon hearing that Kalmar fights for the freedom of his country, "[r]ed with the blood of [his] countrymen," Mr. Fitzpatrick declares that "[w]e're all the same kind here," and Kalmar cries, "Aha, you are of Ireland. You, too, are fighting the tyrant" (72). The two men then exchange tragic tales of their oppression and heroic stories of their resistance to this oppression.

8   As Swyripa points out, moreover, in *Ukrainian Canadians: A Survey of Their Portrayal in English-language Works*, historical inaccuracies "abound" in *The Foreigner*. First, "it is highly improbable that a Russian nobleman would have married a Galician peasant

woman, especially since they were separated geographically and politically into two empires." Secondly, "it is illogical that Rosenblatt, being a Bukovynian, would have been employed in the Russian Secret Service." Lastly, "the names of Kalmar's children—'Irma' and 'Kalman'—were themselves typically Hungarian and most uncommon among both Ukrainians and Russians" (13–14). Swyripa draws attention to these errors in order to argue that Connor knew little about Eastern Europe. I think, however, that regardless of Connor's factual errors, his hierarchical delineation of Slavic characters—Paulina as Galician, Rosenblatt as Bukovynian, and Kalmar, Irma, and Kalman as Russian—serves a deliberate narrative function. The Galician and Bukovynian characters, presented as lowest on the social scale, become foils to the Anglo-Canadian characters, who are presented as highest.

9 See, for example, *From the Heart of the Heartland: The Fiction of Sinclair Ross*, edited by John Moss (1992), and *Sinclair Ross's* As For Me and My House: *Five Decades of Criticism*, edited by David Stouck (1991). Moss's text includes a bibliography of Ross criticism. Stouck's text republishes 1941 reviews of *As For Me and My House*, various writers' and critics' opinions of the novel (originally published between 1952 and 1981), and critical essays on the novel spanning a period of fifty years.

10 The assumption that Philip is the father of Judith's son is not one that all critics make. In "The 'Scarlet' Rompers: Toward a New Perspective on *As For Me and My House*" (1984), David Williams argues that Paul, the local schoolteacher, is the father of Judith's child, and in "Who's the Father of Mrs. Bentley's Child?: *As For Me and My House* and the Conventions of Dramatic Monologue" (1986), Evelyn Hinz and John Teunissen argue that Mr. Finley, Chairman of the Church Board, is the father. Valerie Raoul, in "Straight or Bent: Textual/Sexual T(ri)angles in *As For Me and My House*" (1998), is reluctant to pinpoint the father of Judith's child, but she believes that "there is certainly some room for doubt as to whether it is in fact Philip" (23). Raoul's doubt is grounded in her reading of Philip as gay. "That Philip is attracted to young men rather than to women," Raoul writes, "is mutely trumpeted by a copious trail of clues throughout the text" (19).

11 Importantly—and this is a point to which I will return at the conclusion to my discussion of Ross's novel—Steve Kulanich is not the only outsider in Horizon. Indeed, Mrs. Bentley is drawn to Steve precisely because she, like him, does not belong in the town. David Stouck argues, moreover, that "like Philip, Steve is of doubtful birth and an outcast in the town" and that "Steve, as the town's reprobate, provides Philip with a replica of his own youth" ("The Mirror and the Lamp" 99–100). In "Sinclair Ross's 'Foreigners'" (1992), Marilyn Rose suggests "it is possible to see parallels between Ross's foreigners and other kinds of marginalized figures in his fiction" (98). The "figure of the 'other woman'" (Judith West) is one such maginalized figure, as is the "homosexual presence" in Horizon (Philip). Ross's "foreigners," Rose writes, "could be seen as representing, or even standing in for, marginalized groups whom, for one reason or another, Ross has chosen not to foreground" (98).

12 Raoul argues that Mrs. Bentley sees Steve as a rival for Philip's affections because Philip is sexually attracted to Steve (20). Timothy Cramer makes a similar argument in "Questioning Sexuality in Sinclair Ross's *As For Me and My House*" (1999).

13 According to Rose, the "established families of Horizon...subject the foreigner to a kind of cultural 'gaze' which fixes him as the 'barbaric other.'" The Anglo-Canadian establishment, then, can respond in one of two ways. "One possibility," says Rose, "is that the establishment attempt[s] to assimilate the foreigner." Mrs. Bentley makes this attempt when she and her husband take in Steve. But when she "fails in her efforts to civilize him, Mrs. Bentley falls back on the alternate response (which much of Horizon has favoured all along), rigorous gatekeeping: Steve Kulanich is summarily banished from Horizon" (94).

14 Both Ross's and Laurence's writing needs to be situated in the sub-field of prairie literature that burgeoned during and after the Second World War. Part of a general shift toward regionalism in Canadian literature, their texts examine the complex networks of inclusions and exclusions—in terms of gender, ethnicity, and "race"—that characterized small-town prairie life in the era preceding the advent of "official" multiculturalism. As New argues in "The Other and I: Laurence's African Stories" (1983), "through the multicultural world of Manawaka, Laurence traces an historical shift from a generation of "discriminators"— whether Irish, Scots, Protestant, or merely middle class—to the subsequent generations of women writers, teachers, housewives who have rejected the old definitions of themselves and who find their dignity and freedom after they extend themselves to contact others" (134).

THREE Re-reading the Female Ethnic Subject

1 Prior to the re-release of *Yellow Boots* in 1992, the novel was mentioned briefly in three book-length studies of Canadian literature: Laurie Ricou's *Vertical Man/Horizontal World: Man and Landscape in Canadian Prairie Fiction* (1973); Dick Harrison's *Unnamed Country: The Struggle for a Canadian Prairie Fiction* (1977); and E.D. Blodgett's *Configurations: Essays in the Canadian Literatures* (1982). Frances Swyripa provides more extensive commentary on Lysenko's novel in *Ukrainian Canadians: A Survey of Their Portrayal in English-Language Works* (1978).

2 For a more comprehensive discussion of Lysenko's biography, see Alexandra Kruchka Glynn, "Reintroducing Vera Lysenko—Ukrainian Canadian Author" (1990).

3 See Beverly Rasporich's "Retelling Vera Lysenko: A Feminist and Ethnic Writer" (1989) and "Vera Lysenko's Fictions: Engendering Prairie Spaces" (1991); Alexandra Kruchka Glynn's "Reintroducing Vera Lysenko—Ukrainian Canadian Author" (1990); Carolyn Redl's "Neither Here nor There: Canadian Fiction by the Multicultural Generation" (1996); Tamara Palmer Seiler's "Including the Female Immigrant Story: A Comparative Look at Narrative Strategies" (1996); and Sonia Mycak's "Simple Sentimentality or Specific Narrative Strategy? The Functions and Use of Nostalgia in the Ukrainian-Canadian Text" (1998). A revised version of Mycak's essay appears in her book *Canuke Literature* (2001).

4 *A Jest of God* was, of course, published after *Yellow Boots*. My question here is whether or not *Yellow Boots* represents an adequate challenge to the stereotypes of Ukrainian Canadians that existed before she published the novel, and that continued to circulate after it was published.

5 Lysenko doesn't mention precisely when the Landashes immigrated to Canada.

6 Though she makes no explicit mention of Connor's *The Foreigner*, it seems likely that Lysenko was familiar with this book. She may well have written *Yellow Boots* as a response to Connor's intensely negative attitudes toward Ukrainians.

7 Although Lysenko mentions several times that Reiner is Austrian, and hints, too, near the novel's conclusion, that he is Jewish—introducing what could become a provocative subtext to the novel—she never fully capitalizes on the opportunity, i.e. Reiner comes across in the narrative as Anglo-Canadian, *tout court*.
8 Another inexplicable twist in the narrative is the family's sudden loving embrace of Lilli, to whom they never before have showed kindness or affection.
9 This is a point made by Bill Ashcroft, Gareth Griffiths, and Helen Tiffin in *The Empire Writes Back: Theory and Practice in Post-colonial Literatures* (1989). In Chapters Five, Six, and Seven, I discuss the issue of language at greater length.

FOUR Ethnic Revival versus Historical Revision

1 Many Ukrainian Canadian texts published during the 1980s received direct financial assistance from Multiculturalism Canada, or the Office of Multiculturalism, Secretary of State, or Alberta Culture and Multiculturalism, including Andrew Suknaski's *In the Name of Narid* (1981), Jars Balan and Yuri Klynovy's *Yarmarok: Ukrainian Writing in Canada Since the Second World War* (1987), Ludmilla Bereshko's *The Parcel From Chicken Street and Other Stories* (1989), Gloria Kupchenko Frolick's *The Chicken Man* (1989), and Yuri Kupchenko's *The Horseman of Shandro Crossing* (1989).
2 According to Bohdan Bociurkiw, Ukrainian Canadians "undoubtedly played the leading role in the development and dissemination of the ideas and policy demands that eventually crystallized into the policy of multiculturalism" (100). In 1963, when Prime Minister Lester B. Pearson launched the Royal Commission on Bilingualism and Biculturalism, Ukrainian Canadians, many of whom had experienced political oppression in the Old Country, balked at institutionalized anglophone and francophone cultural hegemony: "[a]mong the briefs submitted to the B&B Commission by various ethnocultural organizations, the largest share came from the Ukrainian Canadian community" (Bociurkiw 105). Between 1963 and 1971, groups such as the Ukrainian Canadian Congress (UCC), the Association of United Ukrainian Canadians (AUUC), the Ukrainian Canadian University Students' Union (SUSK), and the Ukrainian Professional and Business Federation, as well as prominent individuals and representatives from the Ukrainian Canadian press, voiced their staunch disapproval of a bipartite model of nationhood. At public forums and conferences, in newspaper articles and scholarly papers, Ukrainian Canadians reiterated the argument that bilingualism and biculturalism would "[condemn]…other ethnic groups to an inferior, 'non-founding' status and their cultures to eventual submersion in one of two 'official cultures'" (Bociurkiw 105). As an alternative to the proposed "B&B" framework, Ukrainian Canadians called for the federal government to "support the efforts of all ethnocultural groups to maintain and develop their cultural-linguistic heritage." They suggested that a federal ministry of culture be established to "recognize and give unlimited support to all the cultures of the Canadian multicultural society" (Bociurkiw 105). Interestingly, when Prime Minister Pierre Trudeau eventually announced his new policy of multiculturalism within a bilingual framework, in October, 1971, he did so at a meeting of the Ukrainian Canadian Congress (Hryniuk and Luciuk 3). For a fuller description of Ukrainian Canadians' attitudes toward multiculturalism, see *The Cultural Contribution of the Other Ethnic Groups* (1969), the fourth volume of the Royal Commission on Bilingualism and Biculturalism (edited by A. Davidson Dunton

and André Laurendeau), and Bohdan Bociukiw's "The Federal Policy of Multiculturalism and the Ukrainian Canadian Community" (1978).

3 NeWest merits special attention here because the press was founded by literary scholar George Melnyk, who is of Ukrainian descent. As Melnyk explains in the second volume of his literary history of Alberta, he established NeWest Press in 1977 "with assistance from academics and writers at the University of Alberta," including Rudy Wiebe and Henry Kreisel (173). The press grew out of *NeWest Review*, founded in 1975 by Melnyk, Julia Berry, and Sam Gerszonowicz as an alternative "monthly tabloid book-review magazine" with a western Canadian focus (179). For a detailed discussion of the Alberta publishing industry, see "Alberta Book Culture: Publishing, Literary Institutions, and Writers' Organizations" (167–90) in Melnyk's *The Literary History of Alberta, Volume Two: From the End of the War to the End of the Century* (1999).

4 See Jars Balan's "Backdrop to an Era: The Ukrainian Canadian Stage in the Interwar Years" (1991) and "Old World Forms, New World Settings: The Emergence of Ukrainian-Canadian Plays on North American Themes" (1998); Alexandra Pritz's "Ukrainian Dance in Canada: The First Fifty Years, 1924–1974" (1983); and Bohdan Rubchak's "Homes as Shells: Ukrainian Émigré Poetry" (1983).

5 The prominent newspapers, all published in Winnipeg, that were established following the first wave of immigration include *Kanadiiskyi Farmer/Canadian Farmer* (1903), *The Word* (1904), *Robochyi Narod/Working People* (1909), *Ranok/Dawn* (1905), *Red Banner* (1907), *The Working People* (1909), *Ukrainskyi Holos/Ukrainian Voice* (1910), and *Kanadiiskyi Rusyn/Canadian Ruthenian* (1911). During the first decades of the twentieth century, a large number of other newspapers in Manitoba, Alberta, Saskatchewan, Ontario, and Québec "appeared and collapsed with startling rapidity" (Gerus and Rea 10): Marunchak discusses these at length (238–96).

6 By "elevated modes of cultural production," I mean literature, fine art, and classical music—as distinct from, say, folk tales, dances, and songs.

7 For more detailed information about Ukrainian dance in Canada during this period, see Alexandra Pritz's "The Evolution of Ukrainian Dance in Canada" (1984), Irka Balan's "Dance Interpretation and Performance" (1984), and Andriy Nahachewsky's "Ukrainian Performing Arts in Alberta" (1988).

8 Canada's National Ukrainian Festival is an annual event in Dauphin that started in 1966. Vegreville's annual Ukrainian *Pysanka* Festival started in 1974.

9 One of the most well-loved Ukrainian Canadian groups to emerge during the late 1960s was "Mickey and Bunny," a Winnipeg-based duo who produced eighteen albums over the course of their musical careers. In 2002, some thirty years after they retired from performing, "Mickey and Bunny" reunited to record a new album, aptly titled "Reunion." Their enduring popularity was brought home to me when I saw them perform at the Vegreville *Pysanka* Festival in July, 2002—the sold-out crowd at the Grandstand Show gave "Mickey and Bunny" a standing ovation.

10 My list of Ukrainian Canadian dance bands is by no means comprehensive. Because albums produced by these bands are difficult to locate (they are only sold in some Ukrainian stores), I've used my parents' collection as a research source. Unfortunately, dates are rarely included on the album covers, so I've also relied on my parents for information about the approximate years in which the albums were produced (they

say that all of the records were produced between 1970 and 1980). Interestingly, while many bands provide English titles for their songs—Bill Boychuk's band performs the "Laughing Polka," for example, "What a Beautiful Day," and "Please Come Back Home"; and Ron Lakusta's band plays the "Hi-Lites Polka," "Come Spring Fox Trot," and "Moonlight Night Waltz"—the songs themselves are based on the melodies of traditional Ukrainian folk songs. For additional information on Ukrainian Canadian dance bands, see Robert Klymasz's "Folk Music" (1984) and Bohdan Zajcew's "Ukrainian Popular Music in Canada" (1984). See, too, the online catalogue of albums provided by the Ukrainian Bookstore in Edmonton (http://www.ukrainianbookstore.com).

11 See Bohdan Medwidsky's "Three Types of Ukrainian Folk Tales in Canada" (1988) for a fuller discussion of Ukrainian Canadian storytelling traditions.

12 See Frances Swyripa's *Wedded to the Cause: Ukrainian-Canadian Women and Ethnic Identity, 1891–1991* (1993) for a discussion of the ways in which the figure of baba (grandmother) became, in the 1970s and 1980s, part of the "grassroots phenomena" that "marked the victory of a cultural ethnic consciousness ... erected on foods and selected handicrafts as the essence of Ukrainian-Canadian identity" (255). Swyripa provides examples of the ubiquitous *baba* in Ukrainian Canadian folk culture—*baba* takes the form of ceramic figurines; she appears in paintings, and on lapel buttons and T-shirts; and her name is used in Ukrainian fast-food restaurants such as "Baba's Best" in Edmonton (241–52). While Swyripa acknowledges that *baba* represents one of the "overwhelmingly self-conscious, symbolic, ceremonial, and stylized" expressions of Ukrainian Canadian ethnicity, she argues that *baba* nonetheless "legitimize[s] ... Ukrainian Canadians' sense of their place and role in Canadian nation building, as founding peoples of western Canada; and she embodie[s] the essence of their Ukrainian peasant heritage" (256).

13 The prominence of the *pysanka* among other symbols of Ukrainian Canadian culture was perhaps best illustrated by the erection in 1974 of "the world's largest *pysanka*" in Vegreville. Oddly enough, the Vegreville *Pysanka* was erected to commemorate the hundredth anniversary of the Royal Canadian Mounted Police. The monument, which weighs 2270 kilograms, is almost nine metres long, and more than five metres wide (Jones 56).

14 Folk art, according to Isajiw, "encodes in carvings, embroidery, drawings, dancing, singing and storytelling a community's conception of the world and serves to validate and teach about its experiences and its struggles with the basic questions of life" (29). The "dividing line," he says, "between folk art and naïve art is not always clear" but naïve art "usually focuses on the community rather than the world around it" (31). Professional art, unlike other ethnic art forms, "raise[s] questions" and "suggest[s] alternative ways of thinking"; Ukrainian Canadian professional art, specifically, addresses "the problems of ethnic experience" (31). Finally, souvenir art—mugs, for example, plates, tablecloths, and spoons—"imitates folk, naïve, or professional art" but it is "usually inexpensive and produced for mass consumption" (34).

15 The Ukrainian Cultural Heritage Village is one example of a museum that recreates Ukrainian Canadian pioneers' way of life. Located forty kilometres east of Edmonton, Alberta, on a 320-acre plot of land, the Village is a replica of a Ukrainian bloc settlement circa 1892 to 1930. It includes farmsteads, churches, stores, a one-room school, and

a grain elevator, as well as an interpretive centre; one of the reconstructed homes at the Village, the "Grekul House," belonged to one of my ancestors. Visitors encounter role-playing guides in period dress who re-enact the daily activities of Ukrainian Canadian settlers. Construction of the Village began in 1976, with private funding and support from Alberta's Department of Culture, and a good deal of research has gone into authentically replicating the past. For a look at the Village, as well as the background research that went into its construction, see the website of the museum (http://collections.ic.gc.ca/ukrainian). See, too, Sandra Thomson's "The Ukrainian Cultural Heritage Village: Interpreting Ukrainian Canadian History" (1988) and Radomir Bilash's *Ukrainian Cultural Heritage Village* (1989).

16 The pop art to which Pohorecky refers emerged in the 1970s. T-shirts and buttons featuring such slogans as "Kiss Me, I'm Ukrainian"; "Baba's Borshch" (superimposed on a Campbell's soup can); "Cute Chick" (with a cartoon of a chicken next to a *pysanka*); and "Hell's Babushkas" (a play on the "Hell's Angels" complete with a drawing of an old woman on a motorcycle). Glasses and ceramic dishes and mugs with decals replicating Ukrainian embroidery were also produced and sold in Ukrainian Canadians stores or at Ukrainian Canadian festivals. More recently, in the 1980s, Ukrainian Canadian versions of "Roots" clothing appeared, with the word Roots translated into Ukrainian on the original Roots logo.

17 Photographs of some paintings by Shostak (1943–) and Kurelek (1927–77) appear in *Art and Ethnicity: The Ukrainian Tradition in Canada* (1991). Kurelek is arguably the best known Ukrainian Canadian artist, but his artwork depicts other ethnic groups as well. Reproductions of his art are collected in numerous books, including *Jewish Life in Canada* (1975), *Kurelek Country* (1975), *Kurelek's Canada* (1975), *The Polish Canadians* (1981), *A Prairie Boy's Summer* (1975), and *A Prairie Boy's Winter* (1973). For more detailed information about Kurelek, see Patricia Morley's *Kurelek: A Biography* (1986).

18 Photographs of works by Husar (1951–) appear in *Art and Ethnicity: The Ukrainian Tradition in Canada* (1991).

19 Harry Piniuta's *Land of Pain Land of Promise: First Person Accounts by Ukrainian Pioneers, 1891–1914* (1978) is an exception. A collection of reminiscences by first-wave Ukrainian immigrants about their early experiences in Canada, the text largely focuses on their hardships rather than their triumphs.

20 In much of their writing, both Kostash and Potrebenko are outspoken about their feminism and socialism. Kostash's feminist politics inform, for example, *Her Own Woman: Profiles of Ten Canadian Women*, co-edited with Melinda McCracken, Valerie Miner, Erna Paris, and Heather Robertson (1975), and *No Kidding: Inside the World of Teenage Girls* (1987). In *Long Way From Home: The Story of the Sixties Generation in Canada* (1980), *Bloodlines: A Journey Into Eastern Europe* (1993), *The Doomed Bridegroom: A Memoir* (1998), and *The Next Canada: In Search of Our Future Nation* (2000), she writes explicitly about her interest in feminism and New Leftist socialism. Similarly, in Potrebenko's novels, short fiction, and poetry, she frequently—indeed, almost ubiquitously—foregrounds the plight of the working class, and of working class women, specifically. In fact, many of her texts—most notably her novels *Taxi!* (1975) and *Sometimes They Sang* (1986); her collection of poetry *Life, Love and Unions* (1987); and *Hey Waitress and Other Stories* (1989)—read like feminist and socialist political manifestos targeted at the capitalist

and patriarchal structures of Canadian society. Kostash, it bears mentioning, espouses New Leftist socialism, whereas Potrebenko's politics are closer to communist socialism.

21 In an interview with Sneja Gunew and Margery Fee (2002), Kostash reflects on many Ukrainian Canadians' hostile responses to *All of Baba's Children*. In her words, the book was attacked "because I didn't read or speak Ukrainian at the time, right, I could only consult English language sources, I didn't really know what was going on. I had a very imperfect understanding of Ukrainian history, and the conclusions I drew from it. That it was basically a very naïve and unsophisticated account of things. That was the kind version. The unkind version was that I had completely misrepresented Ukrainians when I talked about their misogyny and anti-Semitism, and particularly because I valorized the Red, the Commie experience within it. I was a renegade" (128).

Both *All of Baba's Children* and *No Streets of Gold* received mixed reviews from Ukrainian Canadian and non-Ukrainian Canadian scholars alike. Many reviewers saw Potrebenko's text as socialist propoganda rather than objective history. In her review of *No Streets of Gold*, Aritha van Herk suggests that while Potrebenko "pretends to be objective," her "obviously subjective interpretation of historical events" undermines the credibility of her text. "Given her anger and emotional perspective," van Herk writes, "it is necessary to question whether the author is recounting history or using history as a lever for her own ideology" (40). Similarly, G.A. Rawlyk argues that Potrebenko's "unsophisticated Marxist overview" of Ukrainian Canadian history is "studded with basic factual errors" and "far too many irresponsible historical judgments" (39). Reviews of *All of Baba's Children* were somewhat more positive. van Herk, for example, says that Kostash's text "suffers from the same rhetoric and polemicism that *No Streets of Gold* does, but for some reason, it is more palatable" (40); and Rawlyk suggests that, unlike Potrebenko, Kostash is more successful in "drilling into the Ukrainian-Canadian experience and in finding an unusually heterogeneous, and divided community" (40). Zonya Keywan's reading of the two texts is perhaps most interesting, given that she published her own work of Ukrainian Canadian history, *Greater Than Kings*, in 1977. Keywan, who focuses her text on the economic and social achievements of Ukrainian immigrants and their descendants in Canada, objects to Potrebenko's and Kostash's critical perspectives on Ukrainian Canadian history. Keywan argues that "the total picture [*No Streets of Gold*] presents is inaccurate": "[w]hile the Ukrainian immigrants who came to Alberta most certainly did not find streets paved with gold, neither has their 86-year history in Canada been one of unremitting gloom and exploitation" (40). And, according to Keywan, *All of Baba's Children* is a text without focus because Kostash "lashes out in all directions": she "mockingly catalogues the Ukrainians' steps along the road to anglicization, but she is equally scathing about those institutions and individuals who have resisted assimilation and have tried to preserve the Ukrainian language and culture" (40).

FIVE   "We aren't buying black oxfords"

1. Haas has much in common with the narrator of her novel, Maara Lazpoesky: both belong to Jewish families; their fathers (both pharmacists) immigrated to Winnipeg from Ukraine; and their mothers, while also ethnically Ukrainian, came from Poland. Of course, Haas, born in 1920, was a young woman at the time in which the novel takes place (the late 1930s), whereas her narrator is portrayed as an eleven-year-old girl. But in naming her narrator Maara Lazpoesky, Haas nonetheless draws attention to the similarities between author and character. Haas's maiden name was Maara Lazeczko.

    That Haas fictionalizes her experiences as a Ukrainian Canadian Jew is also significant: Jews (and Mennonites) with Ukrainian backgrounds are usually excluded from historical and literary works about Ukrainian Canadians.

2. In a panel discussion at the *Identifications* conference (1978), Haas made the point that multicultural communities existed long before the introduction of official multiculturalism: "when the first fur traders and the first explorers landed on the shores of Canada and integrated with the Indians, we became multiculturalists. So I cannot see why we even use the word" (149).

3. Taras Shevchenko (1814–61) was born a serf and he was orphaned early in his life. In 1838, he was freed from serfdom by a group of intellectuals who recognized his talents as an artist and a writer. Throughout his life, Shevchenko fought for the emancipation of serfs and for the freedom of Ukraine from Russian rule. His poetry and paintings reflect his love for and loyalty to Ukrainians, especially Ukrainian peasants. Exiled for ten years (1847–57) for his political activities, Shevchenko died seven days before serfdom was abolished.

4. In "Art of Intrusion: Macaronicism in Ukrainian-Canadian Literature" (1989), Robert Klymasz explores in greater depth Haas's use of untranslated Ukrainian words and phrases. Klymasz argues that macaronicism is a comic device in *The Street Where I Live*, but he stops short of discussing the ways Haas uses macaronic humour to undermine the dominance of Anglo-Canadian culture.

SIX   "We laugh, but we are sad"

1. As Christopher Innes notes on the back cover of *Politics and the Playwright: George Ryga* (1985), Ryga (1932–87) wrote "over 90 scripts for radio, television, and film, 3 published and 6 unpublished novels, 16 short stories or novellas, a volume of poetry, two oratorios, two folk song albums, and a documentary travelogue." Most notably his novels include *Hungry Hills* (1963) and *Ballad of a Stone-Picker* (1966), and his plays *Captives of the Faceless Drummer* (1971), and *Ploughmen of the Glacier* (1977). For a bibliography of Ryga's work, see Innes's study, and E. David Gregory's *The Athabasca Ryga* (1990).

2. See Balan's "Ukrainian Influences in George Ryga's Work" (1979), Innes's *Politics and the Playwright: George Ryga* (1985), E. David Gregory's *The Athabasca Ryga* (1990), and James Hoffman's *The Ecstasy of Resistance: A Biography of George Ryga* (1995).

3. Ted Galay's *After Baba's Funeral*, first performed in 1979 at the New Play Centre at City Stage, Vancouver, is similar to Ryga's *A Letter to My Son* in many ways. Set in small-town Manitoba during the summer of 1978, *After Baba's Funeral* is a one-act play that explores the conflicted relationships between second- and third-generation Ukrainian Canadians. The text focuses on the Danischuks—Netty, Walter, and Ronnie; mother, father, and

son, respectively—who have recently lost their mother and grandmother (Baba). Joined by Minnie and Bill Horoshko (Netty's sister and her husband), the family gathers in Netty and Walter's kitchen after Baba's funeral. As they talk, the audience learns that Ronnie, a mathematics Ph.D. student living in Vancouver, has disappointed his family by turning away from his Ukrainian heritage. Unlike his father, he has chosen not to farm, and he no longer speaks Ukrainian or goes to church. Ronnie's sister Edie and brother Larry have also rejected their parents' way of life; neither, moreover, has come home for Baba's funeral. Netty, who nursed her dying mother, worries that no one—no child of hers—will tend to her in her old age. So the relationship between Netty and Ronnie in *After Baba's Funeral* is much like the relationship between Old Man Lepa and Stephan in *A Letter to My Son*. While the second-generation characters in Galay's play (Netty, Walter, Minnie, and Bill) speak English as well as Ukrainian (Galay provides a glossary of translations), they are otherwise stubbornly resistant to Anglo-Canadian society. Farm people who, ironically, worked to make a better life for their children, they see their children's social and economic advancement as a betrayal of their pioneer roots.

Yet *After Baba's Funeral* also differs from *A Letter to My Son* in important ways. Galay's play lacks the sorts of structural devices that Ryga uses to reinforce the central themes of his text. Whereas Ryga's play is expressionistic, *After Baba's Funeral* is realistic. With neither music nor other sound effects indicated in the stage directions, it comprises straightforward dialogue against the simple backdrop of the Danischuk kitchen. And the resolution of the Danischuks' conflict is equally simple and straightforward. At the close of the play, Netty urges Ronnie to look through Baba's belongings and to take with him back to Vancouver something that his grandmother once cherished. Ronnie, in choosing Baba's velvet boots, makes peace with his mother: with this gesture, he shows her that he will not forget his Ukrainian heritage. No such easy reconciliation occurs in Ryga's play between Old Man Lepa and Stephan. Of course, the conclusion to *After Baba's Funeral* echoes that of Vera Lysenko's *Yellow Boots* (Lilli Landash, in the final chapter of the novel, dons her mother's boots, and in doing so ostensibly reconciles her ethnic and national identities)—and both conclusions are ambivalent. Lilli's yellow boots become part of the ethnic costume she wears when performing Ukrainian folk songs; Ronnie's velvet boots become a souvenir of his culture. Ethnic identity, for Lilli and Ronnie, is contained in superficial symbols of folk culture.

4 At one point in the play, Ryga draws attention to the phonological similarities between "Lepa" and "leper": Old Man Lepa, describing to Nancy his trip to the eye doctor, says that the receptionist in the doctor's office called him "Mister Leper" (112).

5 As I mentioned earlier, during the first act of the play, the sound of thunder outside Lepa's house becomes progressively louder as a storm approaches. The thunder reaches a climax at the end of the act, just after Lepa admits that he is to blame for his wife's death. In his stage directions, Ryga calls for "*[h]ard crash of thunder and sound of rain deluge on fast blackout*" (90). Neither the thunder nor the rain returns in the second act of the play—so, presumably some of Lepa's inner turmoil dissipates after he discloses his dark secret.

SEVEN "easter bread and clouds"

1. Robert Kroetsch is of German descent, for example, and Eli Mandel's parents were Russian Jews.
2. Ryga and Suknaski have similar backgrounds. Suknaski's father, like Ryga's, was a second-wave Ukrainian immigrant who settled on the prairies. Because Suknaski's mother was Polish, however, and because Ryga's parents immigrated from Carpathia, a region of Ukraine then occupied by Poland, both writers' home lives were shaped, in part, by Ukrainian *and* Polish culture. Given, moreover, that the communities around which their parents settled were by no means ethnically homogeneous, Suknaski and Ryga were surrounded in their childhood and young adulthood by individuals from diverse racial and cultural groups. Ryga grew up around Richmond Park, Alberta, a community that was "mainly Ukrainian" but that also comprised individuals of "Polish, German, Russian, Scottish, and Icelandic" ancestry (Gregory 14). Suknaski was raised near Wood Mountain, Saskatchewan, a town inhabited by Ukrainian and Polish settlers as well as Romanian, Serbian, English, Irish, Dutch, and Chinese immigrants (Balan, "Voices from the Canadian Steppes" 120). Both writers left their families and communities, working a variety of jobs across the country before returning, in their writing, to their roots.
3. Haas also writes about aboriginal cultures in selections from *On Stage With Maara Haas* (1986), suggesting that she too draws a link between the experiences of Native and ethnic minority groups. I hesitate, however, to include her in my discussion of writers who sought to mythologize the prairies in new ways because there is little evidence in her writing to indicate that she shared this goal. A woman writer whose feminist politics are pronounced in *On Stage*, her concerns about gender set her apart from her male prairie counterparts.
4. Later in this chapter, I discuss Suknaski's interest in Native culture and history at length. Robert Kroetsch's *The Stone Hammer Poems, 1960-1975* (1975) and *The Collected Poems of Al Purdy* (1986) are starting points for further reading on these poets' exploration of the First Nations presence on the prairies.
5. In the 1970s, Suknaski published several chapbooks and pamphlets, including *Circles* (1970), *This Shadow of Eden Once* (1970), *Old Mill* (1971), *Suicide Notes Book I* (1973), *Leaving* (1974), *On First Looking Down from Lion's Gate Bridge* (1974), *Blind Man's House* (1975), *Leaving Wood Mountain* (1975), *Ghost Gun* (1978), and *Moses Beauchamp for Mike Olito* (1978). His major collections of poetry are *Wood Mountain Poems* (1976), *the ghosts call you poor* (1978), *In the Name of Narid* (1981), and *The Land They Gave Away: New and Selected Poems* (1982). He also published two poem sequences, *Octomi* (1976) and *East of Myloona* (1979).
6. Scobie makes this statement in his introduction to *The Land They Gave Away: New & Selected Poems*, a collection of Suknaski's poetry published in 1982.
7. According to Balan, Suknaski attended the Kootenay School of Art (1962–63), the University of Victoria (1964–65), the School of Art and Design at the Montreal Museum of Fine Arts (1965), Notre Dame University in Nelson (1967–68) and Simon Fraser University (1968–69) ("Voices from the Canadian Steppes" 121).

8 Suknaski's father, who belongs to the immigrant generation of homesteaders, becomes a recurrent figure in Suknaski's poems. Among the stories Suknaski tells are numerous references to his own, overwhelmingly tragic, family history. Violent and abusive toward his wife and children as a young man, yet frail and vulnerable in his old age, Andrew Sr. appears in Suknaski's poems as "father" and the "other man" (*WMP* 19-26). "Father" is the "lonely spooked" old man, "merely 110 pounds" at the age of eighty-three, who lives alone in a broken-down shack and uses a bindertwine to hold up his pants (*WMP* 21-22). The "other man" is the monster of Suknaski's childhood who beats his pregnant wife with a rolling pin and, "drowning in black rage," tortures his son (Suknaski's brother Mike) on a grindstone pulley (*WMP* 25). Much of the darkness that pervades *Wood Mountain Poems*, *the ghosts call you poor*, and *In the Name of Narid* derives from the poet's struggle to reconcile the two.

9 I borrow this term from Patrick Lane. In "The Poetry of Andy Suknaski" (1980), Lane says that Suknaski is "part of the first generation that sees itself as an actual part of the landscape. In a way, a new Indian" (95).

10 See the following in *Wood Mountain Poems*: "Chaapunka" (43), "Mashteeshka" (44), "Mishmish" (47-51), "Nez Percés at Wood Mountain" (55-58), "The Sun Dance at Wood Mountain" (64-65), "Poem to Sitting Bull and his Son Crowfoot" (66-68), "The Bitter Word" (69-70), "Sandia Man" (71-73), "Neehhreson" (74) and "Soongeedawn" (75). See, too, these poems in *the ghosts call you poor*: "The Indian and the White Man" (18-19), "The First People" (20-25), and "Shugmanitou I" (26-27).

In addition to writing about First Nations (primarily Sioux) people in *Wood Mountain Poems* and *the ghosts call you poor*, Suknaski writes about Dene and Inuit people in *East of Myloona* (a collection of poems published in 1979 that grew out of his travels in the Northwest Territories), and he retells Sioux legends in *Octomi* (1976).

11 In 1876, following the massacre of George Custer's troops by the Teton Sioux at the Battle of Little Big Horn in Montana, Chief Sitting Bull led his people north across the "Medicine Line" into southern Saskatchewan. Seeking refuge from American troops, Sitting Bull appealed to the Royal North West Mounted Police posted in Wood Mountain and Fort Walsh but he received no help from the Canadian government and eventually surrendered to U.S. authorities in 1881.

12 Sharon Pollock's play *Walsh* (1973) also revisits the history of Sitting Bull in Canada. Interestingly, the same image of Sitting Bull is featured on the front cover of Pollock's play and on the original cover of *Wood Mountain Poems*.

13 Although "The First People" is dedicated "*to the memory of nelson small legs jr (23) and eddie bazie (23)*," Suknaski only makes references within the poem to Nelson Small Legs Jr.

14 According to Leslie Monkman, Suknaski "locate[s] guides to a new sense of place in the myths and legends of the prairie Indians" (143). In inventing an "indigenous Western Canadian mythology" (Balan, "Voices from the Canadian Steppes" 124), moreover, the poet becomes a prototype of the "new Canadian"—not an immigrant but "rather part of the first generation that sees itself as an actual part of the landscape" (Lane 95).

15 Fee's list also includes Margaret Atwood, Douglas Barbour, Leonard Cohen, Robert Kroetsch, Margaret Laurence, Keith Maillard, John Newlove, Howard O'Hagan, and others.

16 In "Stop Stealing Native Stories" (1997), for example, Lenore Keeshig-Tobias refers to non-Native authors' interest in Native stories as "cultural theft" and the "theft of voice" (71). In "Who Can Speak for Whom?" (1993), Dionne Brand says, "[t]here can be no question that Canadian culture has marauded the cultural production of First Nations peoples not to speak of their spiritual myths and icons and their land" (18). For First Nations writers and other writers of colour, the tendency of white writers to draw upon non-white cultures in their texts is as baffling as it is enraging. Keeshig-Tobias asks, "why are Canadians so obsessed with native stories anyway? Why the urge to 'write Indian'? Have Canadians run out of stories of their own? Or are their renderings just nostalgia for a simpler, more 'at one with nature' stage of human development?" (73). [See footnote 6 in my Introduction for further discussion of the appropriation issue.]

17 Melnyk's essay appears in his book *Radical Regionalism* (1981). Klymasz's talk, entitled "Crucial Problems in Ukrainian Canadian Studies Today," was delivered in Winnipeg at the Congress of Humanities and Social Sciences. As he outlined topics related to Ukrainian Canadian studies that need further attention, Klymasz said that "we must document and analyze all aspects of intercultural links between Ukrainian and aboriginal Canadians on the prairies."

18 Sioux words are almost always glossed in footnotes or within the poems themselves. In a number of poems, readers encounter chaapunka or mosquito (WMP 43), mashteeshka or rabbit (*WMP* 44), tatanka or buffalo (*WMP* 65; 67; 69), shugmanitou or coyote (*WMP* 71–73), neehhreson or antelope, and soongeedawn or fox (*WMP* 75). Such poems as "The Indian and the White Man" (*ghosts* 18–19) and "Shugmanitou I" (*ghosts* 26–27) contain prayers to manitou or the great spirit; and "The First People" (*ghosts* 20–25), of course, comprises a litany of Sioux words (all translated within the poem) that refer to the Sioux's spiritual way of life.

19 George Melnyk is a Ukrainian Canadian artist, writer, and literary scholar who currently teaches Canadian Studies at the University of Calgary.

EIGHT From Multiculturalism to Transculturalism

1 See Homi Bhabha's *Location of Culture* (1994), Robert Young's *Colonial Desire: Hybridity in Theory, Culture and Race* (1995), and Aijaz Ahmad's *On Communalism and Globalization: Offensives of the Far Right* (2002).

2 See Smaro Kamboureli's *Scandalous Bodies: Diasporic Literature in English Canada* (2000); Rey Chow's *Writing Diaspora: Tactics of Intervention in Contemporary Cultural Studies* (1993); Ien Ang's *On Not Speaking Chinese: Living Between Asia and the West* (2001); Rajagopalan Radhakrishnan's *Diasporic Mediations: Between Home and Location* (1996); Amy Kaminsky's *After Exile: Writing the Latin American Diaspora* (1999); and Pico Iyer's *The Global Soul: Jet Lag, Shopping Malls and the Search for Home* (2000) and *Imagining Canada: An Outsider's Hope for a Global Future* (2001). Sneja Gunew (with Margery Fee) is currently working on *Diaspora, Indigeneity, Ethnicity: The Multiculturalism of Postcolonialisms in Contemporary Canada and Australia*; she is also involved in an international project on transculturalism sponsored by the International Council for Canadian Studies (ICCS).

3 Sneja Gunew and Smaro Kamboureli are two scholars who have examined texts by "invisible" minority writers.

4   Mycak points to several "tangible" and "quite public" examples of the ways in which the prairie pioneer myth circulates within Ukrainian Canadian communities (70). She suggests that the myth is perpetuated by historical studies of Ukrainians in Canada, such as Michael Marunchak's *The Ukrainian Canadians: A History* (1982); by films such as *Legacy to a New Land: A Celebration of Ukrainian Settlement in the West* (produced by the National Film Board of Canada in 1991); and by museums such as the Ukrainian Cultural Heritage Village. Mycak also gestures toward the "striking range of souvenirs and paraphernalia which has been produced, which image the pioneer as a kind of cultural icon" (70).

5   Kulyk Keefer includes Myrna Kostash in her list of "Janus-faced" transcultural writers (15). This is her only direct reference to Ukrainian Canadian literature in "Mosaic to Kaleidoscope."

6   See, for example, these essays by Kulyk Keefer: "'Coming Across Bones': Historiographic Ethnofiction" (1995); "From Dialogue to Polylogue: Canadian Transcultural Writing During the Deluge," (1996); "Home Comings/Border Crossings: Travels Through Imagined and Actual Worlds" (1999); and "Personal and Public Records: Story and History in the Narration of Ethnicity" (2000).

7   In March, 1985, Gorbachev became General Secretary of the Communist Party Central Committee.

8   "Glasnost" has become shorthand for Gorbachev's cultural and social policies of "openness," characterized by his willingness to acknowledge and discuss past and present problems in the country. "Perestroika," roughly translated as "reform," refers to the economic and social policies he implemented in an attempt to transform the centrally-controlled command economy of the USSR to a decentralized market economy.

9   Gorbachev won the Nobel Peace Prize in 1990 for his role in effecting positive social change in Eastern Europe.

10 Eleven states formed the Commonwealth of Independent States in December, 1991: the Azerbaijan Republic, the Republic of Armenia, the Republic of Belarus, the Republic of Kazakstan, the Kyrgyz Republic, the Republic of Moldova, the Russian Federation, the Republic of Tajikistan, the Republic of Uzbekistan, and Ukraine. In December, 1993, Georgia joined the CIS.

   In 2002, eight Eastern European countries were approved for entry into the European Union (EU). The Czech Republic, Estonia, Hungary, Latvia, Lithuania, Poland, the Slovak Republic, and Slovenia joined the EU in May, 2004.

11 See John Allcock's *Explaining Yugoslavia* (2000); Jasminka Udovicki and James Ridgeway's *Burn This House: The Making and Unmaking of Yugoslavia* (2000); and Joyce Kaufman's *NATO and the Former Yugoslavia: Crisis, Conflict, and the Atlantic Alliance* (2002).

12 The "Orange Revolution" took place from November 24, 2004, to January 23, 2005. It began with Ukraine's Presidential Run-off Election, which pitted Prime Minister Viktor Yanukovych against opposition leader Viktor Yushchenko. Allegations of corruption and fraud within the Yanukovych camp led to nation-wide protests, sit-ins, and general strikes. Demonstrators—not only in Ukraine but around the world—wore orange in support of Yushchenko. A second election was called in late December, with international

observers present to prevent further electoral fraud. Approximately 1000 Canadians, including 500 Canadians of Ukrainian descent, traveled to Ukraine to assist in the second election, which was declared legally valid. Yushchenko won with a clear majority.

13 The independence of Ukraine in 1991 coincided with centenary celebrations of Ukrainian settlement in Canada. In the introductions to several books published in 1991 to mark the centenary (including *Art and Ethnicity: The Ukrainian Tradition in Canada*, edited by Ramon Hnatyshyn and Robert Klymasz; *Canada's Ukrainians: Negotiating an Identity*, edited by Lubomyr Luciuk and Stella Hryniuk; and Orest Subtelny's *Ukrainians in North America*), Ukrainian Canadian scholars acknowledge and applaud the sovereignty of their homeland.

14 In April, 2005, at the 2005 Association of Writers and Writing Programs annual conference held in Vancouver, six Ukrainian American and Canadian authors came together to form a panel entitled "Umbilical Ukraine: Canadian and American Writers of Ukrainian Descent Confront the Mother Country in Fiction and Memoir." Jars Balan, Halyna Hryn, Janice Kulyk Keefer, Myrna Kostash, Askold Melnyczuk, and Irena Zabytko took turns speaking about how their experiences traveling to Ukraine, in some cases many times, have influenced their identities and their writing.

15 The image on the first page of Kulyk Keefer's *The Green Library* comes from Husar's "Pandora's Parcel to Ukraine" (1993), one of the paintings in her *Black Sea Blue* series. In *Honey and Ashes* Kulyk Keefer includes a photograph of the same painting alongside an assortment of family photographs.

16 The Canada Ukraine Legislative and Intergovernmental Project, started in 1996, works toward developing and sustaining democratic and economic reforms in Ukraine. Established in 1989, the Peter Jacyk Centre for Ukrainian Historical Research brings together scholars from Canada and Ukraine who cooperate on joint scholarly publications related to Ukrainian history. The centre also organizes international conferences and seminar series. The Stasiuk Program for the Study of Contemporary Ukraine (1990) and the Kowalsky Program for the Study of Eastern Ukraine (1998) support exchange programs between Canada and Ukraine, as well as providing extensive scholarly resources for the study of Ukraine in Canada.

17 For further reading on globalization and anti-globalization movements, see Naomi Klein's *Fences and Windows: Dispatches from the Front Lines of the Globalization Debate* (2002), Alison Van Rooy's *The Global Legitimacy Game: Civil Society, Globalization, and Protest* (2004), and Kevin Danaher and Jason Mark's *Insurrection: Citizen Challenges to Corporate Power* (2003).

NINE   From Canada to Ukraine—and Back

1. Prior to writing *The Green Library*, Kulyk Keefer published three short story collections (*The Paris-Napoli Express*, 1986; *Transfigurations*, 1987; *Travelling Ladies*, 1990), a book of poems (*White of the Lesser Angels*, 1986), and two novels (*Constellations*, 1988; *Rest Harrow*, 1992). She also published two works of literary criticism (*Under Eastern Eyes: A Critical Reading of Maritime fiction*, 1987, and *Reading Mavis Gallant*, 1989). Several of Kulyk Keefer's short stories—including "Red River Cruise" (from *The Paris-Napoli Express*), "Unseen, the Cuckoo Sings at Dawn" (published in *Yarmarok: Ukrainian Writing in Canada Since the Second World War*), and "Prodigals" (from *Travelling Ladies*)—thematize the experiences of Ukrainians in Canada, but *The Green Library* is her first book-length exploration of Ukrainian Canadian ethnicity.

2. I would argue that the collapse of the USSR also made it much easier for Kulyk Keefer to visit Ukraine.

3. Kotelko was the name of Lesia's husband; not unlike Eva, who believed for most of her life that her mother's husband, Garth Chown, was her father, Kotelko also believed that his mother's husband was his father.

4. Kulyk Keefer does not draw on her grandfather's stories because he died in 1964, when she was a young girl.

5. Staromischyna, the village from which Kulyk Keefer's family immigrated, is now part of "Ternopil" (Tarnopil, in Polish), a province in Ukraine. Historically, however, the village was part of a "geographical and political entity" called Galicia (or Halychyna). During the nineteenth century, Galicia fell under Austrian rule; in 1918, it was claimed by Poland; and, in 1939, it became part of the Soviet Union. When Kulyk Keefer's grandparents immigrated to Canada, Staromischyna was part of Poland—and, in fact, while I refer to her grandfather as Ukrainian, he was actually half-Polish.

6. Relations between Ukrainians and Poles have been marked, for centuries, by tension and conflict. As early as the fourteenth century, Polish forces began to occupy the Ukrainian provinces of Galicia and Volhynia. In the sixteenth century, Ukrainian nobles were assimilated to Polish culture and religion (Catholicism) so that the Ukrainian language and Ukrainian customs, as well as worship in the Orthodox church, were increasingly associated with the lower classes of Ukraine. Throughout the seventeenth, eighteenth, and nineteenth centuries, Ukrainians, and especially Ukrainian Cossacks, revolted—often unsuccessfully—against Polish rulers and landlords in Galicia and Volhynia. During the 1918–19 Polish-Ukrainian War, Polish troops easily defeated a Ukrainian army of volunteers. Poland declared to the League of Nations, in 1920, that it would protect the rights of Ukrainians and other minority groups living within its borders. In 1924, however, Polish-occupied Ukraine began to be subjected to rigorous anti-Ukrainian laws: Ukrainian-language periodicals were abolished; Ukrainian cultural organizations were banned; Ukrainian-language schools were shut down; and laws were passed prohibiting the use of Ukrainian in government agencies. In 1930, Poland initiated its "Pasifikatsia" campaign against Ukrainians living in Galicia. Ukrainian buildings and monuments were demolished, and Ukrainians were arrested, beaten, and tortured. In 1934, Poland withdrew its promise to the League of Nations that it would protect the rights of minority groups in Poland; that same year, Polish officials established a concentration camp at Bereza Kartazka for Ukrainian nationalists.

Throughout *Honey and Ashes*, however, Kulyk Keefer is more explicitly concerned with the historical relations between Ukrainians and Polish Jews. The stereotype of Ukrainians as anti-Semitics has its basis in Ukrainians' historical involvement in pogroms. As Kulyk Keefer points out in *The Green Library*, for example, Bohdan Khmelnitsky, a national hero of Ukraine, was also "one of the great pogrom-makers of all time" (113). A sixteenth-century Cossack hetman, and the leader of numerous revolts against the Polish aristocracy, Khmelnitsky and his army allegedly murdered more than 100,000 Polish Jews. During the 1918–19 Polish-Ukrainian War, as Kulyk Keefer mentions in *Honey and Ashes*, Ukrainians massacred "between 35,000 and 50,000 Jews" (177). And many Ukrainians collaborated with the Nazis during the Second World War—at Babi Yar, most notably, where approximately 70,000 Jews were killed. See Orest Subtelny's *Ukraine: A History* (1994) for a fuller discussion of Ukrainian-Polish relations.

7 In *Imaginary Homelands* (1991), Salman Rushdie, reflecting on the mindset of diasporic writers, suggests that "the writer who is out-of-country and even out-of-language may experience…loss in an intensified form. It is made more concrete for him by the physical fact of discontinuity, of his present being in a different place from his past, of his being 'elsewhere'" (12).

8 Rushdie uses the metaphor of the broken mirror in *Imaginary Homelands* to describe the "fragmentary" vision of diasporic writers who look back to the past but are only able to see parts of it (10). Memory for these writers, he says, is incomplete; some fragments of the past have been "irretrievably lost" (11). But the "broken mirror may actually be as valuable," says Rushdie, "as the one which is supposed unflawed" (11). He suggests that "shards of memory" can acquire "greater status" and "greater resonance" in the hands of writers who use the broken mirror not only as a "mirror of nostalgia" but also as a "useful tool with which to work in the present" (12).

It bears mentioning, however, that Rushdie has in mind writers who are in his position—"exiles or emigrants or expatriates" (10). As a Canadian-born Ukrainian, Kulyk Keefer's situation is not quite the same and might be described—in rather more cynical terms—as a case of "ethnic absolutism," an example of an individual who, as Paul Gilroy argues in *Against Race: Imagining Political Culture Beyond the Colour Line* (2000), seeks "quick ethnic fixes and cheap pseudo-solidarities" to reconcile a divided sense of self that is less genuine than affected (6). Gilroy's "enduring distaste" for ethnic absolutism, harsh though it may seem, needs to be acknowledged in the theoretical spectrum on diasporic consciousness (6).

TEN Between Borders, Beyond Bloodlines

1. Kostash was born in 1944, Kulyk Keefer in 1953.
2. Kulyk Keefer's *Honey and Ashes* and Kostash's *The Doomed Bridegroom* were both published in 1998.
3. In 1993, Czechoslovakia was split into two independent states, the Czech Republic and the Slovak Republic.
4. Kostash notes the irony of the "Mother Poland" ("Matka Polska") trope. Members of Solidarity "[g]enuflect, genuflect, genuflect" (132) before the feminized idea of their country, while treating Polish women as subservient and inferior.
5. In private correspondence with Myrna Kostash, I have learned that David and his family are now Canadian citizens, living in Calgary. He still writes in Serbian, however, and maintains a high profile in Yugoslavia.
6. Later, in Yugoslavia, 1988, Kostash identifies a fourth option. At a meeting of intellectuals in Belgrade sponsored by the Writers' Union of Serbia she witnesses "a moment of collective theatre in which the purpose is precisely not to resolve the dilemma of the community's aggrieved helplessness before history but to sustain it" (101). Although the poets, journalists, and dramatists at this meeting ostensibly share the desire to effect positive social change through their writing, Kostash sees that their "martyrdom" makes them "feel good" and that their real goal is to "keep it going" (101).
7. Kostash's career-long interest in writing about significant political and social movements is evident in the books she published both before and after *Bloodlines* and *The Doomed Bridegroom*. *All of Baba's Children* (1977) and *All of Baba's Great-grandchildren: Ethnic Identity in the Next Canada* (2000) examine ethnicity in Canada. *Long Way From Home: The Story of the Sixties Generation in Canada* (1980) and *The New Canada: In Search of Our Future Nation* (2000) engage with leftist and nationalist politics. *Her Own Woman: Profiles of Ten Canadian Women* (1975), co-edited with Melinda McCracken, Valerie Miner, Erna Paris, and Heather Robertson, and *No Kidding: Inside the World of Teenage Girls* (1987) address feminist issues.
8. Wheat, Kostash explains, is the primary ingredient in "kutia," a traditional Christmas Eve dish and the "food of the gods of harvest" (245). On Christmas Eve, an "honorific wheat sheaf" called the "*didiukh*" is placed in the corner of the house (246). While "*kolach*," a braided Christmas bread, and "*paska*," a braided Easter bread, are both sacred to Ukrainians, all bread is holy in Ukrainian culture. A Ukrainian will "kiss the bread knife before she cuts the loaf, she will kiss the piece of bread that has fallen to the ground and beg its forgiveness for her lapse of reverence" (247).
9. Kostash seems to be aware that, in frankly admitting to her attraction to Eastern European "rebel" men, she is engaged in the problematic politics of cross-cultural desire. Numerous postcolonial scholars have drawn attention to the problematic ways in which the self reduces the other to an exoticized and eroticized object. See, for example, Frantz Fanon's *The Wretched of the Earth* (1963) and *Black Skin, White Masks* (1967), Terry Goldie's *Fear and Temptation: The Image of the Indigene in Canadian, Australian, and New Zealand Literature* (1989), and bell hooks's *Outlaw Culture: Resisting Representations* (1994).

   As my discussion will highlight, however, Kostash's ethnicity and gender complicate her status as "self" vis-à-vis the "other" men she becomes involved with. As a result,

The Doomed Bridegroom becomes an extended reflection on the complexities of cross-cultural desire.

10 Kostash's experimentation with different roles is reminiscent of what Suknaski does in his poetry as he plays the parts of historian and shaman.

11 *All of Baba's Children* was published in 1977.

12 For a photograph of Stus, see *Vasyl Stus—A Life Remembered* (http://www.ualberta.ca/~ulec/stus), an online tribute to the poet put together by the Shevchenko Foundation and the Ukrainian Language Education Centre, sponsored by the Canadian Institute of Ukrainian Studies. This website draws substantially on Kostash's writing about him in *The Doomed Bridegroom*.

13 Stus, Kostash explains, was a Ukrainian nationalist from Kiev, outspoken in his objections to Soviet persecution of Ukrainian intellectuals. In the years leading up to his first imprisonment, in 1972, he used various forms of political protest to publicly denounce the "Russification of Ukrainian culture" (37). After witnessing the arrests of his friends and colleagues by Soviet authorities, Stus wrote "a flurry of open letters and appeals" and "stood outside…courtrooms demanding to be let in" (40). At a cinema once, in 1965, following the screening of a new Sergei Paradzhanov film, he stood up in front of the audience and shouted, "All those against tyranny, rise up!" (37). Most importantly, perhaps, despite the KGB's "relentless persecution of Ukrainian intellectuals" (36), he refused to stop writing. In 1970, a collection of his poems, *Zymovi Dereva* (*Winter Trees*), was published by a Belgian press. Two years later, he was arrested "on charges of involvement in an espionage ring" (45), his apartment ransacked, and all of his writing—"virtually everything he had written in the last fifteen years" (45)—confiscated. Sentenced to "five years in special regime labour camp in Mordovian ASSR and three years internal exile" (45), Stus continued—from camp—to mount "verbal attacks on the KGB" (48). And, despite his weakening health—at the time of his arrest he suffered from a gastric ulcer that gradually worsened as a result of the appalling conditions of the labour camp—as well as the "severe constraints" (48) on his writing within the camp, Stus was able to "smuggle out" (47) letters and poetry that soon circulated in the west as powerful testimonies to the injustice of the Soviet regime. In 1980, some seven months after his first prison sentence ended, Stus was arrested again under familiar charges of "anti-Soviet agitation and propaganda designed to undermine or weaken Soviet power" (57). Sentenced this time to "ten years' forced labour and five years' internal exile" (57), he was held, for a full year before his death in 1985, in "an isolation cell on reduced rations in spite of exhibiting dangerous symptoms of kidney malfunction" (61). A man whose faith in the ideals of freedom and justice was unshakable, Stus died "before his term was up"; and, in a telling commentary on the rigid brutality of the Soviet authorities, his family could not bring his body home until 1989, when it had "'served' his entire sentence" (62).

14 As Kostash explains in "Lord, History Falls Through the Cracks," Mennonites share a long, complex history with Ukrainians that can be traced back to the sixteenth century. She begins her narrative of this history in 1553 when, "[o]n the island of Khortytsia in the bend of the lower Dnipro," a *sich* (fortress) was built by Imperial Official Dmytro Vyshnyvetsky to accommodate some five thousand Ukrainian Cossacks (126). For many years the "first line of Russian imperial defence against marauding Tatars from

the Crimean peninsula," the Cossacks had become, by the late 1770s, a "political monstrosity"—at least "in the estimation of the Empress Catherine" (126). They transformed themselves, over time, from an imperial army unit to a loosely-governed, anti-imperial band of freedom fighters. Eventually "overcome by Russian stealth and treachery" in 1775, the "Cossack rank-and-file fled into Turkey and Turkish-held Europe," their officers "were arrested and sent into penal servitude in Siberia," and the *sich* itself was "razed" (127)—all to "clear the way for more tractable settlers, among them the Mennonites from the muggy delta of the Vistula" (128).

Beginning in 1788, then, Mennonites from Danzig "migrated en masse for the steppes of southern Ukraine" (125). Once there, they cleared and cultivated land, built homes and villages; using German words ("Neuendorf, Schonhorst, Rosental, Einlage, Steinbach, and Kronsweide" [129]) to map the countryside, and planting potatoes ("emblematic of German virtue, prudence" [137]) to make their living, they transplanted German culture onto the soil of the former "Cossack lands" (129). During his visit to Khortytsia in 1843, the German traveler Baron August von Haxthausen observed that "[t]he fields are laid out and cultivated in the German manner; the farmlands and meadows are enclosed with German fences" (132). "Everything" about the Mennonite colony, he noted, "is German: the villages with all their individual farmsteads, the gardens and their arrangements, the plants, the vegetables and above all the potatoes" (132). Importantly, however, as Kostash hastens to point out, the "availability of cheap labour"—"to wit: the Ukrainians"—is what guaranteed the Mennonites' success in building a thriving colony at Khortytsia (138). At its core, she says, this moment in Mennonite/Ukrainian history is "about the land that the Mennonites have and the Ukrainians covet but cannot afford" (138).

15 In her readings of Rudy Wiebe's *The Blue Mountains of China* (1970), Al Reimer's *My Harp is Turned to Mourning* (1985), and John Weier's *Steppe* (1995), Kostash identifies a narrative pattern in which Ukrainians are reduced to one of two ethnically-inflected and gendered roles—the "blockhead" or the "slut" (165). Whereas Mennonites (especially Mennonite men) are agents in their own stories—given to order, sensibility, and piety— Ukrainians are passive pawns who cannot think, much less act, for themselves. The Ukrainian man recurs in these texts as the ignorant servant who is prone to drink, and who works best "under threat of violence" (164). Even when he is "[h]alf-awakened by agitprop" (as is the case with Escha in *The Blue Mountains of China*, a Ukrainian character who revolts against his Mennonite master), he has no control over himself or his actions: he "loses all restraint" and "strikes out blindly" (165), undermining his own attempts at altering his fate. The Ukrainian woman, on the other hand, usually a "female servant in the same households" (165) as her blockhead brethren, is the slutty, "sloe-eyed, exotic beauty in the starched white uniform" who "drives sons crazy with the suggestion of her availability" (165). Although she acknowledges that the Mennonite woman in these texts is also constrained by her gender, locked into the role of the chaste wife, Kostash underscores the ways in which the Ukrainian woman is twice-marked as "other" to the Mennonite master by her ethnicity and gender: her identity is solely defined by her "primal Slavic body" (165). Indeed, in their interactions with Mennonites, Ukrainians— and Ukrainian women especially—have the lowest status in what Kostash calls a "political economy of cross-cultural desire" (168). In her analysis of this economy, the

"Mennonite male desires the Ukrainian female, and may have her. The Ukrainian male desires the Mennonite woman but may not have her. There is," however, "no notion of the specific desire of the Ukrainian woman—she'll take anybody—nor of the dignity of marriage between Ukrainians" (168–69).

16 Kostash read excerpts from Makhno's published memoir, *Huliai-Pole*, in a 1991 issue of *Ukraina* magazine. She provides no exact publication date for the memoir, and I have been unable to locate it.

17 In her bibliographic appendix to *The Doomed Bridegroom*, Kostash lists the texts that she consulted as she researched Makhno's story, including Peter Arshinov's *The History of the Makhnovist Movement* (1974); Victor Eichenbaum's *The Unknown Revolution* (1975) (Eichenbaum published under the pseudonym Voline); Victor Peters's *Nestor Makhno: The Life of an Anarchist* (1970); and Michael Malet's *Nestor Makhno in the Russian Civil War* (1982). For a fuller list of her sources, see Kostash's bibliography.

Monumental Culture and the Future of Ukrainian Canadian Literature

1 For a comprehensive list, see Ed Solonyka's website "Large Canadian Roadside Attractions" at http://www.cyberbeach.net/~solonyka/LCRA/main.htm.

2 See Chapter Four, fn. 9.

Works Cited

Abraham, Michael Q. "Cultural Orphans and Wood Mountain: The Poetry of Andrew Suknaski." *Prairie Journal of Canadian Literature* 14 (1990): 24-35.
Ahmad, Aijaz. *On Communalism and Globalization: Offensives of the Far Right*. New Delhi: Three Essays, 2002.
Allcock, John B. *Explaining Yugoslavia*. New York: Columbia UP, 2000.
Ang, Ien. *On Not Speaking Chinese: Living Between Asia and the West*. London; New York: Routledge, 2001.
Appignanesi, Lisa. *Losing the Dead*. Toronto: McArthur, 1999.
Arshinov, Peter. *The History of the Makhnovist Movement*. Detroit: Black and Red, 1974.
Artibise, Alan F.J. *Prairie Urban Development 1878 -1930*. Ottawa: The Canadian Historical Association Booklets, 1981.
Ashcroft, Bill, Gareth Griffins, and Helen Tiffin. *The Empire Writes Back: Theory and Practice in Post-colonial Literatures*. London; New York: Routledge, 1989.
Bhabha, Homi K. *Location of Culture*. London; New York: Routledge, 1994.
Balan, Irka. "Dance Interpretation and Performance." *Visible Symbols: Cultural Expression Among Canada's Ukrainians*. Ed. Manoly Lupul. Edmonton: Canadian Institute of Ukrainian Studies, 1984. 102-4.
Balan, Jars. "Backdrop to an Era: The Ukrainian Canadian Stage in the Interwar Years." *Journal of Ukrainian Studies* 16:1-2 (1991): 89-113.
———, ed. *Identifications: Ethnicity and the Writer in Canada*. Edmonton: Canadian Institute of Ukrainian Studies, 1982.
———. "Old World Forms, New World Settings: The Emergence of Ukrainian-Canadian Plays on North American Themes." *Cultural Identities in Canadian Literature*. Ed. Bénédicte Maugière. New York: Peter Lang, 1998. 5-23.
———. *Salt and Braided Bread: Ukrainian Life in Canada*. Toronto: Oxford UP, 1984.
———. "Voices from the Canadian Steppes: Ukrainian Elements in Andrew Suknaski's Poetry." *Studia Ucrainica* 4:9 (1988): 120-28.

———. "'A Word in a Foreign Language': Ukrainian Influences in George Ryga's Work." *Identifications: Ethnicity and the Writer in Canada*. Ed. Jars Balan. Edmonton: Canadian Institute of Ukrainian Studies, 1982. 36–52.

———, and Yuri Klynovy, eds. *Yarmarok: Ukrainian Writing in Canada Since the Second World War*. Edmonton: Canadian Institute of Ukrainian Studies, 1987.

Beeler, Karin E. "Ethnic Dominance and Difference: The Post-Colonial Condition in Margaret Laurence's *The Stone Angel*, *A Jest of God*, and *The Diviners*." *Cultural Identities in Canadian Literature*. Ed. Bénédicte Maugière. New York: Peter Lang, 1998. 25–37.

Bereshko, Ludmilla. *The Parcel From Chicken Street and Other Stories*. Montreal: DC Books, 1989.

Bhabha, Homi K. "DissemiNation: Time, Narrative, and the Margins of the Modern Nation." *Nation and Narration*. Ed. Homi K. Bhabha. London; New York: Routledge, 1990. 291–322.

———. "Introduction: Narrating the Nation." *Nation and Narration*. Ed. Homi K. Bhabha. London; New York: Routledge, 1990. 1–7.

Bilash, Radomir. *Ukrainian Cultural Heritage Village*. Edmonton: Friends of the Ukrainian Village Society, 1989.

Blodgett, E. D. *Configuration: Essays in the Canadian Literatures*. Toronto: ECW, 1982.

Bociurkiw, Bohdan. "The Federal Policy of Multiculturalism and the Ukrainian-Canadian Community." *Ukrainian Canadians, Multiculturalism, and Separatism: An Assessment*. Ed. Manoly Lupul. Edmonton: U of Alberta P; Canadian Institute of Ukrainian Studies, 1978. 98–128.

Bociurkiw, Marusya. *Halfway to the East*. Vancouver: Lazara, 1999.

———. *The Woman Who Loved Airports*. Vancouver: Press Gang, 1994.

Brand, Dionne. "Who Can Speak for Whom?" *Brick* 46 (1993): 13–20.

Callaghan, Morley. *They Shall Inherit the Earth*. Toronto: Macmillan, 1935.

Chow, Rey. *Writing Diaspora: Tactics of Intervention in Contemporary Cultural Studies*. Bloomington: Indiana UP, 1993.

Coleman, Daniel. "Immigration, Nation, and the Canadian Allegory of Manly Maturation." *Essays on Canadian Writing* 61 (1997): 84–103.

Connor, Ralph. *The Foreigner: A Tale of Saskatchewan*. Toronto: Westminster, 1909.

———. *The Man from Glengarry: A Tale of the Ottawa*. Toronto: Westminster, 1901.

———. *The Sky Pilot: A Tale of the Foothills*. Toronto: Westminster, 1899.

Craig, Terrence. *Racial Attitudes in English-Canadian fiction 1905–1980*. Waterloo: Wilfred Laurier UP, 1987.

Cramer, Timothy R. "Questioning Sexuality in Sinclair Ross's *As For Me and My House*." *ARIEL* 30:2 (1999): 49–60.

Czumer, William A. *Recollections About the Life of the first Ukrainian Settlers in Canada*. Edmonton: Canadian Institute of Ukrainian Studies, 1981.

Danaher, Kevin, and Jason Mark. *Insurrection: Citizen Challenges to Corporate Power*. New York: Routledge, 2003.

Driedger, Leo. "Urbanization of Ukrainians in Canada: Consequences for Ethnic Identity." *Changing Realities: Social Trends Among Ukrainian Canadians*. Ed. W. Roman Petryshyn. Edmonton: Canadian Institute of Ukrainian Studies, 1980. 107–33.

Dunton, A. Davidson, and André Laurendeau, eds. *Report of the Royal Commission on Bilingualism and Biculturalism, vol. 4*. [*The Cultural Contribution of the Other Ethnic Groups*.] Ottawa: R. Duhamel, Queen's Printer and Controller of Stationery, 1969.

Eichenbaum, Victor. *The Unknown Revolution*. Montreal: Black Rose, 1975.
Evanishen, Danny. *Vuiko Yurko: The First Generation*. Summerland: Ethnic Enterprises, 1994.
Fanon, Franz. *Black Skin, White Masks*. New York: Grove, 1967.
———. *The Wretched of the Earth*. New York: Grove, 1963.
Fee, Margery. "Romantic Nationalism and the Image of Native People in Contemporary English-Canadian Literature." *The Native in Literature*. Ed. Thomas King, Cheryl Calver, and Helen Hoy. Toronto: ECW, 1987. 15-33.
Foty, Yurko, and Sviatoslaw Chepyha. *Let's Sing Out in Ukrainian*. Saskatoon: Canuk, 1980.
Fraser, Keath. *As For Me and My Body: A Memoir of Sinclair Ross*. Toronto: ECW, 1997.
Frolick, Gloria Kupchenko. *Anna Veryna*. Don Mills, ON: Maxwell MacMillan, 1992.
———. *The Chicken Man*. Stratford, ON: Williams-Wallace, 1989.
———. *The Green Tomato Years*. Toronto: Williams-Wallace, 1985.
Galay, Ted. *After Baba's Funeral and Sweet and Sour Pickles: Two Plays*. Toronto: Playwrights Canada, 1981.
———. *Tsymbaly!* Toronto: Playwrights Canada, 1987.
Gerus, O.W., and J.E. Rea. *The Ukrainians in Canada*. Ottawa: Canadian Historical Association, 1985.
Goldie, Terry. *Fear and Temptation: The Image of the Indigene in Canadian, Australian, and New Zealand Literature*. Kingston: McGill-Queen's UP, 1989.
Gregory, E. David, ed. *The Athabasca Ryga*. Vancouver: Talonbooks, 1990.
Grekul, Lisa. *Kalyna's Song*. Regina: Coteau, 2003.
Grove, Frederick Philip. *A Search for America*. Ottawa: Graphic, 1927.
Gulutsan, Lena. *The Mosquito's Wedding*. Edmonton: Kazka, 1980.
———. *Snow Folks*. Edmonton: Kazka, 1982.
Gunew, Sneja, Margery Fee, and Lisa Grekul. "Myrna Kostash: Ukrainian Canadian Non-fiction Prairie New Leftist Feminist Canadian Nationalist." *Canadian Literature* 172 (2002): 114-43.
Haas, Maara. *On Stage with Maara Haas*. Winnipeg: Lilith, 1986.
———. *The Street Where I Live*. Toronto: McGraw-Hill Ryerson, 1976.
Hinz, Evelyn J., and John J. Teunissen. "Who's the Father of Mrs. Bentley's Child?: *As For Me and My House* and the Conventions of Dramatic Monologue." Sinclair Ross's *As For Me and My House: Five Decades of Criticism*. Ed. David Stouck. Toronto: U of Toronto P, 1991. 148-61.
Hnatyshyn, Ramon, and Robert Klymasz, eds. *Art and Ethnicity: The Ukrainian Tradition in Canada*. Hull: Canadian Museum of Civilization, 1991.
Hoffman, Eva. *Exit Into History: A Journey Through the New Eastern Europe*. New York: Viking, 1993.
———. *Lost in Translation: A Life in a New Language*. New York: E.P. Dutton, 1989.
———. *Shtetl: The Life and Death of a Small Town and the World of Polish Jews*. Boston: Houghton Mifflin, 1997.
Hoffman, James. *The Ecstasy of Resistance: A Biography of George Ryga*. Toronto: ECW, 1995.
hooks, bell. *Outlaw Culture: Resisting Representations*. New York: Routledge, 1994.
Hryniuk, Stella, and Lubomyr Luciuk, eds. *Canada's Ukrainians: Negotiating an Identity*. Toronto: Ukrainian Canadian Centennial Committee; U of Toronto P, 1991.

Husar, Natalka. "The Relevance of Ethnicity: A Personal Perspective." *Visible Symbols: Cultural Expression Among Canada's Ukrainians*. Ed. Manoly Lupul. Edmonton: Canadian Institute of Ukrainian Studies, 1984. 36-37.

Hutcheon, Linda, and Marion Richmond, eds. *Other Solitudes: Canadian Multicultural Fictions*. Toronto: Oxford UP, 1990.

Ignatieff, Michael. *Blood and Belonging: Journeys Into the New Nationalism*. Toronto: Viking, 1993.

Innes, Christopher. *Politics and the Playwright: George Ryga*. Toronto: Simon and Pierre, 1985.

Isajiw, Wsevolod W. "Ethnic Art and the Ukrainian-Canadian Experience." *Art and Ethnicity: The Ukrainian Tradition in Canada*. Ed. Ramon Hnatyshyn and Robert Klymasz. Quebec: Canadian Museum of Civilization, 1991. 29-36.

———. "Identity Retention Among Second- and Third-Generation Ukrainians in Canada." *New Soil—Old Roots: The Ukrainian Experience in Canada*. Ed. Jaroslav Rozumnyj. Winnipeg: Ukrainian Academy of Arts and Sciences in Canada, 1983. 208-21.

Iyer, Pico. *The Global Soul: Jet Lag, Shopping Malls, and the Search for Home*. New York: Knopf, 2000.

———. *Imagining Canada: An Outsider's Hope for a Global Future*. Toronto: Hart House, 2001.

Jones, Michael Owen. "A Folklorist's Viewpoint on Ukrainian-Canadian Art." *Art and Ethnicity: The Ukrainian Tradition in Canada*. Ed. Ramon Hnatyshyn and Robert Klymasz. Quebec: Canadian Museum of Civilization, 1991. 47-57.

Kamboureli, Smaro, ed. *Making a Difference: Canadian Multicultural Literature*. Toronto: Oxford UP, 1996.

———. *Scandalous Bodies: Diasporic Literature in English Canada*. Don Mills: Oxford UP, 2000.

Kaminsky, Amy. *After Exile: Writing the Latin American Diaspora*. Minneapolis: U of Minnesota P, 1999.

Karafilly, Irena. *Ashes and Miracles: A Polish Journey*. Toronto: Malcolm Lester, 1998.

Kaufman, Joyce P. *NATO and the Former Yugoslavia: Crisis, Conflict, and the Atlantic Alliance*. Lanham: Rowman & Littlefield, 2002.

Keeshig-Tobias, Lenore. "Stop Stealing Native Stories." *Borrowed Power: Essays on Cultural Appropriation*. Ed. Bruce Ziff and Pratima V. Rao. New Brunswick, NJ: Rutgers UP, 1997. 71-73.

Keywan, Zonia. *Greater Than Kings: Ukrainian Pioneer Settlement in Canada*. Montreal: Harvest House, 1977.

———. Rev. of *All of Baba's Children*, by Myrna Kostash. *Quill and Quire* 44:2 (1978): 39-40.

———. Rev. of *No Streets of Gold*, by Helen Potrebenko. *Quill and Quire* 44:2 (1978): 40.

Kirtz, Mary K. "'I am become a name': The Representation of Ukrainians in Ross, Laurence, Ryga and Atwood." *Canadian Ethnic Studies* 24:2 (1992): 35-45.

———. "Old World Traditions, New World Inventions: Bilingualism, Multiculturalism, and the Transformation of Ethnicity." *Canadian Ethnic Studies* 28:1 (1996): 8-21.

Klein, Naomi. *Fences and Windows: Dispatches from the Front Lines of the Globalization Debate*. Toronto: Vintage, 2002.

Klymasz, Robert B. "Art of Intrusion: Macaronicism in Ukrainian-Canadian Literature." *Canadian Review of Comparative Literature* 16:3-4 (1989): 763-69.

———. "Cultural Maintenance and the Ukrainian Experience in Western Canada." *New Soil—Old Roots: The Ukrainian Experience in Canada.* Ed. Jaroslav Rozumnyj. Winnipeg: Ukrainian Academy of Arts and Sciences in Canada, 1983. 173–82.

———. "Folk Music." *Visible Symbols: Cultural Expression Among Canada's Ukrainians.* Ed. Manoly Lupul. Edmonton: Canadian Institute of Ukrainian Studies, 1984. 49–56.

Kostash, Myrna. *All of Baba's Children.* Edmonton: Hurtig, 1977.

———. *All of Baba's Great-grandchildren: Ethnic Identity in the Next Canada.* Saskatoon: Heritage, 2000.

———. *Bloodlines: A Journey Into Eastern Europe.* Vancouver: Douglas and McIntyre, 1993.

———. *The Doomed Bridegroom: A Memoir.* Edmonton: NeWest, 1998.

———. *Long Way From Home: The Story of the Sixties Generation in Canada.* Toronto: J. Lorimer, 1980.

———. *The Next Canada: In Search of Our Future Nation.* Toronto: McClelland and Stewart, 2000.

———. *No Kidding: Inside the World of Teenage Girls.* Toronto: McClelland and Stewart, 1987.

———. "The Shock of White Cognition." *Border Crossings* 13:3 (1994): 4–5.

———, Melinda McCracken, Valerie Miner, Erna Paris, and Heather Robertson, eds. *Her Own Woman: Profiles of Ten Canadian Women.* Toronto: Macmillan, 1975.

Kroetsch, Robert. *The Stone Hammer Poems, 1969–1975.* Lantzville, BC: Oolichan, 1975.

Kruchka Glynn, Alexandra. "Introduction." *Yellow Boots* [1954]. Edmonton: NeWest; Canadian Institute of Ukrainian Studies, 1992.

———. "Reintroducing Vera Lysenko—Ukrainian Canadian Author." *Journal of Ukrainian Studies* 15:1 (1990): 53–70.

Kulyk Keefer, Janice. "'Coming Across Bones': Historiographic Ethnofiction." *Essays on Canadian Writing* 57 (1995): 84–104.

———. *Constellations.* Toronto: Random House, 1988.

———. "From Dialogue to Polylogue: Canadian Transcultural Writing During the Deluge." *Difference and Community: Canadian and European Cultural Perspectives.* Ed. Peter Easingwood, Konrad Gross, and Lynette Hunter. Amsterdam: Rodopi, 1996. 59–70.

———. "From Mosaic to Kaleidoscope: Out of the multicultural past comes a vision of a transcultural future." *Books in Canada* 20:6 (1991): 13–16.

———. *The Green Library.* Toronto: HarperCollins, 1996.

———. "Home Comings/Border Crossings: Travels Through Imagined and Actual Worlds." *Dangerous Crossings: Papers on Transgression in Literature and Culture.* Ed. Monica Loeb and Gerald Porter. Uppsala: Swedish Science, 1999. 15–30.

———. *Honey and Ashes: A Story of Family.* Toronto: HarperCollins, 1998.

———. *The Paris-Napoli Express.* Ottawa: Oberon, 1986.

———. "Personal and Public Records: Story and History in the Narration of Ethnicity." *Tricks With a Glass: Writing Ethnicity in Canada.* Ed. Rocio G. Davis and Rosalia Baena. Amsterdam: Rodopi, 2000. 1–18.

———. *Reading Mavis Gallant.* Toronto: Oxford UP, 1989.

———. *Rest Harrow.* Toronto: HarperCollins, 1992.

———. *Transfigurations.* Charlottetown: Ragweed, 1987.

———. *Travelling Ladies*. Toronto: Random House, 1990.

———. *Under Eastern Eyes: A Critical Reading of Maritime Fiction*. Toronto: U of Toronto P, 1987.

———. *White of the Lesser Angels*. Charlottetown: Ragweed, 1986.

———, and Solomea Pavlychko, eds. *Two Lands, New Visions: Stories From Canada and Ukraine*. Regina: Coteau, 1998.

Kupchenko, Yuri. *The Horseman of Shandro Crossing*. Edmonton: Tree Frog, 1989.

Kurelek, William. *Jewish Life in Canada*. Edmonton: Hurtig, 1976.

———. *Kurelek's Canada*. Toronto: Pagurian, 1975.

———. *Kurelek Country*. Boston: Houghton Mifflin, 1975.

———. *The Polish Canadians*. Montreal: Tundra, 1981.

———. *A Prairie Boy's Summer*. Montreal: Tundra, 1975.

———. *A Prairie Boy's Winter*. Montreal: Tundra, 1973.

Lane, Patrick. "The Poetry of Andrew Suknaski." *Essays on Canadian Writing* 18/19 (1980): 90-99.

Laurence, Margaret. *A Bird in the House* [1963]. Toronto: NCL, 1994.

———. *The Diviners* [1974]. Toronto: Bantam, 1975.

———. *The fire-Dwellers* [1969]. Toronto: NCL, 1991.

———. *A Jest of God* [1966]. Toronto: NCL, 1988.

———. *The Stone Angel* [1964]. Toronto: NCL, 1988.

Lawson, Alan. "Postcolonial Theory and the 'Settler' Subject." *Essays on Canadian Writing* 56 (1995): 20-36.

Legacy to a New Land: A Celebration of Ukrainian Settlement in the West. Dir. William Pettigrew, Halya Kuchmij, Michael Mirus, Dallas Jones, Anne Wheeler, John Paskievich, and James Beveridge. National Film Board of Canada, 1991.

Linkiewich, Emily. *Baba's Cookbook*. Vegreville: K.J. Linkiewich, 1979.

Luciuk, Lubomyr. *Searching for Place: Ukrainian Displaced Persons, Canada, and the Migration of Memory*. Toronto: U of Toronto P, 2000.

———, and Bohdan Kordan. *Creating a Landscape: A Geography of Ukrainians in Canada*. Toronto: U of Toronto P, 1989.

Lysenko, Vera. *Men in Sheepskin Coats: A Study in Assimilation*. Toronto: Ryerson, 1947.

———. *Westerly Wild*. Toronto: Ryerson, 1956.

———. *Yellow Boots*. Toronto: Ryerson, 1954.

———. *Yellow Boots* [1954]. Edmonton: NeWest; Canadian Institute of Ukrainian Studies, 1992.

Malet, Michael. *Nestor Makhno in the Russian Civil War*. London: Macmillan, 1982.

Mandryka, M.I. *History of Ukrainian Literature in Canada*. Winnipeg: Ukrainian Free Academy of Sciences, 1968.

Marunchak, Michael H. *The Ukrainian Canadians: A History*. Winnipeg: Ukrainian Free Academy of Sciences, 1982.

Medwidsky, Bohdan. "Three Types of Ukrainian Folk Tales in Canada." *Continuity and Change: The Cultural Life of Alberta's First Ukrainians*. Ed. Manoly Lupul. Edmonton: Canadian Institute of Ukrainian Studies; Historic Sites Service, Alberta Culture and Multiculturalism, 1988. 174-81.

Melnyk, Bohdan. *Fox Mykyta*. Montreal: Tundra, 1978.

Melnyk, George. *The Literary History of Alberta, Volume Two: From the End of the War to the End of the Century*. Edmonton: U of Alberta P, 1999.

———. *Radical Regionalism*. Edmonton: NeWest, 1981.

Miki, Roy. *Broken Entries: Race Writing Subjectivity*. Toronto: Mercury, 1998.

Mitchell, Katharyne. "In Whose Interest?: Transnational Capital and the Production of Multiculturalism in Canada." *Global/Local: Cultural Production and the Transnational Imaginary*. Ed. Rob Wilson and Wimal Dissanayake. Durham; London: Duke UP, 1996. 219-51.

Miyoshi, Masao. "A Borderless World?: From Colonialism to Transnationalism and the Decline of the Nation-State." *Global/Local: Cultural Production and the Transnational Imaginary*. Ed. Rob Wilson and Wimal Dissanayake. Durham; London: Duke UP, 1996. 78-106.

Monkman, Leslie. *A Native Heritage: Images of the Indian in English-Canadian Literature*. Toronto: U of Toronto P, 1981.

Morgan, Dawn. "Andrew Suknaski's 'Wood Mountain Time' and the Chronotope of Multiculturalism." *Mosaic* 29:3 (1996): 35-51.

Morley, Patricia A. *Kurelek: A Biography*. Toronto: Macmillan, 1986.

Moss, John, ed. *From the Heart of the Heartland: The Fiction of Sinclair Ross*. Ottawa: U of Ottawa P, 1992.

Munton, Anne. "The Structural Horizons of Prairie Poetics: The Long Poem, Eli Mandel, Andrew Suknaski, and Robert Kroetsch." *Dalhousie Review* 63:1 (1983): 69-97.

Mycak, Sonia. *Canuke Literature: Critical Essays on Canadian Ukrainian Writing*. Huntington, NY: Nova Science, 2001.

———. "A Different Story by Helen Potrebenko: The Pioneer Myth Re-Visited." *Canadian Ethnic Studies* 28:1 (1996): 67-88. [reprinted in *Canuke Literature*, 49-77]

———. "Simple Sentimentality or Specific Narrative Strategy?: The Functions and Use of Nostalgia in the Ukrainian-Canadian Text." *Canadian Ethnic Studies* 30:1 (1998): 50-63. [reprinted in *Canuke Literature*, 31-48]

My Mother's Village. Dir. John Paskievich. National film Board of Canada, 2001.

Nahachewsky, Andriy. "Ukrainian Performing Arts in Alberta." *Continuity and Change: The Cultural Life of Alberta's First Ukrainians*. Ed. Manoly Lupul. Edmonton: Canadian Institute of Ukrainian Studies; Historic Sites Service, Alberta Culture and Multiculturalism, 1988. 211-20.

Nazarenko, Tatiana. "Ukrainian-Canadian Visual Poetry: Traditions and Innovations." *Canadian Ethnic Studies* 28:1 (1996): 89-126.

New, W.H. *A History of Canadian Literature*. Montreal: McGill-Queen's UP, 2003.

———. "*The Stone Angel* and the Manawaka Cycle." *Etudes Canadiennes/Canadian Studies* 11 (1981): 23-33.

Ostenso, Martha. *Wild Geese*. New York: Dodd; Mead, 1925.

Padolsky, Enoch. "Canadian Ethnic Minority Literature in English." *Ethnicity and Culture in Canada: The Research Landscape*. Ed. J.W. Berry and J.A. Laponce. Toronto: U of Toronto P, 1994. 361-86.

Palmer Seiler, Tamara. "Including the Female Immigrant Story: A Comparative Look at Narrative Strategies." *Canadian Ethnic Studies* 28:1 (1996): 51-66.

Pensky, Max. Introduction. *The Postnational Constellation: Political Essays.* By Jürgen Habermas. Cambridge: Polity, 2001. i-xix.

Peters, Victor. *Nestor Makhno: The Life of an Anarchist.* Winnipeg: Echo, 1970.

Philip, Marlene Nourbese. "The Disappearing Debate; or How the Discussion of Racism Has Been Taken Over by the Censorship Issue." *Borrowed Power: Essays on Cultural Appropriation.* Ed. Bruce Ziff and Pratima V. Rao. New Brunswick, NJ: Rutgers UP, 1997. 97-108.

Piniuta, Harry. *Land of Pain, Land of Promise: First Person Accounts by Ukrainian Pioneers 1891-1914.* Saskatoon: Western Producer Prairie Books, 1978.

Pohorecky, Zenon. "Ukrainian Cultural and Political Symbols in Canada: An Anthropological Selection." *Visible Symbols: Cultural Expression Among Canada's Ukrainians.* Ed. Manoly Lupul. Edmonton: Canadian Institute of Ukrainian Studies, 1984. 129-41.

Pollock, Sharon. *Walsh: A Play.* Vancouver: Talonbooks, 1973.

Porter, Anna. *The Storyteller: Memory, Secrets, Magic and Lies.* Toronto: Doubleday, 2000.

Potrebenko, Helen. *A Flight of Average Persons: Stories and Other Writings.* Vancouver: New Star, 1979.

———. *Hey Waitress and Other Stories.* Vancouver: Lazara, 1989.

———. *Life, Love and Unions.* Vancouver: Lazara, 1987.

———. *No Streets of Gold: A Social History of Ukrainians in Alberta.* Vancouver: New Star, 1977.

———. *Riding Home.* Vancouver: Talonbooks, 1995.

———. *Sometimes They Sang.* Vancouver: Press Gang, 1986.

———. *Taxi!* Vancouver: New Star, 1986.

———. *Walking Slow.* Vancouver: Lazara, 1985.

Pratt, Mary Louise. *Imperial Eyes: Travel Writing and Transculturation.* London; New York: Routledge, 1992.

Pritz, Alexandra. "The Evolution of Ukrainian Dance in Canada." *Visible Symbols: Cultural Expression Among Canada's Ukrainians.* Ed. Manoly Lupul. Edmonton: Canadian Institute of Ukrainian Studies, 1984. 87-101.

———. "Ukrainian Dance in Canada: The First Fifty Years, 1924-1974." *New Soil—Old Roots: The Ukrainian Experience in Canada.* Ed. Jaroslav Rozumnyj. Winnipeg: Ukrainian Academy of Arts and Sciences in Canada, 1983. 124-54.

Prystupa, Steve. "Museums and Ukrainian Canadian Material Culture." *Visible Symbols: Cultural Expression Among Canada's Ukrainians.* Ed. Manoly Lupul. Edmonton: Canadian Institute of Ukrainian Studies, 1984. 15-17.

Purdy, Al. *The Collected Poems of Al Purdy.* Ed. Russell Brown. Toronto: McClelland & Stewart, 1986.

Radhakrishnan, Rajagopalan. *Diasporic Mediations: Between Home and Location.* Minneapolis: U of Minnesota P, 1996.

Raoul, Valerie. "Straight or Bent: Textual/Sexual T(ri)angles in *As For Me and My House.*" *Canadian Literature* 156 (1998): 13-28.

Rasporich, Beverly. "Retelling Vera Lysenko: A Feminist and Ethnic Writer." *Canadian Ethnic Studies* 21:2 (1989): 38-52.

———. "Vera Lysenko's Fictions: Engendering Prairie Spaces." *Prairie Forum* 16:2 (1991): 249-63.

Rawlyk, G.A. "Discovering Baba." Rev. of *All of Baba's Children*, by Myrna Kostash, *No Streets of Gold*, by Helen Potrebenko, and *Greater than Kings*, by Zonya Keywan. *Canadian Forum* 58:680 (1978): 38-40.

Redl, Carolyn. "Neither Here nor There: Canadian Fiction by the Multicultural Generation." *Canadian Ethnic Studies* 28:1 (1996): 22-36.

Reimer, Al. *My Harp is Turned to Mourning*. Winnipeg: Hyperion, 1985.

Ricou, Laurie. *Vertical Man/Horizontal World: Man and Landscape in Canadian Prairie Fiction*. Vancouver: U of British Columbia P, 1973.

Rose, Marilyn. "Sinclair Ross's 'Foreigners.'" *From the Heart of the Heartland: The Fiction of Sinclair Ross*. Ed. John Moss. Ottawa: U of Ottawa P, 1992. 91-101.

Ross, Sinclair. *As For Me and My House* [1941]. Toronto: NCL, 1989.

Rubchak, Bohdan. "Homes as Shells: Ukrainian Émigré Poetry." *New Soil—Old Roots: The Ukrainian Experience in Canada*. Ed. Jaroslav Rozumnyj. Winnipeg: Ukrainian Academy of Arts and Sciences in Canada, 1983. 87-123.

Rushdie, Salman. *Imaginary Homelands*. London: Granta, 1991.

Ryga, George. *Ballad of a Stone-Picker*. Toronto: Macmillan, 1966.

———. *Captives of the Faceless Drummer*. Vancouver: Talonbooks, 1971.

———. *The Ecstasy of Rita Joe*. Vancouver: Talonbooks, 1970.

———. "Essay on *A Letter to My Son*." *The Athabasca Ryga*. Ed. E. David Gregory. Vancouver: Talonbooks, 1990. 75-79.

———. *Hungry Hills*. Toronto: Longmans, 1963.

———. *Night Desk: A Novel*. Vancouver: Talonbooks, 1976.

———. *Ploughmen of the Glacier: A Play*. Vancouver: Talonbooks, 1977.

———. *Portrait of Angelica and A Letter to My Son*. Winnipeg: Turnstone, 1984.

———. *Sunrise on Sarah*. Vancouver: Talonbooks, 1973.

Scobie, Stephen. "Ghostly Voices." Rev. of *the ghosts call you poor*, by Andrew Suknaski. *NeWest Review* 4:2 (1978): 3-4.

Second Second Story Collective, ed. *Imagining Women*. Toronto: Women's Press, 1988.

Siemerling, Winfried, ed. *Writing Ethnicity: Cross-cultural Consciousness in Canadian and Québécois Literature*. Toronto: ECW, 1996.

Slavutych, Jar. *The Conquerors of the Prairies*. Trans. H. Morrison, Zoria Orionna, Roman Orest Tatchyn, and Rene C. du Gard. Edmonton: Slavuta, 1984.

Slemon, Stephen. "Unsettling the Empire: Resistance Theory for the Second World." *World Literature Written in English* 30:2 (1990): 30-41.

Spak, Harvey. "Shadows of Our Ancestors." *NeWest Review* 4:2 (1978): 3-4.

Stechishin, Savella. *Traditional Ukrainian Cookery*. Winnipeg: Trident, 1976.

Stouck, David. "The Mirror and the Lamp in Sinclair Ross's *As For Me and My House*." *Sinclair Ross's As For Me and My House: Five Decades of Criticism*. Ed. David Stouck. Toronto: U of Toronto P, 1991. 95-103.

———, ed. *Sinclair Ross's As For Me and My House: Five Decades of Criticism*. Toronto: U of Toronto P, 1991.

Subtelny, Orest. *Ukraine: A History*. Toronto: U of Toronto P; Canadian Institute of Ukrainian Studies, 1994.

———. *Ukrainians in North America: An Illustrated History*. Toronto: U of Toronto P, 1991.
Suknaski, Andrew. *Blind Man's House*. Wood Mountain, SK: Anak, 1975.
———. *Circles*. Calgary: Deodar Shadow, 1970.
———. *East of Myloona*. Saskatoon: Thistledown, 1979.
———. *On First Looking Down from Lion's Gate Bridge*. Wood Mountain, SK: Sundog, 1974.
———. *Ghost Gun*. Toronto: League of Canadian Poets, 1978.
———. *the ghosts call you poor*. Toronto: Macmillan, 1978.
———. *The Land They Gave Away: New & Selected Poems*. Edmonton: NeWest, 1982.
———. *Leaving*. Seven Persons, AB: Repository, 1974.
———. *Leaving Wood Mountain*. Wood Mountain, SK: Sundog, 1975.
———. *In Mind Ov Xrossroads Ov Mythologies*. Calgary: Deodar Shadow, 1971.
———. *Moses Beauchamp for Mike Olito*. Winnipeg: Turnstone, 1978.
———. *In the Name of Narid*. Erin, ON: Porcupine's Quill, 1981.
———. *Octomi*. Saskatoon: Thistledown, 1976.
———. *Old Mill*. Vancouver: blewointmentpress, 1971.
———. *Rose Way in the East*. Toronto: Ganglia, 1971.
———. *This Shadow of Eden Once*. Calgary: Deodar Shadow, 1970.
———. *Suicide Notes Book 1*. Wood Mountain, SK: Sundog, 1973.
———. *Wood Mountain Poems*. Toronto: MacMillan, 1976.
———. *Y the Evolution into Ruenz*. Wood Mountain, SK: Anak A-1, 1972.
Swayze, Walter E. "Ralph Connor's *The Foreigner: A Tale of Saskatchewan* and Paradigm Shifts." *Prairie Fire* 20:2 (1999): 42–51.
Swyripa, Frances. "From Sheepskin Coat to Blue Jeans: A Brief History of Ukrainians in Canada." *Art and Ethnicity: The Ukrainian Tradition in Canada*. Ed. Ramon Hnatyshyn and Robert Klymasz. Quebec: Canadian Museum of Civilization, 1991. 11–27.
———. *Ukrainian Canadians: A Survey of Their Portrayal in English-Language Works*. Edmonton: U of Alberta, 1978.
———. *Wedded to the Cause: Ukrainian-Canadian Women and Ethnic Identity, 1891–1991*. Toronto: U of Toronto P, 1993.
Symchych, Victoria, and Olga Vesey. *The Flying Ship and Other Ukrainian Folk Tales*. Toronto: Holt, Rinehart and Winston, 1975.
Thomson, Sandra. "The Ukrainian Cultural Heritage Village: Interpreting Ukrainian Canadian History." *Continuity and Change: The Cultural Life of Alberta's First Ukrainians*. Ed. Manoly Lupul. Edmonton: Canadian Institute of Ukrainian Studies, Historic Sites Service, Alberta Culture and Multiculturalism, 1988. 239–43.
Udovicki, Jasminka, and James Ridgeway, eds. *Burn This House: The Making and Unmaking of Yugoslavia*. Durham: Duke UP, 1997.
Ukrainian Women's Association of Canada, Daughters of Ukraine Branch. *Ukrainian Daughters' Cookbook*. Regina: Ukrainian Women's Association of Canada, 1984.
van Herk, Aritha. "Bitterness and Regret." Rev. of *All of Baba's Children*, by Myrna Kostash, *No Streets of Gold*, by Helen Potrebenko, and *Greater than Kings*, by Zonya Keywan. *Branching Out* 5:3 (1978): 40–41.
Van Rooy, Alison. *The Global Legitimacy Game: Civil Society, Globalization, and Protest*. Houndsmills; New York: Palgrave Macmillan, 2004.
Warwaruk, Larry. *The Ukrainian Wedding*. Regina: Coteau, 1998.

Weier, John. *Steppe: A Novel*. Winnipeg: Thistledown, 1995.

Wiebe, Rudy. *The Blue Mountains of China*. Toronto: McClelland and Stewart, 1970.

Williams, David. "The 'Scarlet' Rompers: Toward a New Perspective on *As For Me and My House*." *Canadian Literature* 103 (1984): 156-66.

Winland, Daphne N. "'Our Home and Native Land'?: Canadian Ethnic Scholarship and the Challenge of Transnationalism." *Canadian Review of Sociology and Anthropology* 35:4 (1998): 555-77.

Woycenko, Ol'ha. *The Ukrainians in Canada*. Winnipeg: Trident, 1968.

Young, Robert. *Colonial Desire: Hybridity in Theory, Culture and Race*. London; New York: Routledge, 1995.

Yuzyk, Paul. *Ukrainian Canadians: Their Place and Role in Canadian Life*. Toronto: Ukrainian Canadian Business and Professional Federation, 1967.

Zajcew, Bohdan. "Ukrainian Popular Music in Canada." *Visible Symbols: Cultural Expression Among Canada's Ukrainians*. Ed. Manoly Lupul. Edmonton: Canadian Institute of Ukrainian Studies, 1984. 57-61.

Ziff, Bruce, and Pratima V. Rao. "Introduction to Cultural Appropriation: A Framework for Analysis." *Borrowed Power: Essays on Cultural Appropriation*. Ed. Bruce Ziff and Pratima V. Rao. New Brunswick, NJ: Rutgers UP, 1997. 1-27.

Index

Aboriginal people. *See* First Nations people
After Baba's Funeral (Galay), 217n3
All of Baba's Children (Kostash), vii–ix, 57–60, 197, 216n21
All of Baba's Great-grandchildren (Kostash), 197–99, 203
Andrishak, Ruth, 49
Appignanesi, Lisa, 123
art
    four categories of folk arts (Isajiw), 56, 214n14
    Husar's paintings, 57, 123–24
    paintings by Shostak and Kurelek, 57
    pop art, 215n16
    in Suknaski's poetry, 97–99, 105–6
    See also folk arts and cultural artifacts
Art and Ethnicity: The Ukrainian Tradition, 55
Artibise, Alan F. J., 209n2
As For Me and My House. See Ross, Sinclair, *As For Me and My House*
Ashcroft, Bill, 70–71, 83
assimilation
    in Anglo-Canadian writers' works: in Connor's *The Foreigner*, 11, 14–18, 31–32; in Laurence's Manawaka cycle, 27, 29–32; in Ross's *As For Me and My House*, 19, 21–22, 24

    binaries of good/evil and Anglo/Ukrainian, 12–16, 23–24, 37–40, 46
    digestion metaphor, 10, 15, 32
    history: of first- and second-wave Ukrainians, 3–5, 7–10; of third wave émigrés, 5–6, 8, 52–54
    identity: ambivalence toward own culture, 51–52, 104, 106–7, 112, 151; desire to pass, 9, 31–32, 129; homeland ties, 115; stereotypes, 7, 21–22, 39, 197–99, 205n2
    in Lysenko's *Yellow Boots*: as cultural and linguistic loss, 34, 41, 43–46; as desire, 41–43
    in prairie pioneer myth (Mycak), 116–18, 222n4
    resistance to: in Haas's *Street Where I Live*, 71–75; in Ryga's *A Letter to My Son*, 83–88
    See also identity, Ukrainian Canadian; languages, Ukrainian and English
Athabasca Ryga, The (Ryga), 79

Balan, Jars, *Yarmarok: Ukrainian Writing in Canada*, 4, 6, 78, 79, 223n14
    on Suknaski, 91, 219n7, 220n14
    on Ukrainian literary production, 49–50

Balkans, 120–21
Bazie, Eddie, 220n13
Beeler, Karen, 30
Begamudré, Ven, 113
Bloodlines: A Journey Into Eastern Europe. See Kostash, Myrna, *Bloodlines: A Journey Into Eastern Europe*
Bociurkiw, Bohdan, 212n2
Bociurkiw, Marusya, xix, 203–4
Bosnia, Kostash's travels in, 154–55
Brand, Dionne, xiv, 221n16
Bukovynian immigrants
　in Connor's *The Foreigner*, 11, 13, 16–17
　in first-wave period (1890s to 1914), 4

Callaghan, Morley, *They Shall Inherit the Earth*, 19, 39
Cameron, Anne, 206n6
Canada Ukraine Legislative and Intergovernmental Project, 125, 223n16
Canadian Institute of Ukrainian Studies (CIUS), 33, 124, 125, 205n1
Centre for Ukrainian Canadian Studies, 205n1
Chepyha, Sviatoslaw, *Let's Sing Out in Ukrainian*, 55
CIUS. *See* Canadian Institute of Ukrainian Studies (CIUS)
class. *See* social class
Coleman, Daniel, 209n6
"'Coming Across Bones': Historiographic Ethnofiction" (Kulyk Keefer), xiii, 129, 205n3
communism
　Kostash and Potrebenko and, 60, 157, 216n20
Connor, Ralph, *The Foreigner*, 11–18
　as assimilationist narrative, 11, 14–18, 23–24, 31–32
　binaries of good/evil and Anglo/Ukrainian, 12–16, 23–24
　nationalism in, 11, 13–16, 19
　reception and influence of Connor's writings, 208n1, 211n6
　romance in, 12–13, 17
Craig, Terrence, 209n5
Cramer, Timothy, 210n12
cultural appropriation, 101–2, 206n6, 221n16
Czechoslovakia
　immigrants from, 120
　Kostash's travels in, 154–58, 160, 162–64, 166
Czumer, William, 58

dance, Ukrainian
　critical studies of, 52, 213n7, 213n10
　dance ensembles and performances, 54–55, 194–95, 197
　and multiculturalism, 54–55
　See also folk arts and cultural artifacts; music, Ukrainian
diaspora and writing, xv, 114, 206n6, 225n8
"Different Story" (Potrebenko), 116–18
Displaced Persons (DPs), 6
drama. *See* Galay, Ted; Ryga, George

Eastern Europe (after 1991)
　economic and social conditions, 120–26, 164–66
　writers and censorship in, 161–62
　See also Kostash, Myrna; Kulyk Keefer, Janice; transculturalism, transnationalism, and globalization; Ukraine
Ecstasy of Rita Joe, The (Ryga), 78, 90
ethnicity
　ambivalence and, 51–52, 104, 106–7, 112, 151
　in Canadian literary studies, x–xvi
　community and, 114–15
　in diasporic writing, xv, 114, 206n6, 225n8
　ethnic, as term, 112

First Nations people and, xv, 90, 94, 103
genealogy and bloodlines, 130-31, 135, 139-41
history as component of, 119, 130-31, 134-35, 139-41
homeland ties and, 115-16, 123-27
prairie pioneer myth (Mycak), 116-18, 222n4
race and, xiii-xvi, 8, 114, 206n4
regionalism and, 89-90, 192, 211n14
and third or fourth generation Canadians, xx-xxi
three themes of ethnic writing, 115-16
transculturalism and, 114, 122-25
Evanishen, Danny, *Vuiko Yurko*, 117
Eyetalian magazine, 197-98

Fabijančić, Tony, 123
Fee, Margery, 101, 216n21, 220n15, 221n2
feminism
    Kostash as feminist, 59-60, 155, 157-63, 176
    in Lysenko's *Yellow Boots*, 34
    and multiculturalism, 8-9, 52
    See also gender
First Nations people
    cultural appropriation of stories, 101-2, 206n6, 221n16
    ethnic minorities and, xv, 90, 94, 103
    in Haas's *On Stage with Maara Haas*, 219n3
    multiculturalism and, 8
    romantic nationalism and, 101
    in Ryga's *The Ecstasy of Rita Joe*, 78
    in Suknaski's works: Biblical and First Nations mythologies, 100; in *East of Myloona*, 92; and history writing, 99; hybrid prairie mythology, 103; Sioux in *Wood Mountain Poems*, 99-104; *in the ghosts call you poor*, 96
folk arts and cultural artifacts
    baba (grandmother) in, 214n12
    folklore, 55, 205n1, 214n11
    four categories of folk culture (Isajiw), 56, 214n14
    in Haas's "folklorama," 63-64
    in Haas's *Street Where I Live*, 63-64, 69, 74
    in Kulyk Keefer's *Green Library*, 132-33
    in Laurence's *A Jest of God*, 27, 31-32
    in Lysenko's *Yellow Boots*, 35-38, 41, 43-44, 74
    multiculturalism and, xiii, 35, 44-46, 50, 55-56, 63-64
    pop art, 215n16
    prairie monuments, 195-97, 203-4, 214n13
    pysanky (Easter eggs), 55, 56, 195-97, 203-4, 214n13
    revival as positive movement, 55-56
    See also art; dance, Ukrainian; music, Ukrainian
"folklorama" (Haas), 63-64
Foreigner, The. *See* Connor, Ralph, *The Foreigner*
Foty, Yurko, 55
Friesen, Patrick
    in Kostash's *Doomed Bridegroom*, 171, 186-88
"From Mosaic to Kaleidoscope" (Kulyk Keefer), 111-14, 118, 122, 222n5

Galay, Ted
    After Baba's Funeral, 217n3
    Tsymbaly!, 116
Galician immigrants
    in Connor's *The Foreigner*, 12, 15, 17-18
    in first- and second-wave periods, 4-5
    in Laurence's Manawaka cycle, 27, 29
gender
    belonging and, 192
    in Haas's *On Stage with Maara Haas*, 219n3
    masculinity in Connor's *The Foreigner*, 16
    multiculturalism and, 8-9, 52

objectification of women in Husar's sculpture, 57
patriarchal structures: in Kostash's *Doomed Bridegroom*, 188–89; in Kostash's travels in Eastern Europe, 158–60; in Kulyk Keefer's *Green Library*, 140; in Laurence's Manawaka cycle, 25; in Lysenko's *Yellow Boots*, 34–37, 40, 43; in Potrebenko's "A Different Story," 117–18; in Ross's *As For Me and My House*, 20
queer studies, xix
regionalism and, 211n14
roles for first-wave immigrants (1890s to 1914), 4
tensions in Ryga's *A Letter to My Son*, 85–86
unity ideals about, xv
See also feminism
generational conflict
in Galay's *After Baba's Funeral*, 217n3
and language in Suknaski's works, 104–5
in Laurence's *A Jest of God*, 31–32
in Ryga's *A Letter to My Son*, 78, 85–88
genres
hybridity: and alienation, 126–27; of Haas's *The Street Where I Live*, 61, 64–67, 71–75, 200–201; of Kostash's *Bloodlines*, 126–27, 154–56; of Kostash's *Doomed Bridegroom*, 169–73, 179–80, 201; of Kulyk Keefer's *Honey and Ashes*, 142–44, 149–51
and identity in Suknaski's works, 61, 95–96, 201
and resistance in Ryga's *A Letter to My Son*, 200–201
Gerus, O.W., 6
Gilroy, Paul, *Against Race*, 225n8
Glendon, Alberta, 195
globalization, as term, 122–23
See also transculturalism, transnationalism, and globalization

Glynn, Alexandra Kruchka, 33–34, 36, 44
Gordon, Charles W. [Ralph Connor]. See Connor, Ralph, *The Foreigner*
Green Library, The. See Kulyk Keefer, Janice, *The Green Library*
Gregory, E. David, 79, 217n1
Grekul, Lisa
Grekul House at Ukrainian Village, 193, 215n15
on *Kalyna's Song*, xx–xxi, 201–3
on *Leaving Shadows*, xvi–xix, 199, 203
life of, vii–xi, xx, 193–97
Griffiths, Gareth, 70–71, 83
Grove, Frederick Philip, *A Search for America*, 19
Gruending, Dennis, 49
Gulutsan, Lena, *The Mosquito's Wedding*, 55
Gunew, Sneja, 216n21, 221n2–3

Haas, Maara, *The Street Where I Live*, 63–75
ambivalence in, 71, 73, 75, 106–7, 112, 118
assimilation resistance in, 71–75
comparisons: with Kulyk Keefer's works, 127, 132, 151; with Ryga's *A Letter to My Son*, 77–78; with Suknaski's poetry, 92–93, 95, 106–7
hybridity: of genre and culture in, 61, 64–67, 71–75, 200–201; of language in, 69–71, 217n4
life of Haas, x, 205n2, 217n1
multiculturalism: as folk culture, 63–64, 69, 74; "official" vs. "grassroots," 61, 66–67, 73
"official history" vs. lived history, 77, 95
power and hybrid "english," 61, 69–71
realism in, 74–75, 88, 90
works: "folklorama," 63–64; *On Stage with Maara Haas*, 63, 219n3
Hairy Hill, Alberta, 193–94
Hinz, Evelyn, 210n10
history. See Ukrainian Canadian immigrants, history of

History of Ukrainian Literature in Canada
(Mandryka), x
Hoffman, Eva, 123
Hoffman, James, 79
Honey and Ashes. See Kulyk Keefer, Janice, *Honey and Ashes: A Story of Family*
Hryn, Halyna, 223n14
Hungary, Kostash's travels in, 154–55
Husar, Natalka, 57, 123–24, 215n18, 223n15
hybridity
   in Suknaski's prairie mythology, 90, 100–103
   and transnationalism, 125
   See also genres; languages, Ukrainian and English

identity, Ukrainian Canadian
   ambivalence and, 51–52, 104, 106–7, 112, 151
   belonging: and language in Kostash's works, 156, 166–69, 184–85, 189–92; as real or imagined, 156–57, 163–64; and writing, 192
   Canadian identity shifts and, 3, 8–9
   divided self, 148–49, 199–201
   genealogy (bloodlines) and, 130–31, 135, 139–41
   in history by Ukrainian Canadians, 57–58; in Kostash's *All of Baba's Children*, vii–ix, 57–60, 197, 216n21; in Kostash's *All of Baba's Great-grandchildren*, 197–99, 203
   identity formation: in Anglo culture, xvi–xvii; and history in Suknaski's works, 92, 107
   literary production and, xii–xiii, 33, 49–52, 201–4
   and multiculturalism: in Haas's "folklorama," 63–64; in Haas's *Street Where I Live*, 61, 66–67, 73
   naming and, 9, 42, 85–86
   official identity: and literacy in Ryga's *A Letter to My Son*, 81–83; and oral history in Ryga's *A Letter to My Son*, 83–87, 201
   as "other" to Anglo-Canadians: in Connor's *The Foreigner*, 12–16; in Laurence's *A Jest of God*, 25–31, 39; in Lysenko's *Yellow Boots*, 37–40; in Ross's *As For Me and My House*, 21–25, 26, 211n14
   "passing": and assimilation, 3, 9, 31–32, 129; and whiteness, xiii–xvi
   in prairie pioneer myth (Mycak), 116–18, 222n4
   as process not product, 201–2
   stereotypes and, 7, 21–22, 39, 197–99, 205n2
   transnationalism and, 125–27
   and writing in Suknaski's poetry, 95–96
   See also assimilation
Ignatieff, Michael, *Blood and Belonging*, 123
immigration. *See* Ukrainian Canadian immigrants, history of
Indian people. *See* First Nations people
Innes, Christopher, 78, 79, 217n1
International Council for Canadian Studies, 221n2
Inuit people, 220n10
Isajiw, Wsevolod W., folk culture categories, 56

A Jest of God. *See* Laurence, Margaret
Jewish Ukrainians
   anti-Semitism and, x
   in Connor's *The Foreigner*, 209n5
   in Haas's *The Street Where I Live*, 217n1
   immigration of, 7
   in Kulyk Keefer's *Honey and Ashes*, 143–44, 225n6
   in Lysenko's *Yellow Boots*, 212n7
   relation with Polish Jews, 225n6
   in Ryga's *A Letter to My Son*, 80, 85
   in Ukrainian Canadian literary studies, xix
Jones, Michael Owen, 56

Kalyna's Song (Grekul), xx–xxi, 201–3
Kamboureli, Smaro, xii, 221n3

Karafilly, Irena, 123
Keefer, Janice Kulyk. *See* Kulyk Keefer, Janice
Keeshig-Tobias, Lenore, xiv, 101–2, 221n16
Keywan, Zonia, 58, 216n21
Kiriak, Illia, *Sons of the Soil*, 116
Kirkconnell, Watson, xii, 19
Kirtz, Mary, 21–22, 26, 28, 50–51
Klymasz, Robert, 53, 103, 217n4, 221n17
kolbasa prairie monument, Mundare, Alberta, 194
Kostash, Myrna
  ambivalence in, 112, 162
  comparisons: with Kulyk Keefer, 153–54; with Suknaski, 191–92
  cultural appropriation and, 101–2, 206n6, 221n16
  as feminist, 59–60, 155, 158–60, 176, 215n20
  on folk culture as multiculturalism, 64
  language and identity, 127, 166–69, 201
  life of, vii, xiii–xiv, 59–60, 119, 153–54, 226n1
  "official history" (historiography) vs. lived history, 59, 156
  as political idealist, 155, 157–63, 188–89
  as second generation Ukrainian, 155, 162–68, 170
  as socialist, 176–77, 215n20
  travels in Eastern Europe, 119, 154–58, 223n14
  on whiteness, xiv
  writing and reinvention of culture, 127, 191–92, 201
  works: *All of Baba's Children*, vii–ix, 57–60, 197, 216n21; *All of Baba's Great-grandchildren*, 197–99, 203
Kostash, Myrna, *Bloodlines: A Journey Into Eastern Europe*, 153–68
  belonging: and language, 156, 166–69, 192; as real or imagined in, 156–57, 163–64
  gender issues, 158–62
  as hybrid genre (history/autobiography), 154–56
  political idealism, 157–63
  second generation experiences in, 162–68, 170
  as travel writing about Eastern Europe, 119, 126–27, 154–58, 164–66
  writing and language, 160–62, 191–92
Kostash, Myrna, *The Doomed Bridegroom: A Memoir*, 169–92
  belonging: and language, 184–85, 189–92; as real and imagined in, 169–73, 175, 177–82, 184, 188–92; and writing, 169, 190–92
  genre and structure: as creative non-fiction, 169–71, 179–80, 201; narrative montage, 172–73
  lovers and male figures in, 170–71; Kostas, 171, 176–78; K (Polish bureaucrat), 171, 173, 182–87; Lenny (Edmonton), 171, 173–77; Nestor Makhno, 188–90; Patrick Friesen (Mennonite Canadian), 171, 186–88; Stus, 171, 178–82; unnamed Serbian poet, 171, 191–92
  travels in Canada and Eastern Europe, 119, 126–27, 170
Kotsiubynska, Mykhailyna, 179–80
Kroetsch, Robert, 219n4
Kulyk Keefer, Janice
  comparisons: with Haas, 127, 132, 151; with Kostash, 153–54; with Ryga, 127, 132, 151; with Suknaski, 132
  on her identity as a writer, 111–12, 129–30, 154, 192
  life of, xv–xvi, 129–30, 143, 153–54, 205n3, 226n1
  on multiculturalism and transculturalism, 111–14, 118–19, 130, 132
  transnational relationships in Ukraine, 130, 143, 154, 223n14
  on whiteness, xv–xvi
  works: "'Coming Across Bones': Historiographic Ethnofiction," xiii,

129, 205n3; "From Mosaic to
    Kaleidoscope," 111–14, 118, 122,
    222n5; "Introduction" to *Two
    Lands, New Visions*, 118; "Personal
    and Public Records: Story and
    History in the Narration of
    Ethnicity," 143
Kulyk Keefer, Janice, *Honey and Ashes: A
    Story of Family*, 142–51, 200–201
  ambivalence in, 151
  desire and longing in, 150–51, 154
  genealogy in, 126, 142–43, 150–51,
    200–201
  history: as knowable/unknowable
    Truth, 142–45, 148–51, 153, 201; as
    romance in, 145–49
  hybrid genre and narrative structure of,
    142–45, 149–51, 167
  turning back to ancestral homelands,
    118, 131, 134–35, 145–51
Kulyk Keefer, Janice, *The Green Library*,
    129–41, 200–201
  folk culture in, 132–33
  genealogy (bloodlines), ethnicity and
    identity, 118, 126, 130–35, 137–41,
    154, 200–201
  narrative structure of, 131, 138–41
  "official history" vs. lived history,
    130–31, 134–41, 153–54, 201
  realism in, 137–38
Kupchenko, Yuri, 116
Kupchenko Frolick, Gloria, 116
Kurelek, William, 57, 215n17
Kyla's Christmas Concert (Woywitka and
    Mueller), 117

Lane, Patrick, 220n9, 220n14
languages, Ukrainian and English
  assimilation as linguistic loss in
    Lysenko's *Yellow Boots*, 34, 41,
    45–46
  generational conflict: in Laurence's
    Manawaka cycle, 31–32; in
    Suknaski's works, 104–6
  hybridity: as ambivalence to language,
    51–52; in Haas's *The Street Where I
    Live*, 69–71, 69–73, 217n4; as
    "otherness," 83–84; in Ryga's *A
    Letter to My Son*, 61, 83–88; in
    Suknaski's works, 94–95, 103–6
  identity and languages: in Kostash's
    works, 127, 166–69, 201; and
    official history in Ryga's *A Letter to
    My Son*, 82–88
  inexactness of: in Suknaski's works,
    96–99
  literary production and languages, 52
  newspapers for first- and second-wave
    immigrants, xvi–xvii, 4–5, 52
  non-standard "english," 61; in Haas's
    Street Where I Live, 69–71, 83–84;
    in Ryga's *A Letter to My Son*, 61,
    83–84; in Suknaski's poetry, 61, 92,
    94–95, 106
  reception of Kostash's *All of Baba's
    Children*, 216n21
  resurgence of learning of Ukrainian, 9,
    56
  transcultural tensions: in Kostash's
    Bloodlines, 160–62, 165–69, 192; in
    Kostash's *Doomed Bridegroom*,
    184–85, 189–92; in Kulyk Keefer's
    Green Library, 147
  translations: effects of untranslated
    words, 70–71, 95, 217n4; in
    Suknaski's works, 104–6
  See also assimilation
Laurence, Margaret
  A Jest of God, 9, 24–32; assimilation in,
    27, 30–32; generational conflict in,
    31–32; Ukrainian as "other" to
    Anglos, 25–31, 39
  Manawaka cycle, 25–26, 28–32, 211n14
  nascent multiculturalism in, 30–32,
    211n14
Lawson, Alan, 102
Lesik, Vera. See Lysenko, Vera, *Yellow Boots*
A Letter to My Son. See Ryga, George, *A
    Letter to My Son*
Linkiewich, Emily, *Baba's Cookbook*, 55

literary studies, Ukrainian Canadian
  cultural plurality and, xi–xii
  ethnicity in, x–xvi
  Jewish Ukrainians in, xix
  literary production, xii–xiii, 33, 49–52, 201–4
  Mennonite Ukrainians in, 217n1
  place in Canadian literary studies, ix–xvi
  race and, xii–xvi, 8, 114, 206n4
Lithuania, 120
Lysenko, Vera
  life of, 33
  as major Ukrainian Canadian writer, 49, 88
  on misrepresentations of Ukrainians, 38–39
  writing and belonging, 192
  works: *Men in Sheepskin Coats*, 33, 34, 38–39, 58; *Westerly World*, 33
Lysenko, Vera, *Yellow Boots*, 33–46
  assimilation: as cultural loss, 34, 43–46; and desire, 41–43; as linguistic loss, 34, 41, 43–46, 61
  binaries of modern/Anglo and backward/Ukrainian, 37–40, 46
  comparisons with Ryga and Haas, 88
  critical reception and publication, 33–34, 36–37
  cultural and religious practices in, 37–38
  nascent multiculturalism: as ethnic performance, 35, 44–46, 200; "official" vs. "grassroots," 61
  nonstandard "english" in, 61
  as romance, 61
  women's roles: and patriarchal structures, 34–37, 40, 43, 200; in preserving culture, 36, 43–46
  yellow boots as symbol, 36, 44–45, 74, 218n3

Makhno, Nestor, 188–90
Manawaka cycle (Laurence). See Laurence, Margaret

Mandryka, M.I., *History of Ukrainian Literature in Canada*, x
Maracle, Lee, xiv, 206n6
Marunchak, Michael, 222n4
Melnyczuk, Askold, 223n14
Melnyk, Bohdan, Fox Mykyta, 55
Melnyk, George, 213n3, 221n19
  on ethnic groups and aboriginal peoples, 103
  his painting in Suknaski's "Paska I Khmary," 105–6
Men in Sheepskin Coats (Lysenko), 33, 34, 38–39, 58
Mennonite Ukrainians
  immigration of, 7
  in Kostash's *Doomed Bridegroom*, 186–88
  representations in literary works, 217n1
Métis people
  in Laurence's Manawaka cycle, 26, 29–30
Miki, Roy, xiv, 206n6
Mitchell, Katharyne, 125–26
Miyoshi, Masao, on globalization, 121–23
Monkman, Leslie, 220n14
monuments, Ukrainian Canadian prairie, 195–97, 203–4, 214n13
Mueller, Randy, 117
multiculturalism
  feminism and, 8–9, 52
  government support for, xii, 50–51, 212n1, 212n2
  in Haas's "folklorama," 63–64
  in Haas's *Street Where I Live*, 61, 66–67, 73
  in Laurence's *A Jest of God*, 30–32
  literary production and, xiii, 50–52
  in Lysenko's *Yellow Boots*, 34, 44–46, 74, 200
  as mutual influence with Anglo culture, 34
  "official" vs. "grassroots," 61, 66–67
  prairie pioneer myth (Mycak), 116–18, 222n4

Swyripa on folk culture as, 50, 55–56
  themes of getting there, being there, and turning back, 115–16
  transculturalism and multiculturalism (Kulyk Keefer), 111–14
  use of term (Haas), 217n2
  See also Ukrainian Canadian culture
Mundare, Alberta, 194
Munton, Anne, 92
music, Ukrainian
  folk songs: in Lysenko's *Yellow Boots*, 35–36; in Ryga's *A Letter to My Son*, 83
  and multiculturalism, 55, 213n9–10
  and stereotypes, 197
  See also dance, Ukrainian; folk arts and cultural artifacts
Mycak, Sonia, x, 33–34, 116–18
mythology
  prairie pioneer myth (Mycak), 116–18, 222n4
  Suknaski's hybrid prairie mythology, 90, 100–103

nationalism
  Canadian nationalism and assimilation, 7, 13, 15
  in Connor's *The Foreigner*, 11, 13–16, 19
  romantic nationalism and First Nations, 101
  transnationalism and, 121
  Ukrainian nationalism in third-wave émigrés, 53–54
  See also transculturalism, transnationalism, and globalization
Native people. *See* First Nations people
New, W. H., xi–xii, 7, 8, 13, 19, 30, 211n14
NeWest Press, 51, 213n3
newspapers
  for first- and second-wave immigrants, xvi–xvii, 4–5, 52, 213n5
Nimchuk, Michael John, 49
No Streets of Gold (Potrebenko), 57–60, 118, 216n21

Onifrijchuk, Roman, 56
On Stage with Maara Haas (Haas), 63, 219n3
Ontario, immigration to, 5–6
oral history
  in history books by Ukrainian Canadians, 58
  and identity in Ryga's *A Letter to My Son*, 84–88, 201
Ortiz, Fernando, 113
Ostenso, Martha, *Wild Geese*, 19

Padolsky, Enoch, xii, 201–2
painting. *See* art
Palmer Seiler, Tamara, 34, 36, 44, 65–66, 73
Paskievich, John, 123
Pavlychko, Solomea, 118
Pensky, Max, 122–23
perogy prairie monument, Alberta, 195
Philip, Marlene Nourbese, xiv, 206n6
Piniuta, Harry, 58, 215n19
poetry
  critical studies of, 52
  prairie poets of 1960s, 89–90
  See also Suknaski, Andrew
Pohorecky, Zenon, 56
Poland
  influences on Ryga and Suknaski, 219n2
  in Kostash's *Bloodlines*, 154–56, 158–61, 163–64, 166
  in Kostash's *Doomed Bridegroom*, 170, 184–86
  in Kulyk Keefer's *Honey and Ashes*, 143–44, 224n5–6
  opening of borders in 1990s, 120
  Polish and Ukrainian relationships, 143–44, 161–63, 184, 224n6
  rule of Galicia, 5
Pollock, Sharon, 220n12
Popeliukh, Valentyna, 181
Porter, Anna, 123
postcolonialism, 90
Potrebenko, Helen, 57–60, 116–18
  ambivalence in, 112

as feminist, 59–60, 215n20
historical works by, 57–60
multiculturalism and folk culture, 63–64
"official history" vs. lived history, 59
prairie pioneer myth (Mycak), 116–18, 222n4
as socialist, 215n20
works: "A Different Story," 116–18; *No Streets of Gold*, 57–60, 118, 216n21
Prairie Centre for the Study of Ukrainian Heritage, 205n1
prairie monuments, 195–97, 203–4, 214n13
prairie pioneer myth (Mycak), 116–18, 222n4
Pratt, Mary Louise, 113
Prystupa, Steve, 56–57
Purdy, Al, 219n4
pysanky (Easter eggs)
multiculturalism and, 55, 56
Vegreville prairie monument, 195–97, 203–4, 214n13
See also folk arts and cultural artifacts

Québec, third-wave émigrés in, 6, 8
queer studies, xix

race
cultural appropriation and, 101–2, 206n6, 221n16
in diasporic writing, xv, 114
ethnicity and literary studies, xii–xvi, 8, 114, 206n4
in Kostash's *Doomed Bridegroom*, 174–75
Métis in Laurence's Manawaka cycle, 26, 29–30, 211n14
regionalism and, 211n14
whiteness and, xiii–xvi
Rama, Angel, 113
Raoul, Valerie, 210n10, 210n12
Rasporich, Beverly, 33–34, 36, 38
Rawlyk, G. A., 216n21
Rea, J. E., 6

realism
acceptance of, 90
in Galay's *After Baba's Funeral*, 218n3
in Haas's *Street Where I Live*, 74–75, 88, 95
in Kulyk Keefer's *Green Library*, 137–38
in painting (Shostak and Kurelek), 57
as replacement for romance, 19
in Ross's *As for Me and My House*, 19, 21–22, 24
in Ryga's works, 88, 90, 95
in Suknaski's works, 91–92, 95–96
regionalism
and gender, ethnicity and race, 192, 211n14
as movement before multiculturalism, 89–90
Reimer, Al, 187
Richmond Park, Alberta, 219n2
romance
in Connor's *The Foreigner*, 12–13, 17
in Lysenko's *Yellow Boots*, 61
and otherness in Laurence's *A Jest of God*, 26
and realism, 19
romanticized history in Kulyk Keefer's *Honey and Ashes*, 145–49
See also Kostash, Myrna, *The Doomed Bridegroom: A Memoir*
Romania, 120
Rose, Marilyn, 210n11, 211n13
Ross, Sinclair, *As For Me and My House*, 9, 19–24
assimilation and realism in, 19, 21–22, 24
Ukrainians as "other" in, 21–25, 26, 211n14
Royal Commission on Bilingualism and Biculturalism
Ukrainian community submissions to, 212n2
Rubchak, Bohdan, 52
Rumania, Kostash's travels in, 154–55

Rushdie, Salman, *Imaginary Homelands*, 225n7-8
Russian immigrants
   in Connor's *The Foreigner*, 12-14, 16-17, 20
Ryga, George
   comparisons: with Galay's *After Baba's Funeral*, 217n3; with Haas's *Street Where I Live*, 77-78; with Kulyk Keefer's works, 127, 132, 151; with prairie poets of 1960s, 89-90; with Suknaski, 92-95, 106-7
   life of, x, 78-79, 205n2, 217n1, 219n2
   "official history" vs. lived history, 77-79
   realism in works, 88, 90, 95
   as writer, 90, 192
   works: *Ballad of a Stone-Picker*, 78; *Night Desk*, 78; *Portrait of Angelica*, 78; *The Athabasca Ryga*, 79; *The Ecstasy of Rita Joe*, 78, 90
Ryga, George, *A Letter to My Son*, 77-88
   expressionism in, 218n3
   gender relations in, 85-86
   hybrid "english" and standard English in, 61, 83-84
   identity: in languages and genres, 61; in official historical records, 81-83; in oral history, 84-88, 201
   "official history" vs. lived history, 77-79, 81-82, 86-87, 95
   "official" vs. "grassroots" multiculturalism, 61
   as play, 79-80, 82, 218n5
   realism in, 88, 90, 95
   resistance: to assimilation, 83; through genre and language, 200-201
   Ryga on autobiographical elements in, 79
   social class, 77-79, 81, 83

sausage (*kolbasa*) prairie monument, Mundare, Alberta, 194
Scobie, Stephen, on Suknaski, 90, 92, 95, 219n5-6
Serbia
   Kostash's travels in, 154-55, 160-61
   in Kostash's works, 170, 191-92
Serwylo, Ray, 49
Shevchenko, Taras, 67-69, 166, 217n3
Shostak, Peter, 57, 215n17
Siemerling, Winfried, 206n4
Sioux culture
   in Suknaski's works, 99-101, 220n10-11, 221n18
Sitting Bull, Chief, 99, 220n11-12
Skarszewy, Ukraine, 147
Slavutych, Yar, *The Conquerors of the Prairies*, 117
Slemon, Stephen, 102
Slovenia, Kostash's travels in, 154-55
Small Legs, Jr., Nelson, 100-101, 220n13
Snow Folks, 55
social class
   in Haas's *Street Where I Live*, 65-66, 72-73
   in Kostash's work, 215n20
   in Potrebenko's work, 215n20
   in Ryga's *A Letter to My Son*, 77-79, 81, 83
socialism
   Kostash and Potrebenko and, 60, 157-58, 176, 215n20, 216n21
Soviet Union
   impact of collapse on travel and writing, 119-22
   See also Ukraine
Spak, Harvey, film on Suknaski, 91-92, 95
Staromischyna, Ukraine, 145-47, 150, 224n5
Stawnichy's Meat Processing, Mundare, Alberta, 194
stereotypes, Ukrainian Canadian
   binaries of good/evil and Anglo/Ukrainian, 12-16, 23-24, 37-40, 46
   identity and, 7, 21-22, 39, 197-99, 205n2
Street Where I Live, The. *See* Haas, Maara, *The Street Where I Live*

Suknaski, Andrew, 89–108
  authenticity of voice, 62, 92, 94–97, 99, 102–3
  comparisons: with Haas and Ryga, 92–95, 107; with Kostash, 191–92; with Kulyk Keefer, 132
  First Nations culture: Biblical and First Nations mythologies, 100, 103–4; in *East of Myloona*, 92; and history writing, 99; hybrid prairie mythology, 103; and Sioux in *Wood Mountain Poems*, 94, 99–104; in *the ghosts call you poor*, 96
  identity in languages and genres, 61, 95–96, 201
  language: hybrid "english," 61, 92, 94–95, 106; inexactness of language, 97–98; translation, 104–6, 221n18
  life of, 89, 91, 102, 219n2, 219n7, 220n8
  "official history" vs. lived history, 92–93, 98
  "official" vs. "grassroots" multiculturalism, 61
  realism in works, 91–92, 95–96
  roles as writer: as historian, 62, 92, 95–99, 103, 106–7, 191; as poet-shaman, 96–98, 101–4, 106–7; as radical poet, 91; as settler subject, 102–3; as writer concerned with writing process, 95–96, 106–8, 192
  second generation status: and ambivalence, 104–7, 112; and assimilation, 102–3; and reinvention of culture, 201
  writing and art, 97–98
Suknaski, Andrew, works
  "ascent," 101
  "descent," 101
  East of Myloona, 92, 220n10
  "failure," 101
  "genesis," 100–101
  "In Memory of Alfred A. Lecaine," 96–100, 104–5
  "Jimmy Hoy's Place," 94
  In Mind Ov Xcrossroads Ov Mythologies, 91
  In the Name of Narid, 92–96, 103–4, 106–8, 212n1, 220n8
  "Neehhreson," 100
  "Paska I Khmary," 104–6
  "Poem to Sitting Bull and his Son Crowfoot," 99
  "prayer," 101
  Rose Way in the East, 91
  "Sat," 93
  "Shugmanitou I," 221n18
  "Shugmanitou II," 94
  "Soongeedawn," 100
  "Suknatskyj Taking a Greyhound North," 94
  "The First People," 100–101, 103–4, 221n18
  "the first people," 100–101
  the ghosts call you poor, 92–96, 99–101, 103–4, 106, 220n8, 220n10
  "The Indian and the White Man," 221n18
  "The Sun Dance at Wood Mountain," 99, 100
  "The Teton Sioux and 1879 Prairie Fire," 99
  "Vasile Tonita," 93
  Wood Mountain Poems, 93–100, 103–4, 106, 220n8, 220n10
  Y th Evolution into Ruenz, 91
Swayze, Walter, 208n1
Swyripa, Frances, *Ukrainian Canadians*, x, 38, 52
  on colonialism and good/evil binaries, 12–13
  on Connor's *The Foreigner*, 209n4, 209n8
  on immigration, 5, 7, 8
  on multiculturalism, 50, 55–56, 214n12
Symchych, Victoria, *The Flying Ship*, 55
Szypenitz, Alberta, 193–94

Teunissen, John, 210n10
theatre, critical studies of, 52
Tiffin, Helen, 70–71, 83
transculturalism, transnationalism, and globalization, 111–27
   cultural exchange in contact zones, 113–14
   globalization, as term, 122–23
   homeland ties in ethnic writing, 115–19, 123–27
   Kostash on, xiii–xiv
   Kulyk Keefer on, 111–14
   metaphors for: Janus, 112–13, 114, 132; kaleidoscope, 113
   nation-state roles, 121–22
   recent trends in, 121–27
   transculturalism, as term, 114
   See also Kostash, Myrna; Kulyk Keefer, Janice
Trudeau, Pierre, 212n2
Tsymbaly! (Galay), 116
Two Hills, Alberta, vii–ix, 193–94
Two Lands, New Visions, ix

Ukraine
   bread as symbol, 168
   economic and social conditions (after 1991), 120–21, 124–27, 135–36, 141, 145–47, 165–68
   history as positive and negative, 133, 162–63, 168; famine in 1933, 168; Nazi collaboration (Babi Yar), 133, 134, 136, 138, 225n6; Polish and Ukrainian relationships, 143–44, 162–64, 184–86
   in Kostash's: *Bloodlines*, 154–55, 162–68; *Doomed Bridegroom*, 170, 188–90
   in Kulyk Keefer's: *Green Library*, 134–43; *Honey and Ashes*, 130
   leaders: Makhno, Ukrainian revolutionary, 188–90; Shevchenko, Taras, as national symbol, 67–69, 166, 217n3
   Orange Revolution, 121, 124, 222n12
   Polish and Ukrainian relationships, 143–44, 161–63, 184, 224n6
   tensions with other groups, 162–64, 186–88, 224n6
   See also Jewish Ukrainians; languages, Ukrainian and English
Ukrainian Canadian immigrants, history of
   assimilation of, 3–10, 53
   generations: Kostash as second generation, 155, 162–68, 170; Suknaski as second generation, 102–7, 112, 201; third and four generation, xx–xxi
   immigration patterns: first wave (1890s to 1914), 3–9, 53, 116; second wave (late 1920s), 3–6, 53; third wave émigrés (1947 to 1950), 3–6, 8, 52–54
   literary studies: cultural plurality and, xi–xii; literary production, xii–xiii, 33, 49–52, 201–4; place in Canadian literary studies, ix–xvi
   Mennonite Ukrainians, 7, 186–88, 217n1
   narratives of progress, 8–9, 58–59, 117
   nationalism, Ukrainian: in third wave émigrés, 53–54; transnationalism and, 121
   need for dialogue on, 199–204
   "official history" vs. lived history, 59; in Haas's *The Street Where I Live*, 77, 95; in Kulyk Keefer's *Green Library*, 130–31, 134–36, 138, 153–54, 201; in Ryga's *A Letter to My Son*, 77–79, 81–82, 86–88, 95; in Suknaski's works, 92–93, 98–99
   in prairie pioneer myth (Mycak), 116–18, 222n4
   religious and political divisions within communities, 6–7, 54
   travel to ancestral homelands by, xix, 123, 135–36
   by Ukrainian Canadians, 57–58; in Kostash's *All of Baba's Children*, vii–ix, 57–60, 197, 216n21;

in Kostash's *All of Baba's Great-grandchildren*, 197–99, 203
See also assimilation; Jewish Ukrainians; transculturalism, transnationalism, and globalization; Ukrainian Canadian culture
Ukrainian Canadiana, The, 55
Ukrainian Canadian Committee, 5–6
Ukrainian Canadian culture
  baba (grandmother) in, 167, 214n12
  food, xx, 168, 194–96, 214n12
  four categories of folk culture (Isajiw), 56, 214n14
  need for dialogue on, 199–204
  prairie monuments, 194–97, 199, 203–4, 214n13
  sculpture and folk culture (Husar), 57
  stereotypes of, 7, 21–22, 39, 197–99, 205n2
  See also assimilation; dance, Ukrainian; folk arts and cultural artifacts; languages, Ukrainian and English; multiculturalism; music, Ukrainian
Ukrainian Catholic Brotherhood, 5
Ukrainian community organizations
  growth of, 5–6, 52
  in Haas's *The Street Where I Live*, 68–69
  submissions to B & B Commission, 212n2
Ukrainian Cultural Heritage Village, Alberta, 193, 195–96, 214n15
Ukrainian Folklore Program, 205n1
Ukrainian Greek-Catholic Church
  ceremonies in Haas's *The Street Where I Live*, 67–68
  and immigration, 5, 6–7
Ukrainian Greek-Orthodox Church, 5, 6–7
Ukrainian National Federation, 5
Ukrainian Self Reliance League, 5
United Hetman Organization, 5

van Herk, Aritha, 216n21
Vegreville, Alberta, 194–97, 203–4, 213n8, 214n13
Vesey, Olga, *The Flying Ship*, 55

Visible Symbols, 55
Vulcan, Alberta, 195

Wakulich, Bob, 49
Warwaruk, Larry, 116
Weier, John, 187
Westerly World (Lysenko), 33
Wiebe, Rudy, 187
Williams, David, 210n10
Winland, Daphne, on diasporic writing, 114–16
Winnipeg, Manitoba
  in Connor's *The Foreigner*, 11–12, 209n2
  in Haas's *The Street Where I Live*, 64–69, 71, 77
  newspapers: for first- and second-wave immigrants, 213n5
Wood Mountain, Saskatchewan, 93–94, 97, 219n2, 220n11
Wood Mountain Poems (film on Suknaski), 92, 95
Woywitka, Susan, 117

Yarmarok: Ukrainian Canadian Writing in Canada (Balan). *See* Balan, Jars, *Yarmarok*
Yellow Boots. See Lysenko, Vera, *Yellow Boots*
Yugoslavia
  ethnic tensions in, 121, 123
  Kostash's travels in, 154–57, 163–64, 166

Zabytko, Irena, 223n14
Zacharko, Larry, 49
Zdorov magazine, 197–98